# The Wisdom of Egypt:

## changing visions through the ages

UCL
PRESS
Institute of Archaeology

Encounters with
Ancient
Egypt

## Titles in the series

**Ancient Egypt in Africa**
*Edited by David O'Connor and Andrew Reid*

**Ancient Perspectives on Egypt**
*Edited by Roger Matthews and Cornelia Roemer*

**Consuming Ancient Egypt**
*Edited by Sally MacDonald and Michael Rice*

**Imhotep Today: Egyptianizing architecture**
*Edited by Jean-Marcel Humbert and Clifford Price*

**Mysterious Lands**
*Edited by David O'Connor and Stephen Quirke*

**'Never had the like occurred': Egypt's view of its past**
*Edited by John Tait*

**Views of Ancient Egypt since Napoleon Bonaparte: imperialism, colonialism and modern appropriations**
*Edited by David Jeffreys*

**The Wisdom of Egypt: changing visions through the ages**
*Edited by Peter Ucko and Timothy Champion*

ENCOUNTERS WITH ANCIENT EGYPT

# The Wisdom
# of Egypt:

## changing visions through the ages

Edited by

**Peter Ucko and Timothy Champion**

UCL
PRESS
Institute of Archaeology

First published in Great Britain 2003 by UCL Press,
an imprint of Cavendish Publishing Limited, The Glass House,
Wharton Street, London WC1X 9PX, United Kingdom
Telephone: + 44 (0)20 7278 8000    Facsimile: + 44 (0)20 7278 8080
Email: info@uclpress.com
Website: www.uclpress.com

Published in the United States by Cavendish Publishing
c/o International Specialized Book Services,
5824 NE Hassalo Street, Portland,
Oregon 97213-3644, USA

Published in Australia by Cavendish Publishing (Australia) Pty Ltd
45 Beach Street, Coogee, NSW 2034, Australia
Telephone: + 61 (2)9664 0909    Facsimile: + 61 (2)9664 5420

British Library Cataloguing in Publication Data
Ucko, P. J.
The wisdom of Egypt: changing visions – (Encounters with ancient Egypt)
1 Egypt – Civilization  2 Egypt – History
I Title
932

Library of Congress Cataloguing in Publication Data
Data available

ISBN 1-84472-005-5

1 3 5 7 9 10 8 6 4 2

Designed and typeset by Style Photosetting, Mayfield, East Sussex
Email: style@pavilion.co.uk

Printed and bound in Great Britain

Cover illustration:   Hermes Trismegistus on the mosaic floor (1488 AD) of the Duomo of Siena,
Italy (© Opera della metropolitana di Siene Aut. n. 9943).

# Series Editor's Foreword

This series of eight books derives from the proceedings of a conference entitled 'Encounters with Ancient Egypt', held at the Institute of Archaeology, University College London (UCL) in December 2000. Since then, many new chapters have been especially commissioned for publication, and those papers originally provided for the conference and now selected for publication have been extensively revised and rewritten.

There are many noteworthy features of the books. One is the overall attempt to move the study of Ancient Egypt into the mainstream of recent advances in archaeological and anthropological practice and interpretation. This is a natural outcome of London University's Institute of Archaeology, one of the largest archaeology departments in the world, being the academic host. Drawing on the Institute's and other related resources within UCL, the volumes in the series reflect an extraordinary degree of collaboration between the series editor, individual volume editors, contributors and colleagues. The wide range of approaches to the study of the past, pursued in such a vibrant scholarly environment as UCL's, has encouraged the scholars writing in these volumes to consider their disciplinary interests from new perspectives. All the chapters presented here have benefited from wide-ranging discussion between experts from diverse academic disciplines, including art history, papyrology, anthropology, archaeology and Egyptology, and subsequent revision.

Egyptology has been rightly criticized for often being insular; the methodologies and conclusions of the discipline have been seen by others as having developed with little awareness of archaeologies elsewhere. The place and role of Ancient Egypt within African history, for example, has rarely been considered jointly by Egyptologists and Africanists. This collaboration provides a stimulating review of key issues and may well influence future ways of studying Egypt. Until now, questions have rarely been asked about the way Egyptians thought of their own past or about non-Egyptian peoples and places. Nor has the discipline of Egyptology explored, in any depth, the nature of its evidence, or the way contemporary cultures regarded Ancient Egypt. The books in this series address such topics.

Another exceptional feature of this series is the way that the books have been designed to interrelate with, inform and illuminate one another. Thus, the evidence of changing appropriations of Ancient Egypt over time, from the classical period to the modern Afrocentrist movement, features in several volumes. One volume explores the actual sources of knowledge about Ancient Egypt before the advent of 'scientific' archaeology, while another explores knowledge of Ancient Egypt after Napoleon Bonaparte's expeditions and the unearthing of Tutankhamun's tomb. The question asked throughout these volumes, however, is how far fascination and knowledge about Ancient Egypt have been based on sources of evidence rather than extraneous political or commercial concerns and interests.

As a result of this series, the study of Ancient Egypt will be significantly enriched and deepened. The importance of the Egypt of several thousands of years ago reaches far beyond the existence of its architectural monuments and extends to its unique role in the history of all human knowledge. Furthermore, the civilization of Ancient Egypt speaks to us with particular force in our own present and has an abiding place in the modern psyche.

As the first paragraph of this Foreword explains, the final stage of this venture began with the receipt and editing of some extensively revised, and in many cases new, chapters – some 95 in all – to be published simultaneously in eight volumes. What it does not mention is the speed with which the venture has been completed: the current UCL Press was officially launched in April 2003. That this series of books has been published to such a high standard of design, professional accuracy and attractiveness only four months later is incredible.

This alone speaks eloquently for the excellence of the staff of UCL Press – from its senior management to its typesetters and designers. Ruth Phillips (Marketing Director) stands out for her youthful and innovative marketing ideas and implementation of them, but most significant of all, at least from the Institute's perspective, is the contribution of Ruth Massey (Editor), who oversaw and supervized all details of the layout and production of the books, and also brought her critical mind to bear on the writing styles, and even the meaning, of their contents.

Individual chapter authors and academic volume editors, both from within UCL and in other institutions, added this demanding project to otherwise full workloads. Although it is somewhat invidious to single out particular individuals, Professor David O'Connor stands out as co-editor of two volumes and contributor of chapters to three despite his being based overseas. He, together with Professor John Tait – also an editor and multiple chapter author in these books – was one of the first to recognize my vision of the original conference as having the potential to inspire a uniquely important publishing project.

Within UCL's Institute of Archaeology, a long list of dedicated staff, academic, administrative and clerical, took over tasks for the Director and Kelly Vincent, his assistant as they wrestled with the preparation of this series. All of these staff, as well as several members of the student body, really deserve individual mention by name, but space does not allow this. However, the books could not have appeared without the particular support of five individuals: Lisa Daniel, who tirelessly secured copyright for over 500 images; Jo Dullaghan, who turned her hand to anything at any time to help out, from re-typing manuscripts to chasing overdue authors; Andrew Gardner, who tracked down obscure and incomplete references, and who took on the complex job of securing and producing correctly scanned images; Stuart Laidlaw, who not only miraculously produced publishable images of a pair of outdoor cats now in Holland and Jamaica, but in a number of cases created light where submitted images revealed only darkness; and Kelly Vincent, who did all of the above twice over, and more – and who is the main reason that publisher and Institute staff remained on excellent terms throughout.

Finally, a personal note, if I may. Never, ever contemplate producing eight complex, highly illustrated books within a four month period. If you *really must*, then make sure you have the above team behind you. Essentially, ensure that you have a partner such as Jane Hubert, who may well consider you to be mad but never questions the essential worth of the undertaking.

*Peter Ucko*
*Institute of Archaeology*
*University College London*
*27 July 2003*

# Contents

Series Editor's Foreword — *v*
Contributors — *ix*
List of Figures — *xi*
A note on transliteration from ancient Egyptian — *xv*

**1 Introduction: Egypt Ancient and Modern** — 1
*Timothy Champion and Peter Ucko*

**2 The Wisdom of Egypt: Classical Views** — 23
*John Tait*

**3 Ancient Egypt in Medieval Arabic Writings** — 39
*Okasha El Daly*

**4 Images of Ancient Egypt in the Latin Middle Ages** — 65
*Charles Burnett*

**5 The Renaissance Afterlife of Ancient Egypt (1400–1650)** — 101
*Brian A. Curran*

**6 Ancient Egypt in 17th and 18th Century England** — 133
*David Boyd Haycock*

**7 Beyond Egyptology: Egypt in 19th and 20th Century Archaeology and Anthropology** — 161
*Timothy Champion*

References — *187*
Index — *215*

Note: No attempt has been made to impose a standard chronology on authors; all dates before 712 BC are approximate. However, names of places, and royal and private names have been standardized.

# Contributors

**Charles Burnett** is Professor of the History of Islamic Influences in Europe at the Warburg Institute, University of London. He has published extensively on a wide range of subjects, including Natural Science and Philosophy, Astronomy and Astrology, Medicine and Psychology, Music, and Magic and Divination. He contributes regularly to the Warburg Institute's own publications, including the *Journal of the Warburg and Courtauld Institutes, Studies of the Warburg Institute,* and *Warburg Institute Surveys and Texts.* He received his PhD from the University of Cambridge.

**Timothy Champion** is Professor in the Department of Archaeology, University of Southampton. His research interests are in later European prehistory, the history of archaeology and the use of the past in contemporary social and political discourse. His recent publications include *Nationalism and Archaeology in Europe* (1996, ed. with Margarita Diaz-Andreu), *England's Coastal Heritage* (1997, ed. with M. Fulford and A. Long) and 'The Appropriation of the Phoenicians in British Imperial Ideology' (*Nations and Nationalism* 7, 2001). He received his D Phil from the University of Oxford.

**Brian A. Curran** is Associate Professor of Art History at Pennsylvania State University, where he teaches courses in Italian Renaissance Art. He worked for several years in the Egyptian Department of the Museum of Fine Arts, Boston, before turning to Art History and Renaissance studies. He has held fellowships at the American Academy in Rome, the Bibliotheca Hertziana, and the Society of Fellows at Columbia University. He has published several articles on the reception of Ancient Egypt in Italian Renaissance culture. He received his PhD from Princeton University.

**Okasha El Daly** has been teaching Egyptology at Birkbeck College, University of London for 10 years. After studying Egyptology at Cairo University and undertaking a season of excavation on the Giza Plateau, he worked as a guide and guest lecturer in the tourist industry. He has translated several books on Ancient Egypt into Arabic and has contributed to and co-edited *Desert Travellers from Herodotus to T. E. Lawrence* (2000). He recently received his PhD from the University of London (Institute of Archaeology, University College London).

**John Tait** is Edwards Professor of Egyptology at the Institute of Archaeology, University College London. He has edited hieroglyphic, hieratic, demotic and Greek papyri, and studies Egyptian literary traditions. His publications include *Papyri from Tebtunis in Egyptian and in Greek* (1977) and *Saqqara Demotic Papyri* (1983, with H. S. Smith), and he has made several contributions to the work of the Project for the Publication of the Carlsberg Papyri (Copenhagen). He received his D Phil from the University of Oxford.

**David Boyd Haycock** was a Junior Research Fellow at Wolfson College, Oxford. He has published on aspects of The Royal Society in the 18th century (with G. S. Rousseau), and his book on *William Stukeley – Science, Religion and Archaeology in Eighteenth-Century England* was published in 2002. He received his PhD from Birkbeck College, University of London.

**Peter J. Ucko** is Director of the Institute of Archaeology, University College London, and Professor of Comparative Archaeology. He first published a book on predynastic Egyptian anthropomorphic figurines in 1968 and recently returned to this subject ("Mother, Are You There?", *Cambridge Archaeological Journal*, 1996). He has published on *Palaeolithic Cave Art* (1967, with A. Rosenfeld), and on the prehistoric site of Avebury in Wiltshire (1991 with M. Hunter, A. J. Clark and A. David). He has also edited several books on domestication, on settlements, and more recently on *Theory in Archaeology: a world perspective* (1995) and *The Archaeology and Anthropology of Landscape* (1999, with R. Layton), and was Editor of the *One World Archaeology* series. He obtained his PhD in Prehistory and Egyptology from the University of London (University College and the Institute of Archaeology).

# List of Figures

Figure 1:1　'View on the Nile. Isle of Rhoda and the ferry of Geezeh' (1838) by David Roberts (1796–1854). On 7 October "while he waited for the mainsail yard to be replaced ..., he passed the time by drawing the Giza ferry, with the Pyramids in the background" (Bourbon 1996: 36; Roberts 1855).　7

Figure 1:2　Bronze 'Coptic bowl' from the early seventh century royal burial at Sutton Hoo, Suffolk, England (British Museum 1939–1010. 109). Diameter 38.5 cm.　13

Figure 1:3　President Anwar Sadat of Egypt standing in front of pyramids (1977) (© David Hume Kennerly/Getty Images).　20

Figure 2:1　Two columns of demotic astrological text showing two aspects of the moon, one "being a black [disk] around it, you are to say about it: Great fighting shall happen (in) the entire land" (Parker 1959: 39, pl. 4).　28

Figure 2:2　The court of the temple of Horus at Edfu. Note that the 'library' was situated immediately behind the right hand corner of the porch (© Okasha El Daly).　30

Figure 3:1　The Lighthouse of Alexandria by Al-Gharnati (d. 1169 AD) (Paris BN MS Arabe 2168 fol. 17 recto) (after Hamarneh 1971: 87, fig. 1).　46

Figure 3:2　Twelfth Dynasty stela with the name of King Amenemhet II, as recorded in the 14th century by Abu Al-Qassim al-'Iraqi (British Library MS Add. 25,724, fol. 50a).　49

Figure 3:3　The 'Scala Magna' with Coptic inscriptions, as recorded by Abu Al-Barakat (Budge 1928: 81; British Library MS Add. 24,050).　57

Figure 4:1　The ca. 1300 AD Hereford Map indicating a representative example of those places which were significant within Egypt in Medieval eyes (© Hereford Cathedral Library).　67

Figure 5:1　The Great Pyramid and Sphinx of Giza as described by Cardinal Marco Grimani in ca. 1535–1536 (Serlio 1540; Marquand Library, Princeton University, SAPX N2510. S49q).　104

Figure 5:2　Hermes Trismegistus on the mosaic pavement (1488) of the cathedral of Siena, Italy (Opera della metropolitana di Siene Aut. n. 9943; © Alinari/Art Resource).　110

Figure 5:3　The marble 13th–15th century Columna Osiriana in the Museo Civico Viterbo, Italy, described by Annius of Viterbo as "Egyptian sacred letters" (© B. Curran).　113

Figure 5:4     Woodcut of elephant and obelisk from the                        114
               Hypnerotomachia Poliphili, Venice, 1499 (fol. b. vii-v
               Marquand Library of Art and Archaeology, Princeton
               University).

Figure 5:5     One of a pair of granite lions originally inscribed for King    115
               Nectanebo I in the fourth century BC, and relocated to
               Rome by the end of the 12th century AD.

Figure 5:6     Drawing attributed to Baldassare Peruzzi or Simone del          116
               Pollaiuolo, studies of the Vatican obelisk (Hassan 2003:
               Figure 2:22) and of the hieroglyphs on a small obelisk now
               in Berlin (© Bonnat Museum, Bayonne, France).

Figure 5:7     Cronaca–Peruzzi depiction of 'Four Roman Obelisks' with         117
               accurate renditions of their hieroglyphs (ca. 1510). The first
               (from the left) is an obelisk of Ramesses II, with part of it
               restored in the drawing; the second is the obelisk moved in
               the 18th century to the Piazza della Rotunda; the third is
               another reconstruction first located in the façade of a
               building; and the fourth, an obelisk originally standing on
               Tiber island (Christ Church, Oxford, inv. no. 0814v).

Figure 5:8     Frontispiece for the Mass of St John the Baptist (ca. 1530–     120
               1538) (John Rylands University Library, Manchester,
               England, MS 32, fol. 79r).

Figure 5:9     Inlaid bronze table top, Mensa Isiaca (de Montfaucon 1719–      122
               1724: pl. 138 (Special Collections, Pennsylvania State
               University)).

Figure 5:10    John Greaves' (1646: pl. opposite 106) measured "inside of      125
               the first and fairest pyramid", the first accurate
               representation of a pyramid's cross-section (Churchill and
               Churchill 1744–1746: 632).

Figure 5:11    Gianlorenzo Bernini and Ercole Ferrata's 'Obelisk and          130
               Elephant' (1666–1667), Piazza di S. Maria sopra Minerva,
               Rome (© B. Curran).

Figure 6:1     William Stukeley's (15 May 1724) representation of the          146
               winged serpent penetrating a circle which epitomized the
               true trinitarian belief of the Druids (Bodleian Library,
               Oxford, Gough Maps 231 f. 31).

Figure 6:2     Engraving of 'A mummy brought from Egypt' (Pococke             150
               1743–1745, 1: pl. XLVI).

Figure 6:3     Norden's 'colossal head of the sphinx' in front of a pyramid    151
               at Giza (Norden 1755, 1: pl. XLVI).

Figure 6:4     William Stukeley's drawing of "Ancient Symbols of the           157
               Deity" (Stukeley 1743: pl. XL), which includes a
               comparison of Chinese with Ancient Egyptian symbols.

Figure 7:1    William Stukeley's (1743: pl. VII) drawing of a                    164
              "scenographic view of the druid temple of Avebury in
              north Wiltshire", in which he interprets the Overton Hill
              end as the head of a snake, Avebury itself as the snake's
              coiled body, and the Beckhampton Avenue as its tail.

Figure 7:2    Title page of Gliddon 1849 with a hieroglyphic dedication        171
              to Zachary Taylor, President of the United States of
              America.

Figure 7:3    Profiles of pharaonic portraits used to demonstrate the         173
              Caucasian identity of the Ancient Egyptians (Nott and
              Gliddon 1854: figs. 44–47).

# A note on transliteration from ancient Egyptian

The ancient Egyptian scripts convey 24 consonants, no vowels. Fourteen of these occur in modern English, written with one letter: b, d, f, g, h, k, m, n, p, r, s, t, w, y. Three more are also found in English, but usually written with two letters: to keep transliteration as direct as possible, these are transliterated by Egyptologists as follows:

š     'sh' as in 'sheep'

<u>t</u>     'ch' as in 'chin'

<u>d</u>     as in 'j' and 'dg' of 'judge'

The other seven Egyptian consonants do not occur in written English, and are transliterated by Egyptologists as follows:

ꜣ     the glottal stop (faintly heard if you start a sentence with a vowel in English)

i     a sound varying between glottal stop and y

ꜥ     the 'ayin' of Arabic, a deep guttural clenching of the throat

ḥ     a stronger 'h', found in modern Arabic

ḫ     found in Arabic, the 'ch' of Scottish 'loch'

ẖ     a sound varying between ḥ and š

q     a form of 'k' pronounced deeper in the throat, and found in Arabic

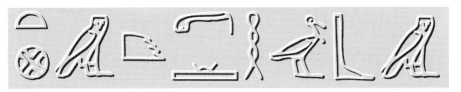

# CHAPTER 1

# INTRODUCTION: EGYPT ANCIENT AND MODERN

*Timothy Champion and Peter Ucko*

## Fascinating Egypt

All the books in this series are, in some way or another, concerned with why and how Ancient Egypt has exercised such a fascination for other societies. They show how many societies from the ancient world to the present day have been inspired, or at times even obsessed, by Egypt. Some of the books examine how specific events triggered such enthusiasm, such as Bonaparte's invasion of Egypt in 1798 or the discovery of Tutankhamun's tomb in 1922, but, as the chapters in this book show, there has always been what must have appeared to those concerned as a long history of knowledge of and interest in Egypt. It is a particularly intriguing aspect of this history that in some ways it has been a more or less continuous history. This is not to suggest any kind of homogeneity of interest; indeed, this interest has many different manifestations: in visiting Egypt, in writing about Egypt and its culture, or in collecting or imitating its antiquities. It also, at different times, draws on very different sources of evidence about Egypt, from the contemporary knowledge of trading partners and resource-obtaining expeditions to the personal experiences of Greek and Roman historians and geographers, preserved in the classical tradition; to the pioneering discoveries of Renaissance scholars in Italy; to the first-hand experiences of travellers; and, later, to the discoveries of archaeologists. Though this fascination with Egypt has proved a durable feature of western and Islamic thought, it has persisted through many different social and intellectual contexts, and served many different ideological purposes. As the following chapters relate, Egypt has been many things to many people. Thus, for example, the Greek and Roman worlds, which frequently expressed a sense of amazement at the culture and wisdom of pharaonic Egypt, could vary their approach from emphasizing the strangeness or perversity of Egypt to seeing Egypt as the natural precursor of all later human developments and achievements – and these two strands were not mutually exclusive. Ancient Egypt also played a major role in the Judaeo-Christian biblical tradition. Though to some it was a place of oppression, it was again mostly seen as a source of civilization. Such interpretations of 'Egypt', however, were not socially or politically innocent, but were deeply embedded in the intellectual structures of their time, not just in the evidence available at any specific point. The interpretations were situated in an ideological context in which such evidence could be used and within the cultural institutions through which such interpretations could be projected and disseminated. Egypt's varied past provided a large repertoire of ideas and physical remains that could be selected or rejected in constructing an image of Egypt, and its changing role in the classical, medieval and early modern eras gave many different contexts in which Egypt, both contemporary and ancient, could be viewed.

Although societies have constructed their image of Egypt according to their own concerns and on the basis of the evidence available to them, Egypt's own geographical location and its historical fate, not unrelated to its location, seem to have made it particularly adaptable to such varied representations.

## Egypt at the crossroads

Egypt has occupied an ambiguous place in many different visions of the spatial ordering of the world, whether in geographical, political or cultural terms. Ancient Egypt perceived itself as lying at the centre of the cosmos, but to other eyes its location in the world has been very different. Thus, for example, Herodotus (II.15–17) discussed the place of Egypt within a three-continent system comprising Europe, Asia and Libya (Thomas 2000: 80–88). Archaic Ionian tradition had adopted a division based on physical features, with continental land masses separated by major rivers, but Herodotus regarded it as absurd to divide Asia from Africa along the line of the Nile, thus bisecting the homeland of the Egyptians. Instead, he proposed to adopt contemporary political or cultural divisions and to align the boundaries of the continents with the boundaries of the Egyptians. His primary concern at this point, however, was to criticize the three-continent scheme itself and to emphasize the unity of the occupied earth, and hence he avoided the question of which continent Egypt really belonged to.

This argument recalls contemporary concerns about the place of Egypt in Africa and therefore the role of Africa in the development of civilization (O'Connor and Reid 2003a: 1–10; Wengrow 2003). Since Egypt lies (mostly, in terms of modern political borders) within the physical boundary of Africa, it is possible to insist on Africa as a meaningful entity for the cultural analysis of the human past, and thus to affirm the importance of Africa's role in that past by virtue of Egypt's civilization. O'Connor and Reid (2003b: 2–3) write:

> On the face of it this appears to be a rather simple question to resolve: geographically Egypt is indisputably situated in Africa. Yet this statement immediately throws up the question, What exactly is Africa? and the logical corollary, What is African? The geographical division of the world into continents is a consequence of European geographical traditions and its fixation with categorization. Mazrui (1986) for instance presents a provocative case for redrawing the continent's boundaries to include the Arabian peninsula ... [T]he definition of what is African, and what it is to be African, is still more complex ... these are constructs which have been generated by European discourse and their definition ... helps to define the opposite of 'European', with implicit notions of civilization and sophistication equally important to this definition ... Hence, the dominant perception of Ancient Egypt, particularly in western thought, has long been 'in Africa, but not of Africa'.

An alternative configuration of the world in Greek and Roman thought placed the Mediterranean at the centre, with the civilized peoples round its coast: "living round the sea like ants and frogs round a pond" in Plato's famous phrase (*Phaedo* 109B). Hellenistic geographers from Eratosthenes onwards often saw the world beyond the Mediterranean margins as divided among the Celts in the west, the Scythians in the north, the Indians in the east, and the Libyans in the south. Here too, Egypt belongs implicitly to the inner circle of Mediterranean lands, clearly distinguished from the less well known and barbarian world of Libya, though not part of the Greek *koine*, at least until Alexander the Great's conquest in 332 BC. The same geographical frame of reference, placing the Mediterranean centre stage, has been adopted by modern historians, most notably Braudel (1972) in his study of the times of Philip II of Spain in the 16th century, and by Horden and Purcell (2000) in their study of Mediterranean history in the classical and early medieval periods. It is interesting to see the part played by Egypt in these lengthy works. Egypt appears throughout Braudel's study of the Mediterranean, but the 16th century was a time of comparative economic and political decline, and it receives less attention than other areas such as Turkey. Egypt is similarly present in Horden and Purcell's work, but it plays a relatively minor role in comparison to Spain, Italy, Asia Minor and the Levant. Here too, Egypt seems to be geographically part of the Mediterranean world, but historically and culturally peripheral.

If Egypt's location in the spatial ordering of the world is ambivalent, then its location on the frontiers of Asia and Africa and on the coastline of the eastern Mediterranean has played a major part in its changing historical fortunes. For more than two millennia the various kingdoms and dynasties that dominated some or all of the Nile Valley, and occasionally further afield, remained independent, but from early in the first millennium the area came increasingly under pressure from external powers in Europe and in Asia. Conquest by Assyria in 671 BC initiated a long and almost unbroken sequence of domination by foreign powers, including Achaemenid Persia (twice), Macedonia, the Roman, Byzantine, Islamic and Ottoman empires (Matthews and Roemer 2003a, b; Warburton 2003; Warburton and Matthews 2003), France and Britain – before eventual independence again in the 20th century AD. Thus, at first, Egypt was squeezed between a succession of power blocks emanating from Europe and from Asia: the dominant polities might change, but Egypt's location at the junction of the continents, and its wealth of productive resources, made it perpetually vulnerable. Later, as European expansion led to the creation of overseas empires, Egypt's location gave it a new, critical importance in global geopolitics, as the key to speedier communications between western Europe and India and the Far East, whether by the so-called 'overland route' between Alexandria and the Red Sea or later, from 1869, via the Suez Canal. Like central Asia, Egypt became a pawn in a 'great game' of imperial competition (Jeffreys 2003a, b). Napoleon's invasion was designed to hinder Britain's links with its richest possession and inevitably provoked an immediate response, resulting in naval disaster and eventual withdrawal; the Suez Canal became a major factor in the politics of the later 19th century, and as late as 1956 Britain intervened militarily in an attempt to retain control of it as a gateway to the empire east of Suez.

This chequered political history has produced a similarly complex cultural mixture in Egypt. After the millennia of political independence and autonomous cultural development, the indigenous Egyptian tradition was diverted by its incorporation into the Greek world of Alexander's empire and its successor states

(La'da 2003). The foundation of Alexandria on the Mediterranean coast was not only a symbol of the importance of the conquered territory in the Macedonian empire, but its very location represented Egypt's reorientation towards the north and the significance of its integration into the hellenistic world. Egypt was of enormous economic and strategic importance to the Greco-Roman world, but it also had a value as the source of ancient wisdom and as a contemporary centre of scholarship. Alexandria became the leading Greek city of the eastern Mediterranean, at least up to the foundation of Constantinople, and its lighthouse and its library (Butler 2003: 260–261; El Daly, Chapter 3) were wonders of the ancient world. With the Arab conquest in 641 AD, just three centuries after its adoption of Christianity, all was changed. Egypt was incorporated into an Islamic world that included the Middle East and North Africa; though it made inroads into Europe, especially in the Balkans and in Spain, its progress there was largely blocked by the forces of Christian Europe, and it achieved greater success in its attempts to expand eastwards. Egypt reached the peak of its economic and political importance in this world under the Ayyubid and Mameluk dynasties in the 13th and 14th centuries (Abu Lughod 1989). When an Egyptian city once again played a major role as a place of world importance, it was Cairo, not Alexandria, and its importance lay not in its connections to the Mediterranean and Europe, but in its role in a network of economic and political relationships embracing the Indian Ocean, the Red Sea and the Arabian Gulf, and stretching to the east coast of Africa and the Far East (Chaudhuri 1985, 1990). Egypt was a centre of Islamic culture and scholarship, as well as of economic power.

The later centuries of Ottoman Egypt were a period of comparative decline as the Indian Ocean was increasingly penetrated by western European traders and armies. By the 18th century Egypt's importance was for strategic reasons of communications rather than economic or cultural significance. Europe's commercial and military power was outstripping that of the Islamic world, and the industrial revolution was creating real differences in the wealth and productive potential of nations on a scale that had simply not existed in the pre-industrial world. Though the terminology of 'development' and 'under-development' lay far in the future, Egypt was becoming a third-world country in comparison to western Europe. By the 19th century Egypt was again turning to the west, and to the United States as much as to Europe, as Mohammed Ali initiated a policy of modernization and industrialization, often at the expense of the surviving remains of Egypt's past. Overseas trade was vital, as was the role of foreign consuls: the United States Consul, George Gliddon (Champion, Chapter 7: 168–175), came to sell industrial machinery and ended up purchasing mummies and other antiquities to supply to collectors and scholars abroad.

## Where exactly was Egypt?

When Herodotus (II.15) took issue with some Ionian geographers who applied the term 'Egypt' only to the area of the Delta, he was implicitly recognizing the important fact that such terms are not neutral or objectively given, but culturally constructed in a specific intellectual milieu. He poked fun at them by asking where the Egyptians would have lived before the formation of the Delta, but their perception of the meaning of the name is quite understandable. In the seventh and sixth centuries BC, under the Saite rulers of the twenty-sixth Dynasty, Egypt's political and economic centre of gravity had shifted to the Delta region and contacts with archaic Greece were expanding. The most important locations in Egypt were the cities of the Delta, such as Sais itself, or the Greek colonial enclave at Naukratis. Just as important as the political setting were the prevailing modes of representing geography in the early Greek world: one of the major genres was the *periplous*, or description of the coastline from the point of view of a navigator, which inevitably gave prominence to the coastal region at the expense of the hinterland. Herodotus, however, was writing in, or perhaps developing, a different mode of enquiry and was interested in a much wider range of historical and cultural evidence; he quite naturally took a broader view of what constituted Egypt, defining it in human terms as the area where Egyptians lived (Harrison 2003; Tait, Chapter 2). Although he did not define specific limits, it is clear that he regarded the core of Egypt as comprising the Nile Valley northwards from Elephantine and the First Cataract. The bulk of his Egyptian ethnography is then devoted to the area of the Nile south of the Delta; when he finally turns to the Delta and the very different life of the inhabitants of the marsh lands there (Herodotus II.92–95), his treatment is much briefer and reads like an obligatory appendix to a discussion of the real Egypt.

Most subsequent discussions of Egypt have, for the most part implicitly, followed the pattern established by Herodotus. Egypt was defined by reference to its core rather than to any borders; regardless of whatever contemporary political boundaries may have existed, that core territory was seen as the middle Nile Valley from Memphis to Aswan. The effect of this dominant representation of the whole of Egypt by a selected part has been to exclude other regions of what was once Egypt from equal consideration, and to relegate them to positions of little or no significance. Perhaps most important was the whole area of the Delta. The environment was, of course, as Herodotus had observed, completely different and monuments survived far less well there than further south, but the whole region was by its very location more outward-looking and more cosmopolitan than the more isolated and introverted valley to the south. Cities such as Naukratis, Tanis, Sais and then Alexandria, and later still Tinnis and Damietta, were all subject to influence from the Mediterranean and must have presented very different characters from those further up the Nile.

Also missing from the selective image of Egypt were the areas of desert, especially the Eastern Desert, with the mineral resources so important in the Roman period, and the Red Sea coast. The conceptual southern boundary of Egypt at Elephantine also acted to preclude any consideration of Egypt's further expansion up the Nile, though from the time of the Old Kingdom onwards, albeit not continuously, Egyptian power had regularly extended into Nubia and in the time of Tuthmosis I reached as far as the Fifth Cataract. The significance of this geographically blinkered view of Egypt is not just that it obscures the extent of Egyptian power and authority, but it presents a partial and flawed version of the nature of Ancient Egypt. By concentrating on the cities, tombs and monuments of the Nile Valley, the military and expansionist nature of the Egyptian state is minimized. At its maximum extent, Egypt's rule extended from the Fifth Cataract in the south to beyond the Euphrates in modern Syria, but that is not a perception that sits easily with a narrow focus on the Nile.

This geographically metonymical representation of Egypt was, of course, shaped by the survival of distinctive monuments in that region. From at least the time of Augustus, large Egyptian monuments have been exported or imitated, and the monumental architecture has become the standard iconic representation of Ancient Egypt, in particular the distinctive forms of the pyramid (Hassan 1998: 205–206; Humbert 2003) and the obelisk (Hassan 2003). Only mummies can rival these monuments as icons of Egypt (Lupton 2003). Even before Renaissance scholars turned their attention to Egyptian monuments, as recounted by Curran (Chapter 5), or travellers began to return with more reliable accounts of Egypt in the later 17th century (Haycock, Chapter 6), western Europe knew of the pyramids as distinctive features of Ancient Egypt (Burnett, Chapter 4). As graphic representations of Egyptian and Egyptianizing monuments became more common, first from Rome and later from visits to Egypt itself, so the visual imagery of Egypt as a land of monuments clustered along the Nile was created and regularly reinforced.

In the 19th century it was possible for many more people to experience this symbolic landscape. As travel to Egypt became more common, a standard itinerary was developed to meet the needs of the European and American tourists (Reid 2002). They moved rapidly from Alexandria to Cairo, and from there directly upstream to Aswan, where they turned and sailed downstream at a more leisurely pace, visiting the monuments en route (El Daly 2003: 142–144). Here again, the visitor experience of Egypt seldom extended to more than the Nile Valley from Cairo to Aswan. For those who could not travel personally, there were many published accounts of such visits. This image of Egypt was further reinforced by visual representations, whether the grand lithographs of monuments by David Roberts (Werner 2003: Figure 5:10) or the more humble wood cuts produced to illustrate the many travel books. Another image was now created to add to the repertoire, that of feluccas sailing on the Nile (Figure 1:1), and the narrow fertile corridor between the deserts; although it was an image of modern, not ancient, Egypt, it served to reinforce the idea of Egypt as being synonymous with the middle Nile Valley. Archaeology has also re-emphasized this vision of Egypt. By its concentration on the better preserved monuments of the area to the south of the Delta, it too has projected an image of Egypt as synonymous with the Nile Valley and its desert margins. Numerous accounts and photographs of excavations revealing monuments from under the encroaching sand have once more projected this stereotypical image of Egypt (Rice and MacDonald 2003: Figure 1:9).

## When was Egypt?

In much the same way as Egypt has come to be symbolized and represented by one of its geographical parts, so also has it come to be predominantly represented by one segment of its chronological past: the Ancient Egypt of the pharaonic period has come to stand for Egypt as a whole, the 'real' Egypt. One very obvious manifestation of this phenomenon is the current structure of academic disciplines, and the emergence of Egyptology as a distinct area of expertise with all the trappings of a separate identity, including specialist knowledge and training, university departments and institutes, conferences, journals and distinctive jargon. Egyptology as currently constituted in European universities has defined its subject area as the period from the Predynastic

Figure 1:1 'View on the Nile. Isle of Rhoda and the ferry of Geezeh' (1838) by David Roberts (1796–1854). On 7 October "while he waited for the mainsail yard to be replaced ..., he passed the time by drawing the Giza ferry, with the Pyramids in the background" (Bourbon 1996: 36; Roberts 1855).

to the Ptolemaic, leaving earlier periods to prehistorians and later periods to classical or Islamic archaeologists. It is easy to understand why there was such a rapid growth of archaeological and historical research in the period of intellectual excitement following the decipherment of the hieroglyphs, and how this led to Egypt becoming the focus for one of the first areas of specialism and of professional employment within the emerging discipline of archaeology. The setting of such academic boundaries has, however, only reinforced more popular perceptions of the image of Egypt, through a variety of media such as museum displays and non-specialist publications. In a wider sense, it also reflects and perpetuates a pervasive western vision of the history of Europe, seen in terms of not a simple continuity, but a continuity punctuated by major turning points: in this scheme, the pre-classical, classical, medieval and modern worlds are separated by the key events of the rise of the classical world, its decline into the Dark Ages, and the subsequent Reformation. In the case of Egypt, its pagan past was demarcated from the period of its incorporation into the Greco-Roman and later Christian world, which was in turn distinguished from its Islamic era by the Arabic conquest in the seventh century.

The Islamic conquest of Egypt also removed it firmly from any possible role in the history of Europe. The medieval conception of Europe as equivalent to Christendom (Hay 1968), in opposition to the alien Islamic world to the east, marginalized even those regions of a geographical Europe that had been subject to Islamic rule, such as Spain or the Balkans, let alone those areas further afield that had once been part of the Greco-Roman world. It may seem ironic that the period when Egypt played its most significant role in European history, as one of the wealthiest provinces of the Roman world and a focus of early Christianity, is the one most forgotten in popular western images. The contemporary situation that all western travellers encountered, from early medieval to modern times, of Egypt as Arabic and Islamic, conditioned one image of the country, while classical and biblical knowledge of its pagan past shaped another. Classical and Christian Egypt, however, quite apart from leaving far less in the way of distinctive monuments, fitted less comfortably with western constructions of the past. Even at times when Egypt played a critical role in debates about the history of Christianity (Haycock, Chapter 6), its importance revolved not around its significance in late Roman and Byzantine times and its part in the growth of the monasteries, but around Egypt's pagan religion as the origin of true belief and the precursor of Christianity.

From the Renaissance onwards, then, interest in Egypt has focused primarily on the pharaonic period, despite the ever growing range of evidence for Egypt's past and present. Prior to the Renaissance, knowledge of Egypt was drawn almost entirely from classical and biblical sources, and it was inevitable that attention should focus on the period of the pharaohs and the pyramids. The centre of interest was, therefore, on the earliest periods of Egyptian history, periods that had a precise chronology in terms of the king lists and had regularly been regarded as the oldest known episode of human civilization.

The king list preserved through the writings of Manetho (Tait, Chapter 2) demonstrated a chronology for Egyptian royal dynasties going back to approximately 3000 BC. Although there has been extensive argument about the exact reliability of these computations, a date for the start of centralized state authority in Egypt in the centuries around then has been broadly agreed. Until comparatively recent advances in archaeology had established more reliable dates for the emergence of civilizations in Mesopotamia, the Indus Valley and China, the Egyptian chronology was therefore the only one, other than that derived from the Bible, that could be extended back before the classical period of Greece, and Egypt therefore enjoyed a uniquely privileged status as the only ancient society.

The idea of Egypt as the oldest of human nations, and as the origin of human knowledge, was a particularly pervasive one. As Tanner (2003: 118) points out, both the origins of monumental sculpture and architecture and those of painting were attributed by Herodotus (II.4) and Aristotle (Pliny *Historia naturalis* VII.205, XXXV.15–16) to Egypt.

The dynastic chronology became acutely problematic when set alongside calculations for the biblical tradition, such as those of Archbishop Ussher, who dated the Creation to 4004 BC; here again, although there were disputes about details, the idea of a six thousand-year-old world was widely accepted. Egypt, therefore, was nearly as old as creation. When 17th and 18th century religious controversy relied heavily on chronology, as Haycock (Chapter 6) explains, Egypt occupied a position of antiquity and authority that allowed it to be seen as the origin of true knowledge and belief, reversing its traditionally accepted relationship with Hebraic culture. The dynastic chronology was also critically important in another debate, as Champion shows in Chapter 7; the polygenist anthropologists of the ante-bellum United States argued that the markedly different representation of physical types in Egyptian tomb paintings (cp. O'Connor and Quirke 2003: Figure 1:6), reliably dated by the accepted dynastic scheme, showed that there was insufficient time for the human species, if the product of a single creation, to have diversified by that time. A multiple human creation and the immutability of the races were therefore demonstrated, giving 'scientific' support to the ideology of inequality and the institution of slavery. The chronology of the Egyptian pharaohs may now seem an abstruse topic, but it played a key role in diverse political and religious debates.

## Egypt in the Mediterranean

Understanding of the early classical world's attitudes to Egypt is shaped by the survival of Herodotus' writings (Tait, Chapter 2). Although his is the longest of the surviving treatments of Egypt, and was undoubtedly influential in establishing a genre of ethnographic work, Herodotus was by no means the earliest writer to be fascinated by Egypt, and concentration on him alone obscures the fact that there was a long-lasting Egyptian discourse in ancient literature (*aigyptiaka*), constituting a classical 'Egyptology' (Hartog 1986). From early inclusions of its location in seafaring manuals of the Mediterranean coast, the discourse was shaped by the Ionian tradition of scientific enquiry, which Herodotus inherited through others such as Hecataeus of Miletus. This was not, however, a neutral, objective tradition of writing: Herodotus wrote to produce a 'mirror' (Hartog 1988) to focus attention on Greek society. His treatments of Egypt and Scythia represented a symmetrical ordering of the physical and moral world, the northern and southern opposites around a central Greece. Herodotus was fascinated by the natural phenomena of the Nile and the formation of the Delta, but his treatment of the people and their culture was shaped by the rhetorical tropes of opposition. The Egyptians did things the opposite way from the Greeks, but that did not imply any relationship of inferiority and superiority (Harrison 2003); indeed, the very fact of constructing this series of oppositions served both to divide Greece from Egypt and to unite Greece and Egypt in opposition to the very different peoples further from the Mediterranean. Herodotus attributed to Egypt the origin of such cultural achievements as architecture and writing, and therefore recognized a Greek debt to Egypt, but this too did not imply Greek inferiority. Greek knowledge of Egypt was increasing with greater contact, and the Greek image of Egypt was moving from a fascination with the country as a land of wonders and knowledge to a more matter-of-fact acceptance of it as a part of the world in which the Greeks lived and travelled. Herodotus had, however, firmly fixed some of what were to be the recurrent motifs of Egypt, including the Nile and its physical properties, Egyptian wisdom and knowledge, and hieroglyphic writing.

In the meantime, another vision of the place of Greece in the wider world had developed with a clearer sense of a Greek identity and the invention of the idea of the barbarian (Hall 1997). This polarization of identities took place as the Greek world expanded through colonization, but was sharpened in the political conflict with Persia. In addition to the basic linguistic meaning of the term (barbarians spoke incomprehensible languages, not Greek), the major distinguishing factor was a political one: Greeks had the advantage of civilized rule through the institutions of the city-state, or *polis*, while barbarians were subject to the autocratic rule of monarchs. On the basis of such a criterion, the Egyptians were clearly barbarians. One powerful medium for the construction and dissemination of such ideas was the stage, and especially the Athenian tragedies (Hall 1989). The representation of foreigners included the use of ethnic stereotypes, and these certainly did convey an implication of Greek superiority: the Egyptians were regularly portrayed as charlatans. Though ethnic abuse of this sort is largely absent from the more philosophical, ethnographic or historical genres of writing, it is found again in different media such as the satires of Juvenal (Maehler 2003; Tait, Chapter 2; Walker 2003). It is difficult to judge whether the 'popular culture' of satire and stage represented something nearer to the views of the general Greek and Roman publics than the 'high culture' of other literary genres.

Though characterized in this way as barbarians and charlatans, the Egyptians seem never to have been exposed to the same force of antagonism as the Persians. Egypt in fact occupied an ambivalent position: though clearly non-Greek, and traditionally ruled by an autocratic monarchy, Egypt had been drawn close into the Greek world. The colony at Naukratis was the gateway for increasing commercial contacts, while Greek mercenaries served in the armies of the Saite pharaohs. Egypt had also been a major donor in response to an appeal for the rebuilding of the Greek sanctuary at Delphi. Above all, Egypt had been conquered by the Persians, and any enemy of the Persians was an ally of the Athenians, who in the 460s BC launched an ill-fated attempt to assist an Egyptian revolt. In these shifting commercial, political and military circumstances, Egypt could not be simplistically characterized as barbarian, especially in comparison to Persia, even if the word had little of the meaning of the modern word 'barbarity'.

In the generations after Herodotus, the opposition of Greek and barbarian was still a potent theme for thinking about the world, but the distinguishing criterion became less strictly one of the mode of government, and more one of culture, education and intellectual and moral qualities. Some writers began to see the simpler ways of non-Greek peoples as preferable to those of the Greeks. In the hellenistic world, there was also a change of attitude towards the institution of monarchy, and the accession of a Greek dynasty of pharaohs, ruling from a Greek city at Alexandria, had brought Egypt even further into the orbit of the Greek world. The accounts of wonders and marvels disappeared, as did the theme of Greek/Egyptian opposition, and one of the key features of the Herodotean discourse prevailed – that of Egypt as a source of wisdom. The evidence was still the same, and the Greek tradition of historical and ethnographic writing had changed little, but the political and intellectual context was very different. In the first century BC, Diodorus Siculus visited Egypt to carry out the research for his universal history, but his version of the Egyptian debate included accounts of the origin of language and astronomy, of Osiris as the one who spread agriculture around the world, and of the pharaoh as a wise and just king.

Thirty years later, in the 20s BC, the Greek geographer Strabo also visited Egypt, staying for a long period in Alexandria and travelling up the Nile. By then, however, Egypt had been incorporated as a Roman province, the special preserve of the emperor. Strabo's account of Egypt, though giving considerable attention to the monuments of the Egyptian past, is little more than a topographical description. He stresses not so much the mysteries and wisdom of Ancient Egypt as the long tradition of civilized life and the progress made in establishing good order.

Throughout this half millennium of written accounts of the Greek and Roman worlds' encounters with Egypt, during which it was transformed from a distant place of wonder to a much-visited and well-known province of the Empire, the theme of Egypt as the origin of knowledge and the special guardian of wisdom is a prevalent one. But it is important to ask, as Tait (Chapter 2) does, whether the reality of classical knowledge of Egypt matched the apparent literary interest. It is not just a matter of what evidence was available to them, or a question of physical and linguistic access. There is a more fundamental problem of whether the classical world was really interested in Ancient Egypt. To take a specific example, hieroglyphs play a significant role in this long discourse, from Herodotus onwards, but it is striking how intellectually incurious the various writers seem to have been. Few other than the late Roman historian Ammianus Marcellinus showed any interest in how this writing system actually worked, despite its prominent appearance in the literature and despite the fact that hieroglyphic inscriptions could have been seen in Rome itself from early imperial times (Hassan 2003; Iversen 1993). Classical writers were keen to deploy Egypt, the Nile and its revered tradition of knowledge as literary motifs, but seldom (perhaps with the exception of Herodotus) showed much interest in the people or the culture of Egypt.

## The lost civilization

> Dynastic Egyptian literature, the written documents of a whole civilization, historical and religious, monumental and cursive fell silent. All that remained was a faint remembrance and a widespread and deeply rooted notion of the symbolic nature of Egyptian writing ...
>
> (Junger with Behlmer 2001: 265)

Somewhere around the early fifth century AD the last person with the knowledge to write a hieroglyphic inscription died. The use of hieroglyphic and demotic scripts had been in decline for some centuries, but had still formed a significant part of the living culture of Egypt. Pagan religious practices similarly lingered in remote outposts such as Philae, but these too succumbed to Christianity. The last hieroglyphic inscription is dated to 390 AD; use of the demotic script persisted into the fifth century, but then the tradition finally failed. For more than a millennium the hieroglyphs would remain mute and inaccessible. Ancient Egypt had been a part of the contemporary Mediterranean world of Greece and Rome; visitors such as Herodotus, Diodorus or Strabo could, if intellectual curiosity moved them, talk to living exponents of Egyptian knowledge, but from the fifth century onwards, Egypt was known not through its living descendants or its own literary tradition, but through the images constructed of it by others.

The brief centuries of Christian Egypt before the Arabic conquest coincided with the decline of the Roman empire in the west and the onset of the so-called Dark Ages. It is an episode now largely forgotten outside the academic sphere, elided between visions of Ancient and Islamic Egypt. Connections between Egypt and the west were important, however; the so-called 'Coptic bowls', bronze basins probably made in Alexandria and found in some rich graves of the seventh century as far west as Anglo-Saxon England (Figure 1:2), are the physical symbol of Egypt's significant role in the early Christian world. From the Arabic conquest, however, Egypt was removed from the Christian world of the Mediterranean and incorporated into the Islamic world of the Near East: Christian Europe opposed to Islamic East became the dominant vision of the new world order.

Nevertheless, western Europe retained a memory of Egypt, as Burnett (Chapter 4) shows, but it was a memory filtered through classical and biblical traditions. Travellers from the west, especially en route to the Holy Land, continued to visit Egypt, but what they saw was a very partial view. They were familiar only with the Mediterranean coast and the Delta region, as far south as Memphis, and the monuments they inspected were the Pharos at Alexandria and the remains of Christian Egypt; the whole of the Nile Valley south of Memphis remained unknown. The only relics of Ancient Egypt they saw were the pyramids, and even there the persistent myth that they were the pharaohs' storehouses shows how far the Bible had eclipsed all other sources of knowledge about the past. In accordance with the biblical account of the peopling of the earth after the Flood, the Islamic population of contemporary Egypt were traced to a descent from Ham, the son of Noah, thus severing any biological link with the people of Ancient Egypt.

An imagined Ancient Egypt emerged from the Bible, the surviving classical texts and later from translations of Arabic sources. From the Bible, it was the very opposite

Figure 1:2   Bronze 'Coptic bowl' from the early seventh century royal burial at Sutton Hoo, Suffolk, England (British Museum 1939–1010. 109). Diameter 38.5 cm.

of Israel, a land of exile, or possibly flight from oppression, and the home of pagan idols. From the classical tradition, it was the location for the popular romances about Alexander. Despite the fact that the writings of the Neoplatonists were unknown and very little of the hermetic tradition was available, Egypt still retained its reputation as the origin of philosophical, scientific and medical wisdom: Ptolemy's astronomy was widely known, and Egypt was the source for *mummia*, medicine derived from mummies. The borders between science and magic were unclear, and it was to Egypt that the origin of the practice of alchemy was assigned in the Arabic texts increasingly available in translation. Egypt was a recurrent motif in western thought and imagination, but what they actually knew of Egypt's past was little more than science, magic, pyramids and mummies.

The Egyptian literary tradition was equally impenetrable to Islamic scholars, but, with the advantage of easier access to Egypt, they showed much greater interest in and familiarity with the monuments (El Daly, Chapter 3). The meanings attached to these remains were very similar to those seen in the West: the temples were sites of knowledge and magic, and the hieroglyphs were symbols encoding that special wisdom. What was different was that Arabic scholars sought to make links between the language of Ancient Egypt and contemporary Arabic, and between ancient Egyptian thought and Islamic philosophy. Thus a sort of kinship was created which was unthinkable in the west, where the Christian tradition looked to a Hebrew origin for its religious ideas, leaving Egypt in an ill-defined ancestral role as a source of wisdom and science.

The outburst of intellectual activity devoted to Ancient Egypt in the Renaissance, especially in Rome, was a remarkable phenomenon, as Curran (Chapter 5) shows, and its results were of the greatest importance. Egyptian monuments and their imitations were discovered and recognized in Rome, and the increased flow of travellers to Egypt began to bring back more antiquities, including mummies. Knowledge of the ancient Egyptian past grew rapidly. More of the classical authors became available as manuscripts were discovered or translated, especially the bulk of the *Corpus Hermeticum* and the writings of the Neoplatonists. These reinforced the image of Egypt as a source of wisdom, of which the hieroglyphs were the material symbol.

Renaissance scholarship, however, was by no means politically innocent, and the study of the ancient past played a significant role in the cultural politics of Italy (Schnapp 1996). A key part was played by the Jesuit priest, Athanasius Kircher (Burnett, Chapter 4), who produced a Coptic grammar and his own mistaken decipherment of hieroglyphs. He repeated once more the idea of Egypt as the source of wisdom and religious belief, but now in a very different context. Appealing to the great antiquity of Egypt, and drawing on the authority given to Egypt's knowledge and contemporary knowledge of Egypt by the scholastic effort of himself and others, he sought to install Egypt as the true origin of religious belief: the Catholic Church, represented by his own order of Jesuits, was the true inheritor of this tradition, and thus claimed the right to unify the human species under its rule.

This linking of Egyptian research and Christian religious debate dominated the discourse of Egypt for two centuries. As scholarly research continued, it gave ever greater authority and significance to Ancient Egypt, which in turn became a more plausible and venerable ancestor for Christian belief. The study of Egypt and the study of Christian theology were inextricably intertwined, as Haycock (Chapter 6) demonstrates. Many of the same scholars operated in what we might now see as two distinct spheres of intellectual activity, but which to them was a single disciplinary field of debate. Even as late as the 1830s, an English ethnologist such as Prichard (Champion, Chapter 7), whose self-appointed task was the defence of Christian belief, devoted much attention to Egypt and the chronology of the ancient world.

During these centuries, the traditional Christian view of the origins of its beliefs in the Hebrew world was overturned, and more and more scholars looked to Egypt as the true source. Renaissance scholarship had undoubtedly played a major role in the rehabilitation of Egypt as a worthy ancestor for Christianity rather than the antithesis of Israel. Ironically, the first advances in archaeological knowledge of the monuments helped to give value and meaning to the Egyptian past, but the interpretation placed on Egypt was still shaped by the classical literary tradition, established by Herodotus, and reinforced by the rediscovery of texts, especially those of the hermetic tradition.

## Egypt and the uses of archaeology

From early in the 18th century, detailed reports of the Egyptian archaeological evidence began to be produced and published in growing numbers. Early travelling scholars such as Pococke, Norden, Niebuhr and Volney laid the foundations, but it was only after the successful decipherment of hieroglyphs that the full potential of the resource was released and the flow of new knowledge turned into a flood. The rise of archaeology provided dramatically different sources of knowledge from the limited range of textual sources and the small number of antiquities known in Europe, and therefore very different opportunities for the exploitation of this new form of intellectual capital.

One means of exploitation was to make possession of Egyptian antiquities a matter of national and personal prestige (see several chapters in Jeffreys 2003a). Another was as the basis for the development of a professional and academic discipline of Egyptology. This was not only a means of establishing personal prestige for individuals within the burgeoning universities and institutes of 19th century Europe, but also a matter of national authority and of European domination of the cultural history of Egypt. Egyptology was, with very few exceptions, the exclusive preserve of European scholars (El Daly, Chapter 3; Haikal 2003: 123–125; Reid 2002), not least by the exclusion by Anglo-American scholarship of any (Arabic) views not expressed first in English. When Egypt's policy turned against the export of its antiquities, it was a Frenchman, Auguste Mariette, who set up the Antiquities Service (Jeffreys 2003b), while fieldwork was dominated by French, Italian, German and later British workers. Egypt plays a central role in Said's theory of orientalism (Said 1978), and the western European control of Egypt's past was a major part of this relationship.

## Egypt in ruins

> Yet all were Babel vanities. Time sadly overcometh all things, and is now dominant, and sitteth upon a sphinx, and looketh unto Memphis and old Thebes, while his sister Oblivion reclineth semisomnous on a pyramid, gloriously triumphing, making puzzles of Titanian erections, and turning old glories into dreams. History sinketh beneath her cloud. The traveller as he paceth amazedly through these deserts asketh of her, who builded them? and she mumbleth something, but what it is he heareth not.

> Egypt herself is now become the land of obliviousness and doteth. Her ancient civility is gone, and her glory has vanished as a phantasma. Her youthful days are over, and her face hath become wrinkled and tetrick. She poreth not upon the heavens, astronomy is dead unto her, and knowledge maketh other cycles.

(Browne 1931: 460)

This wonderfully evocative passage is taken from a 19th century literary fragment by James Crossley.[1] Although the style is reminiscent of Sir Thomas Browne's 17th century beautifully measured English, and he was certainly familiar with a range of Renaissance sources on Egypt, the sentiment does not match his otherwise very scholarly approach to history or his religious meditation on human frailty. The lament for the lost glories of Egypt is, in fact, much more in tune with the romantic sensibilities of a later age. It has much in common with the illustrations of ancient Egyptian ruins set in desert landscapes (but see Werner 2003: Figure 5:10) produced by David Roberts (1796–1854), but perhaps its closest literary parallel is Shelley's sonnet, *Ozymandias* (Werner 2003: 88). He wrote it in 1818, taking his inspiration from a colossal granite bust of an Egyptian ruler, now known to have been Ramesses II, which had been dragged from the temple at Thebes to be put on show in the British Museum (Hamill and Mollier 2003: Figures 11:2, 11:3 col. pls.):

> And on the pedestal these words appear:
> 'My name is Ozymandias, king of kings:
> Look on my works, ye mighty, and despair!'

Nothing beside remains. Round the decay
Of that colossal wreck, boundless and bare
The lone and level sands stretch far away.

To the romantic intellect of the early 19th century Egypt was a land of ruins, a ghostly reminder of a power and a civilization now vanished. In the aftermath of the French Revolution and in the political and economic upheavals of the period in Europe, the collapse of civilization was a terrifyingly real possibility, and writers and artists were obsessed with ruins as a metaphor for Europe's future. Apocalyptic visions of Babylon, Athens, Rome, even London in ruin were wildly popular (Woodward 2001). Though Egypt did not figure in anything comparable to Mary Shelley's (1826) novel, *The Last Man*, set in the plague-stricken and abandoned ruins of Rome, it did nonetheless play a significant part in these doom-laden fantasies.

This new concern for a lost and ruined Egypt marks a major break in Europe's attitude to the country. Previously Egypt had been valued as the origin of knowledge and religious wisdom, and its legacy in later systems of thought and belief was the focus of scholarly concern. Despite the waning of temporal power and the collapse of the temples, the wisdom of Egypt survived; despite later generations' inability to decipher the hieroglyphic inscriptions, the essence of Egyptian thought had survived in the hermetic tradition (for the *Corpus Hermeticum* and the identification of Hermes with Thoth and Imhotep, as well as the influence of the hermetic tradition more widely, and in particular via alchemists to the Rosicrucians, see Burnett, Chapter 4; DuQuesne 1999: 36–40, 43 ff). The mystery of Egypt had been its mystical tradition of religious thought, through which a continuity could be traced to the present. Now, however, Egypt was seen as ancient and lost, a mysterious land about which little was known except that it was a symbol of ruin and destruction.

## Egypt's national past

Britain's occupation of Egypt in 1882 and the emerging sense of Egyptian nationalism that developed in the context of, and in opposition to, that period of colonial rule fostered very different constructions of the relationship between contemporary Egypt and the various phases of the Egyptian past, but emphasized the importance of knowledge about the past, and in particular the ability to control and manipulate that knowledge. In 1910, the then British Prime Minister, Arthur Balfour, addressed the British parliament on "the problems with which we have to deal in Egypt" (Said 1978: 31). Balfour argued that "you may look through the whole history of the Orientals in what is called, broadly speaking, the East, and you never find traces of self-government" (Balfour, quoted in Said 1978: 32–33); whatever had been achieved in the East had been achieved under absolute rule, as one conqueror succeeded another; Britain had assumed the responsibility for exercising this rule, "the dirty work, the inferior work, of carrying on the necessary labour" (Balfour, quoted in Said 1978: 33). This task, so selflessly accepted, benefited everyone: "we are in Egypt not merely for the sake of the Egyptians, though we are there for their sake; we are there also for the sake of Europe at large" (Balfour, quoted in Said 1978: 33). Though Balfour stressed the importance of Britain's knowledge of Egypt's past, this strange and very partial view of Egyptian history is not expounded in detail, but the reference to the more recent periods of Islamic and Ottoman rule is clear. With the collapse of Ottoman rule, Britain regarded Egypt as devoid of any indigenous institutions of power, but also as a place with no autonomous identity, an empty place, lost in time; it could only be administered from outside and its identity could only be reconstructed through intervention from the outside.

In the ensuing period of colonial rule, all administrators were appointed from England or were non-Egyptian; Egyptians were deprived of even minor political and administrative roles. This was in sharp contrast to British practice elsewhere, in India or in Africa, where either an administrative colonized class was encouraged or indirect rule policies were pursued. This administrative exclusion is matched by the almost total absence of Egyptians from positions of academic significance in the field of Egyptology. Knowledge was power, and Britain, and western Europe more generally, had ordained themselves as the only fit exponents of both (Wengrow 2003). The European and American travellers who had ventured to Egypt in the early 19th century had been horrified at the conditions of contemporary Egyptian life that they witnessed, and compared the people to animals (Champion, Chapter 7); they found it difficult to accept any relationship between the present-day Egyptians and the people responsible for the construction of the monuments they had come to see. Just as some people seeking to retain the Parthenon marbles in the British Museum in London rather than return them to Athens have denied any relationship between the ancient Greeks and the contemporary occupants of Greece (Hitchens 1997: 88–90), so too denial of any connection between ancient and contemporary Egyptians has justified the physical and intellectual control of the Egyptian past by Europe, and its political domination in the colonial period by Britain.

The burgeoning nationalism in Egypt from the later 19th century was increasingly concerned, therefore, with developing a distinctive idea of an Egyptian identity and of what it meant to be Egyptian. It is difficult, if not impossible, to imagine a national identity that does not in some way involve a vision of the national past, whether couched in biological, cultural or territorial terms, and Egypt's past offered a rich variety of themes that could be selected to construct such a vision (Gershoni and Jankowski 1986). Three facets of the Egyptian past proved especially useful as paradigms for the future: Egypt's recent role in the Islamic world of the Ottoman empire, her place in a different Islamic world, that of the Arab or Arabic-speaking peoples, and finally an independent Egypt drawing inspiration especially from its remoter pharaonic past. The first of these options was attractive in the years after World War I, when Turkey under Ataturk was beginning to establish a post-Ottoman identity as a secular, modernizing, westernizing state, but this soon gave way to a more pharaonic Egypt, especially after the discovery of the tomb of Tutankhamun in 1922. Since then Arabic and pharaonic visions of Egypt have co-existed, not always easily and sometimes very violently.

The dominant ideology of Egypt in the post-Tutankhamun period up to 1952 was one that emphasized its long period of independence and its ancient splendours, seeing a historical and cultural continuity, rooted particularly in the territory of Egypt and the Nile. With Egypt politically and financially dependent on Europe, another important theme of this period was Egypt's cosmopolitan past and its orientation towards the Mediterranean and the West. It was certainly the Western view of Egypt that prevailed, as cosmopolitan and on the civilizational crossroads between the ancient Near East and Greco-Roman world. Egyptology was supported as the disciplinary formation that provided the ideological evidence linking the civilizations of East and West. The period from the 1930s to 1952 was also the high point of Alexandria as a cosmopolitan Mediterranean city, where King Farouk had his summer residence; there were many thousands of Greeks living there, and nearly as many Italians, French, English and Lebanese. Alexandria, evoking memories of its founder, one of Europe's favourite conquering heroes, and of its later history as a centre of learning and the major city of the Greek East, was the perfect symbol of Egypt's position at the crossroads, and the western obsession with Ancient Egypt, and Egypt's own need to celebrate the cultural achievements of its pre-classical past were quite compatible with this idea of Egypt as Mediterranean.

While the western-supported regime and its royal family projected a western image of Egypt rooted in a concept of historical continuity and Egypt's role at the junction of East and West, the growing opposition to the British presence in Egypt emphasized a vision of the past that ignored these elements, looking rather to the more recent past and to Egypt's potential role in an Arabic community. At the outbreak of World War II in 1939, Britain's chances of victory were not obvious, and the emerging nationalist groups in Egypt recognized their opportunity but bided their time, waiting for the victor to emerge. The Allied victory over the Germans denied the nationalists an easy way forward, and in the following years the elite around King Farouk re-emphasized the former ideology, rejecting the view of Egypt as an Islamic society and as part of the Arab world.

By contrast, after the army officers' revolt of 1952, Nasser's regime (Hassan 1998: 207–208) stressed the Arab and Islamic identity of Egypt and therefore its remoteness from Europe. Nasser's strategic aim was to establish Egypt as an independent nation at the centre of the Arab world and as part of the 'non-aligned movement', outside the polarized conflict of the USSR and the USA in the Cold War. For Nasser, it was important to stress the Arab and Islamic identity of Egypt, and his anti-imperialist stance aligned Egypt with liberation forces in Algeria and with the Palestinians in Israel. It was natural, therefore, to emphasize the modern Islamic cultural identity of Egypt rather than its ancient past. Egyptian victory in the Suez campaign of 1956 led to the end of the British presence in Egypt, and to the withdrawal of non-Egyptians elsewhere. There was an exodus of Greeks, Italians, English and French from Alexandria in the late 1950s as part of the centralization of power in Cairo and of an Egyptianizing campaign. For Nasser, Egyptology was a Western interest and not Egyptian, yet it was also a means of gaining economic support from the West, in particular from the USA. The nationalization of the Suez Canal had been an attempt to raise finance for modernization through the construction of the Aswan Dam after funding had been withdrawn by western states, yet Egypt was happy to accept Unesco assistance in saving the Abu Simbel temples from its rising waters. Culture was an important part of the politics of the Cold War era and of international aid, and Egyptology was thus a means of encouraging economic development and aid from the West.

Egypt's disastrous defeat by Israel in the 1967 war brought home the military and political realities of the weakness of the Arab world and raised questions about the viability of Egypt as a non-aligned Arab state. When Anwar Sadat (1918–1981) took over after the death of Nasser in 1972, he consciously moved Egypt back to its other identity, embedded in its ancient past. His policies were to make peace with Israel and recognize its right to exist, and to crack down heavily on Islamic fundamentalists and in particular the Muslim Brotherhood. Since his death, Egypt has followed a very similar line, but with more concessions to its Islamic past. The rise of mass tourism in the last decades of the 20th century, however, has reinforced the significance of archaeological monuments to the Egyptian economy and to external images of Egypt. Sadat, it is alleged (Hassan 1998: 210–211), often had himself shown as if the leader of Ancient Egypt (Figure 1:3). He was assassinated by a Muslim extremist, representing those who thought they were acting on behalf of the true Islamic and Arab Egypt. His assassin, it is said, cried out, "I have killed Pharaoh" (Hassan 1998: 210). In 1997 Islamic fundamentalists killed 58 foreign tourists at Luxor, striking a blow not only at Egypt's economy but also at the image of Egypt as rooted in its pre-Islamic past. Pharaonic and Islamic images of Egypt sit very uncomfortably with each other.

## 'Wisdom', 'myth' and 'reality'

Today, the term 'wisdom' represents not only itself, as cultivation of knowledge, but also a peculiarly *positive* gloss on that knowledge. The very word implies social approval of the pursuit of knowledge, and appreciation of the 'wise' who master more knowledge than others in the society. Yet Ptahhotep (P. Prisse, 19th century BC, trans. Lichtheim 1975: 63) warned against any simplistic appreciation of 'wisdom': "do not be proud of your knowledge." Science and knowledge can be seen most purely as an index of power when its full-time practitioners are among disciplines too often claiming political innocence, despite their historical role as the shock-troops of colonialism.

As Tait (Chapter 2) observes, there exists a body of ancient funerary compositions directly concerned with relations between knowledge and power. Each of these compositions may be expanded by any or all of four types of 'paratextual' phrases, in order of frequency: declarations of the benefits accruing from knowledge of a formula; instructions for the recitation or copying of a formula; information on the mythic discovery of a formula; instructions to exclude all but a select few from access to the formula. The power of 'wisdom' is sometimes made explicit:

> Guard greatly against doing this for anyone except for yourself, your father, and your son, because this is a great secret of the underworld.
>
> (P. Nu, ch. 137 A; trans. in Lapp 1997: pl. 77)

A further ancient Egyptian slant on the nature of knowledge/'wisdom' is found in P. Westcar (Lichtheim 1975: 215–222) where it is recounted that Hordedef brings a wise man named Djedi to the palace, and the king attempts to learn from him the whereabouts of sacred/secret chambers of the god Thoth:

> Then the king Khufu true of voice said:
> 'What about the report that you know the whereabouts of the chambers of the sanctuary of Thoth?'
> And Djedi said:

Figure 1:3   President Anwar Sadat of Egypt standing in front of pyramids (1977) (© David Hume Kennerly/Getty Images).

'If it please you, I did not know their whereabouts, O sovereign (alive, prosperous and
well!) my lord, but I know the place where that information is.'
Then His Power said:
'So where?'
And Djedi here said:
'There is a chest of flint in the chamber called Inspection in Iunu (Heliopolis) – in that
chest.'
And then Djedi said:
'O sovereign (alive, prosperous and well!) my lord, note that it is not I who is to bring
it to you.'

(trans. column 9, lines 1–7 in Blackman and Davies 1988: pl. 9)

The wise man Djedi then reveals to King Khufu that he will be given the information
he wants by one of three sons of a priest of Ra, slipping in the unwelcome detail that
all three are to succeed to the throne, though only after the son and grandson of Khufu.
In this way a thirst for secret knowledge leads to unwelcome knowledge, that the
family of Khufu will cease to rule Egypt after two generations. As knowledge expands
into the realm of the divine, there is a price to pay, even for the divine king. Although
he makes no direct appearance in the tale, in a sense the central figure is Thoth himself,
the god of writing and knowledge who was to live on into the Greek and Latin world
as Hermes Thrice Great (Trismegistus). The tale gives vivid expression to a belief that
human knowledge cannot be, and should not try to be, as broad as divine knowledge.
The bulk of European, if perhaps not Arabic, commentary from antiquity to the recent
past has focused on the liminal domain of religious composition, and much of the
power of 'Ancient Egypt' is as a motif drawn from this ambiguous character of
communication torn between the accessible and inaccessible.

The lesson to be learnt by the contemporary museum and university is that in
practice they seem most adept at reinforcing existing barriers between social classes
(Bourdieu and Darbel 1966). Relations between knowledge and power are revealed in
every one of the following chapters, as determined by the extent to which the
knowledge obtained on 'Ancient Egypt' in each century depends on, and seems
secondary to, the formations of methods of circulating and developing the
knowledge. Dominant institutions in these histories – Greek *mouseion*, Coptic
monastery, Islamic *madrasa*, medieval Latin university, or early modern European
academy – are the places of learning and the places of storage, the latter often taking
in part the form of places of display.

It is the received wisdom of today that 'truth' is in the eyes of beholders – what is
perceived is what is considered to be relevant to a particular period or social context;
the concept of an objective reality – about Ancient Egypt or anything else – is out of
favour. As Foucault might have said, what we see are constructed fragments in time,
surrounded by areas about which we are largely ignorant. Thus, it should not be
particularly surprising to find the striking differences made by late 19th century Spain
(Sevilla Cueva 2003) and by medieval Christianity (Burnett, Chapter 4) of Potiphar's
wife Lotha (from a sexually deprived, strong-willed queen to a despised Jew) –
although their sources of information would presumably have been the same.

Before the growth of travel to Egypt and the rise of Egyptology in the 18th and
19th centuries, detailed knowledge of Egypt was very limited. However, before and

after Egyptian archaeology was developed, awe was inspired by Egypt despite the self-evident fact that the cultures of Ancient Egypt had themselves changed several times in character over time, as had 'others" perceptions of it. Perhaps the classical views passed on to medieval and Renaissance scholars about Ancient Egypt's skills with regard to anatomy and medicine were of such a generalized nature that they did not need to be confirmed by the examples of the treatment and attitudes revealed by Egyptian text and the actual archaeological discoveries in Egypt (Ritner 2001: 353–356). Similarly, perhaps, the high value placed by Greeks on the quality of ancient Egyptian thinking and 'philosophy' did not need the interpretations of hieroglyphics to provide the actual examples of Egyptian discussion of theological and ethical topics (see e.g. Hornung 1982). No doubt such evidence was not needed to support the Greek tradition that some of their philosophers had studied with Egyptian priests, and it is well established how this 'myth' became the 18th century 'reality' of some Freemasonry orthodoxy (Hamill and Mollier 2003; Lefkowitz and Rogers 1996).

The main concern of the chapters in this book is not to analyze the changing cultural traditions within Egypt, but to explore the ways in which Egypt has been known and valued by other societies – how and why Ancient Egypt has been 'good to think with' for both western and non-western successor cultures. It presents a multi-vocal array of combinations of places and periods. Clear examples of the use of Ancient Egypt exist from 16th century Italy where Annius of Viterbo used Ancient Egypt and contemporary Egyptology as political legitimation for claims of descent, and Jesuits used it to demonstrate the unity of humankind. Societies have taken their inspiration from Ancient Egypt, or have pretended to do so, or have unconsciously done so. A core issue is to assess the extent to which real 'legacy' is in question, as opposed to a convenient or conventional use of 'Egypt' as a label. Another is, why did the magic of Egypt – rather than other ancient cultures – enter the bloodstream of the west and remain there (DuQuesne 1999: 32)?

## Notes

1   This fragment is sometimes included in the collected writings of the 17th century English scholar and antiquarian Sir Thomas Browne, but is now known to be the work of a minor 19th century literary figure.

## Acknowledgments

We thank Stephen Quirke, Michael Rowlands and Jeremy Tanner for allowing us to make use of some of their unpublished thoughts.

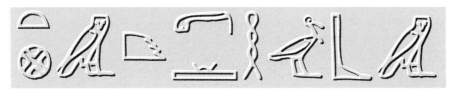

# CHAPTER 2

# THE WISDOM OF EGYPT: CLASSICAL VIEWS[1]

### John Tait

It is widely accepted that the classical world held the civilization of Egypt in awe, and that classical writers sometimes expressed admiration cannot be denied. For example, Herodotus of Halicarnassus (fifth century BC) devoted the second book of his *Histories* to Egypt (Lloyd 1975). When he had disposed, at length, of the geography of Egypt (chiefly the peculiarities of the Nile), he proceeded (Herodotus II.35): "I shall have a great deal more to say about Egypt in itself, because of the number of amazing features that the land contains, and because more monuments that defy description are to be found in it than anywhere else in the world."

The views of Greek and Roman authors concerning Egypt have often been discussed as part of larger studies, for example Iversen (1961, 1993) and Hornung (2001), while Assmann (2000) has dedicated a whole book to the subject. Griffith (1980) has concisely surveyed the way in which Greek authors 're-interpreted' the Egyptian deities. Several contributions to the volumes in this 'Encounters with Ancient Egypt' series highlight the attitude of this or that writer to the Egyptian people or to Egyptian culture (Harrison 2003; Maehler 2003). This chapter rather looks at a few issues and some representative sources. These chiefly involve views of Egypt as extremely ancient, as having pioneered ideas and techniques, and as a source of profound if mysterious wisdom.

The classical perception of Egypt certainly was not uniform. It is easy to point to some very derogatory treatments of the country and its inhabitants. Egyptian 'worship' of animal gods is a crucial issue in the classical view of a deeper hidden wisdom in Egyptian religion. Yet the Latin satirist Juvenal in the second century AD devoted his 15th satire to the bizarreness and barbarities of Egypt (Highet 1954: 28–31; Haycock Chapter 6: 133, this volume). He sneered that not only did the Egyptians venerate animals, but they also worshipped different animals in different parts of the country, and even recognized sacred plants: thus they were fortunate that "sacred beings (*numina*) grow in their gardens" (Juvenal XV.10–11). The core of the satire is an account of a supposed fight between the men of the Upper Egyptian towns of "Ombos" (probably Naqada) and "Tentyra" (clearly Dendera), deriving from their hatred of each other's gods. When the combatants from Dendera are routed, one of them "slips", is captured, torn apart, and completely devoured, raw, by the men of 'Ombos'. Fortunately, Juvenal commented sarcastically, it was a less sacrilegious event than if "sacred fire" (sacred in the classical world, but, despite its ritual use and symbolism, not in the same way for the Egyptians) had been used to cook the body. After various reflections on the extremes to which humans may be driven (although the Ombites had had no such compulsion), the satire ends with the thought that Pythagoras (who would not eat even a bean (*legumen*)) would have been appalled at the sight of such eating of human meat. Juvenal would of course be aware that Pythagoras was one of the Greeks most frequently claimed to have been a visitor to Egypt. Juvenal was engaged in writing satire, not social history, but he seems to be reacting to the view that the Egyptians were "exceptionally religiously observant, more than all human peoples" (Herodotus II.37), and that there was a hidden truth behind their animal worship.

Lucian of Samosata (second century AD) was said to have held a post in Egypt towards the end of his life (Baldwin 1973: 17–20). His *Dialogues of the Dead* adopted an elaborately ironic tone throughout (Hall 1981). The dialogue between Diogenes and Alexander (like that between Philip and Alexander) mocked Alexander's divinity and immortality, recalling the story of his acceptance by the oracle at Siwa as the son of the sun god, Amun-Ra. Diogenes begins the dialogue:

> Diogenes: What is this, O Alexander – you too have died, just like all of us?
>
> Alexander: You can see for yourself, O Diogenes; but it is no great surprise if, as a human being, I died.
>
> Diogenes: So of course Ammon lied in saying that you were his, and really you *were* Philip's (son)?

(Lucian 389–390)

Later in the dialogue, Diogenes comments, "Even now, in Hades, you are out of your mind, and hope to become Anubis or Osiris" (Lucian 392). In Alexander, Hannibal, Minos and Scipio, Hannibal alludes both to Alexander's visit to the oracle at Siwa and to the 'Alexander Romance' myth of how Alexander's mother came to conceive him: "And I did all this without being named the son of Ammon, or pretending to be a god, or recounting the dreams of my mother" (Lucian 382).

## The reality

It is important to understand to what extent classical writers could have had direct access to Egyptian 'wisdom' – and what there was for them to discover. A serious difficulty is that this last question has usually been approached in the reverse direction: the evidence of the classical and patristic writers has been used to try to estimate the state of thought and scholarship in Greco-Roman Egypt. Thus the famous description in the *Stromateis* (i.e. 'Patchwork') by Clement of Alexandria (born about 150 AD) of the systematic nature of the Egyptian corpus of medical books (*Stromateis* VI.37.3) has often been taken to indicate what would actually be found in an Egyptian medical library. The context is an account of the Egyptian priesthood as the guardians of Egyptian philosophy, and the passage ends:

> There are, then, forty-two essential books of Hermes, of which the aforementioned (i.e. the Egyptian priests) learn (or 'study'?) thirty-six which encompass the whole philosophy of the Egyptians, while the *pastophoroi* (i.e. relatively low-ranking priests)

learn the remaining six, which are medical (*iatrikoi*), concerning the structure of the body, and concerning diseases, and concerning instruments and medicines, and concerning eyes, and the last concerning women.

In fact it is difficult to find unanimous or unequivocal evidence for such a strict organization of the subject matter in the handful of surviving Egyptian medical papyri (Grapow 1959: 1; Harris 1971: 113–114; Westendorf 1980: 1,274, 1999: 80–100). Any hints of Clement's system that can be seen in the papyri have on occasion been greeted with enthusiasm. Similarly, the limited evidence that highly specialized doctors could exist in pharaonic Egypt has been stressed by some. Herodotus understood that this was (at least in his own day) the situation: "The practice of medicine they divide into separate spheres, and each doctor is responsible for the treatment of just one disease. There are as a result innumerable doctors, some specializing in diseases of the eyes, others of the head, others of the teeth, others of the stomach, and so forth ..." (Herodotus II.84). Nunn (1996: 191) comments, "No doubt this statement is an exaggeration but the titles of some specialists are known to us", and he devotes a whole chapter (1996: 191–205) to the topic. Unlike Clement, Herodotus made no mention of medical books. A number of studies of Egyptian medicine, such as that of Lefebvre (1956), have, in a sense, followed Clement in as much as they have chosen to discuss Egyptian practice as though divided up into medical specialisms that we would recognize today: for example, anatomy and physiology ("Anatomie et physiologie": Lefebvre 1956: ch. 4). In any case, Clement is likely to have described material (however traditional in origin) available in his own day, and it has been at the least hazardous to use his comments to discuss realities of one or two millennia earlier.

What the Egyptians themselves of the first millennium BC and of the Roman period would have regarded as their store of wisdom has been much discussed, often in connection with post-classical perceptions of Egypt, and above all the hermetic and alchemical tradition (Burnett Chapter 4, this volume; DuQuesne 1999; Hornung 2001; Iversen 1993). The Egyptian tradition gives the appearance, at least, of having been wholly a written one. It is in no way unlikely that religious, technical and craft know-how were also handed on in oral form. Diodorus Siculus (who probably visited Egypt in the mid-first century BC) perhaps implies that skills in writing were passed down from father to son in saying, "The priests train their sons in two kinds of writing, one called 'sacred', and one which concerns more widespread education" (Diodorus Siculus I.81.1). Later in the same passage (I.81.7) he states, "The rest of the mass of the Egyptians learn from childhood from their fathers or family the skills (epitēdeusis) for each way of life – just as we have already stated them; but they teach writing only up to a point – and not all (of them do this), but chiefly those who are engaged in technical skills".

Egyptian textual sources themselves do not suggest this kind of family education in the particular case of learning to write, but rather give the impression that this belonged within the remit of schools. On the other hand, the duty to educate one's own son in *wisdom* is clear in late first millennium BC demotic wisdom texts (see P. Insinger, below). An explicit instance is 'The Instructions of 'Onchsheshonqy' (Lichtheim 1980: 159–184, 1983: 13–92; Thissen 1984). In the narrative introduction to this wisdom text, 'Onchsheshonqy is imprisoned by pharaoh for having been on the fringe of a treasonous conspiracy. When 'Onchsheshonqy despairs of release, he asks his jailer: "Please will you grant me this: may I be brought a writing palette and a papyrus roll. I have a son whom I have not been able to instruct (i.e. educate in person). I shall write down an Instruction (i.e. wisdom text) for him, and have it carried to Heliopolis to instruct him through it" ('The Instructions of 'Onchsheshonqy' 4.10–12). Indeed, if it had been normal to learn to write in schools, schools would have had to be rather numerous, even if the much-discussed suggestion of Baines and Eyre (1983) is accepted, that literacy in the pharaonic period could have been *at most* one per cent. In fact, schools are singularly hard to find, although (from textual references) there is little doubt that some existed from the Middle Kingdom onwards (Brunner 1957). It was once thought that the abundance of so-called 'school' ostraca found at Deir el-Medina provided good evidence for elementary education, but this has begun to be seriously doubted, and the ostraca should probably be seen as the work of more advanced students – the products of trainee scribes working, individually, as apprentices to an elder scholar (McDowell 1995, 1999: 128–129).

By the middle of the first millennium BC, the proportion of the Egyptian elite who held at least some kind of priestly office seems to have increased beyond anything known from earlier Egypt (Lloyd 1983: 301–309). It is even plausible to see the educated, literate elite as closely corresponding in extent to the priesthood. There is no evidence to establish that any written material circulated except within the priesthood, even if conversely it is far from proven that there could have been absolutely no literate circles outside the temples (Tait 1992: 306–308), as many well-preserved and well-known manuscripts have no provenance. The best evidence for the wealth of texts held in priestly communities comes from finds at Dime and at Tebtunis, both in the Fayum oasis, dating to the first three centuries AD. The milieu and written resources of the temple of Sobek at Tebtunis are also known (Osing 1998: 19–23; Zauzich 1991).

This Egyptian recording of knowledge can appear impressively extensive and methodical. The texts that today are called 'wisdom literature', such as the demotic 'The Instructions of 'Onchsheshonqy', are of considerable length, but they vary greatly in the degree to which they are thematically organized. P. Insinger is the most elaborate example (Lichtheim 1980: 184–217, 1983: 107–234). It is divided into 25 numbered sections, each dealing with a particular theme. For example, section 8 is devoted to gluttony, and its links with greed in general, and lust. Section 10 is "The teaching not to weary of instructing your son". The text generally consists of pairs of short, interrelated maxims. For example, from section 10: "The foolish son whom his father has failed to instruct – he is a statue of stone; it is a son's good and fortunate inheritance to receive instruction and to enquire" (P. Insinger 8.22–23). The best-preserved manuscript has lost almost all of the first five sections, but still runs to 35 columns of text.

Among other material, the enormous hieratic 'onomasticon' published by Osing (1998) is perhaps the largest-scale example. It is a compilation of religious and cult information of great variety. Although it is only partly preserved, the edition runs to 22 plates in A2 format. The hieroglyphic 'Book of the Fayum' (Beinlich 1991) is another very extensive text, sections of which give the impression, at least, of a highly systematic listing of cult centres (Tait 2003a). Other examples of long and highly structured texts are found in demotic listings of the forms of personal names (P. Kairo

31169 verso) (Spiegelberg 1906–1908, 1: pls. 109–111, 2: 279–280; Zauzich 2000a, b), while other modest fragments of demotic lexical and grammatical texts hint at a degree of conscious structuring (Tait 2000). The demotic 'Hermopolis Legal Manual' (from the second century BC) is an extensive catalogue of typical disputes that judges in the Egyptian-language courts of the mid-Ptolemaic period might encounter, with straightforward instructions as to how to handle each case (Donker van Heel 1990; Mattha 1975). For the most part, cases dealing with similar topics (e.g. inheritance, disputes between neighbours) are clearly arranged together. Fragments survive of a Greek translation of this text (*P. Oxy.* 3285) from the second century AD (Rea 1978: 30–38): this is usually interpreted as having served a practical purpose, to allow the Greek-language courts of the Roman-period administration access to the traditional state of indigenous Egyptian law, when Egyptians came before them, rather than as revealing any Greek academic interest in Egyptian law. Nevertheless, the mere existence of the papyrus shows that this information would have been available in Greek in the second century AD, a time when other problematic 'translation literature' from Egyptian into Greek was in circulation in Egypt (Thissen 1977). Numerous fragments of another such demotic compilation exist (Chauveau 1991) and a further single small fragment of a similar manual hints that such a text could be even more lengthy than the Hermopolis example (Tait 1991b). The most impressive medical book from the relevant period so far published is the hieratic manual of ophiology (the 'Snake-Charmer's Handbook'), edited by Sauneron (1996), which shows a consistent organization and a wealth of practical detail. Demotic medical texts tend to be fragmentary, and have been little studied. However, small fragments survive of a herbal, in which the numbering given to each herb indicates that over 90 individual plants and their uses were recorded (Tait 1991a). Systematic books of dream-interpretation survive, deriving from an Egyptian tradition, but owing their methodical organization to Babylonian models (Oppenheim 1956; Volten 1942). Elaborate demotic astrological texts have been preserved, including a substantial papyrus drawing omens from the appearance of the sun and moon (Parker 1959; Figure 2:1). Surprisingly little survives of demotic mathematical papyri, but the available material (Parker 1972) suggests that they were as systematic as the earlier Egyptian texts, such as P. Rhind (Peet 1923; Robins and Shute 1987).

Modern views of the 'wisdom' or scientific value of this material have quite often been decidedly jaundiced. Nevertheless, if we rely simply on the indications provided by actually surviving Egyptian manuscripts (however patchy or fragmentary the evidence), it seems clear that a visitor who gained access to an Egyptian temple community from the sixth century BC to the second century AD could have been shown an immensely impressive range of substantial and apparently methodically organized manuscripts demonstrating Egyptian 'wisdom'. Perhaps, at the time of Herodotus, only in the lands where the cuneiform literary traditions lived on could collections have been found that could have rivalled such a range of materials. After the founding of the Alexandrian Library (Butler 2003: 257–258) and its rivals, a Greek could certainly take pride in the sheer quantity of Greek manuscripts held there (Casson 2001: 34–36; Fraser 1972, I: 305–335).

COLUMN VIII　　　COLUMN VII

Figure 2:1　Two columns of demotic astrological text showing two aspects of the moon, one "being a black [disk] around it, you are to say about it: Great fighting shall happen (in) the entire land" (Parker 1959: 39, pl. 4).

## Access

We cannot be sure what it was that classical writers might have read, seen or heard that might have given substance to their respect for Egypt. The history of the Greeks in Egypt before the Ptolemaic period has frequently been described (e.g. Braun 1982; Harrison 2003; Lloyd 1975: 1–60; Pernigotti 1996). It is still much disputed whether or not Herodotus himself visited Egypt, and, if so, how far south he actually travelled (e.g. Armayor 1985; Lloyd 1975: 61–76; Spiegelberg 1927). For the present purpose, this problem does not greatly matter. In Herodotus' generation, a Greek *could* travel in Egypt. He could have done the things that Herodotus claims to have done. He could have visited fully operational, large and wealthy temples continuing the traditions of earlier Egypt. Priests at all levels would have been literate, and, at least in major centres, they would have had free access to an extensive range of written texts. Within the priestly community, manuscripts do not seem to have been kept private or secret. Some of the priests, at least, used this material, and could not only copy it, but also exploit it in the composition and compilation of new texts. Presumably, a foreigner would have been no more able to penetrate far into the interior of an actual temple than an 'impure' (i.e. non-priestly) Egyptian (Ritner 1993: 203). However, Egyptian priests to varying degrees moved widely in their surrounding communities.

It is not known whether Herodotus himself was able to consult higher-ranking priests (Harrison 2003) – or if indeed his information might have come second hand from Greeks resident in Egypt. He states that some of his information came from "the priests" (Lloyd 1975: 89–113; Moyer 2002), and he does not present it as though it derived from mere doorkeepers; but there is the possibility that he talked with the priests of Greek temples in Egypt. In matters of cult, there was a long-standing Egyptian tradition, not quite of secrecy, but that some information should be revealed only to those fit to know of it (Baines 1990; Ritner 1993: 202–205). Thus there might have been a reluctance among Egyptians to reveal to Greeks such as Herodotus the line-by-line contents of religious texts, but their existence would not have been secret. This may be reflected in Herodotus' curious statements, such as "I am reluctant to repeat what I was told about Egyptian religion, apart from merely the names of the deities, as I do not think that any particular nation knows more about these things than any other" (Herodotus II.3) and "This is how they depict him (i.e. Pan – the Ram of Mendes), I should rather not mention the reason" (Herodotus II.46; cf. Derchain 1999). Herodotus (II.47) writes, concerning the sacrificing of pigs, "there is a myth among them (i.e. the Egyptians), but, although I know of it, I think it would be more appropriate not to relate it"; and "Here also in the enclosure of Athene (i.e. the Egyptian goddess Neith) at Sais is the tomb of someone whose name I prefer not to mention"; and "On this lake (i.e. near the temple of Neith at Sais) the Egyptians carry out by night their so-called mysteries of the suffering of the god [whose name he will not mention] ... Similarly I shall remain silent about the mystery-rites of Demeter" (Herodotus II.170–171).

Although access to active Egyptian temples may have been restricted (Figure 2:2), it would not have been difficult to obtain a clear impression of many of them, and much statuary and some relief wall-scenes would have been accessible. Abandoned or ruined monuments would have afforded even better opportunities, perhaps the most famous during the Greco-Roman period being the Colossi of Memnon, the pair

Figure 2:2   The court of the temple of Horus at Edfu. Note that the 'library' was situated immediately behind the right hand corner of the porch (© Okasha El Daly).

of statues that were nearly all that remained from the dismantled mortuary temple of Amenophis III in Western Thebes (Porter and Moss 1974: 449). The Egyptian 'Labyrinth' at Hawara could be thoroughly explored (Tait 2003a: 198–200). Writers who attempted to describe the sights of Egypt (whether from their alleged own first-hand experience, or from the accounts of others), particularly Herodotus, Strabo and Diodorus, give some idea of what it was relatively easy to see: unlike more modern travellers, none of them mentioned having to undergo any particular hardships.

## Topics

Several Greek historians were concerned to know which was the most 'ancient' human nation or race. This was not a matter that troubled the Egyptians (Allen 2003; Uphill 2003). Their views of the cosmos comprised several ideas of the creation of the world, and of the emergence of humankind, but Egypt itself was for them always the site of creation, and at the centre of the cosmos. Other peoples, however troublesome, had been brought into being so that the Egyptian king could make use of them in his relationship with the gods, and in his rule over Egypt (O'Connor 2003). Herodotus, whose chief aim was to explain the war between the Greeks and the Persians (Herodotus I.1) began his survey of Egypt in his second book (Herodotus II.1–2), after a brief mention of the death of Cyrus, the Persian king, and his son Cambyses' preparation for an invasion of Egypt, with an account of an enquiry into this matter, about one generation before Herodotus' own time. He then (Harrison 2003) gave an account of an alleged experiment carried out by Psammetichos to discover who had the best claim to antiquity, by confining two new-born infants without access to human speech to see what their first spoken words might be. Unfortunately, they first uttered, and repeated in the presence of the king, the Phrygian word for bread, thus shattering the claims of the Egyptians. Herodotus states that his source for his form of the story was the priests of Hephaistos (Ptah) at Memphis, although Greeks had various other improbable versions of the story:

> The Egyptians before Psammetichus thought that they were the most ancient of all peoples in the world, Psammetichus, however, when he came to the throne, had the idea of settling this question of priority and ever since his time the Egyptians have accepted that the Phrygians have the priority in antiquity, and that they come second.

Plato (ca. 427–348 BC) (*Laws* 656; cf. Diodorus I.98.5–9) praised Egyptian art and music, both that of "long ago" and that of his own period, for not permitting any innovation, or allowing artists to "create forms different from the traditional ones". He explained that this was self-evident: "If you look, you will discover that works that were painted or carved there ten thousand years ago (I do not just mean 'ages ago', but actually ten thousand years) are in no way better or worse than present-day products, but were executed with the same skill."

Diodorus (I.7), in introducing the scope of his *Universal History*, dealt at length with the creation of life upon earth, and then described the life of humans as bestial, before the emergence of languages, which he saw as spontaneous developments in different places (Diodorus I.8). He then (I.9.1) gave an idea of the range of history: "However, concerning deeds that have been committed to memory, and happened in the known places of the world, we shall try to review them." He (I.9.2) asked who were the first kings, and this seems for him to have corresponded to the beginning of real history: "Since myths place the creation of the gods in Egypt, and the earliest observations of the stars are said to have been invented there, and in addition to these matters noteworthy and numerous deeds of great men are recorded, we shall make the beginning of our History with the activities in Egypt" (Herodotus I.9.6).

Antiquity is one thing, but another source of admiration was the idea that the Egyptians were the *first* to have done something. This may or may not have been explicitly linked to the belief that the classical world then borrowed from Egypt. Herodotus (II.4) stated, "the Egyptians were the first of all humankind to discover the yearly cycle, dividing the year into twelve parts". He regarded the Egyptian calendar of twelve equal months of 30 days, with five added days at the end of the year, as superior to contemporary Greek systems, which depended upon a lunar basis for the calendar. There is good evidence from Egypt itself in the Ptolemaic period that the 'Macedonian' lunar calendar was something of a nightmare for its users; indeed it is not clear whether it was employed out of habit or for its prestige. Other clear statements of borrowing are: "They said that the Egyptians were the first to fix the names of the twelve deities, and the Hellenes took them over from them" and that they were the first to determine cult and to carve stone images (Herodotus II.4); "The names of almost all the gods came to Greece from Egypt" (Herodotus II.50).

The invention of writing was often ascribed to Egypt: for example, Plato (*Philebus* 18B–C) offered a highly theoretical view of the beginnings of the alphabet and of linguistic study:

> Socrates: When some god or god-like man realized that sound was without boundaries – a story in Egypt says that this one was Theuth – he was the first to realize that the vowels(?) in that continuum were not one but many ... until he established the number of them (i.e. vowels and consonants), and gave a name to each and all of them as 'letters'.

He (Plato *Phaedrus* 274C–275A) also commented upon the consequences of the invention of writing:

> Socrates: I have heard then (i.e. that long ago?) that at Naukratis (i.e. the famous Greek trading settlement established early in the Saite period), in Egypt, there was one of the ancient gods there (i.e. of Egypt) whose sacred bird was called the Ibis, and that the name of the divinity (*daimon*) was Theuth. It was he who first discovered numbers and calculation, and geometry and astronomy, and also draughts and dice, and, indeed, writing (or 'letters'). The king then of all Egypt was Thamos, at the great city of the Upper Country, which the Greeks call Egyptian Thebes, and the god was Ammon. Theuth came to him to demonstrate the Arts (i.e. fields of knowledge), and he said that they ought to be handed on to the rest of the Egyptians. He (Thamos) asked what use each of them had, and, as he (Theuth) enumerated them, he would criticize one and commend another, as he thought the account of each good or bad. Thamos is said to have spoken much about each 'Art', tending either way, but it would take a long speech (for me) to go through them. But when it came to writing, 'This learning, O king', said Theuth, 'will render the Egyptians wiser and grant them better memories, for I have discovered a tonic for memory and wisdom'. But he said 'O most skilled Theuth, one man is capable of creating arts, but another of judging what proportion of harm and utility each has for those who are going to use them. And now you, being the father of writing (letters), through affection for them are saying the opposite to their

real effect. For this invention will produce forgetfulness in the minds of those who learn it, through lack of exercising the memory'.

The dialogue (*Phaedrus* 275B) then turns light-heartedly to throw doubt on the apparent earnestness of the whole story:

> Phaedrus: O Socrates, you facilely make up stories about Egypt, or any other place you fancy!

In his dialogues, Plato frequently has Socrates tell fables or stories to help make his point, the most notable being the accounts of 'Atlantis' in the *Timaeus* and *Critias* (Froidefond 1971: 285–290). In the *Phaedrus*, Socrates immediately turns to the subject of the Oracle at Dodona, which had been a *topos* in Herodotus (II.54): "About the oracles, that of Dodona in Greece and of Ammon in Libya, the Egyptians have the following legend: according to the priests of the Theban Zeus (i.e. Amun), two women concerned with the rites of the temple were carried away by the Phoenicians and sold as slaves, one in Libya and the other in Greece, and these women founded the oracles in those two countries." Herodotus stated that he had made enquiries about these legends, and that he had found different versions among Greeks and Egyptians; he was inclined to accept the Egyptian version, although clearly thinking that it was supported by the very existence of Greek variants.

Diodorus was one of several writers who listed supposed Greek visitors to Egypt, and he gave an indication – in line with what other writers imply – of what kind of figure allegedly travelled to Egypt, and their motive:

> For that reason, those of greatest repute for learning desired to visit Egypt, so as to learn of the customs and usages, as being worthy of attention. Even though the country was difficult of access for foreigners – for the reasons previously mentioned – yet, amongst the earliest, Orpheus and the poet Homer were eager to visit it, and, among later generations, so were many others, including Pythagoras the Samian, and again Solon the law-giver.
>
> (Diodorus I.69.3–4)

The 'visitors' to Egypt were consistently philosophers, 'scientists' and artists, especially poets: political figures were included in the lists only when they were seen as law-givers (Diodorus I.96–98; Herodotus I.30; Strabo X.4.19, XVII.29).

The view that the Egyptians had always lived an orderly life could easily be transferred to the idea that they could provide a model of how a state should be run: Strabo (ca. 64 BC–19 AD) stated of the Egyptians, contrary to the position among the Ethiopians: "from the beginning they have lived in an ordered state (politicōs), and in a civilized fashion" (Strabo XVII.1.3). Clearly, Plato's interest in Egypt was chiefly a result of his admiration for a stable society.

Cicero (106–43 BC), in a passage in *De Natura Deorum* (I.29.81–82), contrasted Egyptian with Greco-Roman attitudes to their gods. At first he did not seem to confine himself to the Egyptians, speaking of "neither the Egyptians, nor the Syrians, nor virtually any uncivilized peoples (*cuncta barbaria*)". He maintained that they had more principled religious ideas about dumb animals (*de bestiis*) than the attitude that the classical world took towards its temples and divine images. Thereafter, however, he plainly had Egypt at the front of his mind. He asserted that, in the classical world, shrines and divine images might be plundered; yet there were no instances of an Egyptian committing sacrilege against a crocodile, or an ibis, or a cat; the Egyptians believed as much in the Apis Bull as the Greco-Roman world did in the pantheon. He went on to emphasize just how varied were the depictions of the classical gods, clearly responding to a view that it was the Egyptians who had a ridiculous variety of deities.

Clement of Alexandria's *Protreptikos*, ostensibly addressed to the Hellenes (i.e. pagan Greeks), reviewed at length the numerous tales of the immoral behaviour of the classical gods (ch. 2). He pointed out that the nature of individual gods could vary from place to place. The Egyptians worshipped "better gods" when "they honour irrational animals, village-by-village, and city-by-city". Further, "Even if they (the Egyptian deities) are wild beasts, at least they are not adulterers". Clement proceeded to admit that Egyptian cults vary from place to place. However, he followed this by finding examples of Greeks, in particular places, honouring birds and animals and even, "they record", ants. In these passages (33–34), he affected to show no appreciation of the very considerable difference between Egyptian deities, partly or wholly in animal form, major sacred animals such as the Apis Bull, only one incarnation of which was recognized at any one time, and sacred animals associated with deities, such as ibises, which were mummified in their thousands. Naturally, his account of classical pagan religion, his chief target, is no more nuanced.

In Book VI of his *Stromateis*, Clement explored the relationship between wisdom and true religion. In chapter 4, he discussed the debt in philosophy that the Greeks owed to the Egyptians and to the Indian Gymnosophists (the latter in just one bizarre story in which they were quizzed by Alexander the Great). He concluded (at the beginning of chapter 5), "And it is sufficiently obvious from much evidence that the Greeks are found out as thieves of all kinds of written texts" (*Stromateis* VI.39.1).

Clement's curious account of Egyptian philosophy takes the form of a description of the priesthood and temple ritual. The titles of the priests that he mentions are mostly those in common use in the Greek language within Egypt in the Roman period. His description here, as is the case with his allusions to Egypt elsewhere, evidently includes some correct information, but it is difficult to assess which parts are based on reality:

> We shall find another kind of evidence as confirmation in that the best of the philosophers have appropriated from us (i.e. Christians) their finest tenets (*dogma*) as their own, and yet boast to have derived some which are relevant to each sect rather from the barbarians (i.e. non-Greeks), especially from the Egyptians: that is, various matters, and in particular the tenet concerning the transmigration of the soul. For the Egyptians follow a particular philosophy of their own. Actually, this is especially demonstrated by their religious observances:

> First, the Singer advances, bringing one of the symbols of Music. They say that this priest must master two books from those of Hermes, of which one contains the hymns of the gods, the second the reckoning of the life of the king.

> After the Singer, the Astrologer advances, with a *horologion* in his hand, and a palm-branch, the symbols of astrology. He needs to have on the tip of his tongue the astrological works from the books of Hermes, which are four in number. Of these, one is about the arrangement of the fixed stars, one is about the positions of the sun and the

moon and the five planets, one is about the conjunctions and brightness of the sun and the moon, and the remaining one is about their risings.

Next, the *Hierogrammateus* ('Sacred Scribe') advances, having wings on his head, and a book in his hands and a measuring-rod, in which are the black ink and the rush with which they write.[2] This priest needs to know what are called 'hieroglyphics', concerning cosmography and geography, and the topography of Egypt and the chart of the Nile [cf. Tait 2003a], and about the equipment of the rituals and the places purified for them, and about measures and such things as are useful in the rituals.

Then the *Stolistes* (i.e. 'the one who robes' the god) follows those already mentioned, having the cubit-rod of justice and the libation-cup. This priest knows all matters of training, and the 'sealing' of calves (i.e. assessing the purity of animals to be offered to the deity). There are ten books which concern the honour paid by them to the gods, and containing the Egyptian religious observances, such as concerning sacrifices, offerings, hymns, prayers, processions, and matters like these.

After everyone else, the Prophet[3] comes forth, with the water-jar in his arms for all to see, and there follow him those carrying the issue of loaves. As superintendent of the temple, he studies the ten books called 'hieratic': they include information about the laws (or 'customs'?) and the gods and all the training of the priests. For the Prophet is, among the Egyptians, the superintendent even of the distribution of revenues.

There then follows the passage concerning the medical books of the Egyptians, already cited, and then Clement abruptly concludes, "And such are the practices of the Egyptians, to speak briefly".

A common theme seems to have been that 'barbarian' societies operated differently from Greek societies not because barbarians were intrinsically different, nor because of their environment(s) – except when this provided some kind of practical stimulus – but as a phenomenon of cultural diversity. This thinking could be applied both to Greeks and barbarians, as Strabo (*Geography* II.3.7) clearly illustrates: "For example, it is not by nature (*phusis*) that the Athenians love literature, but the Spartans do not – and the Thebans who are even closer (i.e. geographically, to Athens(?)), but rather by custom/habit (*ethos*). So, also, neither are the Babylonians nor the Egyptians philosophers by nature, but by application and custom." Similarly, "The Sidonians are reckoned to be skilled in many and fine arts, just as The Poet (i.e. Homer *Iliad* XXIII.743) shows. In addition, they are wise (*philosophos*) concerning astronomy and arithmetic, deriving these from calculation and navigation at night, as these concern trade and shipping. Just so, the Egyptian discovery of geometry is said to come from the measurement of land, which the Nile imposes, when it floods boundaries at the Inundation" (Strabo *Geography* XVI.2.24; cf. Diodorus I.81). Lucian (*De Luctu* 21) also compares different nations: "However, after that (i.e. after the mourning process), they have shared out, nation by nation, the styles of funerals: the Greek burns the corpse, the Persian buries it, the Indian encloses it in glass, the Scythian eats it, the Egyptian pickles (salts) it."

## Conclusions

It is clear that writers in the classical tradition – those who admired the wisdom of Egypt – were frequently aware of the work of their predecessors. If not simply reacting to an earlier account, most commonly they rephrased the text of an earlier writer, or openly copied it. Rarely, however, there was a frank admission that one writer had read another's book: "So that the whole of Egypt was plausibly said by Herodotus to be *the gift of the river*", where Strabo (*Geography* I.2.23) accurately reported what Herodotus had said at II.5.

The approach to Ancient Egypt in the classical writers was largely prescribed by the particular context – or literary genre – within which Egypt was mentioned. The classical genres cited above have been very disparate: satire, philosophy, history, etc. Even within the genre of history, the classical writers were torn between different views: to show Egypt as alien and bizarre, or as primeval, or as the fount of all wisdom, or as simply extraordinary. There is little hint, however, of sheer prejudice against Egyptians – or of straightforward racism – even if that may be found in other kinds of text (Harrison 2003). The issue emerges at all periods as to what extent people who thought of themselves as Greeks and people who thought of themselves as Egyptians really met each other in Egypt between the fifth century BC and Late Antiquity, or lived in different 'Egypts' (La'da 2003). As seen above, it is not even agreed what kind of 'priests' Herodotus spoke with within Egypt. The Greeks occasionally noted the failure of 'Egyptians' to speak Greek properly; but Greek and Latin authors rarely seem to have been interested in what an 'Egyptian' looked like. Herodotus (II.22) does mention the fact that "the people [of the Upper Nile] are black because of the heat", among some rather strained arguments against the idea that the Nile flood could derive from snow.

Classical writers were seemingly very ready to use Egyptian themes in their writings, but had little interest in the Egyptians as people. Herodotus may be the one exception – for which he was much criticized in Antiquity, for being an admirer of non-Greek culture (*philobarbaros*). His account of Egypt stands in strong contrast to that of Strabo, who for the most part confined himself to the monuments – although Strabo, of course, was engaged in writing a 'Geography'.

Finally, there is the question of where the classical writers who did admire the wisdom of Egypt thought that the source of this wisdom lay. In part the answer relates to the overt themes discussed above. The antiquity and the apparent stability of Egyptian culture contrasted with the Greek experience of the classical and hellenistic periods. The classical writers who survive to us (however atypical of society in general) were rarely fascinated by the latest achievements of their own culture – and those who were naturally had little reason to mention Egypt with enthusiasm. Pliny the Elder (*Historia naturalis* XXXVI.75, cf. 82) remarks: "The Pyramids – also in Egypt – must be mentioned in passing, too: an unnecessary and stupid display of royal wealth."

That the Egyptians were in some way closer to the gods seems to underlie some classical views: the names of the gods came from Egypt, and writers appear generally to have taken quite seriously the view that the Egyptians worshipped the *same* deities as the *real* gods – the Greek pantheon. Attempts to argue that the Egyptian gods in fact derived from the Greek were rare and have an air of the contrived about them. Similarly, the idea that some 'gods' were originally human (clearly a Greek idea, but hardly to be seen as a commonplace Egyptian one) appears to have been a minority view. Even if the Egyptians thought that some of their texts were written by the gods

– Thoth, for example – this does not seem to have carried much weight with the Greeks. Egyptian 'wisdom' therefore relates to a view – however unrealistic – of Egyptian society.

## Notes

1  Translations from Egyptian, Greek and Latin in this chapter are by the author.
2  This clearly reflects some knowledge of the traditional rectangular form of Egyptian scribal palette, with cakes of black and red ink attached, and a slot to hold the thin brushes of rush used by pharaonic scribes – although the rush pen had given way to the reed in Clement's time, and the palette was obsolete.
3  The Greeks called the highest rank of Egyptian priest prophētēs, simply because of their status, and not because of any similarity in their activities to those of Greek 'prophets'; modern studies of the Egyptian priesthood often use the term 'prophet' for simplicity, as the literal meaning of the Egyptian *ḥm-nṯr* is uncertain; it can be interpreted, for example, as either 'servant of the god' or 'body of the god'.

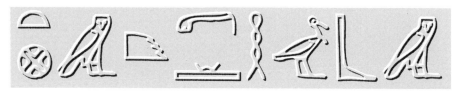

# CHAPTER 3

# ANCIENT EGYPT IN MEDIEVAL ARABIC[1] WRITINGS

*Okasha El Daly*

## Introduction

Until the late 18th century, little was known in the west about the ancient civilizations of Egypt and the Near East, except what had been recorded in the Bible and by the ancient Greeks and Romans (Tait Chapter 2, this volume; Trigger 1989: 39). If this was the case in the west, it was very different in the east in spite of the assertion made recently that:

> Any continuity from ancient to Islamic Egypt was irretrievably and doubly cut off, first by the adoption of Christianity in Egypt in the fourth century and then, three centuries later, by the Islamic conquest. Memories of the world of the pharaohs had long since been forgotten by Egyptians who had been incorporated into the Greek, the Roman, the Byzantine, and, by the seventh century CE, the expanding Islamic world.

> (Haarmann 2001: 191)

This is a surprising view from a scholar who has contributed so much (e.g. Haarmann 1980, 1982, 1996) to our knowledge and understanding of some of the medieval Muslim scholars and their works on Ancient Egypt. The quotation demonstrates a eurocentric view which sees the culture of Ancient Egypt only through a European prism. But even among modern Egyptian scholars, for example El-Shayyal, there are those who reached an over-hasty conclusion that Muslims did not have much appreciation of the history of Ancient Egypt before the 19th century writings of the Egyptian scholar, Rifa'a Al-Tahtawi:

> Ancient Egyptian history was never given its due appreciation by Muslim historians. First because they knew very little about it, and secondly because that period represented, in their opinion, a period of idolatry which stood in direct contradiction to the monotheism of Islam.

> (El-Shayyal 1962: 32)

As a result of such views, the study of Egyptology, which since Napoleonic times has been led by European and American scholars and institutions, has almost totally ignored the vast medieval Arabic and other contributions between the seventh and 16th centuries. The Arabic contribution to some degree fills the void between the classical period and the period of the European Renaissance (Curran Chapter 5, this volume).

Cook (1983) has suggested that medieval Egyptians were not as interested in their ancient heritage as were their counterparts in Iran (cf. Crone and Cook 1977: 114). It is true that medieval Egyptians may not have displayed a chauvinist nationalism, but there can be no real doubt of their interest in ancient matters in general and in Ancient Egypt in particular, as can be seen from the list of Egyptian historians who wrote almost exclusively on the history of Egypt from as early as the first century of Islam (Donner 1998: 225; Enan 1969).

## Medieval Arabic sources

A huge corpus of medieval writings by scholars and ordinary people exists, dating from long before the earliest European Renaissance. This reveals not only a deep interest in the study of Ancient Egypt, but also a desire to learn from such study. The interest covers language (including scripts), history, religion, science and monuments. Much of the available evidence is still only in manuscript form, scattered in collections worldwide.

## Arabs in Ancient Egypt

Egypt was not a strange or distant place to the Arabs, who had long been trading with and working in Egypt (Muhammad 1977). Arabia appears in demotic literary narrative under the name $p\beta\ t\beta\ \beta lby$, in a story set in the twelfth Dynasty (Zauzich 1991: 6), and relations between Egypt and Arabia probably began much earlier (Hitti 1970: 32 ff). Arab names occur frequently in Egyptian records from the Middle Kingdom (Posener 1957) through to the New Kingdom (e.g. Hoch 1994: 567), and up to and including the Greco-Roman period (see e.g. Hanson 1992). Military texts and campaigns in the Near East should not blind us to the long peaceful and cordial periods that also existed between Egypt and its neighbours (Matthews and Roemer 2003b).

Arabs established their own cult centres in Egypt and also participated in the worship of Egyptian deities (Grelot 1972: 338 ff). Some even entered the Egyptian temple service, for example a trader from South Arabia (Yemen) named Zaidullah Ibn Zaid may have worked as a $w^cb$-priest for a temple in Memphis, where he died ca. 263 BC during the reign of Ptolemy II (Vittmann 1998: 1,241 ff). This South Arabian working in Egypt was in a long established tradition of Egyptian acceptance of foreigners in various high offices of government (Murnane 2000: 109). A well-established relationship between South Arabia and Ancient Egypt was maintained and even developed after the advent of Islam, as many Yemenite tribes migrated to Egypt, seeing common bonds between the two countries as centres of ancient civilizations, and regarding themselves, as did Egyptians, as heirs of these civilizations (Fodor and Foti 1976: 160 n. 13). This relationship is also clear in the medieval Arabic epic story of the pre-Islamic hero of Yemen, Saif Ibn Zi Yazan, who, according to the narrative, travelled extensively in Egypt. In his travels he records Egyptian place names, obelisks, tombs and mummies throughout (Khourshid 2002: 84–90).

The historical relationship between Egypt and Arabia was close enough for the classical writer Apollodorus of Athens (first or second century AD) (*Bibliotetheca* II.1, 4) to state that Belus, son of the god Poseidon, settled his son Aigyptos in Arabia. Indeed, earlier writers had suggested that parts of eastern Egypt were called 'Arabia' (Hoyland 2001: 2–3). These old ties may partly explain the similarities between some of the stories in the 'Arabian Nights' and ancient Egyptian ones (Golenischeff 1906).

A major spur to Arab interest in Ancient Egypt, and other ancient civilizations, is the advice in the Quran which urges Muslims to visit and study other lands, cultures and languages, and specifically to study ancient civilizations such as Egypt.

Do they not travel through the land, so that their hearts may thus learn wisdom and their ears may thus learn to hear? For it is not the eyes which are blind, but the heart in the breast.

(Q22: 46)[2]

Say: Travel through the earth and see how creation started.

(Q29: 20)

Do they not travel through the earth and see what was the end of those before them (who) were more numerous and superior in strength and monuments in the land ...

(Q40: 82)

Egypt is often mentioned, or clearly alluded to, in the Quran (e.g. Q2: 61; 10: 87; 12: 21, 99; 43: 51); as a result, many medieval commentators on the Quran researched and interpreted these references, a number of them in the context of the stories of Joseph, and of Moses and the Israelites. Indeed, the Quran makes it clear that Muslims must believe in and treat with equal respect all previous religions and their prophets without any distinction (Q2: 285).

The Quran no doubt afforded the motivation for the Egyptian scholar Abu Ja'far Al-Idrisi[3] (d. 1251 AD)[4] to write what is now the oldest known extensive study on the pyramids of Giza. In this, he tells the story of the Moroccan man who went on pilgrimage to Mecca and, on his return home, hurried to attend the lessons of his master, the Sage Shaikh Abu Zakaria Al-Biyasi who taught medicine and other sciences. His teacher welcomed him back warmly, then said:

Tell me about what you have seen of the pyramids of Egypt but not what you were told.

The student replied:

O teacher, I have nothing of direct sightseeing to tell you.

To this the teacher responded angrily:

Despicable is the student of knowledge and wisdom whose endeavour does not arouse his determination to see the like [of the pyramids], nor stirs his eagerness and passion to see whatever can be seen of marvels. There was nothing to prevent you from informing [us] about them and from [speaking] as a witness here of what you saw, but a swift ride, or a push of a boat. The sluggish one does not deserve to be adorned with the essences of wisdom.

The student immediately departed back to Egypt for no other reason than to see the pyramids (Al-Idrisi 1991: 15).

Egyptian monuments were visited regularly by Muslims and non-Muslims alike, to judge from the number of travel accounts and the amount and variety of graffiti (Vachala and Ondráš 2000: 76). Al-Idrisi (1991: 13–48) devoted a whole chapter to a list of famous visitors to the pyramids of Giza; among them were several pre-Islam prophets, many companions of the Prophet Muhammad and many Muslim kings and caliphs. Medieval Arab poets were much inspired by these monuments where they used to spend their leisure time (Badawi 1965).

Economic benefit also played a role in securing interest in ancient Egyptian sites, as the state, at times, came to be largely dependent on exploiting gold from pharaonic tombs. For example, during the ninth century, Ibn Tulun discovered huge amounts of pharaonic gold (Al-Balawi 1939: 76), estimated to weigh about 4,000 kg (Al-Shurbagi 1994: 106). Having realized the economic potential for the state treasury, he made the exploitation of these gold sources a state monopoly (Rabie 1972: 169), and decreed that no one was allowed to dig anywhere without first seeking permission from the authorities (Al-Balawi 1939: 195). Such a tradition of exploiting ancient treasures can also be seen in Strabo (*Geography* XVII.1.8–9), who records that a Ptolemaic king stole the gold sarcophagus from the tomb of Alexander the Great and replaced it with one made from 'crystal' or 'glass'. Al-Mas'udi (d. ca. 956) (1988, 1: 212) narrated the story of Alexander's funeral but said that it was Alexander's mother who replaced the golden coffin (perhaps reflecting the idea of an alabaster sarcophagus) during the funeral proceedings because she was afraid that later kings might usurp it. Medieval Arabic sources (e.g. Al-Sawi 1938: 243; Anon. author, 10th century ?) appreciated ancient Egyptian exploitation of hidden treasures for the national good of the country.

Protection of ancient materials and ancient sites could be based on a variety of reasons. Thus, for example, Al-Baghdadi (d. 1232) (1985: 110) expressed his admiration for Muslim kings for looking after and protecting monuments, while Ibn Iyas (d. 1542) (1982–1984, 2: 91–92) recalled a case that had taken place under Sultan Al-Ashraf Barsbay (1422–1437 AD), in which the accused was mummifying recently deceased individuals and selling them to Europeans as *mummia*. He also (1982–1984, 4: 275) reported that in the year 1513 AD, a man was arrested for desecrating ancient tombs and selling the dead to foreigners from Europe as *mummia*. In both cases the men were sentenced to death.

There was also a genuine interest in the heritage of Ancient Egypt following the guidance of the Prophet to seek knowledge wherever it may be. The Prophet did not in any way qualify or specify where the search for wisdom and science should take place. He went further, making it "incumbent on every Muslim man and Muslim woman to seek knowledge" (Nasr 1968: 65; Soliman 1985: 3–4), thus encouraging the search for and appreciation of wisdom for its own sake, and allowing Muslims to form their own understanding of the past. The Prophet was himself married to an Egyptian named Maria who was sent from Egypt, accompanied by her sister and a servant, carrying with them various gifts. About a dozen of the Prophet's *Hadith* (15th century sayings attributed to him) are reported in praise of Egypt itself, its produce and its people (Ibn Zahira 1969: 74 ff). According to this tradition, the Copts had kinship (*silat rahim*) with the Arabs and hence enjoyed a close relationship with the new regime (Bashear 1997: 69). A whole genre of literature known as the *Fadail Misr* ("Virtues of Egypt") was produced, which held the wisdom of the ancient Copts (the Egyptians) in great esteem, and glorified Egypt's past. For example, the author of *akhbar al-zaman* spoke of ancient Egyptian priests as

> the most learned and deserving of priesthood, [who] show that even the Greek Sages were aware of their debt to the Egyptians.

(Al-Sawi 1938: 101)

Medieval Muslim/Arab writers used the word *qipt* or *gypt* (Copt) to denote both ancient and contemporary Egyptians, reflecting their assumed continuity between the past and the present. Respect for the Copts derived from admiration for their heritage, and was not merely an emotional response to the Prophet's praise. This very early interest in Egypt on the part of no less an authority than the Prophet encouraged writers and travellers not only to observe Egypt's monuments, but also to study its history and, additionally, contemporary knowledge and practice. For example, while Al-Mas'udi's (1988, 1: 363) narrative of ancient Egyptian wonders is mainly concerned with marvels of the past, he still observed and admired contemporary Egyptian innovations:

> We mentioned the production in Upper Egypt, close to Abyssinia, where they produced crossbreeds from bulls and she-asses, and also from donkeys on cows ... We gave account of their genetic [?] engineering (*droup al-tawlidat*), in animals and plants in our book titled 'Book of Matters and Experiments'.

Al-Mas'udi's works had a significant influence on almost all Arab writers with an interest in Ancient Egypt. The medieval Muslim/Arab view of Ancient Egypt as the land of wisdom and science was influenced by classical writers (Hornung 2001; Tait Chapter 2, this volume), who were well known to, and quoted by, Muslim/Arab readers from Arabic translations, some from the seventh century, the first century of Islam.

Muslims were encouraged to study the history of earlier prophets, thereby creating a body of historical writings known as the 'History of Prophethood'. Knowledge of these histories is an essential part of the duties of the believer (Ferro 1984: 53). It also led to the creation of universal histories in which Muslim historians treated pre-Islamic materials with respect, and made extensive use of them, for example Jewish stories then circulating among Muslims. All this was in keeping with the Islamic view that treated the history of humanity as one universal history in which each group or people had its own culture and place.

In spite of this, Haarmann (1980: 56) notes as a serious obstacle facing Muslims who wanted to develop a deeper interest in the history of Egypt, "the undeniably sombre image of pharaonic Egypt in the Quran and in Islamic tradition". In making this assessment, Haarmann may have been making too much of the Quran's references to *fir'un*, which referred only to the pharaoh who oppressed the Israelites as well as the rest of the population of Egypt. In fact even this pharaoh was portrayed in several Arabic sources (e.g. Al-Minufi (d. 1524) n.d. MS 48076 ff: 56a) as a pious and caring king before his encounter with Moses and some even claimed that he became a Muslim, a view widely held and appreciated in some Sufi circles (Gril 1978). Others (e.g. Al-Mas'udi 1988, 1: 345; Ibn Zahira 1969: 121 ff) portrayed the kings of pharaonic Egypt in general as models of efficiency and kindness, dedicated to the well-being of their people. Thus, the perceived image of the pharaoh as the archetype of tyranny is not founded on either the Quranic portrayal of Egyptian kingship nor on a common medieval Muslim view but on a narrow interpretation of the Quranic story of a single king.

The Muslim/Arab fascination with the pharaohs of Ancient Egypt is clearly displayed in Arabic sources and was extended to later rulers of Egypt such as Alexander the Great and Queen Cleopatra. Arab authors speak with passionate admiration of Alexander (Christides 2000; Mazzaoui 1991), and a great many volumes were produced in what could be termed 'Arabic Alexanderomania'.[5]

Muslim/Arab writers were fascinated by Cleopatra's scientific knowledge as a scholar and scientist, and there is no reference to her sexuality or seductive power; it is her administrative ability and her intellectual power which the Arabic sources admire. In these, she is seen holding scholarly seminars with fellow scholars in the subjects on which she was an expert: alchemy, medicine, and mathematics (El Daly 2003b; Ullmann 1972b).

## Medieval Arab methodology in archaeology

Medieval Muslim/Arab interest in history and archaeology from before the deluge to their own time was not limited to Egypt but covered other known ancient cultures as well. For example, Abu Al-Hassan Al-Hamadani of Yemen (d. 945 AD) was a distinguished geographer who wrote one of the earliest and most complete geographies of Arabia (Faris 1938: 1). His work includes *al-iklil*, an encyclopaedic work on the archaeology and history of South Arabia. Unfortunately, much of it is lost, but book eight was dedicated to his own archaeological works and those carried out by people whom he knew in Yemen. His archaeological methodology consisted of:

- observing and describing the site;

- excavation and recording of finds with descriptions and measurements;

- analyzing the finds based on religious and historical texts and oral history; and

- using knowledge of ancient writings to read ancient Himyarite inscriptions.

With regard to the latter interest, Al-Hamadani also set out to write a manual of palaeography which may be the first such manual ever attempted. His reason for writing it was this:

> Most of the disagreement among people with regard to Himyarite inscriptions centres on the variations in the forms of the character [of its alphabet]. A character or letter may have four or five forms, while the person who reads it is familiar with only one form. Since, as a result, mistakes have crept in, we have decided to record underneath each letter in the alphabet the various forms of its Himyarite equivalent.

> (Al-Hamadani in Faris 1938: 72)

Abu Ja'far Al-Idrisi (d. 1251 AD) was an Egyptian historian who made an extensive study of the pyramids and whose methods and interests included:

- reasons for the importance of the study of the pyramids;

- description of the route to the site;

- description of the pyramids and their inscriptions;

- measuring, and checking previous measurements;

- analysis of the form of the pyramid and reasons for building, with critical review of literature (more than 22 authorities) on the subject (Haarmann 1996: 608);

- study of sediments as an indication of the flood level (Haarmann 1996: 609);

- chemical analysis of clay in building material, by studying its mineral content in order to check places of origin (Al-Idrisi 1991: 118);

- regular visits to the site to see it in different conditions, and to recheck measurements.

The methodologies of some of these early Arab investigators (even including the so-called 'manuals' of 'treasure hunters') contain drawings of sites and specific tombs (e.g. Paris BN, MS Arabe 2764 fol. 71a and MS Arabe 2661 fol. 72b).

A sketch of the famous Lighthouse of Alexandria (Butler 2003) by the Andalusian traveller, Abu Hamid Al-Gharnati (d. 1169), was based on personal observations during his visits to Alexandria in 1110 AD and again in 1117. He described the lighthouse (Figure 3:1) as having three tiers:

> The first tier is a square built on a platform. The second is octagonal and the third is round. All are built of hewn stone, *sakhr manhut*. On the top was a mirror of Chinese iron of seven cubits wide (364 cm) used to watch the movement of ships on the other side of the Mediterranean. If the ships were those of enemies, then watchmen in the Lighthouse waited until they came close to Alexandria, and when the sun started to set, they moved the mirror to face the sun and directed it onto the enemy ships to burn them in the sea. In the lower part of the Lighthouse, a gate about 20 cubits above the ground level; one climbs to it through an archway ramp of hewn stone.
>
> (Al-Gharnati 1993: 99–100; cf. Hamarneh 1971)

## Medieval Arab knowledge of ancient Egyptian religion

### Temples

Medieval Arabs used the word *birba* or *barba* (pl. *barabi*)[6] to refer to an Egyptian temple. Occasionally it was also used to denote pyramids, which would accord with the Coptic word *brbr* – "pointed top of a pyramid or obelisk derived from the ancient Egyptian *bnbn*" (cf. Černý 1976: 26).

According to Ibn Al-Nadim (d. 920) (1988: 418, 425):

> In Egypt there are buildings called *barabi* made of immensely large great stones. The *birba* are temples of different designs, and have places for grinding, pounding, dissolving, assembling and distilling, showing that they are built for the craft of alchemy. In these buildings are reliefs and inscriptions in Chaldean and Coptic; their meanings are not known ... the known *barabi* are the temples of Wisdom.

Figure 3:1   The Lighthouse of Alexandria by Al-Gharnati (d. 1169 AD) (Paris BN MS Arabe 2168 fol. 17 recto) (after Hamarneh 1971: 87, fig. 1).

And according to Al-Qazwini (d. 1283 AD ?) (1960: 139) a *birba* is

> a temple in which a tree or talisman was established. The *birba* of Akhmim is a temple
> which has images depicted in the stones sticking out (i.e. reliefs) still visible until now.

Apparently, medieval Muslim/Arabs were not only very familiar with Egyptian temples, which dotted the landscape around them, but some even took up residence in them. For example, Ibn Umail (10th century AD), an Egyptian alchemist, was a regular visitor to ancient Egyptian sites as is seen in his account of his repeated visits with two different groups of friends to a chapel at Abu Sir (Stapleton *et al.* 1933: 119). Whatever his reasons for going there, Ibn Umail presents a full description of the chapel he visited, and from this Stricker (1943) was able to study, identify and reconstruct the chapel, assigning it to the cult of Imhotep which was popular in medieval Arabic writings (Wildung 1977: 110ff).

In another work Ibn Umail (Paris MS Arabe 2609) presents an account of meetings held with colleagues to discuss an ancient Egyptian object obtained from a temple and presumed to hold the secrets of alchemy. To explain the meanings of the object and its symbols, he wrote a poem in which he spoke of his intellectual curiosity about the statues of the Egyptian temples and of pursuing scientific knowledge about them. He also described reliefs and paintings from ancient Egyptian temples, which he associated with alchemical symbols. He then explained that he was moved to write this poem because while he was at the house of Abu Al-Hassan 'Ali Ibn Ahmad, he found Sa'adah Ibn Rakan Al-Shu'abi and Abu Al-Qasim Al-Nahawandi, discussing an ancient Egyptian stela (*surah barbawiyah*). These colleagues had asked him for his opinion of the stela, saying that a group of astronomers, with knowledge of the functions of the stars, had previously suggested to them that the stela depicted images of planets, but his colleagues could not comprehend the mysterious language used by those astronomers. Ibn Umail suggested that the reason for interpreting the images as planets was a picture on the stela of a person holding a sword and about to strike the neck of another person whose head he was holding (a tied prisoner?). When Ibn Umail gave an alchemical explanation they asked for evidence to support his claim, which they doubted. Ibn Umail then said:

> Our friend Abu Al-Hassan Al-Siqili (of Sicily) brought that book which has the
> paintings and statues from Upper Egypt, where he found it in the possession of a Greek
> monk (*rahib min al-rom*) and he took it from him.

Ibn Umail departed and returned the following day with his poem in which he invoked Hermes and attributed some of his own knowledge to Morienus, the seventh century Alexandrian alchemist. Ibn Umail associated alchemical operation with every Egyptian motif. For example, he explained a female with a crescent on her head as the moon and a crowned male as the sun. In alchemy these stand for silver and gold and by marrying them together, he alluded to mixing them to make an alloy. He ended the poem:

> See what the [ancient] people painted for you
> So that you know what they associated with hair
> They smoothed the roadless terrain
> And showed the truth by drawing [these] paintings.

Thus it is clear that in medieval times, not only were there groups of like-minded scholars interested in ancient Egyptian temples and objects, but such scholars were hoping to further their knowledge of alchemy by studying actual Egyptian objects (one good example from the 14th century being the interpretation by Abu Al-Qassim al-'Iraqi of a twelfth Dynasty stela – Figure 3:2).

Dhu Al-Nun Al-Misri of Akhmim in Upper Egypt (d. 861 AD) lived most of his life inside the *birba* of Akhmim and studied its ancient script. It was he who established the links between ancient Egyptian religious ideas of books, like the 'Book of the Gates' and the 'Book of the Hours', and some of the earliest ideas in Muslim Sufisms, e.g. *'ilm al-ahwal wa al-maqamat*. This temple may have been the one visited and described by the Andalusian traveller Ibn Jubayer in May 1183 AD, when it was almost intact and was a popular destination for travellers in Upper Egypt. It was also popular with local people because of a famous statue of the god Min. Ibn Jubayer's detailed description of the temple enabled Sauneron (1952: 126) to study it and calculate its dimensions as 115 × 85 m (based on a cubit of 52 cm):

> The most remarkable of the temples of the world talked of for their wonder is the great temple east of the city and below its walls. Its length is two hundred and twenty cubits, and its breadth one hundred and sixty. The people of these parts knew it as *birba*, and thus too are known all their temples and ancient constructions. This great temple is supported by forty columns, beside its walls, the circumference of each column being fifty spans and the distance between them thirty spans. Their capitals are of great size and perfection, cut in an unwonted fashion and angulated in ornate style as if done by turners. The whole is embellished with many colours, lapis lazuli and others. The columns are carved in low relief from top to bottom. Over the capital of each column and stretching to its neighbour is a great slab of carved stone, the biggest of which we measured and found to be 56 spans in length, 10 in width, and 8 in depth.

> The ceiling of this temple is wholly formed of slabs of stone so wonderfully joined as to seem to be one single piece; and over it all are disposed rare paintings and uncommon colours, so that the beholder conceives the roof to be of carved wood. Each slab has a different painting. Some are adorned with comely pictures of birds with outstretched wings making the beholder believe they are about to fly away; others are embellished with human images, very beautiful to look upon and of elegant form, each image having a distinctive shape, for example holding a statue or a weapon, or a bird, or a chalice, or making a hand sign to someone, together with other forms it would take too long to describe and which words are not adequate to express.

> Within and without this great temple, both in its upper and its lower parts, are pictures, all of varied form and description. Some are of dreadful, inhuman forms that terrify the beholder and fill him with wonder and amazement. There was hardly the space of an awl or needle-hole which did not have an image or engraving or some script which is not understood. This remarkable decoration which can be wrought from hard stone where it cannot be worked in soft wood, covers the whole of this vast and splendid temple, in wonder at which the beholder might conceive that all time spent in its adornment, embellishment, and beautifying would be too short.

(after trans. by Broadhurst 1952: 53–55)

Another aspect of ancient Egyptian temples noted by Muslim and Arab sources was the concept of purity and cleanliness which had to apply in places of worship. For

Figure 3:2 Twelfth Dynasty stela with the name of King Amenemhet II, as recorded in the 14th century by Abu Al-Qassim al-'Iraqi (British Library MS Add. 25,724, fol. 50a).

example, King Ashmoun built a temple to the east of his town, having four gates
decorated with faces talking to each other and in this temple:

> whoever enters that temple impure, (these faces) blow at him, afflicting him with an
> illness that stays with him until death. It is said that in the middle (of this temple), there
> is a constant column of light and whoever embraces it never fails to see and hear the
> spirits.

(Al-Sawi 1938: 176)

## Magic

Medieval Arab writers associated magic with temples. For many of these writers, *sihr*
refers to the arts and sciences which were part of the responsibilities of kings, priests
and priestesses in the service of Egyptian society. As Ibn Khaldun (d. 1406) (1967, 3:
156) put it:

> These are sciences showing how human souls may become prepared to exercise an
> influence upon the world of the elements, either without any aid or with the aid of
> celestial matters. The first kind is sorcery. The second kind is talismans.

Magic is treated in Arabic sources as a fundamental part of ancient Egyptian religion,
and also of ancient Egyptian government. One source describes an ancient Egyptian
priestess called Qunia acting as a judge:

> She sits in her court on a throne of fire. If a person seeking her judgement was truthful,
> he would walk through the fire unaffected. She built a palace with hollow walls of
> copper, and on each of its pillars wrote the name of a specific craft on which people
> would seek her advice. People will come to the pillar and speak their mind, asking
> questions, and they will be answered.

(Al-Sawi 1938: 104)

The same source also understood the magical function of some of the idols, which
were used to pass judgment on disputants. They were to

> stand before a statue of black stone [basalt?] called 'Abd Afroys which means Servant
> of Zuhul (Saturn); if the disputant strayed from the truth he got stuck in the place and
> could not move.

(Al-Sawi 1938: 105)

'Magic' was practised by various Caliphs and Sultans, using similar objects. For
example, Ibn Iyas (1982–1984, 1/1: 202), quoting Ibn Khalikan, recounts the case of Al-
Hakim, the most famous of the Fatimid Caliphs, who ruled from 996 to 1020 AD:

> The Al-Hakim Bi-Amr Allah obtained an idol, it is hollow and inside it is the spirit
> (*ruhani*), who looks after it. It spoke like humans do, and this statue used to recover lost
> objects and tell where they were ... Then people who lost objects were called to Al-
> Hakim, the idol was brought out and everyone who had lost anything stood before it
> and said 'O Abu Al-Haul I have lost such and such a thing'. The Spirit inside the statue
> then said: 'Your lost object is in such and such place at such and such address'. So Al-
> Hakim sent his servants to the place, they brought back the lost item and all the thieves
> were then hanged. From then on nothing was ever stolen.

It can also be assumed that many Arab writers must have been familiar with that part
of the Alexander Romance where the Egyptian king Nectanebo used magic to carry

out his plans (Burnett Chapter 4, this volume). Another magical episode is recounted by Al-Mas'udi (1988, 1: 359) about an ancient Egyptian queen who built

> temples and equipped them with magic tools and pictures of whoever may come from any direction and their animals, camels or horses, and the ships that may come from the sea of Morocco or Al-Sham (Syria), and she assembled in these great glorious temples, the secrets of nature, the properties of stones, plants and animals ... All was done at certain times of astronomical movements and contacts with higher influences. If an army invaded, she damaged their picture on the temple wall so those who are in that army are wounded. This is why the Kings and Nations feared and respected Egypt.

That the Muslim/Arab writers recognized at least some of the ancient Egyptian beliefs regarding the relationship between deities and good health and well-being is reflected in the account of a king the Arabs called 'Shadat', who built new towns on the east bank of the Nile. In one, he erected what was presumably a statue of the god Min:

> a standing statue with an erect phallus: if one who is impotent and cannot have an erection for any reason came to this statue and held it with both hands, he will recover and obtain the desired erection and the strength to copulate.

> (Al-Sawi 1938: 166)

Al-Maqrizi (d. 1442 AD) (2002, 1: 651) quoted a description of this statue as

> standing on one leg and has only one arm which is raised high. There are inscriptions on his forehead and around the body. He has a prominent phallus.

He then referred to the popular use of this stone phallus for treating male impotence provided the user succeeds in extracting it from the statue without damage and wears it around his waist. King 'Shadat' is said to have erected "a statue of a cow with two large udders [in another town]; if a woman whose milk has decreased or dried up touches it, her milk will flow" (Al-Sawi 1938: 167).

> Another king, called by the Arabs 'Menqaus', is recorded (1938: 169) as having built

> a temple with statues that cure all illnesses, and wrote on top of the shrine of every statue what it would cure, so people benefited from this house for a time until some kings spoiled it.

## Deities

Several medieval writers claimed a relationship between ancient Egyptian religion and its deities, with the religious practices and deities of pre-Islamic Arabs. For example, basing his work on Ptolemy, Al-Hamadani (ninth/10th century), claimed (1996: 42) that Isis was widely worshipped in south-west Arabia and that Amun was worshipped in the Western Desert between Egypt and Libya. Indeed Isis was popular in other parts of Arabia as well (Donner 1995) and, similarly, the names of Horus and Bes were known in Arabia, where they were believed to have originated (Brugsch 1902: 54; Kamal 1902). Bes had a cult centre in Arabia and various Egyptian deities such as Osiris and Isis found their way into Arabic folklore and popular magic (Ray 1994).

Al-Baghdadi (1985: 109 ff) explicitly recognized a sense of continuity between past and present Egyptian culture:

> and as for the idols, they were very common in the ancient world even with the Christians, most of whom, Copts and Sabaeans, were inclined towards their origin in the old tradition of their ancestors of adopting icons in their places of worship. They can even go as far as depicting their god surrounded by angels. All these are remains of the traditions of their predecessors, although the predecessors elevated god beyond any logical or physical reach or comprehension, let alone depiction.

Other medieval Muslim writers tried to reconcile the image of a particular king as depicted in the Quran with their view that Ancient Egyptians were believers in the oneness of God. Thus, Al-Shahrastani (d. 1188 AD ?) (1948, 2: 329) argued that the Egyptian pharaoh of Moses' time was

> formerly of the Sabaean Sect but left it and declared himself the Great God.

It seems that Al-Shahrastani was aware of the many sects within the Sabaean, a creed that is respected in the Quran alongside Judaism and Christianity (Q2: 62). According to the anonymous author (Al-Sawi 1938: 126, 190), the religion which Egyptian priests were teaching their people was that of "the first Sabaeans" and that a particular pharaoh had been "indeed a monotheist".

Al-Mas'udi (d. 956 AD) (1988, 1: 39–40) links the biblical Prophet Akhnukh, 'Enoch' (the Quranic Prophet Idris), with Egyptian Hermes. Somewhat similarly, Al-Ya'qubi (d. ca. 905 AD) (1960, 1: 187–188) recounts that Akhnukh/Idris was "the first to write" and also claims that

> The Sage (Hakeem) of the Copts is Hermes the Copt. They are the builders of the temples who write in the script of the temples ... And in our time, nobody knows how to read it, because only the elite among them were writing in it; they would not allow the common people to do so. The ones in charge of it were their sages and priests. It had the secrets of their religion and the origins of sciences which nobody was allowed to see but their priests, who did not teach it to anyone unless ordered to do so by the king ... Their religion was the worship of planets/stars. From their sayings: The souls are old and were in Paradise and every thirty-six thousands years all that is in the world will perish ... Then nature will bring back to life from every kind and the world will return after its demise. They had of these spirits, deities who descend into the idols, causing the idols to speak which was a craft made by the priests and the drugs that they use; tricks they utilise until it whistles and screams as if the idol was indeed a bird or an animal. Then the priests translate that sound of the idol according to whatever they like to judge, according to their astronomical signs and physiognomy. They tell that when souls depart, they go to these deities who are the planets, so they wash them and purify them if they had sins. The souls then go up to paradise where they belong.

> They say that their prophets were spoken to by the planets which informed them that the Spirits descend into the idols and take residence inside, and foretell events before they happen. They had such precise and wondrous astuteness with which they instilled into the common people the illusion that they were conversing with the planets, which then foretell to them what will happen.

This text reflects many themes of ancient Egyptian belief, such as the keeping of sacred knowledge within certain circles, cyclic creation, priests using mechanical devices to make divine statues move and talk during oracles (DuQuesne 2001: 16 n. 67), and the concept of the souls of the dead united with the stars in the heavens. Al-Ya'qubi apparently admired the knowledge and beliefs of these ancient Egyptian priests. He also, like many other Arab writers, was familiar with hermetic and Gnostic literature and ideas, which had a long tradition in Islam (Corbin 1986: 1) and had great influence on the Arabs (e.g. Scott 1985, 4: 248 ff), and particularly on the Sabaeans (Yates 2002: 52 ff). Al-Mas'udi (1894), who knew the Sabaeans very well, stated that the Sabaeans of Harran were descendants of the Egyptians. The Sabaeans believed that they had links with the Ancient Egyptians, asserting that they were co-religionists and that they originally came from Egypt (Drower 1937: 10, 261). Moreover, they commemorated the souls of Egyptians who were said to have drowned during the Exodus: "for these Egyptians are thought to have been Mandaean by creed" (Drower 1956: 234–235). Some of their magical talismans seem to show Egyptian hieroglyphic signs (McCullough 1967: 43).

Such apparent links may explain attempts by, among others, the anonymous 10th/12th century author (Al-Sawi 1938: 166) to bring the Ancient Egyptians closer to Islam, claiming that the Ancient Egyptians' belief

> in the oneness of God, and their praise of functionary mediums (for example stars) does not affect [the status of] their Creator for they glorify these mediums to worship God and get nearer to him as do the Indians, the Arabs, and many other nations.

It is well known that one of the oldest forms of ancient Egyptian worship was that of cow and/or bull deities. The author (Al-Sawi 1938: 172–174) apparently did not differentiate between cows and bulls. According to this writer, the Egyptian king Menaus was perhaps the first pharaoh to worship cows:

> the reason for this was that he became ill and despaired. He saw in his sleep a great Spirit speaking to him thus: Nothing will cure you but your worship of cows, because the Zodiac at the time was in the Sign of the Bull which is in the image of a bull with two horns.When the King awoke he gave orders and they got a handsome piebald Bull and made a shrine for it in his palace with a gilded dome ... and he worshipped him secretly and was cured. Later on, a bull talked to the King and directed him to worship and look after the Bull and in return the Bull will look after the King's interests and strengthen him and cure him. So the King established a shrine for the Bull and arranged servants to care for him and hold the service of its cult.

Various ancient Egyptian themes can be noted in this text: royal dreams and divine oracles, and the cults of the cow goddess and of Apis/Serapis, the Bull of Memphis and other bull cults.

Medieval Arabic sources also showed awareness of the importance of certain cults in Ancient Egypt. As suggested (Al-Sawi 1938: 109), the head of all the High Priests of Egypt, constantly in the company of the king, was the High Priest of Ashmunen (city of the god Thoth) because it was the oldest city in Egypt.

It is clear that Arab writers sought, and found, close relationships and affinities between their own beliefs and those they perceived to have originated in Ancient Egypt, and such commonality was ascribed to a common origin, or source, of religious ideas in the form of the Prophet Idris/Hermes/Thoth.

## Holy sites

Medieval Arabs regarded many ancient Egyptian sites as holy places, some of which continued as pilgrimage sites during the medieval period. Furthermore, the Nile continued to be celebrated as a holy river in medieval Egypt (Lutfi 1998). Feasts and ceremonies were celebrated by medieval Egyptians and others at and around holy sites, and contemporary writers described many of these festivals, and suggested that they had originated in Ancient Egypt.

Al-Idrisi (1991: 28) was told by a friend of his that he found in various books on and by Ancient Egyptians that the pyramid site was known as 'The Holy Land', and that it was because of its sacred nature that the Egyptians had chosen it as a burial site for their greatest kings and sages.

The Scribe of Salahdin, Al-Emad Al-Isfahani (d. 1201) (1979: 118), reports a leisure trip that he took to the pyramid area at the invitation of the Chief Judge Diau Al-Din Al-Shahruzuri, where they toured the pyramids and debated, among other issues, the identity of their builders and their functions. On their way to the site, Al-Isfahani saw a group of people "dressed in the manner of Iraqis and Syrians wearing head scarfs" and he thought they were students, from the manner of their gathering in a circle, but as his company approached them, they fled. It is possible that these may have been Sabaean worshippers of whom Al-Maqrizi, much later, says that they did not cease to worship Abu Al-Hul (Sphinx) where they sacrificed white roosters and burned incense of sandarac-wood (cf. Scott 1985, 4: 254 n. 4). One reason for the Sabaean belief that Hermes is buried in this area may be the story told by Pliny that the sphinx contained the tomb of the legendary King Harmakhes (*Hor-em-akhet*, the name of the sphinx meaning 'Horus of the Horizon', which may later have been corrupted into Hermes). The sphinx was venerated as a god by the Ancient Egyptians and was known as a place of pilgrimage well into the fourth century (Hassan 1951: 10). Foreigners living in Memphis saw in the sphinx their god Hurun and worshipped it (Wildung 1977: 19). Some urn-burials, which may have belonged to Babylonians, were found around the sphinx by Hassan (1951: 33), who also found that many of the offerings were presented to the sphinx by foreign worshippers who lived in the vicinity of the sphinx, in the area known now as Harrania Village (Hassan 1951: 96). This may well have been the place where Sabaeans from Harran gathered during their pilgrimage. It is clear from Arabic sources that similar veneration continued throughout the medieval period (cf. Haarmann 1978). Al-Idrisi (1991: 151) informs us that there is "a certain day of the year when visitors who aspire to senior jobs with the Sultan offer incense to the Sphinx".

The site was also very popular with many of the rulers of Egypt, such as Ibn Tulun (868–884 AD) (Al-Balawi 1939: 194), who was said to be a regular and frequent visitor (e.g. Al-Idrisi 1991: 35 ff). During the Fatimid dynasty, the national celebration known as 'Night of Fire' was started by setting alight a huge fire on the top of the pyramid (Al-Idrisi 1991: 38).

As reported in Al-Sawi (1938: 174), once the cow/bull cultic rite had been established, its locale became a pilgrimage site:

later on after the Holy Bull was buried people from all over Egypt and neighboring areas flocked to his shrine with offerings to his statue and he would tell them whatever they wanted.

Such ceremonies accompanying burial are well known from Ancient Egypt, where they included processions of large crowds gathering and consulting the oracle. The Serapieion in Saqqarah was one such site. Pilgrimage there may well have continued until the 12th century and even beyond.

The site of *sijn yousuf* ('The Prison of Joseph') at Abu Sir, because of the belief that Joseph received divine revelations while imprisoned there, became in medieval times a pilgrimage centre with annual ceremonies lasting for three days (Ibn Iyas 1982–1984, 1/1: 35). It was very popular among Muslims in general as a holy place where God would answer requests favourably (*yostajabu fih al-du'aa*) (Al-Qalqashandi (d. 1418) 1913–1920, 3: 307). This site has been identified as a cult centre of Imhotep. The pilgrimage would seem to be a continuation of the ancient cult of Imhotep under the name of Joseph, both foretelling future events and interpreting dreams. The surrounding area was associated also with the Oracle of Hermes Trismegistus (Skeat and Turner 1968), a very popular figure in Arabic writings.

Another important holy site was the 'Grand Shrine at Heliopolis' which, according to Al-Idrisi (1991: 109–110), was venerated by both Sabaeans and Egyptians. Al-Maqrizi (2002, 1: 368) also referred to it as a pilgrimage centre not only for Egyptians, but also for people from all over the world. He records that the Shrine was dedicated to seven deities associated with seven heavenly bodies/planets, headed by the sun god who was called Lord of the Gods. Al-Maqrizi (2002, 1: 618) then presented an account of the daily service which included prayers performed three times a day; the first at sunrise, the second at midday and the third at sunset. Al-Maqrizi (2002, 1: 371) also quoted from a lost book by Ibn Al-Kalbi that the Arabic name of the city '*Ain shams,* was derived from the old sun god. Ibn Al-Kalbi (d. 820 AD), an early Muslim historian of religions who wrote several books on various aspects of pre-Islamic Arabia (e.g. *al-asnam*), was clearly aware of the sun cult at Heliopolis. These medieval Arab writers also commented on the ancient Egyptian royal visits to perform religious duties at the Grand Shrine of the city, staying there for seven days. Some Egyptian kings were said to have ordered private chapels to be built at the Grand Shrine for their visit (Al-Maqrizi 2002, 1: 369; Quirke 2001).

Another site connected with Heliopolis and thought by medieval Arab writers to be a holy site was the Muqatam Mountain, *gabal al-muqatam,* to the east of Cairo (Ibn 'Abd Al-Hakam (d. 871 AD) 1922: 157 ff; Al-Maqrizi 2002, 1: 335 ff). This mountain was regarded by Muslims to be so holy that it became the most desired burial ground for their dead, including "'Amr, the first Muslim ruler of Egypt himself, and a number of the 'Companions of the Prophet'" (Ibn 'Abd Al-Hakam 1922: 253). Its soil was used to treat diseases after a woman with a severe eye problem alleged that Prophet Mohammed had recommended it to her in a dream (Ibn Qadi Shuhba (d. 1448) 1977–1997, 1: 522). According to Ibn 'Abd Al-Hakam and Al-Maqrizi, Egyptian kings built a rest-station on the top of this mountain at the halfway point between their palace at Memphis and the cult centre at Heliopolis. This station was also used to announce the departure and arrival of the pharaohs for their regular visits to Heliopolis. These accounts show awareness of the visual connection between Memphis, the Muqatam

Mountain and Heliopolis as well as their religious ties. Observations of a connection between ancient monuments such as the pyramids, sphinx and stars are widely reported in medieval Arabic sources. For example, Al-Idrisi (1991: 151) reported alignments between the sun when it rises in its zodiac and a spot between the eyes of the sphinx, the statue being the major manifestation/idol of the sun.

In general, many of the ancient Egyptian holy sites continued to be treated as such by Muslims even if new myths had to be woven to explain their sanctity. An example was the Temple of Luxor, part of which served as a church, and where later the Mosque and Tomb of Abu Al-Hagag, a Muslim saint, was built. A special festival, still held every year for this Sheikh, recalls the 'Opet Festival' of pharaonic Egypt. All over Egypt today ancient tombs or temples still serve as shrines for local saints, for example the tomb of Sheikh Al-Saman on the Giza Plateau (Porter and Moss 1974 3/1: 235) was originally an Old Kingdom tomb (and see Yamani 2001: 395 for other examples).

## Medieval Arabs and Egyptian scripts

Greco-Roman writers' interest in the scripts of Ancient Egypt has been well documented (Iversen 1993; Parkinson 1999; Pope 1999; Solé and Valbelle 1999; Tait Chapter 2, this volume). In general it seems that the classical commentators believed that hieroglyphic signs were symbols, each representing a single concept. This view prevailed in Europe until the work of Athanasius Kircher in the mid-17th century (Curran Chapter 5, this volume). He suggested that hieroglyphs could represent sounds as well as ideas, and his work began to influence other European scholars, culminating in the work of Champollion. Kircher made use of many Arabic sources (at least 40 Arabic writers) including Gelaledden (Al-Syuti), Aben Regal and Aben Vahschia (Wahshiya). It is difficult at this stage to identify all his Arabic sources but a few are well known. Arabic manuscripts from the 12th century and perhaps earlier which contained Coptic grammars and vocabularies (e.g. the 'Scala Magna' by Abu Al-Barakat, also known as Ibn Kabr; cf. Budge 1928: 79–80; Figure 3:3) were brought to the west by Della Valle and first studied by Thomas Obicini (Thomaso di Nova) in the early 17th century. The contribution of a good knowledge of Coptic, thanks to Kircher's Coptic grammar, to the success of Champollion's work should not be underestimated (Pope 1999: 39).

However, despite the importance of Kircher's work, recent Egyptological literature ignores the contributions made by medieval Arabic scholars to the history of decipherment of Egyptian scripts. It is not generally known that medieval Arabs were fascinated by the problem of deciphering Egyptian hieroglyphs and that, in some cases, they succeeded in identifying the correct meaning of Egyptian signs. Medieval Arabic interest in ancient scripts started as early as the first century of Islam, the seventh century AD (Sezgin 1967, 1: 934).

It should also be noted that Egyptians continued to be interested in and were able to understand the ancient Egyptian scripts long after the Christianization of Egypt, which was in any event a long process. In the Coptic Gnostic materials of Nag Hamadi, Hermes advised his disciple to write his teachings on "a stela of turquoise, in hieroglyphic characters" (Robinson 1996: 326). This interest must have continued

| # | Coptic | Arabic | # | Coptic | Arabic |
|---|--------|--------|---|--------|--------|
| 1 | ⲡⲓⲃⲉⲣⲥⲓⲥ | القطف | 23 | ⲡⲓⲕⲁⲝⲓ | الكرّات |
| 2 | ⲡⲓⲙⲓⲧ | الكرفس | 24 | ⲡⲓⲕⲟⲩⲍⲓⲏ | اللفت |
| 3 | ⲡⲓⲕⲣⲙⲓ | الكرفس البرّي | 25 | ⲡⲓⲃⲉⲣϣⲓ | الكسفرة |
| 4 | ⲡⲓⲥⲉⲣⲓⲛⲟ | المقدونس | 26 | ⲡⲓⲉⲍⲟⲩⲟ | الجزر |
| 5 | ⲡⲓⲥⲧⲁⲡⲓⲛⲁⲣ | الجزر | 27 | ϯⲥⲁⲙⲟⲝⲣⲟⲥ | اللجلاروس |
| 6 | ⲡⲓϩⲙⲓϫⲓ | النعناع | 28 | ⲡⲓⲁⲣⲙⲟⲩⲣⲓ | هنداباري |
| 7 | ⲡⲓϫⲣⲟⲥⲉ | النعناع الجبلي | 29 | ⲡⲓⲕⲩⲣⲓⲟ | سلاب جبلي |
| 8 | ⲡⲓⲁⲙⲓⲣⲟⲛ | اللوف | 30 | ⲡⲓⲕⲍⲓⲟ | سلاب بستاني |
| 9 | ⲡⲓⲃⲱϣⲟⲩ | السلاب | 31 | ⲡⲓⲥⲁⲣⲓⲥ | البرّي |
| 10 | ⲡⲓⲙⲓϯⲟⲩ | النداك الجبلي | 32 | ⲡⲓⲕⲝⲓⲟⲩ | الخنبيز |
| 11 | ⲡⲓⲃⲉⲧⲓϩⲉ | الباذنجان البرّي | 33 | ⲡⲓⲝⲉⲣⲁ | الملاح |
| 12 | ⲃⲁⲝⲁⲛ | الباذنجان | 34 | ⲁⲣⲱⲡⲁⲝⲓⲛ | القلم |
| 13 | ⲡⲉϫⲣⲓⲧ | السلق | 35 | ⲡⲓⲡⲣⲓⲙ | القرظ البرّي |
| 14 | ⲡⲓⲥⲱⲟϭⲓⲛⲕⲟⲩⲁⲣ | الباذنجان | 36 | ϯⲁⲉⲝⲁⲣⲓⲙ | الرجله |
| 15 | ⲃⲉⲧϫⲓ | الباذنجان البري | 37 | ϯⲁⲉⲝⲁ | الرجله |
| 16 | ⲡⲓⲕⲟⲍⲟⲩⲧ | البقطن | 38 | ⲡⲓⲕⲣⲁⲥⲑⲉ | العلق |
| 17 | ⲡⲓⲃⲉⲙⲓⲛⲉ | بنان | 39 | ⲡⲓⲁⲣⲓⲥⲉⲥ | اللسان |
| 18 | ⲡⲓⲝⲣⲟϣⲟⲛ | البقطن البري | 40 | ϯⲁⲣⲧⲉⲙⲓⲥⲓⲥ | الدرمسيسة |
| 19 | ⲡⲓⲕⲟⲥⲉⲕⲓⲛ | الاسفاناخ | 41 | ⲃⲟⲝⲝⲉⲣⲓⲟⲥ | قلبه |
| 20 | ⲙⲟⲝⲟⲩⲓⲁ | الملوخيه | 42 | ⲟⲝⲕⲟⲥ | خذل ابيض |
| 21 | ϯⲃⲁⲝⲙⲟⲁⲩ | الباميه | 43 | ⲃⲟⲝⲃⲟⲥ | غاسول |
| 22 | ⲡⲓⲙⲁⲃ | الخصّ | 44 | ⲃⲟⲝⲣⲓⲃⲁ | غاسول |

ⲟⲝⲟ

A PAGE FROM IBN KABR'S LIST OF VEGETABLES.
(From Brit. Mus. MS. Orient. No. 1325, fol. 117a.)

Figure 3:3 The 'Scala Magna' with Coptic inscriptions, as recorded by Abu Al-Barakat (Budge 1928: 81; British Library MS Add. 24,050).

and expanded so much that it became at times a cause of concern for some in the church hierarchy. In a work ascribed to the Coptic monk Shenoute (d. mid-fifth century AD), there is a monastic invective against hieroglyphs (Young 1981). It has been suggested that knowledge of ancient Egyptian writing survived among the Copts until at least the seventh century AD (Amélineau 1888: xxxix; Butler 1978: 86; Horbury 2003). Coptic magical spells invoked ancient Egyptian deities (DuQuesne 1991; Meyer and Smith 1994: 22–25).

In medieval Arabic writings, Coptic monks were perceived as the keepers of the wisdom and knowledge of the ancient priests. Al-Jobry, who visited Egypt several times in the first half of the 13th century AD, was a regular visitor to Coptic monasteries. On one visit to a monastery in Al-Bahnasa in Middle Egypt, he became acquainted with a monk named Ashmonit, and wrote of him:

> this Elder is a brilliant philosopher who knows the secrets of the ancient priests, and uncovered their symbols and understood their sciences.

(Al-Jobry 1992: 144)

Probably some of the Coptic magical texts were translations of more ancient Egyptian ones and indeed, in some cases, demotic parallels to these Coptic texts have been established (DuQuesne 1991: 11). There are also numerous claims for the survival of some ritual and magical practices from Ancient Egypt into Coptic Egypt (e.g. Kákosy 1989, 1999: 33 ff). In general, Coptic literature preserved a great deal from its pharaonic heritage (Behlmer 1996; Krause 1985). The same pharaonic influence can also be identified within Jewish magic (Bohak 1999: 31–32).

There can be no doubt that much pharaonic/Coptic magic material did indeed pass into Arabic with the result that many of the ancient Egyptian symbols were known to a wider Arab readership (e.g. Bilabel et al. 1934). Symbols and motifs of ancient Egyptian art were adopted into Islamic arts (Grube 1962) either for their aesthetic or their magical value. Extensive re-use of decorated ancient Egyptian stones in Islamic architecture, especially mosques, brought Muslims face-to-face several times a day with pharaonic scenes and hieroglyphs (Meinecke-Berg 1985). Hieroglyphic signs were extant in Arabic talismans and became familiar in the west through the Latin translation of medieval Arabic magic and hermetic works such as 'Picatrix'. Hieroglyphs were also much used as symbols in Islamic manuscripts (Blochet 1907: 215 ff) and in decorating pen-boxes, blazons and shields (Artin 1889).

Another source of knowledge of ancient Egyptian came through the Arabic translations (e.g. Ibn Al-Nadim 1988: 315; Ibn Fatik 1958: 54; Ibn Abi Usaybi'ah 1998: 50) of many of the classical writers whose works included references to ancient Egyptian language and scripts (Tait Chapter 2, this volume).

The writings of the Egyptian historian Manetho were also known to medieval Arabic scholars (e.g. Al-Biruni (d. 1048) 1923: 90 ff); Agapius (ca. 940 AD) (Agapius 1954: 16) referred to him as "The Egyptian Sage, the Astrologer" and cited a book by Manetho, *On The Stars*. He also noted that the Haraneans (Sabaeans; see e.g. Corbin 1986: 132 ff), who "worshipped the idols", cherished Manetho's work, perhaps in keeping with their traditions of Egyptian ancestry.

There can be no doubting the considerable interest of medieval Arabs in ancient Egyptian scripts. More than a dozen names were used in Arabic sources to refer to them. The most common were *birbawi* 'temple script', *musnad* and *himyarite* 'South Arabian scripts' and *huruf al-tayr* 'letters of birds'. As has been seen, the curiosity of medieval Muslim/Arab intellectuals in this subject manifested itself in seminars held to discuss ancient Egyptian materials and inscriptions.

An Arabic manuscript attributed to Ayub Ibn Masalama (early ninth century AD) (fol. 3) advocated the merits of learning ancient scripts for no material gains:

> And keep what had reached you of the science of these scripts. For even if the virtues of this science was limited to its carrier, the one who deals in it is able to reach the secrets of the Sages and Philosophers, and what they wrote to the Kings and Caliphs, which they kept from the ordinary and ignorant, and he does not miss out on any of their affairs, for this is the science that must be passed on and only kept from those who are not worthy of it.

Many of these scholars may have learned Coptic in their quest for knowledge. Ibn 'Abd Al-Hakam (1922: 30 n. 11) accurately quoted a Coptic phrase. Ibn Al-Dawadari (d. 1335 AD) (1981: 214–215) referred to a Coptic book widely available for those interested in the history of Egypt, and recorded that Al-Mas'udi used it, as he had himself (Haarmann 1982: 207). Al-Idrisi (1991: 118) also mentioned a Coptic book on Egyptian chronology translated in ca. 840 AD into Arabic. At that time it is important to remember that many native Egyptian writers must have been more or less trilingual, being conversant with Coptic, Greek and Arabic (Atiya 1986: 92). Al-Maqrizi's account of Coptic monasteries in Asiut (Diab 1998: 170) includes a very important linguistic observation about the local dialect. He noted that in the early 15th century AD, while Upper Egyptian Copts conversed in Saidic Coptic, they also had perfect knowledge of Greek. He also reported that they knew Boharic dialect but that Saidic was the original Coptic. Indeed already during the 13th century AD, there was a school of native Egyptians dedicated to producing religious texts, and studies of Coptic grammar and vocabularies in Greek-Coptic-Arabic languages (e.g. Bauer 1972; Mallon 1906, 1907; Vycichl 1991a, b).

There is every possibility that more than one of the ancient Egyptian scripts may have been known to early medieval Arabs. There are numerous ancient objects and texts with Egyptian hieroglyphic writings or motifs which combine one or more of Coptic, Greek, Carian, Latin, Hebrew, Aramaic, Akkadian, Elamite and Old Persian inscriptions, making it possible for someone with a knowledge of any of these to have tried to decipher ancient Egyptian. Objects with inscriptions range from large texts such as the Rosetta Stone (in hieroglyphic, demotic and Greek), to small tags such as mummy labels (in demotic and Greek), or foundation tablets (in hieroglyphic and Greek – Empereur 1998: 97). There are also Egyptian texts in Greek characters. Other examples of multi-language texts include a scorpion spell where the text is written in demotic and Aramaic with easily recognizable Arabic elements (Porten 1992), and a quadrilingual papyrus, which includes Greek, Latin, demotic and an unidentified script (Coles 1981). Sometimes, Egyptian hieratic was used in combination with Hebrew (e.g. Aharoni 1966).

It is clear that some Arab scholars recognized that the ancient Egyptian language was written in three different scripts. Ibn Fatik (10th/11th centuries) wrote of Pythagoras' quest for knowledge during his stay in Egypt:

> He attached himself to the priests in Egypt and learned wisdom from them. He excelled in the language of the Egyptians with the three types of scripts: the script of the commoners, the script of the elite which is the cursive one of the priests, and the script of the kings.

> (Ibn Fatik 1958: 54)

It is therefore likely that the Arabs were also able to identify the scripts of demotic, hieratic and hieroglyphic. Besides personal observation, such knowledge may have derived from the writings of Clement of Alexandria (d. 220 AD) who had already reported that the Egyptians used those three kinds of writing (Budge 1929: 180).

In the 15th century, Al-Minufi al-Fayd (fol. 49b) quotes the 10th century account by Al-Mas'udi (1988, 1: 347 ff) of the story of the Old Copt hosted by Ibn Tulun in the ninth century in order to quench his thirst for knowledge of the past of Egypt. The Old Copt said that "Coptic script was a mixture of the ancient native letters and those of Greek", so there is evidence of awareness of the origin and nature of Coptic persisting into some medieval Muslim/Arabic sources. Thus, Al-Maqrizi (2002, 2: 425–427) quotes an early account about one of the gates of the Fatimid palace in Cairo, "Bab al-bahr". This palace was built by Al-Hakim Bi-Amr Allah at the end of the 10th century and demolished in 1273 AD during the reign of Al-Zahir Rukn Al-Din Baybars (1260–1277 AD):

> While demolishing this gate to take away some of its columns for some Sultanate building, they uncovered a box in a wall built around it[,] and immediately witnesses and a large crowd came and the box was opened. A statue was found in it. It is hollow yellow copper on a seat similar to the pyramid; its height is about a hand span with four legs supporting the seat. The idol sat cross-legged with his hand raised high. He holds a document, *sahifa*, about three hand spans wide and in this document are standing figures. In the middle there is a picture of a head without a body encircled with writings in Coptic and *Qalfeteriat* (magic signs?).[7]

> Next to it is a figure in the shape of an ear of wheat bearing two horns. On the other side is a figure with a cross on his head, and another with a walking stick in his hand and a cross on his head. Under their feet are figures of birds. Above the heads of the figures, is some script. Also found in the box with this idol, was a boy's writing palette of the type used for writing in the *makatib* (these are small classes to teach youngsters the Quran with lessons in reading, writing and reciting poetry and language skills).

> One of its sides was painted white and the other red, on which most of the writing has fallen off because of the long passage of time. The palette has deteriorated and so has the writing. The white side was written in the same Coptic script as the written remains on the red side, in the following account (line order 1–13):

> Line 1   Alexander ...
> Line 2   the land he gave to him
> Line 3   he tried for all
> Line 4   companions
> Line 5   and he guards
> Line 6   and his strong holding

**Line 7**   the king is begged and gates
**Line 8**   changed his house seven
**Line 9**   wise scholar knowledgable in his mind
**Line 10**   its description so do not spoil
**Line 11**   remover of every evil and the one who shaped it/them women
**Line 12**   walled also all Lion's antiquities Baybars and it is one of
**Line 13**   Baybars king of time and wisdom, the word of Allah, the Glorious.

It was said that this palette is in the handwriting of Caliph Al-Hakim. The most peculiar thing about it is that it contains the name of Sultan Baybars, who saw it and ordered it to be read, so it was shown to the 'Readers of the Scripts' and was read. It is in the Coptic script and its content is a talisman made for Al-Zahir, son of Al-Hakim, in which his mother's name was written together with names of angels, spells, incantations, spirits' names and images of angels most of which for the protection of the land of Egypt and its ports, and to repel enemies ... This talisman was carried to the Sultan and remained among his treasures. It was also seen in an old book called by its writer 'The Will of The Imam Al-'Aziz Bi-Allah, father of the Imam Al-Hakim Bi-Amr Allah, for his above mentioned son'. He mentioned in it the talismans made on the palace gates to give power to the sun king over his enemies.

Al-Maqrizi (d. 1442) (2002, 2: 427–429) narrates the story of another gate demolition in the same palace, the 'Gate of the Wind', which took place in his own time:

A statue of a person was found and when that news reached me I went to the Emir in charge of the demolition, Emir Jamal Al-Din Yosef Al-Istadar, and asked him to bring it. He told me that he was brought a person of stone, short, with one eye smaller than the other. I said, 'I have to see it', so he ordered the man in charge of constructions to bring it while I was with him at the site of the gate, after the demolition of the whole building. The man said he had thrown it into the building stones and that it broke and got mixed up with the rest of the stones and that he could not distinguish it. The Emir pressed the man hard but they failed to bring it, so I asked the man to describe it. The man said that they found a circle with writing in it, and in the middle was a short person with one of his eyes smaller than the other. This sounds very much like the Emir Jamal Al-Din just mentioned.

Al-Maqrizi was therefore clearly aware of the many issues that an archaeologist nowadays takes into account: description of the object, offering interpretation of it, and postulating a purpose and function. Al-Maqrizi's analysis is sited within the framework of the available knowledge about magic and angels. His limited historical knowledge did not stop him from sharing his interest with his readers. The most important feature is his attempted accuracy in recording the words on every line and noting the breaks, lacunae and damage. There is also internal textual criticism, in the form of wondering in disbelief at the supposed existence of the contemporary ruler's name on the stela.

## Conclusion

Muslim/Arab writers drew on rich and varied sources which included, in addition to Muslim/Arab writings, others, both pre-Islamic and contemporary. Their approach to the written sources is at times, but not always, critical. Visiting sites and talking to local people also feature as a major source of information. But even eyewitness accounts were not always accepted uncritically, as Al-Baghdadi's writings have shown.

The fabric of many of the ancient Egyptian temples was almost intact in medieval times and they were perceived by writers as institutions of wisdom, learning and magic. These writers also believed that the Egyptian kings had been concerned with the well-being of their subjects and had utilized all available sources, including magic, to achieve this. Egyptian magic for Arab writers was a 'science' practised by kings, queens and priests, as part of the formal structure of Egyptian religion.

The medieval writers also recognized the sanctity of Egyptian religious sites, especially the pyramid area. Not only did they describe the survival of some ancient Egyptian practices among medieval Egyptians, but, as seen above, many Muslim writers tried to find common ground between Islamic teachings and ancient Egyptian religion, as do some modern scholars (e.g. Al-Sayar 1995: 153 ff).

Many place names in Egypt still show their ancient origin, and modern Egyptians and their medieval forebears, Muslims and Christians alike, regard as holy, places which their ancient ancestors sanctified.

The whole process of the decipherment of ancient Egyptian hieroglyphics was undoubtedly assisted by the view that ancient Egyptian and Arabic languages had so many features in common. It has been suggested that ancient Egyptian was the basis of the Arabic alphabet (Gardiner 1916) and even of the Arabic language (Kamal 1917: 331).

For two and a half centuries the study of Egyptology has been dominated by a eurocentric view, which has virtually ignored over a thousand years of Arabic scholarship and inquiry, encouraged by Islam. This European dominance may have resulted in part from the seeming lack of interest in Ancient Egypt by modern Egyptians and Arabs. The main reason for this was probably the marginalization of interested Egyptians by early western Egyptologists and others who discouraged their participation in any Egyptological study (e.g. Haikal 2003: 123–127; Hassan 2003: 19–27, 65–68; Jeffreys 2003b: 10, 14–18; Reid 1985, 1990, 2002). Young Egyptian scholars complain bitterly, even today, about the western dominance of Egyptology (Said 1999). It seems that there has been a trend among some westerners to object to the teaching or promoting of native Egyptians. There may also have been a desire, subconscious perhaps, on the part of Europeans to claim Ancient Egyptians as proto-Europeans, by showing that only Europeans were interested in the study of their ancient past (Fletcher and Montserrat 1998: 402). Such a view was not limited to Europeans. Ismael Pasha, the ruler of Egypt between 1863 and 1879, worked to make Egypt 'European', styling himself a 'European ruler' at least in appearance (Reid 2002: 96). Even prominent native Egyptian scholars taught Egyptian history as Greco-Roman history at the expense of its pharaonic past (Reid 2002: 211). Indeed, in 1938, Husayn (1938: 24) wrote that it was "utter nonsense to consider Egypt as part of the East".

By affording a glimpse of the richness of medieval Arabic sources and the breadth and depth of their interest in Ancient Egypt, a gap in the history of the study of this ancient civilization is at least narrowed, if not filled.

## Notes

1    I use the word 'Arabic' or 'Arab' in a purely linguistic sense (the language of the source).

2    Texts from the Quran are those of *The Holy Quran: English Translation of the Meanings and Commentary*. Al-Medina, Saudi Arabia: King Fahd Holy Quran Printing Complex. In some cases I have modified this translation.

3    Names of medieval Arab writers are listed alphabetically in the references disregarding 'Abd, Abi, Al- and Ibn.

4    All dates of death of Arab writers in AD; d. = died..

5    Christides (2000: 166) assigned the idea that Alexander was buried under a pyramid down to "certain absurd figments of the imagination of Arab authors like Al-Idrisi who states that Alexander was buried under a pyramid". In fact, Al-Idrisi (1991: 89) was retelling earlier accounts by other authors and, in this particular case, was quoting Ibn Krion whose account ends with the sentence, "Aristotle was buried in one of them [the two pyramids in Giza] and Alexander was not buried in the other".

6    The ancient Egyptian word *p3-r3-pr* means 'the temple', used also in Coptic (cf. Vergote 1964). Yaqut (d. 1228 AD ?; 1995, 1: 362) gives a similar account, namely that *birba* or *barba*, pl. *barabi* is: "a Coptic word, I think it to be the name of the place of worship or the well-ordered closed building, or the place of magic."

7    See Henein and Bianquis (1975: 29) for Ibn Wahishiya, MS Arabe 6805: fol. 112: 116, where one of the ancient Egyptian scripts is called 'Script of the Sage Qalfeterius'.

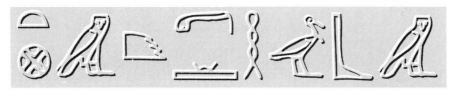

# CHAPTER 4

# IMAGES OF ANCIENT EGYPT IN THE LATIN MIDDLE AGES

*Charles Burnett*

## Introduction

It is commonly thought that the Latin Middle Ages was a barren period for knowledge of and interest in Egypt – between the enthusiasms of the late hellenistic Neoplatonists and the rediscovery of Horapollo and the *Corpus Hermeticum* in the 15th century. The Middle Ages gets exactly one page in Dieckmann (1970)[1] and the brief articles specifically on the Middle Ages tend to emphasize the absence of material (Bober 1980; Cannuyer 1984b). No attempt has been made to bring together the full range of images of Egypt prevalent during this period.

It is undeniable that, at the beginning of the 15th century, a sea-change occurred and new approaches were inaugurated that led to both Egyptology and 'Egyptomania'. Nevertheless the information and legends concerning Egypt in preceding centuries were sufficiently rich to allow us to say that images of that civilization remained alive and creative. This richness was a combination of the motifs that were inherited from classical sources with those taken from Hebrew sacred history, to which were added the direct experiences of travellers to the Orient, and, from the late 10th century onwards, the texts and the images of the Arabs.

## Geography and ethnography

Throughout the Middle Ages, Egypt was generally regarded as part of Asia, not Africa. The desert to the west of the Nile provided the border with Africa. The division of the world into three parts – Europe, Asia and Africa – and the assignation of Egypt and the Nile to Asia is ancient (Pliny *Historia naturalis* VI.38 (209)), and became schematized in the maps of Isidore of Seville (Harley and Woodward 1987, I: 334). But Egypt's western border was also confirmed by the narrower political boundaries of the Roman province of Africa (which corresponded to the Islamic political entity of Ifriqiya), equivalent roughly to the modern state of Tunisia extended eastwards. Egypt's juxtaposition with Asia facilitated the idea that the Nile was one of the four rivers issuing from the Earthly Paradise (Genesis 2:13), which was usually regarded as being in Asia (Scafi 2003), and made Ethiopia border on India, hence facilitating the migration of the supposed kingdom of Prester John from Central Asia to Ethiopia.

The Asian location of Egypt is confirmed by numerous medieval *mappae mundi* (e.g. Harley and Woodward 1987; Westrem 2001: 182, nos. 340, 434, 875), and a medieval reader would have had no problem in imagining where the pilgrim William of Boldensele was when he wrote (in 1336) of monuments "beyond Babylon (i.e. Old Cairo) and the river of Paradise (i.e. the Nile) towards the desert which is between Egypt and Africa" (Graefe 1984: 571).[2]

There was, however, an alternative alignment of the parts of the world: namely, into four quarters, of which Egypt fell into the African quarter. While the inclusion of the whole of Egypt in 'Libya' (= modern-day Africa) occurs in Ptolemy's *Geography* (1540, II: prologue), this opinion would have been much better known in the Middle Ages from the same author's *Tetrabiblos* II.3, where "Libya" is described as the south-western quarter of the world (Ptolemy 1519a; see below). Libya, too, in the narrower sense of being the country immediately to the west of Egypt, was often regarded as belonging to the Egyptian *Kulturgebiet* (see Snape 2003), especially since the most famous Egyptian oracle – that of Amun-Jupiter – was situated there.

For the geographical features within Egypt itself, a medieval scholar could have found information in several classical and patristic works, including those of Pliny, Pomponius Mela, Solinus and Isidore, as well as in works specifically on topography, such as the *Antonine Itinerary* (a third century list of places along particular routes), Jerome's fourth century *Book on the Location and Names of Hebrew Places*, and Julius Honorius' *The Cosmography of Julius Caesar* (written between 312 and the early fifth century). He would not have had access to the *Geographies* of Strabo, or (as has already been noted) Ptolemy. Arabic texts translated into Latin offered a little more information. For example, the *De Causis Proprietatum et Elementorum*, attributed to Aristotle, translated from Arabic into Latin by Gerard of Cremona (1114–1187), and extant in over 100 Latin manuscripts, mentions Alexandria, Damietta and Tinnīs ("Tunix civitas"), and discusses in some detail the course of the Nile, in the context of the question concerning whether the southern side of the earth is elevated and the northern side depressed (and hence whether the Red Sea would flood into the Mediterranean when connected to the Nile by a canal – see Vodraska 1969). "Meroe" (the island of Bagrawiya on the Nile), "Siene" (Aswan) and Alexandria would have been well known as the places between which Eratosthenes measured the size of a terrestrial degree, and after which the lines of latitude for the first three 'climes' were named (Gratwick 1995; Martianus Capella VI.595–598, 876–877; cf. Bubnov 1899: 138–142).

The successive capitals of Egypt are run together in many of the Latin sources.[3] A representative example of which places were significant within Egypt in medieval eyes is given by the Hereford Map (Figure 4:1), which, although dating from ca. 1300, has been shown to belong to a style of world-maps that probably originated in ca. 1100 (Westrem 2001). The places in Egypt on the map include those associated with the exodus of the Children of Israel: Ramesse, Soccoth, Migdol, Phihahiroth, Etham, and Tanis; those referred to in classical sources: Fialus (presumably Philae, the supposed origin of the Nile – Solinus *Collectanea* IX.57), Abydos, the region of Thebes, Ptolemais, the island of Meroe, Memphis, Babylon, Pelusium, Alexandria, Paraetonium, the river Astapum (the Atbara river) and Syene (Aswan); and those associated with early Christianity (the monastery of St Anthony in the desert, next to which "Zosimus", a

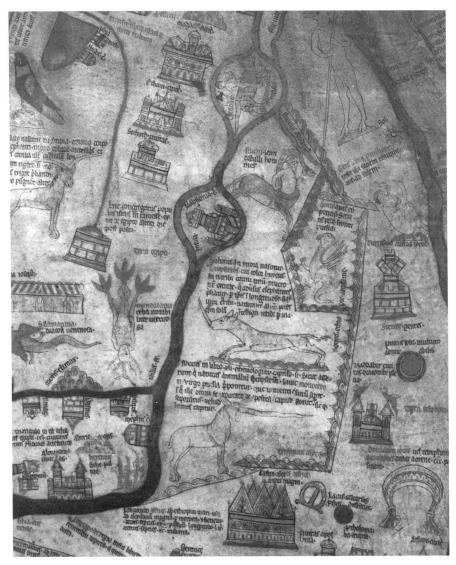

Figure 4:1   The ca. 1300 AD Hereford Map indicating a representative example of those places which were significant within Egypt in Medieval eyes (© Hereford Cathedral Library).

desert father, is named). Also named and depicted within Egypt are the crocodile, the sphinx ("the sphinx has a bird's wings, a serpent's feet and a young girl's face"; Westrem 2001: 135, no. 301), the "granaries of Joseph" (depicted as medieval guildhouses rather than pyramids), the salamander, the mandrake, the unicorn, the rhinoceros, a centaur (a man who is a horse from the waist down), palms, the well of the Sun (Westrem 2001: 182, no. 436)[4] and the lighthouse of Pharos. The Hereford Map shows no knowledge of the new material being brought by the Arabs or by voyagers to exotic places.

While geography placed Egypt in Asia, ethnography tended to make its people Hamites – i.e. the descendants of Ham, son of Noah, who populated the division of the world closest to the Sun (Genesis 10:1, 10:6; Isidore *Etymologiae* VI.6.17 and IX.2.10). A contrast was made between the 'Ancient Egyptians' and the Saracens who lived in Egypt in the Middle Ages. For William of Boldensele, the sultan of Egypt was the "principal champion and disseminator of Muḥammad's impious perfidy" (Higgins 1997: 96). The contemporary experience of Egypt was as a Muslim country. What seems to have got lost is the concept of 'Copt' (Horbury 2003); the term, itself deriving from the Greek word for 'Egyptian' (*Aiguptos*), is not used, and where one would expect it one finds either simply "Christian" (in respect of their religion) or "Egyptian" (in respect of their language).

## Travellers' reports

Egypt was on the itinerary of visitors to the Christian Holy Sites, and several pilgrim reports include brief mentions of the monuments in Egypt (Wilkinson 1977; summarized in Osborne 1986: 114–115).[5] Among the pilgrims were the Spanish nun Egeria (381–384 AD; Wilkinson 1971: 204), a man from Piacenza in ca. 570 AD, the monk Epiphanius (mid-eighth century), an Irish monk called Fidelis (reported in Dicuil's *De Mensura Orbis*, of 825 AD), and another monk called Bernard (870 AD). One journey is that of Burchard of Strasbourg, who was sent by the emperor Frederick Barbarossa on a diplomatic mission to the sultan Saladin in 1175 (Cannuyer 1984a, b; Lappenbeerg 1869: 235–239). He describes the Pharos at Alexandria, the flooding of the Nile, the fertility of the land, hippopotamus, crocodiles, alum and indigo. He distinguishes three 'Babylons':

> the one in which Nabuchodonosor reigned where the tower of Babel (Babylon) was constructed; a second one where the pharaoh used to reign and which was completely in ruins, and the 'New Babylon', six miles away, which was a very important city and is still quite large; it is two-thirds of a mile from the military stronghold and present seat of government, Cairo ('Chayr').

One mile distant from 'New Babylon' Burchard, who, like other travellers, only comments on the larger two of the three pyramids of Giza, saw

> two mountains of square plan, built of very large stones of marble and other materials; they are admirable constructions, an arrow's distance from each other … and of the same height and width. Their height is that of a very strong shot of an arrow; their width, of two such shots. A mile from Cairo, there was a garden of balm trees, irrigated by a sacred fountain, at which the Virgin Mary was said to have washed the infant Jesus.

Burchard gives most space to Christian monuments and the presence of Christians in Egypt, and thereafter to Muslims, especially when they follow the devotions of Christians, or have beliefs that amuse him (such as the fact that those who die in combats against Christians enjoy 10 virgins a day in paradise).

More attentive to the ancient Egyptian monuments, apparently, was an envoy sent in a similar capacity to the Ayyubid sultan in Cairo by Frederick Barbarossa's grandson, Frederick II Hohenstaufen.[6] This envoy, Thomas of Acerra, was shown the archaeological sites in Memphis and Giza, and copied a Latin inscription from a pyramid at Giza. An account of this embassy, however, has not survived in any Latin source, but only in the writings of the Egyptian historian Al-Idrisi (1991: 1,173–1,251), who could have encountered the envoy in person (Haarmann 1990: 29–30).

A century later there is a fuller report on Egypt, within a popular account of his travels written down by a wealthy pilgrim who calls himself Guilielmus de Boldensele.[7] He describes the "new Babylon" of Egypt "which imitates the old Babylon in name and, in a way, in deeds" (Grotefend 1855: 244–246; Higgins 1997: 96); he refers to elephants, a giraffe, a wonderful oblong fruit, called the fruit of paradise which, when cut through the centre reveals the image of the crucifix (i.e. a plantain or banana), and the balm-garden next to Cairo. Then he says that, to the west of the Nile (Graefe 1984: 571, 573),

> towards the desert that is between Egypt and Africa there are very many monuments of the ancients of pyramidal shape, among which there are two of wonderful bulk and height [constructed] from very large and polished stones on which I have found letters belonging to different languages.

He transcribes a Latin poem written in the classical period (evidently the one seen by Thomas of Acerra), and then mentions the common opinion that the pyramids are the granaries of pharaoh, only to refute it on the grounds that they are solid, "except that a small entrance has been left, raised high up from the ground, and a narrow and dark passage along which one descends a certain distance into them" (Graefe 1984: 573).

William of Boldensele's itinerary was one of the two main sources of *Sir John Mandeville's Travels*, composed by an unknown Frenchman in the 1350s entirely from other people's books and reports. But, while following Boldensele's account of Egypt quite closely, the armchair traveller responsible for *Mandeville* refutes the idea that the pyramids are tombs and restores the traditional account of the pyramids being the granaries of Joseph (Higgins 1997: 100; Mandeville 1900: 35–36).

Le Seigneur d'Anglure and his companions in 1395, like Burchard and Boldensele, visited the balm-garden containing the fountain of the Virgin Mary (Bonnardot and Longnon 1878: 56–58), followed by Cairo and Babylon. Babylon is "on the river Nile, which comes from the terrestrial Paradise, passes through the land of Prester John … and flows into the sea at Alexandria" (Bonnardot and Longnon 1878: 64–65). On Wednesday 24 November, they were taken with an interpreter to see the three "granaries of pharaoh". These were the most wonderful things they saw on the whole of their voyage (Bonnardot and Longnon 1878: 65), on account of their size and the fine quality of their construction. Le Seigneur d'Anglure (Bonnardot and Longnon 1878: 67) repeats the legend that:

> they were made by the pharaoh in the time when Joseph, the son of Jacob, was the governor of the kingdom of Egypt. They were made for containing and preserving the grain for the dry period which Joseph had prophesized would come to the kingdom of Egypt, according to the dream of that king pharaoh, as is written more fully in the text of sacred scripture.

What is noticeable is the remarkable consistency of these accounts, from that of Egeria through to the Seigneur d'Anglure's, on the verge of the Renaissance. It is as if there were a set 'tourist itinerary' which was followed equally by pilgrims and political envoys, and which included the wonders of Ancient Egypt (namely, the Pharos and the pyramids of Giza and sometimes the ruins of Memphis), the grove of balm trees,[8] and the Christian monuments. The monuments of Upper Egypt (specifically Thebes) were never visited, and, strangely, although it was adjacent to the Giza pyramids, the sphinx was not mentioned. But these tourists were not notable scholars, and had no time to do research. Most of them would have accepted without question what their 'guidebooks' told them (only Boldensele expresses scepticism concerning the nature of the pyramids as granaries). Their reports sometimes incidentally reveal details that are of interest to the present-day Egyptologist (such as the state of preservation of the cladding of the pyramids), but they did little to change the image of Egypt in the eyes of their readers.

The more educated could have known the true shape and purpose of the pyramids, from several classical and patristic sources, such as Lucan (*Pharsalia* IX.155), Pliny's *Historia naturalis* (Hopfner 1922–1925: 118–122), Servius' commentary to the *Aeneid* (XI.265),[9] Pomponius Mela's *De Chorographia* (I.9.55),[10] Cassiodorus' *Variae* (VII.15),[11] and Isidore of Seville's *Etymologiae* (XV.11.4), but the identification of pyramids with tombs is rarely made. Only the 12th century Master Gregorius (*The Marvels of Rome* 27; Huygens 2000: 297; Osborne 1987) describes pyramids and obelisks as "tombs of important men, of great size and height, coming to a point at the top, making a semi-conoid (?) form", and even he was observing those that had been imported or raised in Rome rather than the original Egyptian monuments (Cannuyer 1984b; Humbert 2003: 26).

## The symbolic concept of Egypt in medieval Christianity

The most widely known references to Egypt in the Middle Ages would have been those in the Bible. The most significant of these is the biblical narrative, spread out over the second half of Genesis and most of Exodus, of the period the Hebrews spent in Egypt and their eventual delivery from the Egyptians through the leadership of Moses, which led to the establishment of a Hebrew state in the "land flowing with milk and honey". For Jews this narrative provides the basis for their religious and national identity. For Christians, this story not only prefigures the flight to and return from Egypt of Joseph, Mary and the baby Jesus, but also tells in an allegorical way the salvation history of the individual Christian, who, having wallowed in the filthiness of worldly society, is baptized by passing through the waters, and eventually achieves a state of blessedness. In the standard commentary to the Bible in use from at least the early 12th century to the age of printing, known as the *Glossa Ordinaria*, the beginning of this story is glossed and commented on as follows:

> **Genesis 39, v. 1:** And Joseph was brought down to Egypt (i.e. Christ was proclaimed throughout the world); and Potiphar, an officer of pharaoh, captain of the guard, an Egyptian, bought him (with the price of faith) of the hands of the Ishmeelites (the people who are chaste in their faith, who sometimes are forced to serve secular rulers), which had brought him down thither (because races had announced Christ to [other races]).

**v. 2:** And the Lord ([God] the Father) was with Joseph (the Son) and he was a prosperous man (in deeds and words); and he was in the house of his master (the Church of God, of which Christ was a servant according to flesh) …

**v. 7:** And it came to pass after these things that his master's wife (Synagogue [i.e. the Jews]) cast her eyes (licentiousness, which attempts to attack chastity, but a chaste man recalls to memory the good things that have been bestowed on him and overcomes the temptation that strikes him) upon Joseph; and she said 'Lie with me'.

(King James version; the interlinear glosses from the
*Glossa Ordinaria* 1992: 92 are given in brackets)

These interlinear glosses are augmented by substantial comments in the margin, e.g.:

**v. 7:** *His master's wife cast her eyes* Isidore: the allegory: This is the figure of Synagogue, who often commits adultery with alien gods and who wished to detain Christ in the crime of her adultery, so that he would deny that he was God and would rather serve the precepts of the Pharisees and Scribes, than those of the Law which was, as it were, his legitimate wife.

(*Glossa Ordinaria* 1992: 92)

Similarly, at the beginning of Exodus, the allegory is explained in interlinear glosses and a marginal commentary:

**Exodus 1, v. 1:** Now these are the names (these names are written in heaven) of the children of Israel (those seeing God), which came into (according to the phrase 'In my innocence I came into' etc.) Egypt (the world); with Jacob (with Christ as leader, who lightens the saints in the darkness of Egypt; hence 'the lord is my illumination and my salvation' etc.), every man with his household (with the imitators or associates of his deeds, thoughts or virtues). Through the twelve sons of Jacob the twelve apostles are signified.

(*Glossa Ordinaria* 1992: 112)

The marginal commentary opens:

Exodus is the most excellent book of the Pentateuch. In it almost all the sacraments by which the Church is instructed are expressed in a figurative way. For through the corporeal departure of the children of Israel from Egypt is signified our departure from the spiritual Egypt. Through the Red Sea and the drowning of pharaoh and the Egyptians, the mystery of baptism and the death of spiritual enemies. Through the sacrifice of the 'typical' lamb and the freedom of the Hebrews, the passion of the True Lamb and our redemption …

(*Glossa Ordinaria*, facsimile: 112)

The allegory may seem strained – the Hebrews are on the side of the righteous, the wife of Potiphar is the despised Jew, Jacob and Joseph are both Christ – but it is carried through the whole of the narrative. Moses eventually emerges as another prefiguration of Christ. But he also acquires the persona of an ancient wise man (see below).

## History and mythology

An account of the geography of an area very often preceded its history (as is the case of Orosius), and, as we have seen, several historical allusions are included on maps and in travellers' tales. In medieval chronicles and histories themselves, we find no systematic history of Egypt. Events in ancient Egyptian history, if mentioned at all, were entirely adjuncts to the history of the Hebrews, and those of the Ptolemaic period to those of the Greeks and Romans. For example, Bede, in the world chronicle included in his *De Temporum Ratione* (725 AD), under the year 1849 from the beginning of the world, and contemporary with the generation mentioned in Genesis 11:22, adds "It is said that [in this year] the Egyptians inaugurated their empire, Visoues being the first to reign over them" (Wallis 1999: 164). This information, in fact, comes immediately from Isidore (*Chronica maiora* 28 (430)), and can be found in several medieval chronicles (e.g. Vincent of Beauvais *Speculum Historiale* I.97). In the story of Joseph, Moses and the Exodus of the Children of Israel, Egypt takes centre stage. But few details other than those already in the Bible are added by medieval chroniclers. Vincent of Beauvais, when he reaches this stage in his *Speculum Historiale*, merely adds to the biblical account names of pharaohs from Eusebius, and some etymologies (*Speculum Historiale* II.4; Vincent of Beauvais 1624, II: 48). Egyptian history becomes progressively more fully documented from the beginning of the Ptolemaic era (323 BC) until Egypt becomes a Roman province in 30 BC, while the exploits of Alexander the Great, and Cleopatra, reached legendary proportions.

The same chronicle of Bede, under the year of the world 2108, the date on which Isaac begat Esau and Jacob, states that "Inachus first reigned over the Argives ... whose daughter Io the Egyptians worship under the altered name 'Isis'" (Wallis 1999: 166; see Ovid *Metamorphoses* I.568–750 and hence Augustine *De Civitate Dei* XVIII.37 and *Mythographus Vaticanus* I.18). This demonstrates how mythology can merge with ancient history.

Considerable information was available in the Middle Ages concerning the Egyptian gods (Hopfner 1922–1925). The brother-sister gods Isis and Osiris and their son Horus, the bull-god Apis, and the dog-god Anubis were all well known. Cicero mentions Ptah (*De Natura Deorum* III.22 (55)) and Thoth (*De Natura Deorum* III.56), while Pliny (*Historia naturalis* VIII.46 (184–186) – hence Solinus *Collectanea* XXXII.21) describes Apis and his worship at Memphis at length. The oracle of Jupiter-Amun in Cyrenaica (in the Libyan desert) was of an importance equal to those of Delphi and Dodona (cf. Cicero *De Divinatione* I.1 (3) – see also Lucretius *De Rerum Natura* VI.849; Juvenal *Satires* VI.555 (Humphries 1958); Solinus *Collectanea* XXVII.45), and the Serapieion, founded in Alexandria by the Ptolemies for the worship of Serapis after the death of Alexander the Great, was often described (e.g. Macrobius *Saturnalia* I.7 (14–17); Rufinus *Historia Ecclesiastica* XI.23). The centrality in Egyptian religion of the lamentation of Isis over Osiris' death led to frequent references to Egyptians as given to weeping (Juvenal *Satires* VI.534 (Humphries 1958); Servius comm. on *Aeneid* III.65; Apuleius *De deo Socratis* 14 (149); Gregorius Nazianzenus *Orationes* 39, 5/6) – to such an extent that Servius states that the Egyptians *invented* lamentation for the dead (comm. on *Aeneid* XI.265).

The Greek mythology inherited by the Romans and the Middle Ages tended to domesticate the Egyptian gods, and make them secondary to the Greek ones (Bede's *De Temporum Ratione* quotation above; for Ovid on Io and Inachus see *Metamorphoses* I.568–750). The story of Osiris being periodically lacerated and his sister Isis searching for his body-parts included the hideous Greek giant, Typhon, as the lacerator (cf. Servius *Commentary on Georgics* I.166). Moreover, the Egyptian gods were viewed simply as counterparts to the Greek pantheon: Thoth was Hermes, Imhotep, Asclepius, and Amun, Jupiter. In the medieval retelling of classical myths, known as *Mythographus Vaticanus I*, Typhon chases the gods into Egypt where Jupiter out of fear is changed into a ram, Apollo into a crow, Liber into a goat, Diana into a cat, Juno into a cow and Venus into a fish, these being what were seen as the animal symbols of the respective Egyptian gods.

Christian interpretations followed classical ones which claimed that the Egyptian gods were men who were elevated to the status of gods after their deaths. So Apuleius (*De deo Socratis* (15) 153–154) gives Osiris as an exemplary hero who was posthumously honoured as a god. Hyginus (*Astronomica* II.20) describes Amun as a certain man from Africa who introduced the domestication of animals to Egypt and was given some land opposite Thebes, and was thereafter commemorated by statues with horned heads. Aries was also made the first sign of the zodiac in commemoration of Amun's deed. Hyginus also (*Astronomica* II.20) attributes the privileging of the sign of Aries to the fact that a ram had led Liber to a spring in the desert which later became the temple of Jupiter-Amun. Augustine (*De Civitate Dei* XVIII.40), following Varro, reports a belief that Isis had come as a queen into Egypt from Ethiopia and, because she had ruled wisely and justly and established the art of writing and other skills among them, she received divine honours after her death, and so much honour that a man is guilty of capital punishment if he says that she was a mortal.

Following such stories, Hermann of Carinthia (*De Essentiis* 71rB–C), a mid-12th century humanist and translator of Arabic, mentions the veneration of Amun in the form of a ram, and Isis in the form of bull, and gives an explanation for the latter:

> It is established that the Egyptians are partly under Aries (with part of Libya), and partly under Taurus, since on this side they worship Aries with their veneration of Amun, and on that side they worship Taurus, under the name of Isis [a mistake for Apis?]. For this reason they used not to permit any slaughter of cattle. The story is not incongruous, then, that a man became a bull, since, when a man lost the use of his reason, he went away after a bull, so that, what had been given to him for his use, he set up to be worshiped and venerated by him, in the same way as one reads about the Chaldeans, who erroneously repaid the gift of fire by setting it up as their highest god.

(trans. Burnett 1982: 170–171)

Already in classical times, the Egyptians were scorned for their beliefs (Tait Chapter 2, this volume). Their veneration of animals was ridiculed both by Cicero (*Tusculan Disputations* V.27) and by Juvenal: "Who does not know what monsters lunatic Egypt/Chooses to cherish? One part goes in for crocodile worship;/One bows down to the ibis that feeds upon serpents; elsewhere/a golden effigy shines – of a long-tailed holy monkey!" (*Satires* XV.1–4 (trans. Humphries 1958)).

In Christian contexts the Egyptian religion was the epitome of idolatry, and was made particularly obnoxious in that the idols they worshipped were not even human, but species of animals (Rufinus *Historia Monachorum* VII; Orosius *Historia Adversus Paganos* I.8 (7–12); Prudentius *Apotheosis* 194–196; Augustine *De Civitate Dei* II.22). When the Hebrews lapsed back into idolatry under Mount Sinai, their Golden Calf was thought to be the Egyptian Apis (Pseudo-Clement *Recognitiones* I.35). Jerome frequently mentions the idolatry of the Egyptians, calling them "an impure race, who venerate images of all beasts" (Jerome *Commentary on Ezechiel* VII.23) and even worship plants, such as "the fearsome and dreadful onion and the stomach-wind which is the religion of Pelusium" (Jerome *Commentary on Isaiah* XII.45).

The classical tradition established certain phrases as formulaic, such as the "barking Anubis" (Propertius IV.10 (11).41; Vergil *Aeneid* VIII.698; Prudentius *Contra Symmachum* V.532), "the seven mouths of the Nile", "horned Amun", the "hundred-gated Thebes" (Pliny *Historia naturalis* V.11; Juvenal *Satires* XV.6 (Humphries 1958)). Thus certain images of Egypt became part of the repertoire of poets of the Middle Ages. The level of sophistication to which the literary tradition could aspire may be demonstrated in the *Architrenius*, written by Johannes de Hauvilla (Wetherbee 1994), a *magister* at the cathedral of Rouen, in 1184. He can refer to 'Sienes' (Aswan, after which the second clime is named) as a metaphor for a remote place (Hauvilla I.5.82); "the shipwreck of the Pharian tyrant" (V.278–279), a reference to the golden breastplate of Ptolemy XIII who drowned in the Nile in 47 BC (Florus *Epitoma* II.13 (IV.2).60); the abundance of soda in 'Pharos' (VII.207) and hippopotamus in the Nile (VII.208–209); and the sistrum as distinctive of 'Pharos' (IX.414). But his most many-layered and elaborate poetic conceit occurs in Book II, lines 239–242, where the satirical poet complains about how people attempt to get ingredients for the tastiest sauces from the most remote regions. Included among these regions are: "the upper reaches of the Nile, and Pharos (the famous lighthouse, here used *pars pro toto* for Egypt) naked under the Sun, where Memphis gazes at the stars with unblinking eye." The last metaphor here should probably be unravelled as follows: Memphis is the most important city of Ancient Egypt; the Ancient Egyptians were the first astronomers; the most famous of the Egyptian astronomers was Ptolemy; therefore, Memphis = Ptolemy.

## Origin myths and the wisdom of Egypt

One branch of mythology common to all peoples tells which god or man was responsible for inventing or introducing particular skills to that people. In regard to Egypt, origin myths take two overlapping forms. The first concerns the invention of the arts within Egypt itself; in the second Egypt is regarded as the origin of the arts for the rest of the civilized world.

In Greek mythology Isis is said to have invented letters, and when she came to Egypt from Greece, she passed them on to the Egyptians (Augustine *De Civitate Dei* XVIII.37; Isidore *Etymologiae* I.3.5); Amun was said to have introduced animal husbandry. Isis, again, was the first to wear a garland of ears of wheat (Tertullian *De Corona* 7). More common, however, is the idea that inventions were made in Egypt. Isidore (*Etymologiae* III.10.1, 13.8, 12.12, 15.1; V.33.2; VI.10.1; XIX.16.2) mentions the opinion that the Egyptians invented astronomy and astrology (the Egyptians are said to have been the first to reckon the day of the month from the course of the sun), geometry, the use of papyrus, representational art, the lyre (invented from the carcass of a tortoise left by the retreating waters of the Nile), and the sistrum (invented by Isis). The phrases *"Aegypti primi …"*, *"Aegyptus primum …"* or *"Aegypti primum …"* run like a litany through Isidore's text.

In other sources Isis is said to have introduced the custom of weaving linen and making clothes, and the use of grain, while that of the vine is attributed to Osiris (Martianus Capella *De Nuptiis* II.158). Grammar was first established in the time of Osiris (*De Nuptiis* III.223), whilst dialectic was conceived by Parmenides, who, fleeing cities and crowds, spent a long time on a rock in Egypt where he thought out the science (*De Nuptiis* IV.330; Klibansky 1941–1943). The arts as a whole are described as being discovered in Egypt by Thoth (Cicero *De Natura Deorum* III.22), while Macrobius credits Egypt with the discovery of "all the teachings of philosophy" (comm. on *Somnium Scipionis* I.19.2).

This priority of the Egyptians, however, did not pass unchallenged by Christian authors. Cassiodorus, Isidore and Rhabanus Maurus rather claim that the Hebrews, especially Abraham (whose sojourn in Egypt was known from Genesis 12), taught the arts to the Egyptians. Their ultimate source is Josephus (*Antiquitates* I.8.2), who recounts that the arts survived the flood because the sons of Seth, warned by Adam's prediction of the world's destruction by fire and water, erected two pillars, one of stone, the other of clay, on which they inscribed all that was known of the arts. In a unique gloss in one of the oldest manuscripts of Remigius of Auxerre's ninth century commentary on Martianus, the sons of Noah are credited with having set up the two columns preserving the arts: "by means of this, when Abraham was in exile in Egypt, he taught astronomy, and from this all the other arts were originally discovered in Egypt and taken from there to Greece" (Lutz 1956: 41; Taylor 1961: 210–211). Isidore (*Etymologiae* III.25.1) acknowledged Josephus as his source for the opinion that Abraham taught the Egyptians astronomy in particular.

These origin myths were repeated in the Middle Ages; for example, in the *Didascalicon* of Hugh of St Victor, composed in Paris in the late 1120s, in which there is a chapter entitled "the authors of the arts" (*Didascalicon* III.2; Buttimer 1939: 49). Hugh himself depends largely on Isidore of Seville and Remigius' commentary on Martianus Capella. But it was the priority of the Egyptians in geometry and astronomy (with the accompanying arts of astrology and magic) that is most frequently mentioned in the Middle Ages.[12]

Martianus Capella (*De Nuptiis* VI.595–598) refers to the "surveyors of king Ptolemy" who established the rules of geometry, and Isidore (*Etymologiae* III.10.1) describes how the Egyptians invented geometry as the result of the force of circumstances: the yearly inundations of the Nile obliterated the land-boundaries, which therefore had to be redrawn by means of accurate measurements. Isidore's statement is frequently repeated in works of geometry in the Middle Ages (e.g. *Geometria incerti auctoris* IV.60, Bubnov 1899: 362, lines 7–8; *Geometria Gerberti* I.2; Bubnov 1899: 49; Pseudo-Boethius *Geometria* I; Bubnov 1899: 50; and Hugh of St Victor *Didascalicon* III.2). In the most elaborate form of the Arabic-Latin version of Euclid's

*Elements* attributed to Adelard of Bath, that known as 'Adelard III', the introduction begins:

> In geometry, just as in the other arts, practice preceded theory. The practice developed among the Egyptians; for when the flooding of the Nile every year wiped out the boundaries of the fields, they instituted certain rules of measurement by which they might recover the earlier dimensions of the fields.

(Busard 2001, I: 31)

It might seem surprising that in this context the construction of the pyramids is not mentioned.

For such accomplishments the wisdom of the Egyptians was proverbial. It was enshrined in verses from the Bible: "Moses was learned in all the wisdom of the Egyptians" (Acts 7:22); and "Solomon's wisdom excelled … all the wisdom of Egypt" (I Kings 4:30). For Servius (comm. on *Aeneid* III.68), the Egyptians are "skilled in wisdom". This wisdom is echoed in the first words of the Alexander Romance (see below).

Beneficiaries of the wisdom of Egypt were not only Moses, but also Vergil (Servius, Prologue to comm. on *Aeneid* VI) and Plato. According to Remigius (Taylor 1961: 211 n. 36), Plato, after the death of Socrates, emigrated to Egypt, whence, having acquired liberal studies, he returned to Athens and, taking to himself disciples at the Academy, his villa, turned his efforts to the study of philosophy. Once again, Christian writers alter a traditional story to make the Hebrews appear to be the original source of true wisdom. For example, Augustine (*De Civitate Dei* VIII.11) writes:

> Some people are surprised when they hear or read that Plato has such thoughts about God, that they agree greatly with the truth of our religion. Hence they thought that he, when he went to Egypt, heard Jeremiah the prophet or read prophetic scriptures on the same journey (*Augustine casts doubt on this*) … unless, by chance, because (Plato) was of the most piercing intellect, just as he learnt the Egyptian (writings) so also he learnt [the Jewish] through an interpreter.

According to the 12th century historian Peter Comestor, Plato, when he went to Egypt, read the books of Moses (comm. on Genesis 7; Migne, pl. CXCVIII, col. 1061). Because of these stories from Antiquity it was quite natural that Egypt should be on the itinerary of medieval scholars. Constantine the African, the pioneer in translating Arabic works on medicine at the end of the 11th century, is said by Peter the Deacon to have travelled to India, Ethiopia and Egypt (Bloch 1986, I: 171), while Leonardo de Pisa, the 13th century founder of modern arithmetic, states that he voyaged as a young man to Syria, Egypt and Sicily (Boncompagni 1857–1862, I: 1). There could be an element of truth in these tales. Under the Tulunids, Fatimids and Ayyubids there were some fine Arabic scholars, and rumours of their excellence may have encouraged western scholars to consider that the tradition of the wisdom of Ancient Egypt was still alive. Two of the 'contemporary' scholars in Egypt, in particular, could have fostered this impression. The first, Aḥmad ibn Yūsuf ibn Ibrāhīm al-Dāya, lived in Cairo in the late ninth and early 10th century, and was the author of two important texts on geometry, translated into Latin in the 12th century, as well as of the commentary on Pseudo-Ptolemy's *Centiloquium*. It is possible that he was the real author of the *Centiloquium* itself (see Lemay 1978). In both the geometrical texts Aḥmad ibn Yūsuf evokes the dramatic situation of a symposium of scholars and princes in the Tulunid palace, and relates a heated discussion over how to interpret Euclid's *Elements*, as if it were of common occurrence. In a comment to a sentence about talismans in *Centiloquium* IX (1519b: 97v), he talks of a Christian convert to Islam who became expert in geometry by staying in Egypt, made statues that artificially moved, and knew the (secret) nature of stones and plants. Aḥmad ibn Yūsuf was often confused in the Latin context with an even greater Cairene mathematician, ʿAlī ibn Riḍwān (d. 1068), chief physician to the Fatimid caliph al-Mustanṣir; both were known in Latin as 'Haly'. Ibn Riḍwān composed an extensive commentary to the *Tetrabiblos* of Ptolemy, which, in its late 13th century Latin translation, was extensively used by western astrologers. In it he refers several times to his own experience in Egypt, in ways that would confirm the impression of the stories of mathematics and magic from Ancient Egypt.[13]

However, in spite of the reputation that these Arabic scholars may have won for contemporary Egypt, for one reason or other western scholars who searched for ancient wisdom preferred to seek out their manuscripts, and the masters to interpret them, in Spain, Sicily and the Crusader States.[14] An English scholar of the turn of the 13th century, Alexander Neckham, goes so far as to assert that there were *no* schools in Greece and Egypt in his day (Thorndike 1934–1958, II: 190).

## The Egyptian script and language

The Middle Ages has been regarded as a dark period in the history of Egyptology, particularly with regard to the absence during this period of knowledge of Egyptian writing (Dieckmann 1970: 30–31; Iversen 1993: 57–59). As with Egyptian monuments, so with the writing systems used by the Egyptians, there were hints concerning their nature in classical and patristic texts that were read in the Middle Ages. These included Macrobius' *Saturnalia* (I.19 (13)): "When the Egyptians wish to indicate 'earth' with hieroglyphic letters, they put the image of a bull"; Origen (comm. on *Epist. Pauli ad Romanos* II.13): "Also only a circumcised man used to learn those priestly letters of the ancient Egyptians which they call 'hieroglyphs'"; and Isidore (*Etymologiae* I.3.5): "Among the Egyptians the priests have one kind of letters, the common people another, the priestly letters are called *hieras*, the popular, *pandemos*." A vivid description of these "priestly letters" is given in Apuleius (*Golden Ass (Metamorphoses)* XI.22):

> The priest brought out of the secret place of the temple certain books written with unknown characters, partly painted with figures of beasts, declaring briefly every concept, partly with letters whose tops and tails turned round in the fashion of a wheel, joined together above like unto the tendrils of a vine, whereby they were wholly strange and impossible to be read by the common people.

> (adapted from Adlington 1915: 579)

The Neoplatonic works which saw a symbolic and profound mystical nature in the hieroglyphs were not known in the Middle Ages (e.g. Plotinus *Enneads* V.8.6; Iversen

1993: 45–46), but the association of hieroglyphs with magic was already present in a passage in Rufinus' *Historia Ecclesiastica* (XI.26):

> Who can number the superstitious evil acts of Canopus, where, under the pretext of [teaching] the letters of the priests – for thus they call the ancient letters of the Egyptians – there was virtually a school of the magic art open to all-comers?

The classical sources that were known in the Middle Ages were not sufficiently informative as to give medieval scholars the possibility of reading Egyptian script (whether hieroglyphs, hieratic, demotic or Coptic). Some medieval manuscripts contain 'Egyptian letters' along with other real or fanciful alphabets (Bischoff 1981: 142). They are often accompanied by 'Chaldean', Hebrew and Greek letters, and are given made-up names (Bischoff 1981: 142). However, they have nothing to do with any form of Egyptian letters.

But while the scripts remained a mystery throughout the Middle Ages, medieval scholars had some experience of the Egyptian language itself. For them the 'Egyptian language' was Coptic, which they did not know under this name. But it was not inappropriate to call Coptic 'Egyptian', since it descended directly from the language of the Ancient Egyptians, and would in later centuries (e.g. through the grammar written by Athanasius Kircher – see Curran Chapter 5, this volume) provide clues for the decipherment of the hieroglyphs. The names of the Egyptian months were known from Isidore of Seville's much copied *De Rerum Natura* (VI.7), and from the basic text for computing the church calendar in the Middle Ages – Bede's *De Temporum Ratione* (725 AD; ch. 11; Jones 1934; Wallis 1999: 45), and were reintroduced in 12th century translations of Ptolemy's *Almagest* and Arabic astronomical tables, where they were regularly used for the conversion of astronomical data to and from the Alexandrian calendar (of which the starting date is the Seleucid era: 1 October 310 BC). In Petrus Alfonsi's version of the astronomical tables of al-Khwārizmī (1116 AD) the heading is "Table for knowing on which weekday falls each of the months of the Egyptian year, which in Arabic are called *Kephtian*" (Neugebauer 1962: 86), and the names are written as: *tot, hobbe, haton, kihac, toba, amsir, barhamech, barmuda, bessir, thona, abib, macere* (compare the ancient names in the Bohairic dialect: 'Thōut', 'Paopi', 'Athōr', 'Khoiak', 'Tōbi', 'Mekhir', 'Phamenōth', 'Pharmouthi', 'Pakhōn', 'Paōni', 'Epēp', 'Mesōrē').

Other Coptic words would have been known through the synonyms for different plants given in Dioscorides' *Herbal* (first century AD), and in the fourth century Latin herbal attributed to Apuleius (Howald and Sigerist 1927), both of which depend on a list drawn up by a certain Pamphilos (first century AD).[15] But Europeans added to their knowledge of Coptic also by direct experience. Two manuscripts (Vat. Reg. lat. 755 (ninth century) and Reg. lat. 123 (1056 AD)) of the ninth and 11th centuries respectively give the Coptic numeral words in the Sahidic dialect (Bischoff 1967: 232). And, as a result of the Crusades, a *lingua Franca*-Coptic glossary was composed in the 12th century (Aslanov 2002).

## Nectanebo

The evidence for the images of Egypt that have been given so far have tended to show that, although much accurate information in classical sources was available to medieval scholars, it was used selectively, and there was a bias towards regarding the Egyptians as idolatrous, as the foil to the ancient Hebrews, and at best as holding quaint ideas about the gods, which should rather be interpreted as entertaining myths. Ancient Egypt could only be seen through the prejudiced filter of Latin authors, the Bible, and the Church Fathers. There were, however, two late classical sources that provided a much more direct and positive view of the religion and culture of Egypt, namely, the 'Alexander Romance' and the *Asclepius* of Hermes Trismegistus.

The 'Alexander Romance' was one of the most popular stories in the Middle Ages; it existed in several Latin versions and numerous vernacular translations (Ross 1963, 1985; Thorndike 1934–1958, I: 551–565, ch. 24). It is the story of the life of Alexander the Great, of which the earliest extant version was written in Greek and attributed to Callisthenes, one of Alexander's generals. The Greek text was translated into Latin, first in a very free version by Julius Valerius Alexander Polemius some time after 300 AD, and then by the archpriest Leo in the second half of the 10th century. Three interpolated versions of Leo's text – which is referred to as the *Historia de Preliis* – appeared on the scene between the 11th and early 13th centuries (known respectively as J$^1$, J$^2$ and J$^3$). It is clear that the biography ultimately derives from Egyptian material which was designed to show to native Egyptians that Alexander was the legitimate ruler of the country. For this to be the case, like every pharaoh, his true father had to be the national god, who impregnated his mother in the guise of the reigning pharaoh; thus the last native Egyptian pharaoh, Nectanebo II, who fled from the kingdom in the face of a Persian invasion in 343 BC, had to be the human form through which the Egyptian god operated (Merkelbach 1977; Pritchard 1992). In the course of transmission this political motif was embellished, especially by developing the theme of magic, but authentic ancient Egyptian elements remained.[16] Most of the images of Egypt and Egyptians that were to become stereotyped occur already in the first chapters of the *Liber de Preliis*, which is worth summarizing in detail (Bergmeister 1975). The text begins by characterizing the Egyptians:

> The Egyptians, being the wisest of men, since they know the measurement of the earth [Perhaps an allusion to Eratosthenes' measurement of a terrestrial degree; see above], they have control over the waters of the sea, and understand the arrangement of the celestial bodies (i.e. they compute the course of the stars), have handed down this knowledge to the whole world because of the sublimity of their teaching and through magical arts.

The Egyptians themselves single out Nectanebo, their 'king', as an intelligent man, skilled in astronomy, astrology and magical powers. When he was told that a Persian army was advancing on his kingdom, instead of preparing his army, he resorted to lekanomancy (divination by interpreting images on the stirred surface of water in a dish). By waving a bronze wand (the versions vary between 'eneam' ('bronze') and 'ebeneam' ('ebony')) and reciting magical incantations he summoned demons to his aid, and by this means he was able to see the ships of the enemy in the water of the dish. Dismissing terrified messengers who reported, as eyewitnesses, the vast number of enemies congregating on the borders, Nectanebo continued his magical pursuit. He then placed little wax models of ships in the dish, and through his wand-waving and spell-chanting, he managed to see (horror of horrors!) the Egyptian gods themselves at the helms of the enemies' ships. So he changed his clothes, shaved his head and his beard, took as much gold as he could carry and everything he needed for practising astronomy, astrology and magic, and fled from Egypt to Ethiopia. Then he put on linen clothes and, thereby impersonating an Egyptian priest (the Latin word is *propheta*, which matches the standard Greek term of the period for the highest rank of priest in an Egyptian temple: 'prophētēs'), arrived in Macedonia, where he told people's fortunes. When the Egyptians realized that their king had fled they consulted Serapis, their greatest god,[17] concerning his whereabouts. The god replied that Nectanebo had fled, but that, after a short time, he would return as a young man and avenge them on their enemies. So the Egyptians immediately erected a statue of Nectanebo made from black stone, and inscribed the god's reply on its base.

When Philip, king of Macedon, happened to depart on a campaign, Nectanebo went up to the royal palace; on seeing Olympias, Philip's queen, he was smitten with ardent love. When they started to talk to each other, the first question the queen asked was "Is it true that you are an Egyptian?", to which Nectanebo answered: "O Queen, in calling me an Egyptian you have spoken most beautifully and royally. For the Egyptians are wise, since they even interpret dreams, explain portents, understand birds, know and uncover secrets, and tell the fates of the new-born. I, too, am experienced concerning all these things, because of my most subtle sensibility, being just like a prophet or divine person." The queen then asked what he was thinking as he looked at her so passionately. He replied that he remembered a prediction of the gods, that he should once be looking at a queen. Then he brought out from his breast a wonderful ebony and ivory tablet mixed with gold and silver, on which three circles were depicted. The first contained the ten intelligences,[18] the second, the twelve animals,[19] the third, the Sun and Moon. From an ivory casket he produced seven gemstones, one for each of the seven planets, "which explore the hours and the nativities of men".[20] The queen tested him by asking him the exact time of Philip's birth, and what would become of her marriage to him. Having obtained her confidence, Nectanebo came to the point: Amun, one of the most powerful gods, would lie with her. On being asked what form Amun would take, the Egyptian replied that he would be middle aged, with a ram's horns on his brow, and a beard decorated with white hairs; that he would come to her that very night, and she would see him and sleep with him in her dreams. Nectanebo reverted to his magic, this time collecting herbs and extracting their juices, again using incantations and diabolic inventions so that Olympias would see in her dreams Amun sleeping with her. But after this he promised more: she would see Amun face to face in a waking state. Nectanebo promised that the god would come to her, first in the form of a snake, and then in Nectanebo's own form. And thus it came to pass, through further magic procedures, that Olympias "was deceived into sleeping with a man as if with a god" (Bergmeister 1975: 14b).

The outcome of this union was, of course, Alexander. Other magical scenes occur. Philip in a dream sees Amun sleeping with his wife and afterwards a gold ring sealing the entrance to her womb inscribed with the head of a lion, a symbol of the sun's course, and a sword, which are explained to him by his soothsayer.

The significance of the image of Nectanebo can be seen from his frequent occurrences in medieval literature. Gerbert d'Aurillac, who died as Pope Silvester II in 1003, but who was renowned as the greatest mathematician in the Latin west in the late 10th century, is called 'Neptanabus' in a poem written by Adalberon de Laon soon after Gerbert's death (Carozzi 1979, V: 166). A curious text attributed to Galen, entitled *De Spermate* or *Microtegni*, which first appears in Latin manuscripts in the 12th century, but may have been translated from a lost original Greek or Arabic text in the late 11th century (Burnett 1994: 109–110; Pahta 1998), is devoted to the questions of how the human embryo is formed and what determines the character of the child. The latter includes the influence of the environment, and especially of the stars, and a chapter devoted specifically to this topic is entitled, in the printed edition: "About [cases in which] the conceptions of children are differentiated by the stars, not by the parents" (Galen 1542, VIII: cols. 144–145). This chapter includes, precisely, the example of Alexander:

> It also happens sometime that the child is similar to neither of its parents. This occurs because of the nature of the planets. For it is sometimes born dumb, or lacking feet, hands, eyes etc. But philosophers assert confidently, calling Hippocrates to their witness, that every animate corporeal substance is joined and bound to the planets and signs of the zodiac and the bonds of the four elements. I agree with this on the authority of Alexander, the emperor of Macedon, who says as much; for his father, Natanabus, king of the Egyptians, lay with his mother Olympias according to the operations of the planets, and through his mathematical and astronomical reasoning he made sure in advance that he would not 'know' her except at those times at which he (Alexander) would take his form from the operation of the planets and signs and not from his father or mother. For he waited for the time when the Sun would enter Leo, and Saturn, Taurus – being the signs from which above all he wished his son-to-be to derive his form and nature. From Leo, then, he derived the curliness of his hair, his tawny colour and his fierce gaze, irascibility and strength …

The description continues, very much as an elaboration of the *Historia de Preliis*, with the addition of the relevant astrological details.

Finally, in MS Oxford, Bodleian, Digby 67, a manuscript of the end of the 12th or early 13th century, there is on fol. 78r a short piece entitled "the opinion of the philosophers on the hours on which talismans should be made", which begins with the names of the philosophers concerned: "*Ypocras et Nectanebus Philosophus …*"

## Hermes Trismegistus

The second late classical text that was to have a significant influence on medieval views on Egypt was the *Asclepius* of Trismegistus. Before the translation of 14 texts of the *Corpus Hermeticum* by Marsilio Ficino in 1463 this was the only antique text on theoretical *Hermetica* known in the west. Its Greek original is lost, but the Latin version was already known to Augustine, and was copied and quoted frequently in the Middle Ages (Porreca 2001). There is no doubt about the Greco-Egyptian origin of the *Asclepius* (as with the Greek *Corpus Hermeticum* – Copenhaver 1992: iii–xxxii; Fowden 1986), and the Egyptian background is clear also from words in the *Asclepius* itself. The *dramatis personae* are Amun and Tat, who both have Egyptian names, and Hermes Trismegistus and Asclepius, whose are the Greek equivalents of Thoth and Imhotep. The Egyptian context of the conversation is presumed from the beginning, but the first explicit mention is in section 24, when the conversation turns to statues "ensouled and conscious, filled with spirit and doing great deeds, foreknowing the future, and predicting by prophecy, dreams and other means". "Do you not know," says Trismegistus to Asclepius, "that Egypt is an image of heaven or, to be more precise, that everything governed and moved in heaven came down to Egypt and was transferred there? If truth were told, our land is the temple of the whole world." Immediately after this, in *Asclepius* 24, Trismegistus apostrophizes Egypt in a prophecy that rang all too true in the ears of his medieval readers:

> O Egypt, Egypt, of your reverent deeds only stories will survive, and they will be incredible to your children! Only words cut in stone will survive to tell your faithful works, and the Scythian or Indian or some such neighbouring barbarian will dwell in Egypt.

> (Copenhaver 1992: 81)

A note to this passage in a 12th/13th century manuscript of the *Asclepius* comments that "Here (Trismegistus) prophesies about the time of Christ and about Muḥammad, who concocted a heretical religion for himself out of the Old and New Testament – a religion which the Egyptians, Chaldeans and all the Saracens presently hold to" (MS Copenhagen, Kongelige Bibliothek, Fabricius 91 4°; Porreca 2001: 246).

In *Asclepius* 37, Trismegistus, within an account of the euhemeristic explanation of the worship of the Egyptian gods, says:

> Take your ancestor, for example: he was the first to discover medicine, Asclepius. They dedicated a temple to him on the Libyan mountain near the shore of the crocodiles. There lies his material person – his body, in other words. The rest, or rather, the whole of him (if the whole person consists in consciousness of life) went back happier to heaven. Even now he still provides help to sick people by his divine power, as he used to offer it through the art of medicine. And Hermes, whose family name I bear, does he not dwell in his native city that was named for him (i.e. Hermopolis), where mortals come from all around for his aid and protection? Isis, wife of Osiris: we know how much good she can do when well disposed, when angered how much harm! Anger comes easily to earthly and material gods because humans have made and assembled them from both natures. Whence it happens that these are called holy animals by the Egyptians, who throughout their cities worship the souls of those deified while alive, in order that cities might go on living by their laws and calling themselves by their names.

> (Copenhaver 1992: 90)

The passages concerning Asclepius and Isis are quoted by Hermann of Carinthia, but Hermann paraphrases the intervening sentence as: "Concerning Hermes the case is the same – whether, as most men think, he was a demon embodied at a particular time, or a man who became a demon" (*De Essentiis* 73rF–G; Burnett 1982: 186).

In this paraphrase Hermann shows a good understanding of the *Asclepius*. For one of its leitmotifs is that, while the gods of the ancients may have been exemplary men and women, there are such things as divine spirits (called, in the *Asclepius*, *daemones*), which are obedient to men, and which man can call down into appropriate matter in order to make living statues which have the power of looking after things and foretelling the future through lots and divination. These are the same demons as those that Nectanebo invoked (Leo presbyter and *Historia de Preliis* I (2) – Bergmeister

1975: 4–5), and the formulae for summoning them, although not given in the 'Alexander Romance' or in the *Asclepius,* must have been similar.

The *Asclepius* started to be copied in large numbers of manuscripts during the 12th century, which was when the second version of the *Historia de Preliis* ($J^2$) was produced. It is probably not by coincidence that this rise in popularity of both 'Egyptian' works coincided with discovery, through translations from Arabic, of technical hermetic texts which *did* give the rules for summoning demons (now called *spiritus*[21]) and making statues (now called "talismans") for protection and for effecting good and evil. It is, then, to the influence of translations from Arabic that we next turn.

## The influence of Arabic literature

The massive translation of Arabic texts which began in the late 10th century but reached its apogee in the 12th and 13th centuries – during which one can speak of a *translatio studii* from the Muslims to the Christians – was bound to add to, and to modify, the western image of Egypt. This was not only because many of the texts came from that region, but also (and more important) because certain scholars writing in Arabic had deliberately preserved and perpetuated an Egyptian heritage. From the western scholar's point of view the very fact of taking wisdom from the infidels was analogous to Hebrews taking the spoils of the Egyptians. Thus Daniel of Morley (*Philosophia*, Pref. 6 – Maurach 1979: 213) justifies his action in introducing Arabic learning to his Christian audience by comparing it to the enrichment of the Hebrews from the gold and silver of the Egyptians. The question of the validity of "spoiling the Egyptians" was often raised in the Middle Ages: for example Vincent of Beauvais (*Speculum Historiale* II.6) states that "the Hebrews spoiled the Egyptians by divine permission or dispensation, as if in recompense for their wages, because they had served them freely and for a long time with their labour and had been paid nothing; so they also took from them clothing, gold and silver, so that the tabernacle could be made from them", and he quotes Augustine in further justification. The transference of this metaphor was facilitated by the fact that the contemporary Egyptians *were* Arabs,[22] and their wealth was still legendary (William of Tyre *Chronicon* XII.12; Huygens 1986: 573; cf. Hebrews 11:26).

But before considering the contents of translations from Arabic, one must tackle the perennial problem of the translation of proper names, in respect to Egypt. The commonest Arabic word for Egypt – 'miṣr' – also had the sense of 'capital town' (note 3 above), and it is translated simply as *'civitas'* in the Arabic/Latin portion of the mid-13th century Arabic-Latin/Latin-Arabic glossary compiled in Spain, and known from the title of its first edition as the *Vocabulista in Arabico* (Schiaparelli 1861: 188, 294). The capital of Egypt itself was often referred to in Arabic sources as miṣr, and this usage survives in the map of the Delta of Sebastian Münster (1550): "Memphis vulgo Messer" (Hornung 1990: fig. 4). Even miṣr as 'Egypt' was at first not always understood by the translators. In Abū Maʿshar's *Abbreviation of the Introduction to Astrology* (trans. Adelard of Bath in ca. 1120), the phrase "according to the school of the Egyptians" is translated "secundum Medorum philosophos/secundum Medos" (MS Sloane 2030, fols. 83r and 87r), and only corrected in later manuscripts to "secundum Egyptiorum philosophos" (Burnett *et al.* 1994: 88–89, 92, 136–138).[23] That miṣr was regarded as equivalent to 'Egyptus' can be seen from the Latin/Arabic portion of the same *Vocabulista in arabico*: Egiptus = "miṣrī qibṭī, miṣr, qibṭ". But it is noticeable here that "qibṮ" (= Copt) is also translated by the same term.

In the Latin translation of the *Great Conjunctions* of Abū Ma'shar, "al-qibṭ" is at first transliterated ("Alchibit/Alhabat"), then, in a revision, translated "Egiptii" (II 805, V 1000), but for the chronological era "years of the Copts", "Egiptii" is used throughout (Appendix II: 35, 36, 38), and the phrase "al-qibṭ min al-miṣr" (Appendix I: 37) is translated "Alchibt (*glossed*: scilicet Egiptiorum) de Egipto" (Burnett and Yamamoto 2000: 87, 143, 146–147, 204). In the *Picatrix*, translated in the court of Alfonso X, king of León and Castile, from a Castilian version of the Arabic "Ghāyat al-Ḥakīm", in the late 1250s, one finds considerable variation and confusion concerning the various names of oriental authorities (Pingree 1986: book, chapter and section numbers):

1   "qibṭ" is usually translated "Caldei", except when it is misread as "nabaṭ" and transliterated as "Naptiones" (II.2.4), "Naptini" (II.5.1), "Neptei" (III.5.2), and "Neptini" (III.8.1). The connection with Egypt of this misunderstood ethnic term is retained in *Picatrix* II.5.1, where "Naptini de Egipto" translates "qibṭ miṣr", but in III.5.2 "al-qibṭ min al-miṣrīyīn" ("the Copts among the Egyptians") is separated into two races: "Neptei" and "Egyptii".
2   The only occasion on which it looks as if "qibṭ" has been transcribed is in III.5.2 ("Capteos" preceding "Nepteos"); but here the Arabic gives "al-kāldānīyūn min al-nabaṭ" ("the Chaldeans among the Nabataeans"), and it is tempting to see in "Captei/Neptei" etc. an indication that "nabaṭ" and "qibṭ" (which, in unvowelled Arabic, differ only in their first letters – n and q – which in the written Arabic of the Maghreb are very easy to confuse) were regarded as the same word.
3   However, "nabaṭ" is translated "Chaldean" whenever the title of Ibn Waḥshiya's *Nabataean Agriculture* is mentioned (III.8.2–4; IV.7 *passim*).
4   But "Caldeus", aside from translating "qibṭ" and "nabaṭ", also translates "al-kasdānīyūn" (another word for "Chaldeans"; II.3.2, 5.1), "al-fāris/fārisīya" ("the Persians"; III.7.27, 9.16) and "al-akrād" ("the Kurds"; IV.2.1), and only once translates "al-kāldānīya" ("the Chaldeans"; IV.7.60).
5   Finally, whilst Egiptus/Egiptius usually translates "miṣr/miṣrī", on one occasion it translates "al-ḥabasha" ("Ethiopia": IV.2.1; the term 'Ethiopia' itself is never used in *Picatrix*), and on another, "al-fir'awnī" ("of pharaoh": II.10.5).

Bearing problems of interpretation in mind, we can now turn to two areas in which translations from Arabic had an important effect on the European image of Egypt: namely the science of the stars, and hermetic literature.

## Astronomy and astrology

As has already been mentioned, the Ancient Egyptians were regarded as astronomers. Aside from the numerous classical references to Egyptians being inventors of astronomy (Bouché-Leclercq 1899: 51 n. 1), or being particularly experienced and adept at it (Cicero *De Divinatione* I.1.2; Isidore *Etymologiae* III.15.1), they are credited with the equal division of the zodiac into 12 signs of 30 degrees (Servius comm. on *Georgics* I.33) and the designation of signs as houses of particular planets (the *thema mundi*: Firmicus Maternus *Mathesis* III.1; Macrobius comm. on *Somnium Scipionis* I.21, 23–27).

When Arabic works on astronomy were introduced into Europe, their accounts of the origins of astronomy were blended with the native Latin and patristic tradition. In the Latin preface to a late 10th century collection of translations of Arabic texts on the astrolabe Abraham is credited with teaching the Egyptians astrology (Millàs Vallicrosa 1931: 274), and another translator, introducing a compendium of Arabic texts on astrology, implies that Abraham owed his knowledge to his being amongst the Chaldeans (Burnett 1977: 84). The transit of the science of the stars from the Chaldeans to the Egyptians is made explicit in Hermann of Carinthia's free translation of Abū Ma'shar's *Great Introduction to Astrology* (Lemay 1995–1996, VIII: 85–86: italics indicate the passages in Hermann's translation for which there is no equivalent in the original Arabic):

> As Ptolemy and several other men of ancient authority relate in all seriousness, when dealing with the ancient history of the world: after the memory of virtually everything that had gone before had been destroyed by the universal flood which covered the earth, and only a few living beings remained from all the nations of the world, in Chaldea *the study of the movement and the power of the stars was conceived, wisdom was born, and then in the progress of time it grew up and gradually spread through the world.* They say that, after the flood, where dry land first appeared as the waves returned to their former beds, Noah, who had survived with his sons, in his pursuit of more temperate breezes, came out from Armenia to where Babylon was later founded. As the world was being reborn his descendants gradually scattered in all directions from this point along the Tigris to Kascar, and along the Euphrates to Kufa. One of his grandchildren, they say, was Sem, who, first being instructed by remembering what his grandfather said, or being enlightened by the divine gift of his own intelligence, on observing the courses of the stars, began to wonder at their effects … [*the observation of other astrological phenomena is described*]. *As the human race developed, afterwards the nations of the world adopted this wisdom, and by studying it they corrected some things according to the ability of their intelligence, and made great advances. Among these nations it was the Egyptians who contributed most, thanks to the subtlety of the nature of their air.*

AbūMa'shar, being himself a Persian, prefers to see wisdom coming from Persia and India. But Hermann, as we see, makes Egypt the most fertile nation for the cultivation of astronomy, because of the quality of its air. This would be a natural assumption from the fact that the principal authority on the science of the stars was Ptolemy, who, in reality, lived and worked in Alexandria in the second century AD, and whose association with Egypt in the Middle Ages was unquestioned; for his name was the same as those of the hellenistic kings of Egypt. Ptolemy wrote the *Almagest*, which remained until the Copernican revolution the most authoritative theoretical account of the movements of the heavenly bodies, and the *Tetrabiblos* (or *Apotelesmata*), which was equally authoritative in the field of astrology. Other texts were also attributed to him, of which the best known were the *Preceptum canonis Ptolomei* (astronomical tables with their instructions), the *Iudicia* (astrological judgments) and the *Centiloquium* (100 astrological aphorisms). All these texts, with the exception of the Latin *Preceptum canonis* which dates from late Antiquity, became known in the Middle Ages through translations from Arabic in the 12th century (the origins of the *Iudicia* are not yet clear, but its contents are from Arabic sources).

The confusion of Ptolemy with a king goes back at least to Isidore (*Etymologiae* III.26.1), who writes:

> About the teachers [of astronomy]: In each language [i.e. Latin and Greek] different authors have written works on astronomy. The most important author among the Greeks, however, is Ptolemy, the king of Alexandria. He also composed rules by which the courses of the stars can be found.

Isidore's words are echoed in a translator's preface to the earliest corpus of writings on the astrolabe (the instrument *par excellence* of astronomy) translated from Arabic (Millàs Vallicrosa 1931: 274). A title of one of these texts adds the appellation 'king': "Here begin the chapters of the book on the sundial of king Ptolemy", and a work deriving from another text in the corpus begins its description of the astrolabe with the words "King Ptolemy orders [one to make an astrolabe in the following way] ..." (Millàs Vallicrosa 1931: 322). Hugo of St Victor (*Didascalicon* III.2; see above) repeated the statement that "Ptolemy, king of Egypt, revived astronomy ...". Such attributions prompted an astronomer of the mid-12th century, Raymond of Marseilles (*Liber Cursuum*, Burnett and Poulle forthcoming), to state that:

> Astronomers are also wont to argue about which of the twelve kings of Egypt who were called 'Ptolemy' was the inventor of the astrolabe. But since two of the kings are said to have been wiser than the rest, it is said by the more authoritative of astronomers that it was the Ptolemy who was called 'the Great' who invented it.

When the *Almagest* itself was translated from Arabic later in the 12th century, its translator, Gerard of Cremona, following words in an Arabic preface, specified that

> Ptolemy was *not* one of the kings of Egypt who were called 'Ptolemies', as some people think; but Ptolemy was his name, as if someone was called 'Chosroe' [the name of Persian kings] or 'Caesar'.

> (Ptolemy, *Almagest* 1528)

This differentiation of Ptolemy from the kings of Egypt is stated at greater length by ʿAlī ibn Riḍwān, who writes at the beginning of his commentary on Ptolemy's *Tetrabiblos*:

> Abū Maʿshar and those others who wrote histories and only took the [literal meaning of the] text and accepted things on hear-say, because they did not seek out what was the truth and what was not, believed that this Ptolemy was one of the kings of Alexandria who succeeded Alexander, because all those kings were called by this name, and there was among them one king who loved scholars, arts and sciences so much that he sought out and collected as many books on every subject as he could, and attracted as many scholars as he could to his land, by imploring them to come and giving them great rewards, to such an extent that this Ptolemy was called the 'lover of sciences'. But this Ptolemy lived a long time before the Ptolemy who wrote this book (the *Tetrabiblos*). For, in all the histories, we find that those kings of Alexandria which were called 'Ptolemy' lived before the emperors of the Romans, and we find that the Ptolemy who composed the *Almagest* describes the positions of the stars according to their adjustment at the time of the Roman emperors, a long time after the times of the kings of Alexandria. Therefore we understand that Ptolemy the Pheludian ['Pheludianus' has resulted from a mis-reading of the Arabic transcription of 'Claudius', Ptolemy's cognomen] was not one of the kings of Alexandria. Moreover, we have never found that king Ptolemy, the 'lover of the sciences', wrote any book,

although he was very fond of scholars, of listening to [readings on] science, and especially books [translated] from Hebrew. John the Grammarian [this is the usual Arabic designation of John Philoponus, the sixth century Alexandrian Greek philosopher], who was one of the fine scholars of Alexandria confirms what we say. Hence we know for certain that the Pheludian Ptolemy who composed the *Almagest* is the one who wrote this book (the *Tetrabiblos*).

(Ptolemy 1519a: aa4v)

Nevertheless, the feeling that Ptolemy was a king of Egypt persisted, and in illustrations he is commonly depicted wearing a crown (Tezmen-Siegel 1985: 113 n. 69, pls. 13, 15, 38, 55; other references to Ptolemy as a king are given in Burnett 1998: 340–343).

It is significant that Isidore and ʿAlī ibn Riḍwān calls the Ptolemies "kings of Alexandria", not "kings of Egypt", for this hints at the distinction between the Greek culture of Alexandria and a native Egyptian culture, which is implied by Ptolemy himself (as a Greek) when he distinguishes his own theories from those of the "Egyptians". Ptolemy claims that the Egyptians are the most advanced nation in the science of astrology (*Tetrabiblos* I.3; Robbins 1971: 31),[24] but he begs to differ from them in his computation of a particular element in astrology, namely, the 'terms' of the planets. The terms are the divisions of the 30 degrees of each sign of the zodiac amongst the five planets in varying proportions from sign to sign. The term in which a planet is located is one of the criteria for making an astrological judgment, but there were different ways of dividing the degrees. Ptolemy describes those of the "Egyptians", the "Chaldeans", and his own, and criticizes the Egyptians for not being able to give a rational explanation of the division into terms (Robbins 1971: 101–103).[25] In his *Great Introduction* Abū Maʿshar (V: 12) adds a fourth division (that of 'Asṭuwāṭū'; Lemay 1995–1996, II: 327), but, in spite of Ptolemy's criticism, the "terms of the Egyptians" became the preferred division in classical astrology (Dorotheus, Paul of Alexandria and Firmicus Maternus; Bouché-Leclercq 1899: 206–215), in Arabic and, consequently, in Latin astrology. They are the only terms mentioned in Abū Maʿshar's own *Abbreviation of the Introduction*, where they are said to be "according to the school of the Egyptians". Al-Qabīṣī, in his *Introduction to Astrology*, also listed the terms "according the Egyptians", and since his work, in the mid-12th century translation of John of Seville (Alcabitius' *Introductorius*), became the most popular introduction to astrology in the Middle Ages, the *termini Egyptiorum* became generally familiar (Burnett *et al.* forthcoming). The Latin translator, however, added that the "Egyptians said that these terms were those of Hermes" (al-Qabīṣī (Alcabitius) *Introductorius* I.19), evidently because of the association of Hermes with Egypt (see below), and this statement was repeated by Raymond of Marseilles (*Liber iudiciorum*, MS Paris, Bibliothèque Nationale de France, 16208, fol. 14va–b).

Another Egyptian doctrine is that of the 'decans', which is not found in Ptolemy, but was well known in classical astrology. Firmicus Maternus (mid-fourth century), the author of the only classical Latin prose work on astrology to survive into the Middle Ages, refers to an Egyptian authority for the astrological doctrine of decans:

We have said … that each sign of the zodiac is divided into three decans. The decans themselves are of great spiritual force (*numen*) and power, and through them all good and bad fortune is discerned. Thus Nechepso, the most just emperor of Egypt and a

very good astrologer, assigned everything to do with harm and well-being to the
decans, showing what kind of well-being each decan produced and, because one
nature is conquered by another and because one god frequently conquers another, he
discovered remedies for all illnesses [by using] their contrary natures and powers, by
his skills in divine reasoning.

(Maternus Mathesis IV.22)

The decans and their numinous rulers are recognized in modern scholarship as being
a distinctively ancient Egyptian contribution to astrology (Pingree 1963), which was
taken over by Greek, Indian and Arabic astrologers. By the time the doctrine reaches
Abū Maʿshar (*Great Introduction* V.15), however, it is credited not only to the
Egyptians, but also to the "wise men of Persia and Babylon" (Lemay 1995–1996, II:
139, V: 202, VII: 87), whereas al-Qabīṣī (*Introductorius* I.20) no longer gives any
authorities for it. Relics of ancient Egyptian imagery have been discerned in the
descriptions of the "images that ascend in each decan" in the sixth book of Abū
Maʿshar's *Great Introduction*, and the illustrations of these images in a picture-book
dependent on Abū Maʿshar (Gousset and Verdet 1989). Abū Maʿshar (*Great
Introduction* VI.1) attributes the first of three sets of images for each decan to "the
Persians, the Babylonians and the Egyptians" (Lemay 1995–1996, III: 373, V: 215, VII:
96). The image that is said to arise in the first decan of Virgo is a young woman,
identified by Teukros (of Babylonia) as Isis, sitting on a couch, nourishing a child
whose name is 'Īsū' (Abū Maʿshar *Great Introduction* VI.1; Dyroff in Boll 1903: 512–513;
Lemay 1995–1996, III: 380, V: 224, VII: 101). Abū Maʿshar interprets the name as 'Īsā'
('Jesus'), which meant that in the translations of John of Seville and Hermann of
Carinthia, this image in the sign of Virgo was seen as a prediction of the Virgin birth,
and became the most-quoted passage of the *Great Introduction* (Burnett 1982: 246;
Kunitzsch 1970). Nevertheless, in Hermann's version only, and for this image alone,
the authority of the Egyptians for this image is repeated, alongside other ancient
witnesses (Lemay 1995–1996, VII: 101).

At a more popular level of astrology, one finds the doctrine of 'Egyptian days', i.e.
certain days throughout the month which were regarded as inauspicious, and were
connected with the 10 plagues of Egypt (Steele 1919). These, though again they are not
mentioned by Ptolemy, are referred to by Augustine, and appear regularly in works
on the ecclesiastical calendar (*computus*) and medieval Latin astrological works, such
as the *Liber Introductorius* of Michael Scot (MS Munich, Bayerische Staatsbibliothek,
Clm 10268, fol. 68rb).

Firmicus' authority, "Nechepso, the most just emperor (i.e. pharaoh) of the
Egyptians", together with his correspondent 'Petosiris' both typified the "expert
Egyptian astrologer" in classical literature (cf. Ausonius XXV, *Epist.* 19; Juvenal *Satires*
VI.581; Paulinus of Nola *Carmina* III.8–9), and some specimens of the writings of the
two correspondents are known (Pliny *Historia naturalis* VII.49 (160); Servius *Aeneid*
X.272; Riess 1892; Pingree 1978, II: 436–437). Among these is a *Letter of Petosiris to
Nechepso*, which exists in Greek and Latin, and was copied throughout the Middle
Ages. In this Petosiris writes to "King Nechepso" on the subject of predicting the
outcome of an action or event, especially of an illness: the sum of the numerical
equivalents of the name of the client is divided by 29 and the remainder is found in

one of six compartments within a rectangle or a sphere, which are headed "great life, medium life, small life, great death, medium death, small death" respectively.

Texts on the science of the stars provide examples of Egyptian (or alleged Egyptian) doctrine and the Egyptians as authorities, but texts on astrology also give an image of the character of the country and its inhabitants (an element of astrology known as 'chorography'). On this, Ptolemy is the prime authority. In *Tetrabiblos* II.3 he assigns the "four quarters of the world" to the four triplicities of three signs of the zodiac each, within which Egypt falls into the south-western quarter, attributed to the triplicity of Taurus, Virgo and Capricorn, ruled by Venus and Saturn. Amongst the characteristics of this quarter are government by a man and wife who are siblings (the well-known practice of rulers in Ptolemaic Egypt), and ardour in love-making (Robbins 1971: 151). Egypt belongs to the north-east section of this quarter, which is situated near the centre of the inhabited world, and has, in addition, affinity with the north-eastern triplicity of Gemini, Libra and Aquarius, with Saturn, Jupiter and Mercury as rulers. Hence inhabitants of this section are subject to the rulership of all five planets, and so are:

> worshippers of the gods, superstitious, given to religious ceremony and fond of lamentation ... they are polygamous, polyandrous and lecherous, marrying even their own sisters, and the men are potent in begetting, the women in conceiving, even as their land is fertile ... Of these peoples the inhabitants of Cyrenaica and Marmarica and particularly of Lower Egypt are more closely familiar to Gemini and Mercury; on this account they are thoughtful and intelligent and quick in all things, especially in the search for wisdom and religion; they are magicians and performers of secret mysteries and in general skilled in mathematics.

(Robbins 1971: 155–157)

Thus the astrological data support other evidence of the Egyptians' aptitude for wisdom and magic. The assignation of Lower Egypt to Gemini is repeated in the table of signs and regions which immediately follows in *Tetrabiblos* II.3. In subsequent Arabic and Latin astrological works Egypt as a whole is attributed to Gemini (Abū Ma'shar *Great Introduction* VI.9, *Abbreviation* I.21; Lemay 1995–1996, V: 248; Burnett *et al.* 1994: 17, 97; al-Qabīṣī (Alcabitius) *Introductiorius* I.27), while Pisces rules 'Egypt and Alexandria' (Abū Ma'shar *Great Introduction* VI.9, *Abbreviation* I.81; *On the Great Conjunctions*, App. I: 14; Burnett and Yamamoto 2000, I: 517, II: 143; Burnett *et al.* 1994: 25, 101; Lemay 1995–1996, V: 250; al-Qabīṣī (Alcabitius) *Introductorius* I.36). Later astrologers also follow Ptolemy in ascribing Egypt to Mercury, the "lord" of Gemini (Abū Ma'shar *On the Great Conjunctions* II.4; Burnett and Yamamoto 2000, I: 66–67).[26] Hermann of Carinthia, as well as giving this alignment in his translation of Abū Ma'shar (*Great Introduction*), claims that Egypt is "on the edge of the inhabitable world" and consequently is frequently visited by aerial spirits (demons) from the other world (Hermann of Carinthia *De Essentiis* 79rB; Burnett 1982: 226–227).

## Hermeticism and magic

The mention of demons brings us to perhaps the most vivid of the images of Egypt in medieval eyes. While the Egyptian gods may have been explained away as deifications of exemplary men, the presence of demons in ancient Egyptian society was regarded as a fact. We have already seen how Nectanebo used demons to effect his magic deeds, and how, in the *Asclepius*, demons were summoned to vivify statues. In Apuleius' *De deo Socratis* (15 (153)), which accompanies the *Asclepius* in many medieval manuscripts, the difference between a deified human being and a demon is taken for granted:

> People call gods those on whom, when, by the help and offices of good demons, they have justly and wisely ruled their lives, are bestowed temples and ceremonies by men, as if they are divine spirits ...

Egypt was full of demons and the presence of the divine (cf. Macrobius *Saturnalia* VII.10.13). The prime authority for the means by which these demons (good or bad) could be controlled is Hermes. Isidore of Seville states that Hermes was the inventor of magic, as well as of the lyre (*Etymologiae* III.22.8–9), and that he gave laws to the Egyptian people (*Etymologiae* V.1.2). At the end of the 12th century Alain de Lille explains the term "hermeneutic" as deriving from "Hermes" and describing the communication between a Master and a "diabolus" or demon (Alain de Lille *Distinctiones Dictionum Theologicalium*, Migne, pl. CCX, col. 776C).

The problem is that there were several Hermes bequeathed to the Middle Ages both from classical and Arabic sources. Cicero gives five, of whom only the last two have associations with Egypt.[27] A genealogy was sometimes provided. In the *Asclepius* (37) Hermes Trismegistus states that his grandfather (or ancestor) was the god Hermes (Copenhaver 1992: 90). Augustine (*De Civitate Dei* VIII.8) identifies the older Hermes as the son of Maia, daughter of Atlas, whose grandson is Mercurius Trismegistus (Sladek 1988). With the introduction of Arabic works more details were added to this family tree. Abū Maʿshar, in his ʿkitāb al-ulūfʾ (ʿBook of the Thousands'), had stated that the first Hermes lived in Egypt before the flood; the second in Babylon, and revived the sciences after the flood; and the third, once again in Egypt, taught alchemy and passed on his wisdom to Asclepius (Burnett 1976). This account is reflected in the preface by an anonymous translator to an alchemical work attributed to Hermes (*Septem tractatus Hermetis Sapientia Triplicis*) who includes the following words in his preface:

> In the histories of divine matters, we read of three very famous philosophers, each called ʿHermes'. The first of these was Enoch, who lived before the flood, and departed into heaven on a fiery chariot accompanied by angels [for the identification of Hermes with Enoch in Arabic sources, see al-Masʿūdī, ʿMurūjʾ, I: 39–40]. The second was Noah, who escaped from the flood of many waters in the Ark, by the command of God. Each of these was called either ʿHermes' or ʿMercury', in contrast to the Hermes who reigned in Egypt after the flood. For this third very famous man, who, adorned with a royal diadem, reigned for a long time as king of Egypt, was called ʿthrice great' because of a three-fold virtue. For they say he was a king, a philosopher and a prophet, who is said to have been the inventor of every liberal and mechanical art.

(Ruska 1928: 31)

In another anonymous preface, this time to a work on astrological judgments addressed to Robert, Earl of Leicester from 1118 to 1168, ʿMercury' is mentioned together with Ptolemy as a king of Egypt:

What we have found worth relating concerning medicine and the science of the stars in the most venerable books of the ancient philosophers – Mercury and Ptolemy, kings of Egypt and Abū Ma'shar the Indian – and of the modern converts to the Christian faith – al-Zarqalluh, Iohannes Hispaniensis and Iohannes Daysch of Toledo (who with a wonderful effort [translated] the book which Mercury, king of Egypt, composed concerning the faith of the Trinity, which is also entitled the 'Book of Longitude and Latitude') – we have taken care to explain in depth to you, Robert, most reverend Count of Leicester, who are most skilled in these subjects.

> (MSS British Library, Royal 12.E.XXV, fol. 172v and
> Oxford, Bodleian Library, Digby 57, fol. 137v)

Here "Hermes the thrice-great" has become garbled into "Mercury who wrote a book concerning the Trinity"; the identification is assured, however, by the existence of a book attributed to Hermes "of longitude and latitude" (the first part of an Arabic text with this title survives in MS Milan, Ambros. ar. C 86), which is also mentioned in a preface to a 12th century Latin cosmology based on Arabic sources, which adds to a summary of the story of the three Hermes cited above (Ruska 1928) a list of Hermes' books:

In the old histories of divine matters, we read that there were three philosophers. The first of these was Enoch, who was called both Hermes and by another name: Mercury. Another was Noah, who likewise was called Hermes and Mercury. But the third was called Hermes Mercury, the three-fold, because he flourished as a king, a philosopher and a prophet. This one reigned in Egypt after the flood with the greatest justice, excelled in the liberal and mechanical arts, and first explained astronomy. He composed in a lucid style the *Golden Bough* [Burnett 2001b: 280], the *Book of Longitude and Latitude*, the *Book of Elections*,[28] the '*Zīj*', i.e. the Canons for establishing the positions of the planets,[29] [a work] on the astrolabe, and many other works. Among his books this three-fold or thrice-great ('Trismegistus') [scholar] first made alchemy public. Morienus, the great philosopher, studied his (Hermes') writings and began to investigate the secret nature of alchemy with long hard work. Eventually, he put together a work on alchemy, writing about it in a subtle way.

> (Silverstein 1955: 247)

Many more can be added to this list of works by Hermes. In their catalogue of medieval Latin hermetic texts, Lucentini and Perrone Compagni (2001) list 41 different works, extant in some 400 manuscripts. Most of these give instructions on the various materials to be used to make talismans and to summon spirits, so providing the practical aspect to the theory of the *Asclepius* (Burnett 2001a). However, it cannot be immediately assumed that all these works were thought to be by an Egyptian Hermes or to convey Egyptian wisdom. When Hermes is quoted by Abū Ma'shar, he is a Persian, and this is reflected in Hermann of Carinthia's *De Essentiis*, in which quotations of 'Hermes' (or 'Hermes Persa') refer to citations from Abū Ma'shar's *Great Introduction*, whereas quotations of 'Trismegistus' refer to the *Asclepius* (Burnett 2001a: 115).

Modern scholarship has tended to see the origin of much of the Arabic hermetic literature (on which the medieval Latin texts depend) among the star-worshipping Ṣābi'ans of Harran in northern Iraq, whose religious authorities were Hermes and Agathodaimon (Green 1992; Tardieu 1986). The traditional story is that, to avoid persecution by the Muslims, they picked the name 'Ṣābi'an' from the Quran, where

Ṣābi'ans are mentioned alongside Christians and Jews as worshippers of the one true God. The Quranic Ṣābi'ans have been identified with the sect of the Mandaeans of southern Iraq, whose religion includes elements of Christianity, Judaism and Zoroastrianism. But the similar religious importance attached to the stars and the pursuit of astrology among the Mandaeans and the Harranian Ṣābi'ans, which may be due to a common Mesopotamian background, has prompted certain scholars to suggest that there was a closer relation between the two than is suggested by the traditional story (Drower 1937: xvi–xviii; McCullough 1967: xv–xvii). Moreover, in certain Arabic sources, the Egyptian priests are called "the first Ṣābi'ans" and the pharaoh in Moses' time is said to be a Ṣābi'an (El Daly Chapter 3, this volume). Thus it is not surprising if there is some blurring between 'Chaldean' and 'Egyptian' magic. 'Caldei et Egyptii' are often lumped together as generic ancient authorities (e.g. *Picatrix* IV.2.1; Bartholomew of Parma *Tractatus Spere* III.6.1; Bouché-Leclercq 1899: 51 n. 1; Burnett 2001c: 186; Pingree 1986: 178). The coincidence of a Chaldean and an Egyptian Babylon would have facilitated the amalgamation of the two ancient peoples. Moreover, as we have seen, the situation in Latin is further confused by the misinterpretation of the Arabic word for 'Copts' as a word for Chaldean and by the word for Egyptian ('miṣrī') as 'Medes'.

In one passage of the *Picatrix* (II.5.1), however, the magical doctrines of the Ṣābi'ans are associated with the Chaldeans and are differentiated from those of the Egyptians:

> For I tell you that I have seen a great and wonderful [statement] of one of the wise men of Antiquity that pertains to what I have decided to say now. He used to say that this science is divided into three parts. The first is the magical science (in Arabic: 'the science of talismans'), and those who study and operate with it are what we have called the 'Azahabin' (in Arabic: Ṣābi'ans), who are the captive slaves of the Chaldeans (in Arabic: "the Nabataeans among the Chaldeans"). The second is the science of the stars and praying to them with suffumigations, sacrifices, prayers and written [charms]; and those who have studied in this science are Greeks; they are very subtle in this, knowing and understanding it (i.e. astrology), and they have a true science, because the science of astrology is regarded as the root of the whole of the science of magic. The third part is the science which operates by suffumigations, spoken words and [written] words appropriate to those things, and also the science of the spirits that should be joined to the words and those that should be separated from them; and the Indians are especially adept at this science, and certain people from the Yemen and the Naptini [this is a misreading of Arabic 'Qibṭ' (= 'Copts')] in Egypt have especially operated with this part.

> (Pingree 1986: 46; Ritter 1933: 80)

It seems correct that the branch of magic that used spirits (demons) in its operations should be associated with Egypt. The connection of Egyptian and Indian magic, together with the employment of spirits, occurs elsewhere in the *Picatrix* (III.11.126), where a king of India is providing services for the Egyptians. In the first story he prepares for the men of Egypt 12 feasts in as many months (Pingree 1986: 168; Ritter 1933: 278–279); the second and third stories are more explicit in their topical references to Egypt and neighbouring Nubia:

> This same king made an earthen vessel which he filled with water from which the whole army drank, but the water-level did not decrease at all. This king lived at the

time of Alexander the Great, and it is said that he presented this vessel, with certain other wonderful things, to him. The vessel was constructed by [a combination of] man-made artifices, properties of nature and the knowledge of the strengths of the spirits of the planets and of the fixed stars. Moreover, in this way was made a ball which Acaym, king of India made in the gate of the city of Nuba (i.e. Nubia), which was made of black marble and was completely full of water. Whatever amount was taken out of it, nothing [appeared] to be missing; and this was because he attracted the moistures of the air through the power of the artifice by which it was made. He constructed this work to refresh his people, because of the distance of that city from the waters of the Nile, and because of its proximity to the salty sea. From its property it happened that the thick and moist vapours were raised by the rays of the sun from the water of the sea, and the more subtle of them were purified from their saltiness in the air, and descended by the most subtle geometrical artifices and magical sciences (Arabic: "ḥīla siḥrīya") into the ball itself, as if condensing from the air. For this reason [the ball] never lacked [the water], because of the attraction mentioned above – an attraction analogous to that of the 'bloodstone' which attracts [blood] when it is placed above it.

(*Picatrix* III.11.127; Pingree 1986: 168–169; Ritter 1933: 279)

Another story from *Picatrix* finally brings Hermes and Egypt together:

The Chaldeans [the Arabic has "al-qibṭ" "the Copts"; for the confusion of Copts with Chaldeans in Latin see above] … say that Hermes long ago [instead of "Hermes long ago", the Arabic has "the first Hermes"] constructed opposite the Mountain of the Moon a 'house of talismans' (Arabic: "bayt tamāthīl") by which he could know the volume [of water] of the Nile, and he made a house (Arabic: "a temple") for the Sun. He hid himself from the face of men so that nobody in his presence could see him. He also was the one who built the city in the east of Egypt, whose length comprised 12 miles, in which he constructed a fortress which had four doors on its four sides. On the door on the east he placed the figure of an eagle, on the door on the west that of a bull, on the south that of a Lion, on the north that of a dog. He made spiritual spirits (Arabic: "rūḥānīyāt") enter into them, who spoke by projecting their voices [Arabic: "who began to speak when anyone approached them" and adds "and their voices had a terrifying sound"]; nor could anyone enter its doors unless by their command [Arabic: "by the command of the person in charge"]. There also he planted certain trees, in the middle of which stood a large tree which bore all kinds of fruit. On the summit of the fort itself he got a tower built that reached the height of thirty cubits, on whose summit he placed a spherical cupula, whose colour changed every day up to seven days. At the end of seven days it received the colours which it had at first. That city each day was covered with the colour of that copula and thus the city shone each day with that colour. Round the tower there was abundant water in which very many kinds of fish were always to be found. Round the city he arranged different talismans of different sorts, by whose virtue the inhabitants were strengthened and were cleansed from evil and malignant diseases. This city was called 'Adocentyn' (Arabic: Ashmūnayn = Hermopolis).

(*Picatrix* IV.3.1; Pingree 1986: 188–189; Ritter 1933: 309–310)[30]

Certain Latin *Hermetica* derive from a genre of Arabic hermetic writings (Ullmann 1972a: 375), which purports to be the wisdom of Hermes as told by Aristotle to Alexander the Great, his pupil.[31] An extract from one of these Arabic texts, in Hermann of Carinthia's *De Essentiis*, tells how, in the days of the king of the "Medes" (possibly for "miṣrī") a certain man was visited at Thebes by the spirit of Venus in a dream, who gave him instructions on how to summon the spirit by sacrificing a ram, and chanting the correct names of the spirit (Burnett 1981: 167). The immediate Arabic source for this passage has not been found (it was probably in a book entitled 'The Book of the Essences of Talismans'). In the Arabic text closest to the Latin (the "kitāb al-Istamāṭīs") there is no mention of the Medes or of Thebes, which may be an addition of Hermann's, for Thebes quite commonly occurs in Latin texts as the city where magical events happen, or from which magicians originate.[32] Hermann of Carinthia turns the toponym of the ancient sage associated with Hermes, Apollonius of Tyana ("Bālīnūs al-Ṭawāna" in Arabic), into 'Thebanus' (Hermann of Carinthia *De Essentiis* 65vC; Burnett 1982: 130), and Adelard of Bath calls Thābit ibn Qurra, the Harranian Ṣābi'an who wrote a book on talismans, "Thebidis" (in the genitive), as if signifying "the man from Thebes" (Burnett forthcoming). In the 13th or 14th century a work on Solomonic magic, consisting of prayers for obtaining knowledge in all the sciences, was written and foisted on "Honorius of Thebes the son of Euclid" (Hedegård 2002; Thorndike 1934–1958, II: 283–289). Thebes, as the ancient capital of Upper Egypt, was not on the itinerary of western travellers, and its very location seems to have been vague in the eyes of western scholars. William, Archbishop of Tyre (*Chronicon* XIX.24), identifies the ancient 'Thebaid' with the modern Fayum; he mentions a kind of opium that is called 'Thebaicum' because the best opium grows there (Huygens 1986: 897). This perhaps lent it an exoticism that more accessible places in Egypt, such as Alexandria and Cairo, did not have.

For one genre of hermetic texts the specifically Egyptian origin is clear, namely that of alchemy. We have already seen how the story of the descent of the Egyptian Hermes from two other Hermes is told in two prefaces to works on alchemy, and how, in another preface, the Egyptian Hermes is credited with the publication of the earliest writing on alchemy, which Morienus studied (Maryānūs is a legendary alchemical authority). One of the two protagonists in Morienus' *Liber de Compositione Alchemiae* (1564), Calid, is called the king of the Egyptians, and a story is told of Calid's grandfather Macoya, king of the Egyptians (Stavenhagen 1974; Thorndike 1934–1958, II: 216).

There is little doubt that the theory and practice of western alchemy arose on Egyptian soil. While the name of the art most probably comes from Greek *khumeia* rather than the word used by the Egyptians for their fertile black land, *km.t* (DuQuesne 1999: 33), Zosimus, the earliest alchemist to whom we can put a name (third to fourth centuries AD), came from Panopolis (Akhmim). The first Latin texts on alchemy were translated from Arabic in the 12th century, and included the *Septem tractatus Hermetis Sapientia Triplicis* and the *Liber de Compositione Alchemiae* of Morienus. A leitmotif that occurs with respect to the Arabic and Latin alchemical texts is the discovery in an underground chamber or crypt of a stela made of marble, ebony or emerald, with mysterious writing or symbols on it. The Egyptian context of these stelae would have been recognized by Latin scholars of the Middle Ages from the story of Nectanebo and also from a passage in Martianus Capella, which describes:

> certain books coloured with sacred blackness whose letters were believed to be the images of animals. Athanasia, seeing these notes of books, ordered them to be inscribed on certain conspicuous rocks and placed within a cave [entered] through the sanctuaries of the Egyptians, and calling these same rocks 'stelae' she ordered them to contain the genealogy of the gods.

(Martianus Capella *De Nuptiis* II.137)

The best known of these stelae was the emerald tablet of Hermes, on which is written a hymn that encapsulates the mystery of alchemy (Ruska 1926). This first appears in Latin in a mid-12th century translation of the *Secrets of Nature* of Pseudo-Apollonius, made by Hugo of Santalla. Apollonius purports to find a statue of Hermes, under which there is a crypt, which he enters, carrying a torch. There he finds another statue of Hermes, holding the emerald tablet. It has been claimed that the emerald tablet existed and was originally a stela dedicated to the healing god Imhotep which was set up in or near the Anubieion, on the desert edge west of Memphis (Stricker 1943). The fullest account of the discovery of such a stela, however, is that of Ibn Umayl (early 10th century), who was very probably an Egyptian himself. He describes, as a personal experience, the discovery of a marble tablet in an Egyptian temple with 10 symbolic figures inscribed on it, and explains these symbols in two commentaries: in verse ("The Letter of the Sun to the Crescent Moon") and in prose ("The Silvery Water and the Starry Earth"). The whole text was translated into Latin as the "Tabula chemica" of "Senior Sadich/Zadith". The date and author of the translation are unknown, but the work became quite popular in the later Middle Ages, and its author is referred to by Chaucer (Ruska 1934, 1935). The discovery of the tablet is described in the Latin text as follows:

> Senior Sadich, son of Hamil said: Abulchasim and I entered a 'barba' (i.e. a certain underground dwelling),[33] and afterwards Abulchasein and I [entered] the prison of Joseph (which was a treasure-house).[34] I saw on the ceiling nine painted images of eagles, with their wings outstretched as if they were flying, and their claws stretched out and open. Each eagle had in its claws something like a bow, which archers carry, fully drawn [Ronca 1995: 22 explains this image as "the *shenu* or *shen* ring, an object similar to a capital omega (i.e. a fully drawn bow) held by flying vultures in their claws" which "is often found in Egyptian tombs and signifies eternity"]. On the wall of the dwelling to the right and the left of the person entering, were images of standing men, as beautiful and perfect as can be imagined, dressed in [clothes] of different kinds of colour, and with their arms stretched out towards the inner chamber [this word, *thalamus*, is also used by Pliny (*Historia naturalis* VIII.185) for the two inner shrines in Memphis where the sacred bull Apis was worshipped], pointing to a certain statue sitting inside the dwelling on the side next to the door of the inner room, to the left of the person entering, and facing him. It [the statue] was sitting on a chair similar to the chairs of physicians [Ronca (1995: 23) sees in this image "one of the characteristic attributes of the physician-hero Imhotep … seated with an open papyrus scroll across his lap"], but [the chair was] detachable from the statue. [The statue] had in its lap a marble tablet, detachable from [the statue] but supported between its shoulders and its extended arms. The tablet had the length of an arm, and the width of a palm, and the fingers of the [statue]'s hands were wrapped round the bottom of the tablet to look as if they were holding it. The tablet was like an open book for anyone entering [the chamber], as if hinting to him: 'Look at this!' In the part of the chamber in which he sat there were innumerable images of different things and barbaric letters [the Arabic uses the adjective 'barbāwī' ('pertaining to the barbā'), for which "barbarus" is either corruption or a false friend]. In one half of the tablet (for it was divided through the middle by a line), there was an image of two birds, in the lower part, which was supported by [the statue]'s chest [one must imagine the tablet upside down, or as if being read by the statue itself]. One of these had cut wings, the other two wings, and each held the tail of the other in its beak as if the one flying wished to fly with the other, and the latter wished to keep with him the one flying. Those two birds bound together and of the same species were depicted in one circle, as if being an image of two in one;

and next to the head of the flying [bird] there was a circle, and above these two birds, next to the top of the tablet which was closest to the fingers of the statue, there was an image of the crescent Moon on one side and, on the other side of the tablet, another circle, looking towards the birds below. These make five images in all: the two birds and the circle below, and the image of the Moon and another circle above. In the other half, on the top of the tablet towards the fingers of the statue, there was an image of the Sun emitting two rays, like an image of two in one; and on the other side, an image of the Sun with one ray coming down. These make three images altogether. The ray of the two in one and the ray of the one, as they descended, reaching the bottom of the tablet, surrounded a black sphere divided into two-thirds and a third. The third had the form of the crescent Moon, for [this] lower part was white without [any] blackness ... These make five images [in this half] too, and altogether there are ten images, which match the number of those eagles and of the black earth.

(trans. Ronca 1995: 17–20)

## Conclusion

With this vivid evocation of the crypt of an Egyptian temple covered with mysterious symbols, it is appropriate to end this survey. We have seen how the medieval west received different images of Ancient Egypt, depending to a large extent on the status and profession of the recipient. For the common people the predominant image of Egypt would have been as the antithesis of Israel and the epitome of idol-worship. For the scholar educated in classical literature, it was a land of myths and exotic gods, that provided a rich fund of metaphors. For the doctor, it was the source of medicines – including the *mummia* from preserved corpses (Camille 1999; El Daly 2000) – and the land of Cleopatra, whose beauty had qualified her to write on women's cosmetics. For the philosopher and theologian, it was the home of Hermes Trismegistus, who, although a pagan, had a profound understanding of the nature of gods and men (Dronke 1990; Porreca 2001). For the astronomer, Egypt, because of its clear skies and favourable climate, was the cradle of the science of the stars, and nourished its most eminent proponent, Ptolemy. For the magician and alchemist, it was a land of wonders, and the fount and conduit of ancient wisdom. Most of these images were based on classical, biblical and Arabic sources, and first-hand experience of Egypt and its monuments had, to all appearances, little effect. In this respect the period of the Middle Ages in the west could be said to differ not only from the periods that preceded and followed, but also from the contemporary Arabic situation. Nevertheless, the images of Ancient Egypt formed a significant part of western medieval culture, and deserve to be taken into account.

## Notes

1    Note on references: classical and patristic works are quoted from the standard editions (most of the relevant quotations are conveniently provided in Hopfner 1922–1925). Medieval works are listed under the names of their editors where modern critical editions exist; they are quoted under their author when early printed editions or manuscripts are used. Translations of classical, patristic and medieval works are listed under the translator.

2    Similarly, the statement in *Picatrix* "three wisemen of India from Egypt" (*Picatrix* IV.7.23; Pingree 1986: 210) would not have been thought incongruous, nor perhaps would that of

Burchard of Strasbourg, who personally visited Egypt (see below): that the Nile and the Euphrates were the same river (Cannuyer 1984b: 14).

3   In reality Memphis was the northern capital (the capital of Lower Egypt) which only declined when the Arabs conquered Egypt (641 AD) and set up a new capital at Fusṭāṭ 10 miles to the north and on the opposite bank of the Nile. Fusṭāṭ itself was adjacent to the Greek-Coptic town of Babylon (Latin: 'Babylonia'; Arabic 'Bābalyūn'). This 'double-city' was called 'Old Cairo' after the establishment of 'miṣr al-qāhira' (Cairo: the 'conquering city') a little further north on the left bank by the Fatimids in 970. The word 'miṣr' itself could either refer to the administrative centre (as a generic term meaning 'capital town of a conquered province') or the whole country of Egypt. Yet further north, Heliopolis, the city of Imhotep and of the phoenix, was also sometimes included in this conglomeration of cities called 'Babylon'. Thus, in the numerous surviving commercial treatises between European states and Egypt, the letters sent to the Egyptian sultan are always addressed to the "Sultan of Babylon" (Amari 1863).

4   This is the well of Siene (Aswan) in which the Sun was said to shine directly, without a shadow, at midday at the summer solstice (Pliny *Historia naturalis* II.183–186; Gratwick 1995).

5   Although the third and fourth Crusades also included expeditions into Lower Egypt, the Crusaders themselves do not appear to have left records of ancient Egyptian monuments. Typical perhaps is William, Archbishop of Tyre, who, when describing in detail the Egyptian campaigns of Amaury I, king of Jerusalem (1163–1174) in his *Chronicon*, although he devotes a whole chapter to the description of Egypt (XIX.24), and another to Alexandria (XIX.27), mentions no ancient monument, but concentrates on the natural features and the economic state of the country, especially the effects of the flooding of the Nile and the cosmopolitan nature of Alexandria (Huygens 1986: 896–898, 902–903).

6   Frederick II, having been brought up in Sicily, spoke Arabic and was renowned for his curiosity, his disregard for ecclesiastical authority, and his inquisitiveness about Islam and the learning that could be found in Islamic countries. He corresponded with the Ayyubid Sultans in Cairo, al-Malik al-Kāmil and his two successors, al-Malik al-ʿĀdil and al-Malik al-Ṣāliḥ, concerning philosophical and mathematical problems, and brought Egyptian experts to his court (Frederick II *De Venatione cum Avibus* I.106). One such was an Egyptian expert on ostriches whom Frederick summoned to Apuleia (Paulus and Van den Abeele 2000: 113). In 1226/7, in the run-up to his campaign in the Holy Land (the infamous Fifth Crusade), he sent Thomas of Acerra, his *bailli* in Syria, as an envoy to al-Malik al-Kāmil.

7   The text has been edited in Grotefend 1855 and Deluz 1972. A new edition has been promised by Scott D. Westrem. A summary of the Egyptian chapter can be found in Higgins 1997: 96–100. The section on the pyramids of Giza has been edited, translated and discussed in Graefe 1984, 1990.

8   Note that balm is singled out as specific to Egypt also in the magical text *Picatrix* IV.7.53: "Some places have different properties, namely of trees and animals specific [to them] and hardly found elsewhere, as one can see in the balm which is found only in Egypt" (Pingree 1986: 216).

9   "Among men of yore noblemen were buried either under high mountains or inside the mountains themselves: hence the custom arose of raising above the dead pyramids or huge columns (i.e. obelisks)."

10  "Pyramids of 300 feet built from stones, of which the largest (for there are three) occupies almost four *iugera* of earth, where it stands, and is as high as it is broad."

11  "Among the seven wonders … are the pyramids in Egypt, whose shadow, falling on its own surface, cannot be seen anywhere outside their structure." From Bede onwards the pyramids are no longer included amongst the seven wonders of the world (Cannuyer 1984b: 680; Omont 1882).

12  Origen had already picked out these subjects as particularly prominent among the Egyptians: see his comm. on *Epist. Pauli ad Romanos* II.13: "[He who] studied geometry or astronomy, which were especially pursued amongst them (the Egyptians) … [or] investigated the secrets of astrology and nativities, which they thought were the most divine [subjects] of all …" The Egyptian origins of astronomy will be dealt with later.

13  For example, Ptolemy 1519a: 20v: "I will mention the result of an experiment that I have seen in a place which is called 'the eye of the Sun' ["the well of Aswan": the translator confuses two meanings of '*ayn* = 'eye' and 'well'], because in a brief time I saw great wonders."

14  There was no Arabic scholar in Egypt who could boast, as did Kamāl al-Dīn ibn Yūsuf (1156–1242) in Mosul, that Jews and Christians came to hear his interpretations of the

Torah and the Gospels, and who included among his pupils Frederick II's 'philosopher' and translator of texts from Arabic into Latin, Theodore of Antioch (Suter 1922: 1–7).

15    For example, Pseudo-Apuleius, the most popular herbal in the Middle Ages, includes the 'Egyptian' equivalents *asaer (plantago), asufi (quinquefolium), pempemthar (verbenaca), safitho (simfoniaca;* from Dioscorides), *senecon (scelerata), aneses (monoclonos), nym (artemisia tagantes;* from Dioscorides), *eminion (dracontea),* and many others.

16    Jasnow (1997) considered on philological grounds that the Nectanebo episodes could have been translated from demotic, and Kim Ryholt (1998, 2002) has recently identified four fragmentary versions of Nectanebo's dream in demotic. The astrological aspects of the story of Nectanebo are explored in Boll (1950: 344–347, 351–356).

17    J$^1$ gives *'dominus'* ('Lord'), but Leo, J$^2$ and J$^3$ give *'deum'*: Serapis only achieved this position *after* the establishment of the Ptolemies. Leo, and the Greek original, give the more plausible reading *'Hephaestus'*.

18    It is clear from the Greek text that Leo had misinterpreted *'dekanous'* (*'decans'*) as *'deka nous'* ('10 intelligences'), and thus medieval readers could not recognize the distinctively Egyptian astrological division of the *decans* here (see below). J$^1$, J$^2$ and J$^3$ change '10' to '12' intelligences.

19    That is, the signs of the zodiac; again a misleading translation of *'zodia'* (the 'animal [signs]') as 'animals'.

20    Here a fancy version of the apparatus for casting a horoscope is being described. Normally the positions of the stars would be drawn on a symbolic map of the heavens, but here stones representing the planets are to be placed on a tablet.

21    The identity of *Asclepius'* 'demons' with *'spiritus'* is implicit in a note to *Asclepius* 23 in the 12th/13th century MS Copenhagen, Kongelige Bibliothek, Fabricius 91 4°, where *'spiritus'* and *'demones'* are used interchangeably (Porreca 2001: 245–246).

22    Cf. Michael Scot, *Liber Introductorius*, MS Munich, Bayerische Staatsbibliothek, Clm. 10268, fols. 70v–71r gives the different reckonings of time according to various different nations, and brackets 'Egyptians' and 'Arabs' together.

23    That *'Medi'* is a misinterpretation of *'miṣrīyīn'* ('Egyptian') is clear from the fact that the original Arabic is written in transliteration in the margin of the Sloane manuscript on fol. 83r: *'ale elmeizrin'*. But Adelard may be deliberately substituting a similar-sounding biblical and classical term for the Arabic word. See below.

24    An anonymous late 12th century commentary on this passage explains that "It is clear that the Egyptians have demonstrated the greatest effects of the operation [of the stars], since in all [their] books they have joined the science of medicine to the science of prediction, because they realized that they would be like this. But they joined them together at the same time so that they might make incantations and medicines for destroying present and future, general and particular impediments that occur in the surrounded body (i.e. the air), since they thought that what was destined to come about, could not be changed unless it was turned around [by magic]" (MS Vatican, Lat. reg. 1285, fol. 105r).

25    The same late 12th century commentary observes: "Note that certain very ancient magicians and scholars placed terms in certain horoscopes that they had not found by any process of reasoning, but only by experience and by the nature of the planets in those terms. For when they observed Jupiter in the first six degrees of Aries, they saw that it was stronger than in its (Aries') other degrees, and the same for the rest. From these horoscopes the Egyptians accepted these terms, and this is what he (the author) says" (MS Vatican, Lat. reg. 1285, fol. 110v).

26    However, in a chorography added to this work in two Arabic manuscripts, and present in the Latin translation, Egypt, being the third of the seven climes of the northern hemisphere, is assigned to Mars, with Aries and Scorpio (Burnett and Yamamoto 2000, II: 515).

27    "The fourth [Hermes] is the son of the Nile, whom the Egyptians hold that it is blasphemy to name; the fifth is the one whom the Pheneatae in Arcadia worship, who is said to have killed Argus, and for this reason to have fled to Egypt and taught the Egyptians their laws and script. This Hermes the Egyptians call 'Theuth' ('Thoth'), and the first month of the year is called by the same name amongst them" (Cicero *De Natura Deorum* III.56. For the Egyptian months, see above. Servius comm. in *Aeneid* IV.577 lists four Hermes, omitting Cicero's fourth one).

28    This could be Hermes, *'al-kitāb al-makhzūn'* ("the book preserved in a treasury"), included in *'al-kitāb al-Ustuwwaṭas'* in Paris, Bibliothèque Nationale de France, ar. 2577, fol. 24r, from which derive several medieval Greek and Latin texts – see Burnett forthcoming. This book prescribes the most appropriate astrological times for doing or avoiding certain activities, including making talismans for various purposes.

29   No complete set of canons (instructions) for astronomical tables is attributed to Hermes,
     though the presence of 'Egyptian years' might have implied to medieval scholars that such
     canons were written by an Egyptian. Compare Petrus Alfonsi's statement at the end of his
     preface to his translation of the canons to al-Khwārizmī's tables: that he "translated the
     text from Arabic, Persian and Egyptian [sources]" (Burnett 1997: 66–67).

30   The stories in this and the previous quotation can also be found, with more details, in al-
     Maqrīzī (Wiet 1911, I: 145 and 225) and al-Masʿūdī (Carra de Vaux 1898: 169; the second
     story only).

31   Cf. the description of the 'kitāb al-Ustuwwaṭās' as the "book of the activation of spirits by
     Hermes … which Alexander demanded from Aristotle the Wise when he had completed
     the 'kitāb al-Iṣtamāṭīs', which he had composed for Alexander to take on his journey to
     Persia" (MS Paris, Bibliothèque Nationale de France, ar. 2577, fol. 38r).

32   It is a curious coincidence that Abū Maʿshar is reported by Ibn al-Nadīm (Dodge 1970: 657)
     as having died in 'al-Wāsiṭ', which is both a city in central Iraq and the ancient Egyptian
     name for Thebes: Waset (David 1993: 79).

33   The Latin translator adds a gloss to the transliteration of the Arabic loan-word from Coptic
     'barbā'/'birbā', which means both an Egyptian temple and an underground dwelling.

34   Once again the Latin translator adds a gloss – this time to a phrase in the Arabic which he
     clearly did not understand: "entered Būsīr, Joseph's prison, known as Sidr Būsīr, which the
     professional treasure-hunters ('muṭālibīyūn') opened up for us."

## Acknowledgments

I am grateful for the help of Okasha El Daly, David Juste, Christopher Ligota, Zur Shalev, Kevin van Bladel and David Wengrow.

# CHAPTER 5

# THE RENAISSANCE AFTERLIFE OF ANCIENT EGYPT (1400–1650)

*Brian A. Curran*

Herodotus, that most ancient historian, who had searched many lands and seen, heard and read of many things, writes that the Egyptians had been the most ancient people of which there was memory, and that they were solemn observers of their religion if anyone was, and that they adored and recognized their idolatrous gods under the various figures of strange and diverse animals, and that these were fashioned in gold and silver and other metals, and in precious stones and almost every material that was able to receive form. And some of these images have been preserved up until our own day, having been very much seen as manifest signs of these very powerful and fluent people, and of their very rich kings, and further from a proper desire to prolong the memory of them for infinite centuries, and further than this the memory of their marvellous intelligence and singular industry and profound science of divine things, as well as human ... Following these people, I myself can inform you that the art of good drawing and of colouring, and of sculpture and of representation in whatever manner, and in every manner of form, was held in great esteem [by them]. As for architecture, it should not be doubted that they were great masters, as is still seen in the pyramids and other stupendous edifices of their art that survive and will continue to last, as I myself believe, for infinite centuries.

(Adriani in Vasari 1568)

By any system of reckoning, the renewal of scholarly and cultural interest in Ancient Egypt and the recognition of Rome's Egyptian monuments as pharaonic imports 'in exile' (Iversen 1968) should be numbered among the most significant accomplishments of the European Renaissance. But, although intellectual historians have long acknowledged the importance of the 'hermetic' revival for the development of Early Modern philosophy and science, the broader significance of the Renaissance reception of Ancient Egypt is still incompletely understood. The reasons for this are complex, but perhaps the principal problem is the fact that, from the point of view of modern Egyptian studies at least, the self-proclaimed Egyptologists of the 'long' Renaissance (from Annius of Viterbo in the 15th century to Athanasius Kircher in the 17th) seem to have got it all so 'wrong'. In the case of these relatively well-known but controversial figures, who claimed to be able to read, and published now-discredited 'translations' of, hieroglyphic texts, there is the added suspicion that each, in his own way, was engaged in a monumental project of scholarly deception, for which the antiquity and obscurity of Egyptian civilization provided a kind of historiographical shield. For Annius, the Egyptians provided a useful foil for his argument that his ancestors, the Etruscans, were the most ancient (and divinely sanctioned) peoples of Europe, and that their descendants, the Romans and the modern Italians, were therefore entitled to inherit their mantle of sacred kingship. For Kircher, the hieroglyphs and secret doctrines of the Egyptians provided irrefutable evidence for the fundamental unity of human culture and its origins, at the beginning of time, in the revelation of the Christian God. This unity, in turn, provided historical support for the Jesuit argument that all peoples should be united in the common culture of Roman Catholicism.

Of course, 'knowledge', even when wedded to the most honourable and disinterested of intentions, is never entirely innocent, and historical writing and research must always be understood against the backdrop of ideology and culture. In the case of Annius and Kircher, what unites their apparently dubious but otherwise divergent researches to the stream of early modern 'Egyptology' as a whole is an underlying presumption that the European, Christian culture of their day could stake its claim to historical legitimacy, in part, on its inheritance of the 'legacy' of Egypt. This notion, that Ancient Egypt somehow stands at a point of origin for 'western' civilization, has its roots in biblical and classical tradition (Tait Chapter 2, this volume), and has persisted, in various forms, to the present day. Indeed, the debate over 'Who owns Egypt?' is as charged today as it ever was, as the bitter debate over Bernal's *Black Athena* amply demonstrates (see Berlinerblau 1999; Bernal 1987, 1991, 2001b, 2003; Lefkowitz and Rogers 1996; MacDonald 2003). In this chapter, I summarize some of the main currents and illuminate some of the most fascinating corners in this incompletely understood phase in the 'Mnemohistory', to use Assmann's (1997) term, of Ancient Egypt.

Before examining the Renaissance 'afterlife' of Ancient Egypt in depth, it must be acknowledged that, while the period made significant and lasting contributions to western conceptions of Ancient Egypt, the memory of Egyptian civilization and its achievements had never really been lost. The preceding chapters in this book provide a glimpse of the richness and diversity of the sources that were available to Renaissance students of Egypt. As the acknowledged ancestor and progenitor of so many ancient arts, and the site of countless events in the sacred and secular histories of antiquity, the Egypt of the pharaohs retained its grip on the imagination of Christians, Jews and Muslims alike. Egypt was a land of the Bible and of Christian conversion and conflict, and as such, figured prominently in the apologetic writings of the Church Fathers (Lactantius, Augustine) and other late antique and early medieval sources (Macrobius, Isidore of Seville). At the same time, Egypt also survived as a real country that played a central role in the political and economic life of the Mediterranean world, and was visited by generations of pilgrims, merchants, soldiers and other travellers from Europe, Africa and the Muslim east. For these visitors, the obelisk of Heliopolis/Alexandria (which now stands neglected in New York's Central Park – Hassan 2003: Figure 2:6), the pyramids of Giza and Saqqarah, and, for a select few, the great temples in the remote regions of Luxor and Karnak provided indisputable evidence for the power and magnificence of their builders (Dannenfeldt 1959; El Daly 2003: 139–140, 144; Greener 1967: 34–57; Guérin-Dalle Mese 1991; Lumbroso 1879).

As the Florentine academician Giovanni Battista Adriani acknowledges in the quote at the beginning of this chapter, Europeans were well-acquainted with the pyramids and other Egyptian monuments that survived in the home country. Their sources ranged from ancient descriptions (by Herodotus, Pliny the Elder and others) to modern travel accounts. The old 'pilgrim's' identification of the pyramids of Giza as the 'Granaries of Joseph' (see Burnett Chapter 4, this volume) had gone out of vogue by the early 15th century, and virtually all Renaissance commentary on the subject explains the monuments as tombs. Some accounts are more expansive than others, of course. In 1483, the Dominican friar Felix Fabri of Ulm made a pilgrimage to Egypt and the Holy Land that included a stop to see the "admirable pyramids" of Giza (Masson 1975; Murray 1956; Prescott 1950). His account includes an early description of the interior passages of the pyramids, and he also mentions the Great Sphinx, described as an "immense idol of stone which had the shape of a woman" (he presumes it had been dedicated to Isis – Masson, 1975: 448–457). The first reasonably 'accurate' printed description (and illustration) of the Great Pyramid (Figure 5:1) to receive wide circulation appeared in Sebastiano Serlio's 16th century text and is drawn from the eye-witness account of Cardinal Marco Grimani of Venice, who visited Egypt ca. 1535–1536, and took the opportunity to measure, climb and explore the interior of the pyramid. Grimani's measurement of the pyramid's base (in *varchi* or 'paces' equivalent to three *palmi*) determined that it formed a perfect square, "built entirely of tough live stone" and rising in "about two hundred and ten" steps of about three and a half *palmi*, making it very difficult to climb up to the flat plane on the summit, which led him to conclude that the pyramid "was not pointed" as originally constructed (Serlio 1540). The interior is described as containing a stone "staircase" rising gradually to a chamber containing the stone sarcophagus (Hart and Hicks 1996: 184, 442).

Renaissance descriptions of Egypt's southern monuments are much harder to come by. During the 1520s, the Muslim historian Al-Hassan Ibn Mohammed Al-Wazan, Al Fâsi (ca. 1491–ca. 1552), who had been captured by Christian pirates and 'presented' to Pope Leo X in 1520, began writing a history and description of Africa under his assumed name of Leo Africanus. The resulting text, published in 1550, included a short description of Egypt from Alexandria to Aswan, with passing reference to the ancient building and "towers" that could be seen in the southern territories (in Ramusio 1978: 390–429). Even more evocative is the account of an anonymous Venetian traveller of ca. 1589, whose impressions of Karnak, Luxor and Philae may be the earliest eyewitness accounts of these sites by a European traveller of the early modern period (Burri and Sergeron 1971: 7–153). Standing before the great pylon of the Temple of Amun-Ra at Luxor, he compared its great obelisks to the ones he had seen in Rome and Alexandria. Partaking of the acquisitive spirit of his Roman forebears, and anticipating the activities of European plunders to come, he expressed his admiration in acquisitive terms:

> And there is not the equal of these obelisks [*aguglie*] either in Rome, or in Alexandria, or in the whole of Egypt. Those in Rome and Alexandria I have seen and re-seen and measured; these two exceed all the others in size; and they are perfect, and they stand together, where the rare beauty of a variegated granite very pleasing to the eye can be seen, and there are an infinite number of signs, more than I have ever seen, and carved so clearly that they seem to be new, so that my words are incapable of describing their

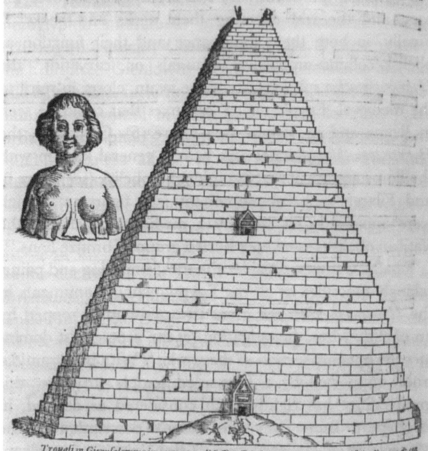

andare. Nella sommità di questa ui è un bel piano di circa otto varchi per ogni quadro, doue si conosce questo essere il piano che fu fatto nel tempo che fu finita la piramide, & che non era mai stata, laquale è ancora tutta intera, eccetto che qualche pietra è uscita a alquanto del suo luogo. Poco discosto dalla piramide è una testa di pietra viua con parte del busto, tutta d'un pezzo, & solamente la faccia sua è da dieci varchi, laqual figura è di brutto aspetto, & dispiaceuole in vista, & in questa ci sono alcune grotte con lettere Egittie, per lequali si comprende che fussero sepolture.

Trouasi in Gierusalemme in vn monte di sasso assai sodo, incauato per artificio di mano & con ferri, vn'edificio di buona grandezza, nel modo che quì sotto è disegnato: & accioche per la grandezza della stanza di mezo ella non hauesse a rouinare; gli furono lasciati quei due pilastri maggiori nel mezo, & quei due mezani dalle bande, & i due minori dinanzi, iquali pilastri tengono vna volta (come ho detto) fatta per forza di scarpello così grossamente. Nella prima entrata ci sono quattro capellette. Nella parte di mezo ci sono diciotto capellette. Nell'altra parte più interiore ci sono due capellette, & vna porta chiusa: laqual dinota che si andaua più innanzi, & queste capellette erano luoghi, doue si sepellinano i Re di Gierusalemme, per quanto mi disse il Patriarca di Aquileia a quel tempo, & hora Cardinale, ilquale di questa cosa mi dette notitia, & si disegna

Figure 5:1    The Great Pyramid and Sphinx of Giza as described by Cardinal Marco Grimani in ca. 1535–1536 (Serlio 1540; Marquand Library, Princeton University, SAPX N2510. S49q).

beauty. Oh what a rare thing it would be to see them placed in a superb piazza such as the one in Venice, which is without equal in all the world, and to see such monuments as these. Countless numbers of people would flock there to see these trophies installed there.

(trans. based on Burri and Sergeron 1971: 90–91; Donadoni *et al.* 1990: 60)

By the time of the Anonymous Venetian's journey, the vogue for obelisks had reached a new peak in the Rome of Pope Sixtus V (Hassan 2003). It is worth noting that in virtually all Renaissance and Early Modern accounts of the antiquities of Egypt, reference is made to comparable monuments that the author had seen in Rome (Humbert 2003: 326). These are the marvels of Egyptian art that Adriani alludes to having "seen for himself" in the opening quote, above, and it is to the fortunes of these Roman Egyptian monuments that much of this chapter is devoted. For the inescapable fact remains that, for the entire span of the Renaissance or Early Modern period, and despite the ongoing and, toward the end of the period, increasing engagement with the Egyptian antiquities in Egypt, the laboratory of Egyptian studies was to be found in Rome.

As Adriani knew, the obelisks, statues and other Egyptian artefacts that he had seen in the Eternal City had been brought to Rome in antiquity as trophies of Augustus' conquest of Egypt or as tokens of devotion to the popular cults of the Egyptian gods. In the centuries of decline that followed the dissolution of the Western Empire, the majority of these monuments had fallen into the dust of the crumbling city. But a few, including some of the obelisks and some statuary groups of lions and sphinxes, had survived above ground. By Adriani's time, many others had been 'rediscovered' as a result of unsystematic excavations in the 15th and 16th centuries. The obelisks and other monuments that survived into the Middle Ages continued to attract the admiration of pilgrims and other spectators, but the memory of their Egyptian origins was, for the most part, lost. Authors of guidebooks like the 12th century *Mirabilia Urbis Romae* (Nichols 1889) praised the obelisks and pyramids as marvels of the ancient Romans, and identified them as tombs and memorials of great figures from Roman history. The obelisk of the Vatican, imported from Egypt by Caligula and raised on the *spina* of his Vatican *circus*, became widely known as the sepulchre of Julius Caesar, and was venerated by pilgrims as "St Peter's Needle" because of its presumed association with the Apostle's martyrdom (Curran and Grafton 1995; Hassan 2003: Figure 2:22). The Roman pyramids of the Vatican and the Porta Ostiense, built by Roman notables in imitation of the sepulchres of Egyptian kings, were identified as the tombs of Rome's mythical founders, Romulus and Remus, and, in some cases, as the monuments of more historical figures like Augustus and Scipio Africanus (Neuerburg 1969; Peebles 1936).

By the early 15th century, however, Italian humanists had begun to study the monuments of Rome from a more exacting and historical perspective. The ruins, while still admired as marvels of ancient technology, came to be considered as a kind of text, whose proper 'reading' could provide evidence for the history, institutions, and lost knowledge of the ancients. The humanists, who were specialists in the study of language, were particularly drawn to the study of inscriptions, which were, after all, the only original, 'authentic' texts that survived from antiquity. At the same time, the humanists and their agents scoured the libraries of the accessible world, east and west, for manuscripts of the ancient authors. From the turn of the 15th century to the end of the decade, a growing corpus of ancient texts was collected, copied, 'corrected' and circulated among the humanists and their noble patrons. These included the works of the Latin authors Apuleius, Pliny the Elder and Ammianus Marcellinus, and the Greeks Herodotus, Diodorus Siculus, Plutarch and Strabo, to name just some of the more important sources of Egyptian lore. From about 1460 onward, these texts also began to appear in printed and, in the case of Greek authors, translated editions (Pope 1999: 20). Collections of inscriptions were assembled, and these too began to circulate and, eventually, came to print as well. In this way, through fits and starts, the modern 'science' of archaeology was born, although it would be centuries before the techniques of systematic excavation would be added to the mix. The point of all this determined activity, according to the intrepid Renaissance inscription-hunter Cyriacus of Ancona (ca. 1390–1455), was quite simply to bring the ancient world back to life, "to wake the dead" (as he put it) and lead "the glorious things which were alive" in antiquity from the "dark tomb into the light, to live once more among living men" (Cyriacus of Ancona 1742: 54–55; trans. Mitchell 1960: 470).

Karl Giehlow (1915: 12–40), founder of the modern study of Renaissance Egyptology, has traced the origins of this emerging 'discipline' to an elite circle of mostly Florentine humanists in the early 15th century. The key figures of this 'movement' were the Florentine humanists Niccolò Niccoli (1364–1437) and Poggio Bracciolini (hereafter, Poggio 1380–1459); the aforementioned merchant and epigrapher Cyriacus of Ancona; the historian Flavio Biondo of Forlì (1392–1463); and the author, architect and polymath Leon Battista Alberti (1404–1472). All were avid students of ancient literature and all were well acquainted with the ruins of Rome. Poggio, Biondo and Alberti were employed for a considerable time by the papal curia, and they all either knew each other or were familiar with each other's work (Alberti, the youngest, came to Florence in the last years of Niccoli's life).

The story begins with the discovery of a manuscript of the *Hieroglyphica*, the self-styled "hieroglyphic dictionary" ascribed to one Horapollo "Niliacus", recently identified as a fifth century Alexandrian scholar named Horapollon the Younger, son of Asklepiades (Boas 1950; Fowden 1982; Maspero 1914). The text provided a description and 'translation' of some 189 hieroglyphic images. A number of these have been shown to derive from Egyptian tradition, including the bee as a hieroglyph of kingship. But despite these scattered authenticities, Horapollo's methodology is almost entirely un-Egyptian, and reflects the late antique and 'Hellenized' conception of the hieroglyphs as allegorical image-signs. He also provides no explanation of how these images and meanings could be joined to form sentences or compound thoughts, a reflection, perhaps, of the fading memory of the original system (Boas 1950: 3–29; Brunon 1981; Iversen 1961: 47–49). In any event, the manuscript (now in the Laurentian library, Florence: MS 69.27) was acquired by the Florentine traveller and manuscript hunter Christoforo Buondelmonti on the Island of Andros in 1419 and was presented to Niccoli around 1422 (Giehlow 1915: 12–18; Sider 1986). As Giehlow has shown, the moment was ripe for a favourable reception of this text, which arrived just as Niccoli was completing his study of Ammianus Marcellinus' description of the hieroglyphs and the obelisks that bore them. In due course, Niccoli sent the original copy of the Ammianus manuscript on to Rome, and his friend Poggio presented it in turn to his employer, Pope Martin V. It appears from the surviving correspondence that Niccoli arrived in the Eternal City soon after, to join Poggio on his perambulations among the city's ruins (Giehlow 1915: 16–19). Giehlow has identified the convergence of these persons in Rome at this time, ca. 1422–1424, as the historical moment when the images carved on the obelisks must have been recognized as the "sacred letters" of the Egyptians, and the obelisks as the Egyptian imports described by Ammianus and Pliny the Elder.

Giehlow's thesis is supported by the fact that Poggio was the first post-antique writer to identify – in print – the carvings on the obelisks as the "sacred letters" of the Egyptians. The relevant passage is found in his description of the ruins of Rome, begun in the 1430s and completed in 1448, when it appeared as the opening section of Poggio's magnum opus, *De Varietate Fortunae* ("On the Vicissitudes of Fortune"), which he dedicated to Eugenius' successor Nicholas V (1447–1453; D'Onofrio 1989: 81–82). At about the same time, Flavio Biondo (1443–1446) produced his much more elaborate topographical study, the *Roma Instaurata*, which includes a lengthy discussion of the obelisks and their hieroglyphs. Biondo's text draws extensively (and frequently verbatim) from Ammianus and Pliny, but Tacitus (*Annals* XI.15) is his source for the observation that these Egyptian monuments were nothing less than "the earliest documents of human history ... impressed upon stone" (D'Onofrio 1989: 121–135).

And so these devoted students of ancient Rome 'found' themselves in a landscape seasoned with Egyptian monuments and inscriptions. There is no evidence that they attempted to decipher these enigmatic carvings themselves, a circumstance which inspired Weiss' (1969: 156) remark that (during the Renaissance) "in the field of epigraphy Egyptian hieroglyphs could scarcely have aroused less interest". But this was not entirely the case. We have, for example, the account of Cyriacus of Ancona, who copied an inscription in 'Phoenician letters' (his term for the hieroglyphs) that he found on the summit of the Great Pyramid of Giza in September 1436. Cyriacus reports that he sent a copy of the transcription to Niccoli in Florence, since he was the "man most interested in these things" (Lehmann 1977; Van Essen 1958). Niccoli would have had little time to study them, in any case, since he died a few months later. After that, the trail of the Cyriacan transcription grows cold. But despite these presumed frustrations, the idea of the hieroglyphs proved too attractive to be abandoned entirely, and soon the attention of many Renaissance scholars shifted from the problem of the inscriptions themselves to the 'idea' of the hieroglyphs as described by the ancient authors. A key document for this shift is a famous passage in Leon Battista Alberti's (1485) treatise on architecture (already in progress by 1452 – see Grafton 2000: 266–269; Grayson 1960):

> The Egyptians employed the following sign language: a god was represented by an eye, nature by a vulture, a king by a bee, time by a circle, peace by an ox, and so on. They maintained that each nation knew only its own alphabet, and that eventually all knowledge of it would be lost – as has happened with our own Etruscan: we have seen sepulchres uncovered in city ruins and cemeteries throughout Etruria inscribed with an alphabet universally acknowledged to be Etruscan; their letters look not unlike Greek, or even Latin, yet no one understands what they mean. The same, the Egyptians claimed, would happen to all other alphabets, whereas the method of writing they used could be understood easily by expert men all over the world, to whom alone noble matters should be communicated ... (In turn) our own Latin ancestors chose to express the deeds of their most famous men through sculpted histories. This gave rise

to columns, triumphal arches, and porticoes, covered with histories in painting, or sculpture.

(Alberti 1485, VIII: 4)

There has been considerable debate over Alberti's sources for this passage; his examples (eye, vulture, bee, etc.) suggest a familiarity with Diodorus and Horapollo, and while his broader interpretation of the hieroglyphs as a kind of universal language of images is more original, it conforms in a general sense to the explanations proffered by his sources. For, with virtual unanimity, the ancient writers described the hieroglyphs as a system of allegorical image-signs whose meanings were rooted in a knowledge of the essential meaning and character of the things depicted. In antiquity, knowledge of the system was reportedly restricted to the Egyptian priests and other members of the elite, who alone possessed the 'secret' knowledge required for understanding the signs (Van der Horst 1982). But since the Egyptian image-signs were non-linguistic, it was at least theoretically possible that they could be understood by the enlightened and educated elites of other cultures (and times). Perhaps it was from this notion that Alberti came to his ultimate conclusion that "Egyptian letters", which stood at the origins of all representational art and monumental writing, held the promise of a universal language of images that could transcend the limitations of speech-derived script and communicate to learned men of any culture or age. The fact that the very same signs could not be understood by the lower classes of the society only strengthened the hieroglyph's appeal for Alberti and his unabashedly elitist cohorts (Finzi 1991).

If the hieroglyphs were good enough for the Egyptians and their Greek and Roman imitators, then they were obviously good enough for Alberti's readers, the noble patrons and princes of the Renaissance. Indeed, as the studies of Giehlow (1915: 138–159), Russell (1986), Volkmann (1923) and Wittkower (1977) have shown, the hieroglyphs provided a useful model for the emblematic inventions of the Renaissance. Alberti took an early step in this direction with his personal 'hieroglyph' of the "winged eye", which he explained as a symbol of the power of vision (see Giehlow 1915: 35–37; Grafton 2000: 105–107; Schneider 1990; Watkins 1960). In broader terms, this general acceptance and 'reclamation', as it were, of the Egyptian tradition also encouraged the 'revival' of monumental Egyptian forms like the obelisk and pyramid for commemorative purposes, and, in some cases, the appropriation and transformation of surviving Egyptian monuments. Alberti was presumably involved, as an expert consultant at least, in one of the earliest and most ambitious of these endeavours, Pope Nicholas V's project to move the Vatican obelisk to the piazza in front of St Peter's (Curran and Grafton 1995; Hassan 2003: 33, Figure 2:22). In this new location, the obelisk was to be reinstalled and transformed, in effect, into a Christian triumphal column. According to the pope's secretary, Gianozzo Manetti, the obelisk would have been held aloft by life-size bronze statues of the Evangelists, with a figure of the risen Christ installed at its summit (Magnuson 1954: 93; Manetti 1734). Drawings of the 1460s show that the base of the obelisk was cleared in possible anticipation of the transfer (Marcanova 1465; for discussion see Curran and Grafton 1995: 237). But the sheer scale of the project must have weighed heavily on the pope's planners (not to mention his treasury), and the plan was abandoned after Nicholas' death. It was reconsidered and abandoned several times thereafter until 1586, when the obelisk was finally moved and re-erected by the unstoppable Sixtus V (see below).

If the hieroglyphs and interest in the obelisks were the major factors in the earliest phase of the Renaissance 'revival', the second phase began with a more direct confrontation with the fabled 'wisdom' of the Egyptians. Once again the catalyst was the fortuitous discovery of a manuscript. In 1460–1462, a Tuscan monk, Leonardo da Pistoia, brought a manuscript containing 14 Greek dialogues attributed to Hermes Trismegistus to Florence. He presented it to his patron, Cosimo de Medici (1389–1464), who immediately ordered a translation from one of his favourite scholars, Marsilio Ficino (1433–1499). At the time, Ficino was immersed in another Medici-sponsored project, a Latin translation of the collected works of Plato, but Cosimo insisted that he give priority to the "older" Egyptian's work. The translations were finished and presented to Cosimo in April 1463, and were printed for the first time in 1471 (Allen 1990; Ficino 1576: 1836–1868; Yates 1964: 1–83). The notion that the Egyptian Hermes had anticipated key aspects of Christian doctrine, including the decline of paganism and the advent of the "son of God", was firmly established in the scholastic tradition in which Ficino had been trained. Hermes' prophetic doctrines had been acknowledged by such Christian authorities as Lactantius and Augustine, and the Latin version of one of the most "prophetic" hermetic dialogues, the *Asclepius*, was already well known in the west. In his influential commentaries, published along with the translation, Ficino described Hermes as a pagan contemporary of Moses and the first among the ancient philosophers to turn from practical matters to "the contemplation of divine things":

> He foresaw the ruin of the antique religion, the rise of the new faith, the coming of Christ, the judgment to come, the resurrection of the world, the glory of the blessed and the torments of the damned. For this reason, Aurelius Augustinus doubted whether he accomplished many things by skill in astrology or by revelation from daemons. Lactantius, however, does not hesitate to number him among the Sibyls and Prophets.

(trans. adapted from Copenhaver 1992: xlviii)

It is in this prophetic capacity that Hermes was granted a place of honour on the 1488 mosaic pavement of the Duomo of Siena (Figure 5:2). He appears in the centre of the nave, just inside the main (royal) portal, at the head of a cycle of the pagan Sibyls. The robed and bearded sage, who wears a tall, pointed hat appropriate to his priestly status, is identified by inscription as *Hermis Mercurius Trismegistus contemporaneus Moysi*. He hands a book, inscribed *Suscipite o licteras et leges Egiptii* (Take up Laws and Letters, O Egyptians), to a pair of men (one of whom wears an "eastern" turban, the other a priestly hood). His other hand rests upon a tablet with an abbreviated rendition of the passage from the *Asclepius* that Lactantius (and Ficino) had identified as a prophecy of Christ (Iversen 1961: 42–43; Yates 1964: 42–43). An "Egyptianizing" touch is provided by the pair of (Greek-looking) sphinxes with their tails intertwined. These creatures may have been included as little more than appropriately antiquarian ornament. But it is possible that they were intended to allude to an ancient thesis – rooted in the *De Iside et Osiride* of Plutarch, that the Egyptians had invented the sphinx as a symbol of their secret doctrines. As Ficino's younger colleague, Giovanni Pico della Mirandola (1463–1494), put it at about this time:

> It was the opinion of the ancient theologians that one should not rashly make public the secret mysteries of theology, except insofar as it was permitted to do so from above ... and it was for this reason that the Egyptians had Sphinxes sculptured in all their

Figure 5:2   Hermes Trismegistus on the mosaic pavement (1488) of the cathedral of Siena, Italy (Opera della metropolitana di Siene Aut. n. 9943; © Alinari/Art Resource).

temples, to show that divine things should be concealed under enigmatic veils and poetic dissimulation.

(trans. Sears 1985: 169–170)

In his later work, Ficino continued to develop the themes of the "ancient theology" and its Egyptian roots. He produced translations and commentaries on the works of the Neoplatonists, and promoted an explanation of the hieroglyphs as "Platonic" images, whose meanings were drawn from the essential meaning of the things represented:

The Egyptians imitated the very nature of the universe and the work of the gods; they also showed the images of the mystic and hidden notions in the form of symbols, in the same way in which nature too expresses occult causes in apparent forms or in symbols, as it were, and the gods explain the truth of the ideas of manifest images.

(trans. Dieckmann 1970: 36)

By the 1490s, the exalted status of the Egyptians as founders of the arts and sciences and possessors of a *prisca theologia* had set the stage for an outbreak of 'Egyptomania' in the visual arts. This trend is exemplified by Pinturicchio's frescoes of the myth of Isis, Osiris and Apis, which cover the vaults of the central audience room in the apartment of the Borgia pope, Alexander VI (1492–1495); and by the hieroglyph-covered, obelisk-sprouting monuments of the *Hypnerotomachia Poliphili*, published in Venice in 1499 (Colonna 1999). The virtually simultaneous appearance of these works has prompted some scholars to link them to a common Egyptianizing culture in the Rome of the 1490s (Calvesi 1980, 1996). In the case of the Borgia frescoes, this connection is clear, since its imagery owes an evident debt to the historical forgeries of Annius of Viterbo, who apparently provided his patron with an Egyptianizing genealogy that paradoxically furthered the Borgia's claim to legitimacy in Italy (Curran 2000; Mattiangeli 1981; Parks 1979; Saxl 1957). As for the *Hypnerotomachia*, while it is evident that its elusive author and illustrator had access to drawings and descriptions of monuments in Rome, the work is best understood in traditional terms as the work of a Venetian friar whose approach to Egyptian matters was rooted in the local tradition of close trade and cultural ties to Egypt and the east (Curran 1998).

As the likely *ispiratore* of Pinturicchio's frescoes (the first large-scale cycle of Egyptian mythological imagery to appear since antiquity), not to mention his claim to be the first post-antique author to publish a 'translation' of a supposedly antique hieroglyphic inscription, the Dominican friar Giovanni Nanni, better known as Annius of Viterbo (ca. 1432–1502), would seem to merit an honoured place among the 'founders' of Egyptology. The fact that he was an unscrupulous forger, a manufacturer of false antiquities, and, according to at least one early source (Rowland 2000), experienced fits of madness and died in a straightjacket made of chains, has perhaps limited his appeal as a forerunner. Indeed, any attempt to evaluate Annius as a 'scholar' in the modern sense would be futile, although it has been noted that his effort to translate Etruscan inscriptions of the type that had frustrated Alberti met with unexpected success. But the fact remains that Annius' 'researches', his forgeries, indeed his entire enterprise was slanted to a pre-determined, political end: to provide historical and archaeological 'proof' for his thesis that the origins of European civilization could be traced to an enlightened kingdom, established in his home town of Viterbo in the period after the Great Flood by no less a figure than Noah himself.

To this end, Annius laboured for years on the forgery of a collection of supposedly ancient texts, which he published under the privilege of Pope Alexander in 1498 as the *Commentaria Fratris Ioannis Annii Viterbensis ordinis praedicator, theologiae professoris super opera diversorum auctorum de Antiquitatibus loquentorum*, "Commentaries on works of various authors discussing antiquities", better known as the *Antiquitates*. Among these texts, which Annius claimed to have obtained – in conveniently 'translated' form – from an Armenian monk in Genoa, were portions of the lost histories of Berosus of Chaldea and Manetho the Egyptian (Italian translation Lauro 1550 – for a list of editions

Stephens 1989: 344–345, App. II). Annius emulated Ficino and the other humanist editors of his time by providing a full commentary for each of his 'rediscovered' texts. The end result is a bewildering conglomeration of falsified text and references to 'authentic' sources such as Diodorus and Pliny.

The main thrust of Annius' narrative was that Noah, whom Annius (following an established medieval tradition) identified with the Etruscan founder-god, Janus, retired to Italy after dividing the kingdoms of the world among his sons. Settling on the site of Annius' native Viterbo, he founded an enlightened kingdom based on the true religion imparted to him by God. Among the most distinguished of Noah's descendants was the Egyptian king Osiris, also known as Apis, whom Annius identified as a son of Noah's least favourite offspring, Cham. In the sixth century after the Flood, Osiris was called to Italy, where the colonies established by his grandfather had been overrun by a race of cannibalistic giants. Osiris campaigned against the giants with the help of his son, Hercules the Egyptian (called Libyus or Aegyptius). Victorious, Osiris ruled in Viterbo for 10 years, re-establishing the rule of law and re-educating the people in the agricultural and other 'peaceful' arts. He then returned to Egypt, where he was killed and dismembered by his jealous brother Typhon. Hercules and his mother Isis reassembled and buried the body of the fallen king, then began another war against Typhon and his allies (another gang of evil giants). Hercules' campaign brought him to Libya (where he killed the giant Antaeus), to Spain (where he founded the ancient line of Spanish kings) and eventually back to Italy, where he restored the kingdoms of his forefathers.

To his modern readers, Annius' 'history' reads as pure fairytale. But in its overall tone and many details, it conforms to a whole genre of mythological or 'euhemeristic' historiography that has its roots in later classical, hellenistic, and medieval traditions. In particular, he draws many of his characters (the Egyptian and other pagan figures, in particular) from the writings of Josephus and the *Bibliotheca Historica* of Diodorus Siculus, which he cites from Poggio Bracciolini's Latin translation, printed in 1472. It is a brilliant strategy, since it allows Annius to frame his own false text with testimony from the authentic sources. But Annius did not stop there. He also took pains to provide archaeological support for his narrative. These included, among other things, the 'discovery' of a series of ancient tablets, inscribed in Greek and, in one case, medieval Lombardic script, that he had manufactured for the occasion (Collins 2000; Emiliozzi 1986; Weiss 1962).

But the most unexpected of all the Annian 'finds' was the *Columna Osiriana*, a marble tablet that he 'discovered' on the *rostra* or pulpit of the Cathedral of San Lorenzo in Viterbo. The piece, preserved and recently restored in the Museo Civico in Viterbo, is a late medieval palimpsest, combining a 13th century lunette with a relief of a tree with twisting vines, a salamander, and some birds with a pair of somewhat later (early 15th century?) profile-heads (Figure 5:3). But according to Annius, these carvings represent nothing less than a historical document, carved in the "sacred letters of the Egyptians" to commemorate the victory of Osiris and Hercules over the giants during the sixth century post-Diluvium (Emiliozzi 1986: 29–31; Mattiangeli 1981: 297–302; Weiss 1962: 119). Annius proceeds to devote a substantial passage to a description and 'translation' of the piece:

Figure 5:3   The marble 13th–15th century *Columna Osiriana* in the Museo Civico Viterbo, Italy, described by Annius of Viterbo as "Egyptian sacred letters" (© B. Curran).

And Pliny, in his *Natural History* says that these images that you see are Egyptian sacred letters. Therefore, on this column there is a space, in the middle of which is the trunk of an oak tree, resembling a compounded sceptre, the tops of whose branches form the image of an eye. These images are particular to Osiris, as Xenophon affirms. Both he and Macrobius, in the first book of the *Saturnalia*, confirm this, saying that to express Osiris in the sacred letters they carved a sceptre, and they [also] represented him with the image of an eye. And by this sign they showed Osiris. Moreover, they placed on this tree trunk not one but many sceptres, because he ruled not only one, but every part of the world, as Diodorus writes ... Therefore, these ... effigies may be read in this fashion: 'I am Osiris the king, who was called against by the Italians and hastened to fight against the oppressors of the Italian dominion ... I am Osiris, who taught the Italians to plow, to sow, to prune, to cultivate the vine, gather grapes, and make wine, and I left behind for them my two nephews, as guardians of the realm from land and sea.'

(trans. Curran 2000: 172–173)

It is difficult for the modern observer to appreciate how Annius came to identify this curious object as an 'Egyptian' or hieroglyphic monument, let alone how he hoped to convince his contemporaries that he was right. But however improbable they may seem today, Annius' researches were embraced by generations of readers, and enshrined by his fellow Viterbese when the *Columna* and the other Annian 'antiquities' were solemnly installed in the city's public palace. However, by the time he published this 'ground-breaking' translation, the study of hieroglyphs had already begun to shift to a more critical and 'archaeologically precise' level.

An early manifestation of this new approach may be glimpsed on one of the woodcuts in the *Hypnerotomachia Poliphili* of 1499. As has long been noted, most of the hieroglyphic inscriptions that the protagonist stops to translate during the course of his 'antiquarian journey' are entirely Roman and/or contemporary in form. It is only in a single case – the hieroglyphs that appear on the obelisk that pierces the body of a black stone elephant-tomb (Figure 5:4) – that the artist

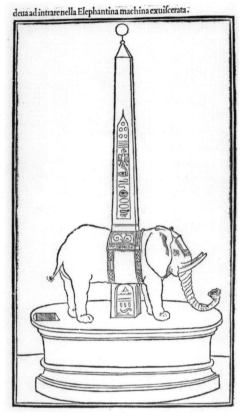

deua ad intrare nella Elephantina machina exuifcerata.

Figure 5:4 Woodcut of elephant and obelisk from the *Hypnerotomachia Poliphili*, Venice, 1499 (fol. b. vii-v Marquand Library of Art and Archaeology, Princeton University).

employed signs derived, however corruptly, from the carvings that could be seen on the obelisks in Rome. In this case, the original model was apparently the broken obelisk of Domitian that lay in the ruins of the Circus of Maxentius near the "Capo di Bove" on the Via Appia. The obelisk is more famous today as the centrepiece of the Piazza Navona, where it was raised in 1652 under the supervision of Athanasius Kircher (Hassan 2003: 47, Figure 2:23; and see below).

But Kircher was not the first to admire and study this broken monument. Its carvings are mentioned admiringly by a number of Renaissance worthies, including Pope Pius II and the sculptor-architect Filarete. And a drawing of the lower part of the monument in the Vatican sketchbook of Giuliano da Sangallo (datable to ca. 1513–1514) provides a glimpse of the sort of model that must have been available to the artist of the *Hypnerotomachia* (Biblioteca Apostolica Vaticano, MS Barberiniano lat. 4424, fol. 70r; cf. Hülsen 1910, I: 72, II: pl. 62r; see Curran 1998: 172–174). Sangallo's is one of the earliest surviving drawings of a hieroglyphic inscription that might be called 'archaeologically accurate' or epigraphic in character. The only earlier specimens may be found in a pair of manuscripts, in Paris and Reggio Emilia respectively, that were compiled by the Carmelite humanist Michele Fabrizio Ferrarini (d. 1492), a self-proclaimed follower of Cyriacus of Ancona. In both cases, the hieroglyphs are copied, not from an obelisk, but from the base of one of a pair of grey granite lions, inscribed for the fourth century BC pharaoh Nectanebo I (Figure 5:5). These lions had been set up in the Piazza della Rotunda in Rome, where they formed a kind of frontispiece for the Pantheon, by the end of the 12th century (they are now in the Cortile della Pigna in the Vatican). In the Paris manuscript (M. Ferrarini, n.d. ca. 1480s, Par. Lat. 6128. fol. CXXXv and CXXXIr) the signs are precisely copied and numbered according to their position on the four faces of the base of the left-side lion. On the Reggio folio (M. Ferrarini, n.d. ca. 1480s, *Antiquarium sive Divae Antiquitatis Sacrarium*, Reggio Emilia, Biblioteca A. Panizzi, MS C 398, fol. XXVv) these same signs are redeployed, carefully and without significant modification, to form a decorative border, in a manner that anticipates (and may even have informed) Giulio Romano's hieroglyphic decorations in the Palazzo del Te, Mantua, ca. 1528 (Curran and Periti forthcoming; Jaeger 1994).

Roughly contemporary with Sangallo's drawing are two remarkable sheets with studies of obelisks, variously attributed to Sangallo's Florentine colleague Simone del Pollaiuolo, called Il Cronaca (1457–1507), and more recently to the Sienese painter-architect Baldassare Peruzzi (1481–1536; Frommel 1991–1992: 174–177). The first sheet (Figure 5:6), now in Bayonne, contains two studies of the Vatican obelisk, along with a careful copy of a hieroglyphic inscription from a small obelisk, now in Munich (Bean 1960: no. 252v (inv. no. 1342v)). The second, in Oxford (Figure 5:7), is more impressive, since it depicts no fewer than four Roman obelisks with remarkably accurate renditions of their hieroglyphic carvings (Shaw 1976: 44–45, cat. no. 41 (inv. no. 0814r)). The artist's intention is clearly archaeological, since each monument is carefully labelled as to location, material and condition. Reading from left to right, the first obelisk is identified as the "*Agulia* di S. Maria in Aracoeli", a small obelisk of Ramesses II that stood at that time on the Capitoline Hill. This obelisk was really only

Figure 5:5   One of a pair of granite lions originally inscribed for King Nectanebo I in the fourth century BC, and relocated to Rome by the end of the 12th century AD.

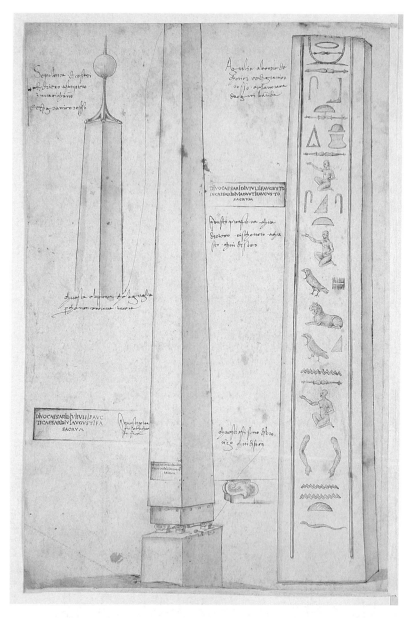

Figure 5:6   Drawing attributed to Baldassare Peruzzi or Simone del Pollaiuolo, studies of the Vatican obelisk (16th century; see Hassan 2003: Figure 2:22) and of the hieroglyphs on a small obelisk now in Berlin (© Bonnat Museum, Bayonne, France).

a fragment; the entire bottom section had been restored during the later Middle Ages with a re-carved column shaft of the same red granite material. In the drawing, however, the artist has gone so far as to 'restore', on paper, the missing section of the monument, by replacing the uninscribed lower part with the corresponding section of a similar monument that stood in the Piazza di San Macuto. The restoration is

Figure 5:7   Cronaca–Peruzzi depiction of 'Four Roman Obelisks' with accurate renditions of their hieroglyphs (ca. 1510). The first (from the left) is an obelisk of Ramesses II, with part of it restored in the drawing; the second is the obelisk moved in the 18th century to the Piazza della Rotunda; the third is another reconstruction first located in the façade of a building; and the fourth, an obelisk originally standing on Tiber island (Christ Church, Oxford, inv. no. 0814v).

described in a short notation: "below this sign from [the obelisk] of S. Macuto." The artist has obviously recognized what it took Egyptologists centuries to discover – that the inscriptions on the upper sections of these little obelisks are virtually identical, and that they probably were fashioned at the same time as a pair (the inscriptions record a dedication by Ramesses II).

Next on the sheet is the S. Macuto obelisk, which was moved, in the 18th century, to the fountain in the Piazza della Rotunda (Hassan 2003: Figure 2:31). It is shown intact, with a full (if somewhat worn) copy of one of its inscribed faces, standing on its base and simple astragal supports. The third obelisk is another 'reconstruction', this time composed of three distinct fragments (from the remains of two distinct obelisks) that were installed, in those years, in the façades of some buildings in the same Piazza di S. Macuto. It is interesting to note that this on-paper reconstruction anticipates the eventual fate of these fragments, which were incorporated into a composite obelisk that was assembled in Urbino in 1737 (Lembke 1992). The fourth and final obelisk on the sheet provides the only relatively complete record of the Roman-era obelisk that once stood on the Tiber Island (only fragments of this monument survive; see Curran 2000: 148–150).

The "Cronaca-Peruzzi" obelisk-drawings shed a tantalizing but incomplete light into an otherwise shadowy corner of early Egyptology. The artist and/or antiquarian responsible for these drawings apparently endeavoured to produce accurate and consultable epigraphic copies of Egyptian inscriptions, and studied them closely enough to attempt to "restore" the missing sections of two of them. For what sort of audience were this draftsman's studies intended? We know from somewhat later accounts that drawings of hieroglyphic inscriptions circulated in humanist circles as far as Venice by the 1520s. And we also know that at least some of the more audacious scholars of the time attempted, however fleetingly, to identify and interpret some of these signs by checking their copies of Horapollo (Curran 2000: 140–146).

Among the humanists of the period (ca. 1500) who apparently looked at 'authentic' Egyptian inscriptions, the Florentine Pietro Crinito (1475–1507) may be considered among the most impressive. Crinito was an early critic of Annius' forgeries (see Angeleri 1955: 459–460; Giehlow 1915: 84 n. 1), and his comments on the subject of hieroglyphs are brief. But his work reveals an impressive awareness of the sources, as well as a familiarity with the sort of images that could be seen on the obelisks (Giehlow 1915: 84–85). He describes several of these, including "scarabs, bees, rivers, bulls, vultures" and the 'rippling water' hieroglyph, among others. Since, as Giehlow has noted, virtually all the signs on Crinito's list can be shown to correspond to ones that could be seen on the Roman obelisks, it seems likely that he drew on visual as well as literary sources, perhaps a drawing like the one consulted by the *Hypnerotomachia* illustrator, who also attempted a version of the 'water' sign (Angeleri 1955: 180–181). If this was the case, Crinito certainly earned the praise bestowed on him by Pierio Valeriano, who listed him as one of the most important early students of Egyptian letters (Giehlow 1915: 79–88; Valeriano 1602: fol. 3r).

By the first decades of the 16th century, then, it would appear that an 'epigraphic' approach to the hieroglyphs had emerged from the humanist and epigraphic studies of the later Quattrocento, and was taken up with enthusiasm by the archaeologically-inclined artists of early Cinquecento Rome. It would further appear that the artists in question belonged to a relatively small and distinguished group with close ties to the papal court, to the new building projects instituted at the Vatican by Pope Julius II (1503–1512), and especially to the circle of collaborators associated with the famous painter, architect, and all-around artist impresario, Raphael (1483–1520). While Julius II himself did not share the Egyptological enthusiasm of his predecessor, Alexander VI, the attitudes of his successors, the Medici popes Leo X (1513–1521) and Clement VII (1523–1534), were of an entirely more receptive nature. It was Leo X who elevated Raphael to a new role as supervisor of Rome's antiquities, and who supported the artist's incredibly ambitious project to reconstruct the appearance of Rome (and all of its monuments) as it appeared in antiquity. But the Medici popes did more than promote the expansion of archaeological studies in Rome; they actively oversaw the restoration and installation (or re-installation) of a number of major Egyptian antiquities in the city. The Egyptian lions at the Pantheon were restored and reinstalled, a pair of sphinxes was added to the steps of the Senatorial Palace on the Capitoline Hill, and the rediscovery of one of the obelisks from Augustus' Mausoleum inspired an ambitious project to repair and re-erect it as the centrepiece of a renovated Piazza del Popolo. At the same time, the decorations of the Vatican palace and other papal or Medici properties were filled with Egyptian imagery inspired by the renewed interest in Rome's Egyptian heritage. The motive for all this Egyptianizing activity is not entirely clear. On the most obvious level, the Medici were doing nothing more than re-appropriating, as it were, the Egyptian 'trophies' that had been brought to the city by Augustus and his successors. Both of the Medici popes, and Leo in particular, were fond of comparing themselves to Augustus, and their claim to inherit his place as ruler of the world was nothing new in and of itself. But the Medicean Egyptianisms suggest a deeper engagement with the mystical and hermetic sources of Egyptian power, a subject that these Florentine 'priest-kings' would have known well from their education at the feet of Ficino and other distinguished luminaries of the 'Egyptian' Renaissance (Curran forthcoming).

The taste for Egyptian motifs extended beyond the papal palace to such non-papal patrons as the Roman-Sienese banker Agostino Chigi, who erected pyramids in his burial chapel in S. Maria del Popolo; the Cesi family, who assembled a collection of Egyptian antiquities and ornamented their family tombs with Egyptian sphinxes; and the Gonzaga of Mantua, who commissioned Guilio Romano's hieroglyphic decorations in the Palazzo del Te (Jaeger 1991, 1994). This Egyptianizing trend soon spread from Italy to France, where royal and princely patrons appropriated motifs from Roman Egyptian statuary as part of a broader Italianate movement. But the culmination of this High Renaissance 'Egyptian Taste' is the astonishing illuminated 'Egyptian Page', actually the frontispiece for the Mass of St John the Baptist, in the Missal of the Roman Cardinal Pompeo Colonna (Figure 5:8), now in the John Rylands University Library in Manchester. Datable to ca. 1530–1535, the page has been described (Barker 2000; James 1921: 18–20, 87–96, pl. 77; Pevsner and Lang 1968: 222–223, 247 n. 58, fig. 29; Syndram 1989: 19 (pl. 1), 389–380 (no. 1/9)) as a visual encyclopaedia of Egyptian imagery known to the Renaissance. What it represents, in fact, is an archaeological excursus on the Colonna family's Borgia-like claim to descend from the Egyptian Osiris.[1] The copiousness of the illuminator's application of Egyptian imagery is unmatched in the period, and comparable exercises would not appear in European art until the 18th century.

Figure 5:8    Frontispiece for the *Mass of St John the Baptist* (ca. 1530–1538) (John Rylands University Library, Manchester, England, MS 32, fol. 79r).

Scholarly interest in the hieroglyphs was not neglected by the humanists in Leo's court. Among the Egyptological studies that emerged from the *milieu* of Leonine and Clementine Rome were the Latin translations of Horapollo's *Hieroglyphica* and Plutarch's *De Iside et Osiride* by the Ferrarese humanist Celio Calcagnini which were published after his death in 1541 (Giehlow 1915: 80–82). And it was under Leo X that a gifted young scholar, Pierio Valeriano (1477–1558), began his lifelong study of the hieroglyphs (Haig Gaisser 1993: 109–113; Rosa 1986). But what began as a self-described effort to decipher the inscriptions on the obelisks and fill the obvious gaps in the hieroglyphic sources like Horapollo expanded over the decades of production to embrace the entire field of symbolic theory and tradition. As a result, the reader is forced to scour the endless pages and chapters of Valeriano's *Hieroglyphica* (1602) for its few traces of 'authentic' archaeological material, which are subsumed by the author's encyclopaedic assemblage of every conceivable meaning for such images as the lion, the elephant, the eyes, and the rest. The motive for Valeriano's all-inclusive approach is fairly easy to grasp, however, for it soon becomes clear that for this author, as for Ficino, the meanings encoded in the hieroglyphs cannot be understood as a specific, historically-determined image-code, but as a trans-historical and universal mode of symbolic thought that is rooted, ultimately, in the divine language of Creation itself (Allen 1979: 115–117; Curran 2000: 140–146, 156–162, 178–179; Giehlow 1915: 113–129; Iversen 1961: 70–73; Pope 1999: 24–27).

Paradoxically, at the very same time that Valeriano and his literary friends were moving away from the monuments to consider the poetics of universal symbolism, new generations of artists and scholars began to develop a more critical and monument-centred approach to archaeological study. The sketchbooks and antiquarian albums of artist-antiquarians like Pirro Ligorio, Étienne Dupérac and Jean-Jacques Boissard include many drawings of Egyptian monuments and copies of hieroglyphic inscriptions. In several cases, these were collected into specifically Egyptian sections or albums, and, since they contain many images that appear to have been copied and passed about, it is at least possible that they provide a glimpse of an otherwise lost plan, however loosely organized, to collect and publish printed copies of these inscriptions. The first printed collection, Johann Herwarth von Hohenburg's *Thesaurus Hieroglyphicorum*, did not see publication until about 1610 (Iversen 1961: 86–87; Whitehouse 1992: 72–73). This important but little known publication, which was originally intended to be accompanied by an interpretive text, included engravings of the inscriptions on the obelisks, the Pantheon lions, and other Roman specimens, as well as a full-page reproduction of the so-called *Mensa Isiaca* (Figure 5:9), an inlaid bronze table-top of Roman date whose images of Egyptian gods and orthographically accurate but literally meaningless hieroglyphic inscriptions were the ironic focus of many hieroglyphic studies of the Renaissance and subsequent periods (Leospo 1978; Scamuzzi 1939). The *Mensa* had been sketched and engraved before, and drawings seem to have been in circulation by the early 1520s, when the tablet entered the collection of the famous Venetian poet (and future Cardinal) Pietro Bembo (1470–1547). Valeriano knew the *Mensa* well, and considered some of its imagery in passing in the *Hieroglyphica*. It was the subject of a full-size engraving (by Enea Vico) in 1559, and some two decades later, the Flemish antiquarian Jan Becan van Gorp's (1580) hieroglyphic treatise included several woodcuts of figures from the *Mensa* (Whitehouse 1992: 70). Hohenburg's engraving described the figures on the *Mensa* as

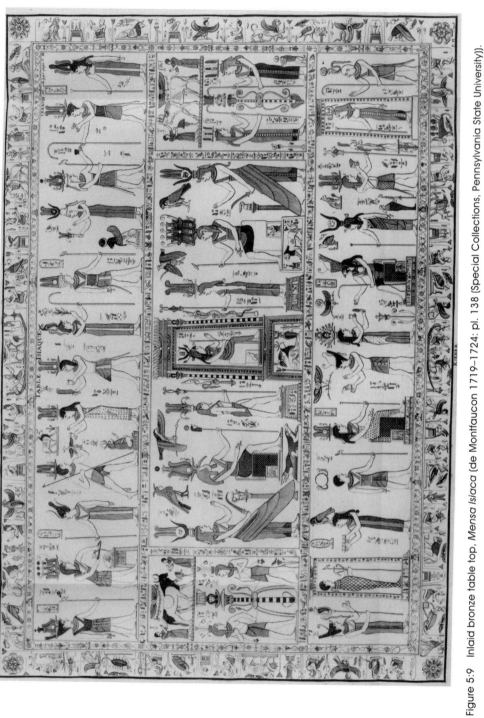

Figure 5:9  Inlaid bronze table top, *Mensa Isiaca* (de Montfaucon 1719–1724: pl. 138 (Special Collections, Pennsylvania State University)).

symbols of the 33 points of the compass. This thesis was elaborated upon some years later when Herwarth's son published a treatise on the *Mensa* as a kind of hieroglyphic nautical map of the world (Herwart von Hohenburg 1623; Whitehouse 1992: 70).

This sort of interpretive license is nowhere to be found in the Paduan humanist Lorenzo Pignoria's monographic study of the *Mensa*, published in Venice in 1605. As has long been acknowledged, Pignoria's approach to the hieroglyphs represents a more critical and even sceptical approach to Egyptian studies, as is only to be expected, perhaps, from this close friend and ally of Galileo. Pignoria begins by admitting that he will not be able to provide a complete decipherment of the images and inscriptions on the tablet, and limits himself to an iconographic description and comparisons to the information provided by the (authentic) classical sources. He also expresses contempt for the expansive proclivities of his predecessors:

> I will describe to the best of my abilities the figures of this tablet, and not allegorically (*non allegorikos*) but rather based upon the ancient accounts. Indeed, I detest more than anyone the far-fetched interpretations of the Platonists, based on tenuous tales and almost ignoring the teachings of their master. And I have chosen to confess my ignorance rather than offend the erudite reader any longer.

(Pignoria 1670: 1–2; trans. Donadoni et al. 1990: 56–57)

Pignoria's text-critical and iconographic approach is indebted to the expanding corpus of mythographic publications that began to appear in the middle of the 16th century (see Allen 1979: 249–278; McGrath 1963; Seznec 1953: 219–256; Volpi 1997). Mythographers of the period were especially fascinated with the bizarre hybrid figures of the Egyptian pantheon: Anubis, for example, and curious vase-bodied images of Osiris that the late antique sources identified as the idol of Canopus (Panofsky 1961). In 1615, Pignoria contributed an updated appendix to Cartari's mythography that included illustrations and descriptions of the "idols" of India, Asia and Mexico, anticipating the diffusionist, 'world-culture' approach of Athanasius Kircher (Cartari 1615; Seznec 1931).

Valeriano's *Hieroglyphica* continued to stand as the most authoritative source on the subject in the late 16th and early 17th centuries. A revised edition, with an appendix of some 90 additional hieroglyphic meanings by Celio Augusto Curio, appeared in 1567, and the work was translated into Italian and French (e.g. Valeriano 1602). Jesuit Nicolas Caussin's (1631) *De Symbolica Aegyptorium Sapientia* is important for his emphasis on the biblical and Christian sources for the concept of Egyptian wisdom (Allen 1979: 118–119; Pope 1999: 28).

A more 'revisionist' work of the period is the treatise on the obelisks of Rome. Mercati (1541–1593), a geologist and physician, was employed as keeper of the papal *Metallotheca*, and was fortunate enough to be 'on the scene' when the indefatigable Pope Sixtus V (1585–1590) embarked on his ambitious policy of moving, unearthing and re-erecting obelisks (Findlen 1994: 233–235, 350–361; Iversen 1961: 84–85; Mercati [1589] 1981: 9–32). As Sixtus' 'official' obelisk expert, Mercati was able to observe first hand the excavation of the obelisks of the Circus Maximus and restoration of these monuments (along with the Vatican and Augustus-Mausoleum obelisks) in the *piazze* of Sixtus' new Rome (Cipriani 1993: 9–75; D'Onofrio 1992: 145–185; Fontana 1590; Iversen 1968: 28–44; Orbaan 1910: 130–172). Mercati scoured the texts of the ancient authors for evidence of each obelisk's Egyptian and later Roman history, and also provided the earliest serious study of the history and meaning of the obelisk as a monumental type. He also addressed the problem of the hieroglyphs in a remarkable chapter (Mercati [1589] 1981: 103–132), where he postulated the thesis that while 'image-writing' had been adopted by many early or 'primitive' peoples (like the Ethiopians and the Mexicans), it was the Egyptians who transformed this rudimentary form of communication into the complex system of concealed allegory described by the ancient authors (and imitated in his own time by the inventors of emblems). Like Pignoria a few years later, Mercati concluded that this system was all too successful in its secretive mission, and that any serious attempt at decipherment would require the discovery of further information.

The sceptical trend in early modern Egyptology reached a kind of peak with Isaac Casaubon's (1614) declaration that the hermetic writings, far from representing the translated doctrines of an Egyptian of the time of Moses, were the products of a late antique 'imposter'. According to Casaubon, the Egyptians' use of terms and ideas derived from later Greek and Hebrew, and even Christian literature represented not a prophecy or prefiguration of revelation to come, but a shameless borrowing from the writings of his contemporaries. For the Calvinist Casaubon, the deconstruction of Hermes was a means to a more important end. As the hermetic prophecies had continued to be cited by Counter-Reformation historians, so the discrediting of these doctrines served to damage the reputation of these Catholic scholars (Grafton 1983; Yates 1964: 432–477).

This interpretive reticence is nowhere to be found in the voluminous works of the most notorious Egyptologist of the 17th century, the Jesuit polymath and 'master of 100 arts', Athanasius Kircher (1602–1680) (Allen 1979: 120–132; Donadoni et al. 2001: 101–141; Evans 1979: 433–442; Iversen 1961: 89–100; Pope 1999: 28–39; Rowland 2000; Stolzenberg 2001: 115–139; Strasser 1988). Like most other Catholic scholars (and Protestants as well), Kircher continued to hold the wisdom of the Egyptian Hermes in the highest regard. Indeed, the hermetic 'prophecies' provided the foundation for Kircher's monumental effort to restore and disseminate the lost wisdom of the Egyptians. Kircher recalled that he was inspired to pursue his hieroglyphic studies after seeing a book with engravings of "all the Roman obelisks" in the library of Speyer in 1628 (Stolzenberg 2001: 115). Since he neglected to provide the title or author of this fateful volume, we can only speculate that it might have been Hohenburg's *Thesaurus*, or Domenico Fontana's treatise on the moving of the obelisks. But it is clear from Kircher's story that, by this time, the printed visual record of Egyptian monuments had expanded beyond the meagre pickings available in the previous century (Whitehouse 1992: 73). In addition to the growing antiquarian literature, travel accounts had continued to proliferate, and printed editions were sometimes provided with illustrations. The woodcuts of pyramids, obelisks, the Great Sphinx, and an Egyptian mummy published by Thevet (1556) were wildly anachronistic (Cannuyer 1985). By the 17th century, however, the Egyptian journey was attracting the talents of intellectuals like John Greaves, a professor of astronomy at Oxford who produced the earliest measured study of the Great Pyramid (1646). Greaves' engravings of the pyramid and its chambers set a new standard for archaeological accuracy for the period (Greaves 1646: pl. opposite 106; Whitehouse 1992: 68–69; Figure 5:10).

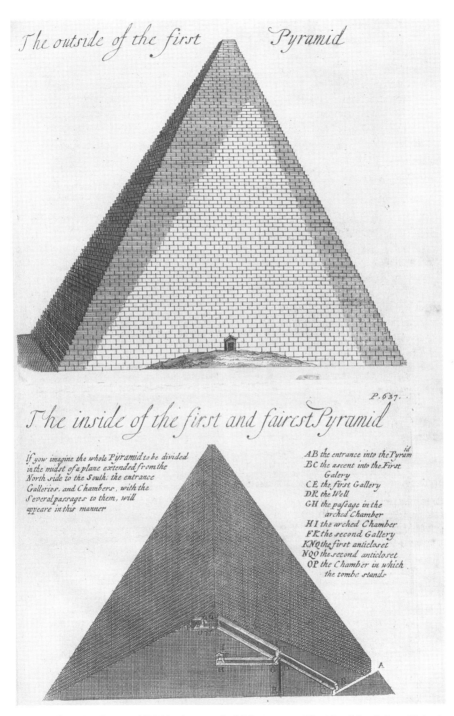

The outside of the first Pyramid

*P. 637.*

The inside of the first and fairest Pyramid

If you imagine the whole Pyramid to be divided in the midst of a plane extended from the North side to the South: the entrance Galleries. and Chambers, with the Several passages to them, will appeare in this manner

AB the entrance into the Pyram id
BC the ascent into the First Galery
CE the first Gallery
DR the Well
GH the passage in the arched Chamber
HI the arched Chamber
FK the second Gallery
KNQ the first anticloset
NQO the second anticloset
OP the Chamber in which the tombe stands

Figure 5:10   John Greaves' (1646: pl. opposite 106) measured "inside of the first and fairest pyramid", the first accurate representation of a pyramid's cross-section (Churchill and Churchill 1744–1746: 632).

Kircher's own publications were even more sumptuously illustrated, although since he collected his images from a bewildering variety of sources, old and new, the overall effect is more than a little incoherent. From travellers' accounts, there are views and diagrams of Egyptian tombs. There are the expected images of the obelisks and ever-proliferating population of Egyptian statues extracted from the ruins of Rome. And there are lots of mummies, accompanied by mummy cases, amulets, statuettes, papyri, and the full range of reasonably portable funerary paraphernalia. These objects, obviously imported from Egypt, had begun entering personal and 'scientific' collections in the previous century, and had become something of a vogue by Kircher's day. Mummies had been coming to Europe for centuries as the powder produced by grinding these desiccated Egyptian corpses had been highly valued for its medical properties since the 12th century (Dannenfeldt 1959; El Daly 2003). Thevet (1556) provides one of the most informative and colourful of accounts of mummy-finding expeditions. It would seem that earliest collectors of mummies were physicians, naturalists, and travelling treasure-hunters. But over time, as these collections of natural 'curiosities' became increasingly systematic and aestheticized, mummies, especially ones that were relatively intact in their painted or otherwise decorated cases, came to be considered more or less as works of art, and as such were displayed in the collections of such distinguished men of culture as the Grand Duke of Tuscany, the painter Peter Paul Rubens, and Cardinal Flavio Chigi (nephew of Pope Alexander VII, one of Kircher's most important patrons – Dannenfeldt 1959: 22–23; Pollès 2001: 33–80; Whitehouse 1989, 1992: 66–69).

Chigi's mummies, a matching male and female pair of the Roman-era 'Fayum Portrait' type, had been brought to Rome in the early 17th century by Pietro della Valle (1586–1652), a wealthy Roman patrician whose travels took him to Egypt, Persia and India. Della Valle's account of the excavation and purchase of these and some other mummies is perhaps the earliest Egyptological 'excavation report' in western literature, and is remarkable for its detail and display of critical acumen. During his tour of Egypt in the autumn and winter of 1615–1616, della Valle visited Giza and explored the interior chambers of the Great Pyramid. From there, he ventured to the mummy pits of Saqqarah, accompanied by a gang of local antiquities hunters. They showed him a number of tombs that were stacked with mummies and other antiquities. But the pair that passed to the Chigi collection had already been dug up by one of the *fellahin*, and della Valle was so impressed by their condition and the quality of their decoration that he bought them on the spot, and had them packed in palm-leaves and brought back to Rome. With their beautiful gold ornament and striking portrait panels, the della Valle-Chigi mummies achieved a kind of celebrity upon their arrival in Italy. In his 1650 'excavation report' (Kircher 1652–1654, 1676), della Valle compared the style of the portrait panels to the ancient figures of saints that could be seen on the walls of the older basilicas in Rome – an astute observation and an early demonstration of art historical style-comparison! (Valle 1672, I: 371–389; trans. Bull 1989: 48–63.) The mummies were restored after passing to the Chigi collection and were sold to agents of the Duke of Saxony in 1728 (they are now in the State Museum of Dresden) (Bedini 1986; Doxiadis 1995: 18–19, 122–125; Whitehouse 1992: 67–68).

The Saqqarah 'couple' were not the only treasures that della Valle brought back from his travels. A cartonnage mummy-mask of Ptolemaic date passed from della

Valle's heirs to the collection of the great antiquarian and art-theorist Pietro Bellori (1613–1696) (it is now in Berlin – Matthiae 2000, II: 521, no. 51). Pietro also acquired some important manuscripts, including several Coptic grammars and a pair of Coptic-Arabic vocabularies. Della Valle entrusted the translation and publication of these works to an Arabic expert, Tomas Obicini da Novara, who died in 1632 after making a promising start (Pope 1999: 36–39; van Lantschoot 1948). At this point, the aristocrat French scholar Nicholas-Claude Fabri de Peiresc (1580–1637) became involved in the search for a replacement. Peiresc was an avid collector of antiquities, and his interest extended to Egypt and hieroglyphic studies. Like della Valle, his collection included Egyptian antiquities, mummies, and some Coptic-Arabic manuscripts. From his base in Aix-en-Provence, he maintained a steady correspondence with some of the leading scientific and antiquarian figures of his day, but his relationship with della Valle was not always easy. Still, through his close contacts with such key Roman figures as the antiquarian Cassiano dal Pozzo, Pope Urban VII, and the pope's powerful nephew, Cardinal Francesco Barberini, Peiresc was described as both well-informed and well-connected as far as the study of Egyptian antiquity was concerned (Aufrère 1990; Iversen 1961: 91–93; Pope 1999: 37–38; Whitehouse 1989).

By 1632 Kircher had made Peiresc's acquaintance, and it was through this connection that he was recommended to della Valle and to Francesco Barberini, who offered Kircher a professorship in mathematics at the Jesuit Collegio Romano in Rome. Upon his arrival in the papal city in 1635, he took up the study of the della Valle grammars, and released his first tentative study of the material, the "Coptic Forerunner" in 1636. This was followed by the more elaborate "Egyptian Language Restored" (1646) which included a complete Coptic grammar and lexicon, translated from the Arabic of the della Valle originals. Kircher's analysis of the Coptic language contained its eccentricities – his idea that the Greek language had derived from Coptic, for example. But his basic argument that Coptic was a later descendant of the language of the pharaohs was entirely correct, and provided some of the basic evidence that was to prove so useful to Champollion.

Kircher (1636) had unabashedly proclaimed that the decipherment of the hieroglyphs was at hand, and even provided a sample decipherment of the human-headed scarab from the *Mensa Isiaca* (Allen 1979: 122–123; Kircher 1636: 5–16, 238–277). And true to his word, he soon began issuing the great Egyptological works that are his most famous legacy. The first (Kircher 1650) was commissioned by Pope Innocent X to commemorate the restoration and installation of the 'Capo di Bove' obelisk as the centrepiece of Bernini's Fountain of the Four Rivers in the Piazza Navona (the site of Pope Innocent's splendid new family palace; Hassan 2003: Figure 2:23). In the 560-plus pages of this amazing publication, Kircher provides a detailed and mostly imaginary history of the obelisk, from its original manufacture by the Egyptian pharaoh Sothis in the 14th century before Christ (1366 BC, 1028 Post-Diluvium, and 2684 since the creation of the world, to be exact). Its transport to Rome is credited to the Emperor Caracalla in the third century AD (the obelisk was actually carved in hieroglyphs for an earlier Roman emperor, Domitian). Through this historical precedent, the present-day restoration by Pope Innocent appears as the logical fulfilment of the monument's history. A long discourse on the origins of the obelisks and on the origins of writing and of the hieroglyphs follows. In its cast of characters and primordial scope, Kircher's history has more than a little in common with Annius', although the details are different. Like Annius, Kircher ascribes the foundation of Egyptian civilization to Noah's son Cham, who in Kircher's version is identical to the Egyptian Osiris. But the origins of Egyptian wisdom are traced even further back, before the Flood, to the sacred doctrines imparted to Adam in the Garden of Eden. These doctrines passed to Noah from the Adamic source, but by this time an alternate, corrupt version of these doctrines, which included the heresies of idolatry and black magic, had been instituted by Cain. It was the great error of Cham to have combined both of these teachings, the good and the bad, which passed in turn to his son, Misraim the Egyptian (Allen 1960, 1979: 124–131; Iversen 1961; Pope 1999: 28–33; Stolzenberg 2001: 115–139).

Inspired by his study of the Arabic tradition (El Daly Chapter 3, this volume), Kircher identified not one but two Egyptian sages known as Hermes. The first of these is credited with the invention of the pyramids (Humbert 2003), which were constructed to preserve the secret doctrines from the effects of calamitous floods. The second Hermes, known to posterity as Hermes Trismegistus, was the author of the *Hermetica*. And it was he who endeavoured to purify the doctrines inherited by his people and return them to their uncorrupted truth. This second Hermes invented the obelisk and the hieroglyphs as his own instruments to encode and preserve the reconstituted doctrines of divine wisdom. But despite his best efforts this tradition was contaminated by the misunderstandings of later generations, who once again fell into idolatry and superstition. Over the intervening centuries, however, the true doctrines were recognized and adopted by the more enlightened sages and philosophers of ancient Greece, Orpheus, Pythagoras, and Plato among them. And so a glimpse, at least, of the true revelation of Adam was preserved in the philosophies and religion of all subsequent non-Hebrew peoples. The restoration and purification of this doctrine was the special task that Kircher had set for himself, as he became, in effect, his own generation's Hermes Trismegistus (Stolzenberg 2001: 127–130 ff)!

Like Valeriano before him, Kircher sought the traces of this true doctrine through the complete inherited knowledge of human civilization. He invoked all the familiar classical and biblical sources and themes, but these are now amplified by Kircher's own access to a bewildering collection of new materials: Hebrew, Arabic, Persian, Coptic, etc., all cited in their original fonts before being translated, lending a visual and linguistic density to this already opaque work. A long discussion of specific meanings and symbols follows, and the text is liberally illustrated with images derived (sometimes rather freely) from Egyptian monuments. The book concludes with a sign-by-sign, illustrated translation of the inscriptions on the obelisk. Each is individually labelled, and the overall meaning, a dense web of esoteric and religious-sounding pronouncements, is provided in a parallel Latin text. The most celebrated example of his method is Kircher's (1650: 557 – Allen 1960: 531–532) improbable decipherment of the cartouche of Domitian as a proclamation of the power of Osiris: "Osiris is the source of all fecundity and vegetation; the Holy Mophta draws this power of generation from the sky into his realm."

Although it is a hefty and lavishly produced volume in its own right, the *Obeliscus Pamphilius* is only a prelude to Kircher's even more spectacular multi-volume epic (it runs to some 2,000+ pages), the *Egyptian Oedipus* (1654), a work whose very title announces the author's claim to have solved the mysterious riddles of the sphinx. Across the vast fabric of this work, Kircher directs his critical eye to the explanation of virtually every known Egyptian theme. He begins with a restatement and elaboration of the historical theses laid out in the *Obeliscus Pamphilius*, and concludes with a copiously illustrated catalogue of virtually every known Egyptian monument and artefact known in his time, and provides, for the majority of them, sign-by-sign translations of their hieroglyphic inscriptions.

These translations are all wrong – wrong, that is from the standpoint of modern Egyptology. For Kircher continued to subscribe to the Classical-Renaissance theory that the hieroglyphs had been invented to encode the Egyptian doctrines in veils of allegory and enigma. In a fascinating variation of this thesis, Kircher argued that the hieroglyphs functioned on a variety or hierarchy of levels. At the first, simplest level, the individual signs stood phonetically (and figuratively) for the thing represented. It was these simple hieroglyphs that served the most elemental and practical functions of language and were suitable for the use of the ignorant masses. They also provided the original models for the eventual development of cursive and alphabetic script, including Coptic and Greek letters. In this section (Kircher 1654: 49), as Iversen (1961: 96–97) has pointed out, Kircher identified several signs as alphabetic equivalents of Coptic letters and words, including the 'rippling water' hieroglyph previously noted by Pietro Crinito (see above). In a leap of inspired reasoning, Kircher associated this water-glyph with the Coptic word for water – *mu* – and established himself as the first post-antique scholar to correctly identify the phonetic meaning of an Egyptian hieroglyph (Stolzenberg 2001: 115–139). But Kircher did not, could not, stop there. For his real interest lay, not in the mundane world of ideograph and alphabetic signs, but in the more lofty realms of wisdom and mystery. And it was to the other three 'levels' of hieroglyphic meaning: the natural-philosophical (level 2); the tropological (level 3); and the anagogical (level 4) that he sought the allegorical method and theological meaning of these Egyptian signs.

In its rich scope and monumental hubris, Kircher's *Egyptian Oedipus* may be said to mark the climax (and fusion) of all the diverse strands – historical, archaeological, philological, theological, etc. – that informed the Renaissance afterlife of Ancient Egypt. Kircher's triumphant synthesis of the 'Egyptian Renaissance' finds its artistic equivalent in Gianlorenzo Bernini's Roman obelisk ensembles: the aforementioned Fountain of the Four Rivers (1648–1651; Wengrow 2003) and, perhaps more enjoyably, the intimate and playful elephant and obelisk group (1666–1667; Figure 5:11) in the Piazza di S. Maria sopra Minerva (D'Onofrio 1992: 288–301; Iversen 1968, I: 76–92; Preimesberger 1974). The discovery of the Minervan obelisk – a diminutive specimen dedicated to the sixth century BC pharaoh Apries (Hassan 2003: Figure 2:34) – in the gardens of the Dominican convent brought Kircher and Bernini together again as scholar and artist. Kircher rushed across the street from his offices in the Collegio to inspect the find, and soon published (Kircher 1666) his translation of the carvings on the obelisk, whose discovery on the site of the ancient Temple of Isis Campensis he correctly noted (Cipriani 1993: 77–167). At the same time, Bernini and his assistant, Ercole Ferrata (who actually carved the elephant) produced a three-dimensional, hieroglyphic analogue of Kircher's fusion of pagan and Christian wisdom, whose form was inspired by one of the most extravagant Egyptianizing confections of the *Hypnerotomachia* (D'Onofrio 1992: 302–323; Heckscher 1947; Iversen 1968: 93–100). The

Figure 5:11   Gianlorenzo Bernini and Ercole Ferrata's 'Obelisk and Elephant' (1666–1667), Piazza di S. Maria sopra Minerva, Rome (© B. Curran).

resulting ensemble provides a fitting ornament for the church of the Minerva. For it was here that the body of the hieroglyph-reading friar Annius of Viterbo had been laid to rest in 1502, in a church whose apse – with the tombs of the Egypt-friendly popes Leo X and Clement VII – rises over the ruins of the Temple of Isis itself. The inscription on the base of Bernini's elephant resounds with the sort of syncretic and triumphalist rhetoric that both Athanasius and Annius were so adept at exploiting:

> In the year of Salvation 1667, Alexander VII dedicated to Divine Wisdom this ancient Egyptian obelisk, a monument of Egyptian Pallas, torn from the earth and erected in what was formerly the forum of Minerva, and is now that of the Virgin who gave birth to God.
>
> (Iversen 1968, I: 97 n. 4)

As a cultural and intellectual 'movement', the Renaissance renewal of Ancient Egypt provides powerful testimony for the enduring appeal of that civilization and its monuments, an appeal that has continued to manifest itself in innumerable ways from antiquity to our own time (Humbert and Price 2003; MacDonald and Rice 2003). Like the protagonists of the Hollywood mummy films (Lupton 2003), Ancient Egypt has refused to lie quietly in its tomb, choosing instead a cycle of resurrection and reincarnation in successive eras, each of which has tried, in its way, to reclaim (and remake) Egypt in its own image.

## Note

1    The Colonna family's descent from Osiris is detailed in the preface of Vallone (1576: 6v–8v) and elaborated by Mugnos (1658). The latter source was first cited by Pevsner and Lang (1968: 247 n. 58). I (Curran forthcoming) have recently completed a patronage-based iconographic study of the missal and its 'Egyptian Page'.

## Acknowledgments

I am indebted to the brilliant detective work of Giancarla Periti of Johns Hopkins University for directing my attention to the Ferrarini materials and to John Ritterbush of Pennsylvania State University for editorial and research assistance.

# CHAPTER 6

# ANCIENT EGYPT IN 17th AND 18th CENTURY ENGLAND

*David Boyd Haycock*

How Ægypt, mad with superstition grown,
Makes gods of monsters, but too well is known:
One sect devotion to Nile's serpent pays,
Others to Ibis, that on serpent preys.

(Juvenal XV.1–4, trans. Dryden (1693))

As the acknowledged source of geometry, mathematics and astronomy, and as the schooling ground for Greek science and philosophy, Ancient Egypt was of obvious interest to European scholars of the early modern period. Isaac Newton (Bodleian Library, Oxford, New College MS 361/2 f. 110) postulated in the late 17th century that "the first great kingdom in the world on this side the Indies seems to have been yt of Egypt", whilst in 1727 his friend the antiquary William Stukeley (1980: 140) wrote that he was studying "the old sages & prophets of Egypt that first disseminated wisdom through the world". Such was the prestige of Egyptian wisdom that in the mid-15th century the Florentine humanist Marsilio Ficino (1576; Curran Chapter 5, this volume) had translated the recovered works of the supposed ancient Egyptian priest-king-philosopher Hermes Trismegistus *before* those of Plato.

The Reformation helped to propel the interest in ancient history even further, particularly in Protestant countries. There scholars hoped that by returning to a closer study of the Bible they would overcome the centuries of 'corruption' of true Christianity by papal dogma – a campaign both assisted and demanded by the re-emergence during the Renaissance of numerous lost classical texts that challenged traditional late classical and medieval scholarship (Burnett Chapter 4, this volume; Gascoigne 1991: 173). In order to fully understand the Bible it became essential to understand ancient history and chronology. These in turn were important subjects for early modern protohistorians of science, who, since Nicholas Copernicus' 16th century astronomical 'revolution', had turned to even older traditions than the Egyptian astronomer Ptolemy of Alexandria's second century AD *Almagest* in order to seek out the 'genuine' wisdom of the ancients. As a true humanist would, Copernicus (1543) had justified his heliocentric theory by presenting it not as a new discovery, but as a re-discovery of ancient Greek astronomical theory (Dear 2001: 34–35).

By the mid-17th century, interest in Egyptian, Babylonian and Chaldean history was resurgent in England, and particularly at Cambridge University. And with this resurgence the traditional interpretation of the relationship between Hebrew and Gentile science and theology came under increasing critical analysis. The Old Testament book of Acts 7:22 had recorded that "Moses was learned in all the wisdom of the Egyptians, and was mighty in words and in deeds". The question was thus raised by some scholars as to whether the Egyptians had learnt their religious customs from the Jews, or the Jews from the Egyptians. The orthodox argument, established by the Church Fathers (particularly Clement of Alexandria) and as stated by the English scholar Theophilus Gale (1669), was that the Egyptians had gained their knowledge from the Jews during the period when Joseph and the other patriarchs had lived in exile in Egypt. According to Gale (1669: 13), when Plato spoke of the traditions of the Egyptians, he had actually meant those of the Jews, "because at that time, when *Plato* was in *Egypt*, the *Jews* resorted thither" (and see Gascoigne 1991). This view, however, was challenged by the great Cambridge Hebrew scholar John Spencer (1685), who pointedly claimed that the Jews had learnt their religious practices and rituals from the Egyptians, and not *vice versa*. Importantly, Spencer's book reflects what was manifestly a burgeoning interest in religious history and chronology at Cambridge University (Gascoigne 1991: 178–179).

This chapter concentrates on the ways in which attitudes in England to ancient Egyptian science, religion, chronology and archaeology shifted through the course of the 17th and 18th centuries, particularly the way in which the study of Egyptian science, religion and chronology were interrelated, and how this fitted into early modern concerns with the growth of freethinking and irreligion, as well as with the development of archaeological studies. This interest in Ancient Egypt also influenced interpretations of the prehistory of Britain in the 18th century. The interest in – and understanding of – Egyptian religious practices changed considerably over these two centuries, moving gradually from a position that accepted Egypt's place in a biblical world of limited age, to one that challenged most of the established Christian beliefs about both the history of religion and the history of humankind.

## The *Corpus Hermeticum* in 17th century England

In early modern Europe the major extant written work attributed to the Ancient Egyptians was the *Corpus Hermeticum*. These were a collection of texts supposedly written by Hermes Trismegistus, the thrice-majestic philosopher, priest and king, who took his name from Hermes, the Greek name for the Egyptian god Thoth, the inventor of writing. Hermes Trismegistus was considered by early Christian scholars to have been a contemporary of Moses, and thus very close to what was believed to be the fount of true theological wisdom which had been passed directly by God to Adam, to Noah and then to Moses. According to ancient tradition, Moses was the author of the Pentateuch, the first five books of the Old Testament, including most importantly Genesis, the account of the Creation of the World and of Adam and Eve, the Fall, the Flood, the lives of the Patriarchs, and the Hebrew slavery in Egypt. As a contemporary of Moses, and showing similar concerns, the hermetic texts were referred to by several of the early Church Fathers, including Lactantius, Augustine,

Eusebius and Origen. They saw them as evidence that Egyptian religion had both anticipated Christianity and influenced Greek philosophy. Through the writings of Hermes Trismegistus, it was believed that Plato had learnt the truths of the Creation; this early patristic viewpoint was summed up in the second century AD by Numenius of Apamea, who asked rhetorically: "What is *Plato* but *Moses Atticus*?" (Patrides 1969: 7). Which is to say, Plato merely reproduced for Greek philosophy what Moses had already established in the Scriptures. Moses, Hermes, Plato and their successors were thus all links in a chain which, it was argued, passed down the divinely-granted secrets of natural philosophy and theology from biblical to more modern times. This was, crudely speaking, the 'pristine theology', which carried with it 'pristine science'. This whole interpretation gave the hermetic texts orthodox respectability (Yates 1964: ch. 1).

This essentially explains why Ficino translated the hermetic texts before the Platonic when these ancient works were obtained for the Medicis in the mid-15th century. They were apparently older, and had seemingly influenced the Platonists and other Neoplatonists (such as the Greek philosopher Plotinus, who in the third century AD wrote an influential text on hieroglyphs). Hermes Trismegistus' works were accepted as important documents containing divine truths which had been passed down through the ages. As Ficino (1474) wrote, "every religion has something good in it; as long as it is directed towards God, the creator of all things, it is a true Christian religion" (Harrison 1990: 13; Walker 1972).

Using Ficino's Latin translations and commentaries, Neoplatonism was increasingly incorporated into 16th and 17th century natural philosophical studies, gradually ousting the Aristotelian philosophy taught in the universities. In England the influence was extensive, and can be seen in the works of Sir Thomas More and Robert Fludd, and, in particular, in the so-called Cambridge Platonists, Ralph Cudworth and Henry More. Equally, the belief in a 'pristine' theology passed down through the ages would be well developed in the 17th century, and would be summed up in the 18th century by Matthew Tindal (1730) in his controversial deistical tract, *Christianity as Old as the Creation*.

It is now, of course, known that the hermetic texts of Hermes Trismegistus were *not* the remote antique Egyptian founts of divine wisdom which Ficino and the Church Fathers had taken them to be. Rather, they actually dated to the first three centuries AD, and reflected the fusion of a wide range of influences upon Greco-Egyptian religion and philosophy, including the writings of Gnostics, Neoplatonists, Pythagoreans, Orphics, Mithraists, Chaldeans, Jews and Christians. Furthermore, this redating of the hermetic texts to the early Christian period was first made in the early 17th century by the Genevan scholar Isaac Casaubon (1614), who was then employed by the English court of James I (Yates 1964: 398–403). But Casaubon's scholarly insights had not spelt the end for Hermes Trismegistus. In Cambridge, Cudworth (1678) and More (1653) circumvented the textual redating problem by arguing that the hermetic works, whilst maybe not *wholly* original, were nevertheless based on an older wisdom that their authors would have had access to, and thus they still manifested the true vestiges of that older wisdom (which is in fact possibly closer to the truth).[1] Nor did Isaac Newton, who knew both Cudworth and More, appear to have been concerned with the dating problem. As late as the early 1680s he wrote a commentary on an alchemical work attributed to Hermes Trismegistus, which apparently contained information on the creation of the world (McGuire 1977; Teeter Dobbs 1991: 54).

This growing interest in Ancient Egypt – like the blossoming contemporary interest in the ancient civilization of China – was fuelled by increasing physical knowledge of North Africa and the Near and Far East. English travellers were starting to journey to Egypt from early in the 17th century (El Daly 2003: 142), and one of the earliest English accounts was by Henry Blount (1636), whose short, popular book had already reached an eighth edition by 1671. John Greaves' *Pyramidographia* (1646), the first treatise by an Englishman solely concerned with Egyptian antiquities, was a relatively brief work, but it remained an authoritative description of the pyramids for over a century (Perry 1743: vii). Interest in matters Egyptian also extended to the practice of mummification. London doctor Thomas Greenhill (1705) unsuccessfully attempted to extract the brains from corpses in the manner described by Herodotus; he suggested that the ancient Egyptians had held the Pythagorean belief in metempsychosis, the transmigration of souls or reincarnation.

One particular challenge posed to western scholars by ancient Egyptian history was that of its extended chronology. This chronology (as well as that of China) challenged the official biblical account of the age of the world. In 1658 James Ussher (1658: 1) had computed that Creation had occurred in 4004 BC (Champion Chapter 7, this volume). This exact date, though disputed, was given official Anglican sanction and was included in the Authorized Version of the Bible from 1701. The date remained authoritative until well into the 19th century (Coburn 1962).[2] Yet the Egyptians' claim for extended antiquity (Uphill 2003) had troubled St Augustine early in the Christian era, and in *The City of God* he had simply accused them of "abominable lyings" in claiming "for their wisdom an age of 100,000 years" (Schnapp 1996: 224). Greaves (1646: 17) had already observed that the precise dating of the pyramids' construction was an inquiry "of much importance, in regulating the various and uncertain traditions of the Ancients, concerning the Ægyptian Chronologie". But he went on to add that if he were to examine all the myriad arguments of just how long this history was, "we shall finde our selves intangled in a Labyrinth, and a Maze of Times, out of which we cannot, without much perplexitie, unwinde our selves" (Greaves 1646: 17). Sir John Marsham (1672) made some headway in untangling the complexities of Old Testament and Egyptian chronology, but speculation, doubt and simple confusion remained rife. As the Royal Society of London's demonstrator, Robert Hooke (Rossi 1984: 16), wrote, the histories of Egypt and China "tell us of many thousand Years more than ever we in Europe heard of by our Writings, if their Chronology may be granted, which indeed there is great reason to question". As long as the view of the short history of the world prevailed, Egyptian chronology would be widely interpreted as much exaggerated. The challenge for the majority of European scholars remained to fit Egyptian history into the Christian cosmology, and not *vice versa*.

## Egyptian science and Newtonian chronology

As well as the concern with its close association to religious history, the 17th and 18th century interest in Ancient Egypt was also intimately tied to the development of scientific knowledge. Early Fellows of the Royal Society of London, founded in 1660, took an interest in hieroglyphs as a route to finding a 'natural' or 'universal' language. This was in the nature of the language first used by Adam, and by which in Eden he had named all the creatures of Creation. John Wilkins (1668), one of the leading lights in establishing the Society, wrote on this subject, and attempted to create a universal writing system in which words would contain the nature of the thing they described, rather than being arbitrary signifiers (and see Singer 1989: 58–62).[3] As a student at Cambridge in 1661 Newton also made notes "Of an Universall Language" (Elliot 1957) and developed his own theory on Egyptian hieroglyphs (see below).

As well as providing a source for the retrieval of lost knowledge (for those who believed in this tradition), Ancient Egypt was also closely connected with the corruption of philosophical and theological practice. Thomas Sprat (1667: 5) ascribed the origins of astronomy and geometry to the traditional locus of the Assyrians, Chaldeans and Egyptians. But

> as to them we owe the *Invention*; so from them proceeded the first *Corruption* of knowledge. It was the custom of their Wise men, to wrap up their Observations on Nature, and the Manners of Men, in the dark Shadows of Hieroglyphicks; and to conceal them, as sacred Mysteries, from the apprehensions of the vulgar. This was a sure way to beget a Reverence in the Peoples Hearts towards themselves: but not to advance the true *Philosophy* of *Nature*.

Following Sprat, the Irish pantheist John Toland (1720: title page) explained that "the Exoteric and Esoteric Philosophy" was "the *External and Internal Doctrine* of the antients: the one open and public, accommodated to popular Prejudices and the establish'd Religions; the other private and secret, wherein, to the few capable and discrete, was taught the real TRUTH stript of all disguises". In ancient times the priesthood, the original possessors and protectors of the true divine wisdom of Creation which God had granted to Adam and his descendants, had come to fool themselves with their own deceptive stories. Eventually they had allowed idolatry to corrupt the divine religious and philosophical truths that had once been theirs.

These arguments were developed by the Cambridge scholar Thomas Burnet (1684), who, rejecting the Mosaic account of Creation, attempted to explain Earth's origin from the perspective of modern philosophical practice. Burnet utilized the idea of the two-fold philosophy, arguing that Moses had only given an account of Creation in Genesis that would be understood by the ignorant masses, whilst retaining the 'true' account for himself. He (Burnet 1692) went on to write that "it appears from the sacred Scriptures, that the Egyptian Wisdom was more ancient than [Moses'] and he was the Disciple rather than the Teacher of that learned Nation" (Gascoigne 1991: 182). He also argued that this "Barbaric Philosophy" could be traced back to "the Deluge, and Noah the common Father of Jews and Gentiles" who had "delivered the Lamp of learning" from the ante- to the postdiluvian worlds (Burnet 1736: 241–246). This notion appears to have had some currency outside the walls of academe, for the Norfolk physician and antiquary Sir Thomas Browne (1643) alluded to it, reflecting on the "great deale of obscurity" he found in reading Genesis, which suggested to him that "perhaps the mysticall method of *Moses* [was] bred up in the Hieroglyphicall Schooles of the Egyptians" (Martin 1964: 33–34).

The whole question of the relationship between biblical history and natural philosophy was of particular interest to Burnet's Cambridge colleague Isaac Newton, the foremost mathematician and natural philosopher of the age. Newton, like Burnet, believed that the corruption of ancient religion had proceeded hand in hand with the corruption of scientific knowledge. The priests of the ancient world had been the holders of both theological *and* philosophical wisdom – a situation essentially unchanged in 17th century England, where university Fellows were obliged to become ordained priests of the Church of England. This, in a nutshell, was Newton's problem. Probably in preparation for the taking of holy orders in the early 1670s Newton began pursuing biblical studies, reading the Scriptures and the Church Fathers. By the middle of the decade these studies had led him to the conclusion that the Church's doctrine of the Holy Trinity of God the Father, the Son and the Holy Ghost was a falsehood (Snobelen 1999; Stewart 1996). In Newton's opinion the Trinity had been grafted erroneously on to an earlier, pristine, Christianity: whilst Christ *was* the son of God, he was neither co-eternal nor consubstantial with Him. Yet, ever since Athanasius' defence of the doctrine of the Trinity at the Council of Nicaea in 325, the Trinity had been a pillar of orthodox belief, and an antitrinitarian opinion such as Newton's was heretical. Newton was careful to keep his unorthodox beliefs largely to himself, and through a special dispensation from the king in 1675 was exempted from taking holy orders: ordination would have forced him either to falsely affirm a belief in the Trinity, or to declare his Arianism and lose his university position.

In his hostility to the antiquity of the doctrine of the Trinity, Newton was taking a position in opposition to that of other contemporary English writers. Gale (1669: 346) had written that the idea of the Trinity was "scattered up and down in the *Oriental Parts*, especially *Phenecia* and *Egypt*", whilst Cudworth (1678) argued that the idea of the Trinity was everywhere to be found in pagan theology (Harrison 1990: 33). This knowledge, Cudworth believed, had been possessed by the Jews, and had been communicated by them to the Egyptians and other pagan nations; his reading of the ancient sources thus indicating that trinitarian theology could be found in Orpheus, Pythagoras and Plato, and in the arcane theology of the Egyptians, Persians and Romans. More (1653: 1) had, like Cudworth, defended the antiquity of the Trinity, which he considered to be "not a mere Pagan invention" but "from Moses originally" and not "from Pythagoras or Plato".[4] Stukeley would argue in the following century that it was a misinterpretation and corruption of the doctrine of the Trinity that had led the ancients into polytheism (Haycock 2002).

Newton believed that all heathen religions and their practices were based upon the ancient corruptions of an earlier, postdiluvian and divinely inspired theology which had first been practised by Noah and his sons after the Flood (Gascoigne 1991: 185; Harrison 1990: 114; Sailor 1988). This theology had been brought to Egypt by Noah's son Ham, who, it was traditionally supposed, was subsequently venerated by the Egyptians as their god Amon (Iversen 1993: 38–41). As Newton (sometime in the 1670s) wrote in his 'Philosophical origins of Gentile theology', "ye Mosaical religion concerning ye true God contains little else besides what was then in use among the Egyptians" (Force and Popkin 1990: 11; Westfall 1982).[5] There the one true religion had been corrupted by the onset of idolatry and polytheism. Newton described this true religion of Noah's as being "The religion of loving God and our neighbour". He suggested that the ethics taught by Noah and his sons was also subsequently taught to "the heathens by Socrates, Confucius and other philosophers, the Israelites by Moses and the Prophets and the Christians more fully by Christ and his Apostles" (McLachlan 1950: 28, 52). Newton also noted, "it's certain that ye old religion of the Egyptians was ye true [Noachian] religion tho corrupted before the age of Moses by the mixture of fals Gods with that of ye true one" (Newton, quoted in Gascoigne 1991: 190). In Newton's opinion, Moses had begun a "reformation" of these corruptions "but retained the indifferent elements of the Egyptians", and then Christ had come in turn and "reformed the religion of Moses" (Turnbull 1959–1977, 3: 338).

Newton (1733: 204–205) believed that Christianity had been further corrupted in the fourth century, when Pope Gregory the Great had facilitated the conversion of the pagans by replacing the festivals of their gods with "annual festivals to the *Saints* and *Martyrs* ... By the pleasures of these festivals the *Christians* increased much in number, and decreased as much in virtue". The corruption of the most ancient, true, Noachic religion was, therefore, later paralleled by the pattern of corruption of Christianity and its descent from the fourth century onwards into the idolatry of the worship of saints: this was in essence no different from the pagans' earlier adoration of dead kings and heroes. Added to this was the polytheistic taint of trinitarianism: Newton, of course, did not consider *himself* to be a heretic. So in Newton's eyes, the clear waters of true theology and natural philosophy had been muddied through a continuous process of corruption, before returning by gradual steps of reform and rediscovery back to truth again. The 16th century Reformation had been one step in this process. In Newton's scheme, this reformation was still incomplete.[6]

Newton thus remained committed throughout his life to the idea that originally all Mankind had worshipped one God and one fundamental law, but that the corruption of this religion had brought with it a corruption of scientific knowledge. This was reflected in the design of ancient temples. As early as the fifth century BC Herodotus (Harrison 2003; Tait Chapter 2, this volume) had recorded – in remarks of considerable subsequent authority given their sheer antiquity – that, according to the priests at Memphis with whom he conversed, it was the Egyptians who

> first brought into use the names of the twelve gods, which the Greeks adopted from them; and first erected altars, images, and temples to the gods; and also first engraved upon stone the figures of animals. In most of these cases they proved to me that what they said was true.

> (Herodotus II.4)

Newton was interested in why the Egyptians had used animals as templates for their temples. From reading Lucian, he noted how "the Temples of Egypt are beautiful & large being built of costly stones but if you seek a God within you will find either an Ape or a Stork or a Swallow or a Cat. To represent things by". He (Bodleian Library, Oxford, New College MS 361/2 f. 108v) explained that these "beasts wch the Egyptians honoured were nothing else than the symbols or hieroglyphics of their first fathers propagated down to their several tribes". He also perceived an analogy between the Egyptians' use of hieroglyphs and the language of the biblical prophets who, he wrote, "frequently used" "the same language", so that birds, animals and insects were used by both to represent "kingdoms & bodies politic, fire to signify warr wch consumes them, the sun moon & stars to signify the king & his people" (Bodleian Library, Oxford, New College MS 361/2 f. 108r).

Newton proceeded to suggest that this was the reason the Egyptians had apparently worshipped animals and animal-headed gods, and had built temples in their shape, for

> under these characters or hieroglyphics the several tribes or Nomes honoured their first fathers & worshipped them as Gods. And this I take to be the reason of the Egyptians worshipping their Gods in the shapes & species of Birds, Beasts, ffishes & Plants ... ffor the making & worshipping such images was referred to & prohibited in the second commandment when Israel was newly come out of Egypt & there fore was older than ye days of Moses ...

> (Newton, Bodleian Library, Oxford, New College MS 361/2 f. 108r)

This was the commandment as stated in Exodus 20:4, "Thou shalt not make unto thee any graven image, or any likeness of any thing that is in heaven above, or that is in the earth beneath, or that is in the water under the earth". Undoubtedly Newton was also here reminded of St Paul's remark (Romans 1:22–23) concerning the Gentiles' corruption of divine worship: "Professing themselves to be wise, they became fools. And changed the glory of the uncorruptible God into an image made like to corruptible mortal man, and to birds, and fourfooted beasts, and creeping things." For Newton, Egyptian hieroglyphs did not hide wisdom, they hid spurious religion in the form of ancestor worship.

Newton believed that the idolatrous practices of the Hebrews had been learnt directly from the Egyptians. And it was the Egyptians also who had spread the knowledge of temple building round the Mediterranean and into Europe. In 'The Originals of Europe' Newton (Bodleian Library, Oxford, New College MS 361/2 f. 104r) wrote that the Phoenicians had traded on the Red Sea until "the revolt of Edom from Judea", from when they "began to sail upon the Mediterranean & built Carthage & some towns in Spain ... & going out of the straits discovered Madera & Britain till then unpeopled". Stukeley (1980: 70) recorded Newton telling him how "when the Pastors were ejected [from] Egypt in great numbers, some went to Syria, to Greece, to Mauritania, to Spain, Italy, &c, under the conduct of the Egyptian Hercules, who passd the Straits, built Carteia, Cadiz, & was thence calld Melcartus, & this man first found the tyn trade to Brittan". Stukeley (1727) also wrote that Newton had told him that the Greeks had "borrowd their architecture, as they had their religious rites" from the Egyptians.

In this way the practice of erecting standing stones and open-air temples such as Stonehenge had been brought to Britain. Newton proposed that the religion "most ancient & most generally received by the nations in the first ages [i.e. after Noah] was that of the Prytanea or Vestal Temples" (quoted in Iliffe 1989: 81). These temples, he suggested, were circular structures with a burning flame at their centre representing the Sun. Newton believed that these vestal temples showed that the ancients had originally understood the heliocentric universe as 'rediscovered' by Copernicus. As Newton (Yahuda MS 41 f. 8r) explained, it

> was one designe of the first institution of the true religion in Egypt to propose to mankind by the frame of the ancient Temples, the study of the frame of the world as

the true Temple of the great God they worshipped ... And therefore that a Prytanaeum might deserve the name of his Temple they framed it so as in the fittest manner [to] represent the whole systeme of the heavens. A point of religion then which nothing can be more rational.

Furthermore, from his reading of travel writers, Newton found that such vestal temples existed around the world, and examples had been reported in China, India and Ireland. He (Newton, Yahuda MS 41 f. 3r–3v) also observed that "In England neare Salisbury there is a piece of antiquity called Stonehenge wch seems to be an ancient *Prytaneum*. For it is an area compassed circularly wth two rows of very great stones wth passages on all sides for people to go in and out at". He continued, "Tis said there are some pieces of antiquity of ye same form & structure in Denmark". He also believed that the Hebrews had espoused this same heliocentric belief in Solomon's Temple, "placing ye fire in the common center ... framing ye Tabernacle & Temple so as to make it a symbol of the world" (Newton, Yahuda MS 41 f. 6r).

Newton was of the opinion, therefore, that circular stone temples such as Stonehenge, and more sophisticated structures such as Solomon's Temple, scattered across the globe, were all vestiges of the cult of the vestal flame, and were the physical remains of the most ancient religion of all (Gascoigne 1991: 188). This religion, based upon the Noachic moral philosophy, had been corrupted by later generations, who had turned to the worship of the stars (which they named after their dead kings and heroes) and to 'hieroglyphical figures'. Over time, through the corrupt practices of their priests, they had confused the meaning of the vestal fire representing the sun which burnt at the centre of the *prytanae*, taking it instead to be a fire at the centre of the earth. Hence, through religious corruption, they had lost the truth of the heliocentric universe. Their new system, which placed the world at the centre of the universe, had subsequently been elaborated in the geocentric system of Ptolemy of Alexandria, an erroneous system which had dominated western astronomy until Copernicus' rediscovery.

As can be seen in his writings of monotheism and the rituals of worship practised in Egypt, Babylonia, India and Chaldea after the Flood, Newton saw an intimate relationship between science and religion in the early centuries of the world. Monotheism had existed alongside a correct interpretation of the universe, as expressed in ancient temples representing the true form of the heliocentric universe. So it was that the onset of the corruption of religion through polytheism was intimately tied to the corruption of knowledge of the natural world (Manuel 1974: 43). Newton's natural philosophical and theologico-historical studies shared the same goal, that is, to restore the true understanding of God's relations with humanity and the natural order that had been gradually lost by the growth of idolatry after the Flood. He believed that the recovery of true natural philosophy also implicitly involved a recovery of true (natural) religion (Gascoigne 1991: 188–189). Newton made this belief publicly clear:

And no doubt, if the Worship of false Gods had not blinded the Heathen, their moral Philosophy would have gone farther than to the four Cardinal Virtues; and instead of teaching the Transmigration of Souls, and to worship the Sun and Moon, and dead Heroes, they would have taught us to worship our true Author and Benefactor, as their

Ancestors did under the Government of Noah and his Sons before they corrupted
themselves.

(Newton 1721: 379)

Newton thus held that his discoveries in natural philosophy were in fact the
rediscovery of an ancient, but lost, wisdom.

In the *Classical Scholia* Newton (Casini 1984) stated his belief that the Pythagoreans
had known his inverse square rule, "and adumbrated it by the harmony of the
celestial spheres ... measuring the intervals of the spheres by the intervals of the tones"
(McGuire and Rattansi 1966: 115). Newton passed his notes for the *Scholia* on to
Oxford Professor of Astronomy David Gregory (1715: iii–iv, xi) who examined and
'proved' the argument that Newton's discovery of universal gravity "was both
known and diligently cultivated by the most ancient Philosophers". Gregory
explained that Pythagoras had understood "that the Gravity of the planets towards
the Sun (according to whose measures the Planets move) was reciprocally as the
Squares of their Distances from the Sun" (Casini 1984, 1988; Iliffe 1995; McGuire and
Rattansi 1966). Through Gregory and others, the intimate connection that Newton
made between ancient and modern science and religion became clear (Iliffe 1995: 164–
165). Stukeley (FM MS 1130 Stu (1) f. 179), who was close to Newton in the 1720s, duly
described him as "the Great Restorer of True Philosophy".

Newton's interest in ancient history and the wisdom of the ancients was further
explicated in three posthumously published works (1728a, b, 1733). He (Newton
1728a: 8) declared his intention "to make Chronology suit with the Course of Nature,
with Astronomy, with Sacred History, with *Herodotus* the Father of History, and with
it self". He claimed that his chronology of the ancient history was accurate within five
or ten years, or "sometimes twenty, and not much above". He explained how the
Ancient Egyptians had understood the heliocentric system, though they had
disseminated this knowledge "under the veil of religious rites and hieroglyphick
symbols" (Newton 1728b: 2).

Yet despite the strong tradition from which he developed his thesis, Newton's
accounts of ancient history and religious chronology received a mixed response.
William Warburton told Stukeley (10 February 1733), "Though he was a prodigy in
his way, yet I never expected great things on this kind (which requires a perfect
knowledge of antient Literature, History, and Mankind), from a man who spent all his
days looking through a telescope" (Nichols 1817, II: 21). Such was the poor reputation
of Newton's biblical studies that by 1732 the Oxford antiquary Thomas Hearne (1732:
100–101) could (inaccurately) observe that "Sir Isaac Newton, tho' a great
Mathematician, was a man of very little Religion, in so much that he is ranked with
the Heterodox men of the age".

In addition to these 18th century critics of Newton, not all 17th century English
scholars accepted the belief in the wisdom of the ancients. Sir Francis Bacon rejected
the worth of ancient knowledge that so preoccupied Newton. He (Bacon 1620) did not
consider it relevant "whether the discoveries to come were once know to the ancients
... than it should matter to men whether the New World is the famous island of
Atlantis which the ancient world knew ... For the discovery of things is to be taken
from the light of nature, not recovered from the shadows of antiquity" (see Dear 2001:

58–60; Jardine and Silverthorne 2000: 122). Nevertheless, Bacon (1701) did recognise an important but short-lived period of Presocratic philosophy in ancient Greece, writing how the "Antiquities of the first Age (except those we find in Sacred Writ) were buried in Oblivion and Silence: Silence was succeeded by Poetical Fables; and fables again were followed by the Records we now enjoy ... But concerning Human Wisdom, I do indeed ingenuously and freely confess, that I am inclined to imagine, that under some of the Ancient Fictions lay couched certain Mysteries and Allegories, even from their first invention". Bacon did not believe that the tales told by Homer and Hesiod were invented by them, but that they were the "abstracted Airs of better times, which by Tradition from more Ancient Nations, fell into the Trumpets and Flutes of the *Græcians*".

Bacon thus accepted the same two-fold philosophy described by Newton, Toland and many others. But he did not believe that the ancients had deliberately intended to hide knowledge beneath the veils "of Fables, Enigma's, Parables, and Similies of all sorts". Rather, by these methods they had "sought to teach, and lay open ... especially seeing the Understandings of Men were in those times rude and impatient, and almost incapable of any Subtilties ... for as *Hieroglyphicks* preceeded Letters, so Parables were more ancient than Arguments" (Bacon 1701: 11–12; Singer 1989: 49–70). For Bacon, the Sphinx was an allegory for 'natural philosophy'. Its wings stood for the swift passage of knowledge and inventions, whilst its sharp talons represented "the Axioms and Arguments of Science" which "so fasten upon the mind, and so strongly apprehend and hold it". The Sphinx can only be overcome by a lame man because those "too speedy of Pace, in hasting to *Sphynx* her *Ænigma's*", become "distracted by Disputations", instead of learning "by Works and Effects" (Bacon 1701: 86–89). And Bacon made at least one concession to the Greek debt to the Egyptians. In his discussion of the Greek myths concerning "Pan, or Nature", he suggested that the Greeks "either by intercourse with the *Ægyptians*, or one way or other" had "heard something of the *Hebrew* Mysteries; for it points to the state of the World, not considered in immediate Creation, but after the fall of Adam, exposed and made subject to Death and Corruption" (Bacon 1701: 27).

Bacon's attitude to ancient wisdom was thus complex. However, by the end of the century there were English scholars prepared to reject ancient claims with more determination. William Wotton (1694: chs. IX, X) dismissed theories of ancient wisdom, arguing that the claimed extent of Egyptian and Chaldean knowledge did not stand up to critical scrutiny. But perhaps the most extensive attack against ancient wisdom was that made by John Woodward (1777: 10, 17, 30), Professor of Physics at Gresham College, London, and a leading antagonist of Newton. He believed that in modern times the only supporters of the idea of Egyptian wisdom were those who bore "no good-will to Christianity", and who claimed that Moses' knowledge had come from them, and not directly from God. For Woodward (1777: 10, 17, 30), the Egyptians were "the most ostentatious, boasting people in the universe", so sunk in idolatry "that they seem to have known little if anything of God". In his opinion, Egyptian wisdom was superior only in so far as it was relative to the poor learning of the nations around them, and it had, anyway, been exaggerated by over-respectful ancient writers such as Herodotus, Diodorus and Plutarch. He also adopted the stance that Egyptian architecture was nothing particularly extraordinary or aesthetically interesting. The pyramids were no more than a "great many vast stones" placed one on top of another "without any consideration of order and beauty; the whole speaking much more the industry and labour of the undertakers, than their ingenuity of contrivance" (Woodward 1777: 20). Their temples were equally "confused, barbarous, and ill-contrived"; in their painting and sculpture they "aimed at something that was hideous, deformed, and monstrous" (Woodward 1777: 22, 24). Mummification was a pointless practice that succeeded as well as it did only because of Egypt's arid atmosphere – he pointed out that mummies (as well as other antiquities) brought back to England's damp and smoky climate quickly deteriorated and rotted away. He (Woodward 1777: 26–27) did not see the purpose in removing the brain and entrails of the mummified corpse, thus leaving the returning soul either with "a very indifferent habitation" or obliging it to reframe these organs anew, "and then nobody will be well able to imagine why the rest of the body might not as well have been framed by the same means, without all this trouble of preserving it, and, in truth, but in a very sorry manner after all".

It was hieroglyphs alone that gave the impression that the Egyptians "were masters of some mighty knowledge". This false perception survived because no-one, not even the Greeks, could actually read them. In fact, Woodward declared, the hieroglyphs – with their clear obsession with birds and serpents – concealed not great philosophy at all: they were chiefly "an historical representation" of their absurd religious customs. As a system for passing down knowledge they had nothing on Greek letters, and were "vastly more defective than even the Chinese" (Woodward 1777: 10, 13–14):

> It is a reflection one has but too often occasion to make, that no persons fall into so many and enormous soloecisms as men of learning and much reading. There are, in the numerous and almost endless shoals of books at this day extant, so many things that are obscure, perplext, and inconsistent, so many that are dubious and uncertain, and so many finally that are not true, that few readers have capacity, attention, and strength of mind, sufficient to make a fit choice of things, and rightly to digest and dispose of them.
>
> (Woodward 1777: 70)

Woodward's final recourse was Scripture; it was Scripture alone that could be trusted in this uncertain world of half-truth, speculation and error.

## The 18th century approach

In the 17th century scholars such as Burnet, Spencer and Newton established the scholarly approach to Egyptian history and biblical chronology that would be continued into the first half of the 18th century. Stukeley was one of the most influential writers to carry forward this tradition. Significantly, the study of religious chronology became increasingly important in 18th century England as a potential solution to what many considered the dire threat of a tide of irreligion sweeping the country. Sir Matthew Hale (1677) expressed his doubt that there was "so much speculative Atheism abroad in the World as many good men fear and suspect: But if there be but one quarter of that Atheism in the World, I do not know any better Cure of it, or Preservative against it, next to the Grace of God, than the due consideration of the Origination of Mankind" (Hunter 1990; Redwood 1996). It appeared that the salvation of true Christianity lay in chronology – and it was as a part of chronology that Egyptian history was most closely studied in this period.

This was certainly how the Cambridge-educated physician and Newtonian philosopher David Hartley saw things. In December 1735 he inquired of Stukeley, who was then in the midst of his researches on the stone circles of Avebury and Stonehenge (Nichols 1817: 805),

> How go your Chronological affairs on? As far as I am a judge, you gentlemen who have abilities and inclination to defend Revelation ought not to be idle. There seems to be a general doubt at least of Christianity prevailing amongst all the moderately learned of the world; and some of good learning and abilities are quite Infidels. I have no fear but the History and Chronology of the Scriptures can never be too much studied, because the arguments of that kind, when once explained rightly, are level to all capacities, and yet so convincing, that I think nothing can resist them ...

(Hartley to Stukeley, 19 December 1735)

As a long-lived, prolific and influential writer, diarist and sociable 'networker', Stukeley and his legacy was at the centre of English antiquarian studies through a large part of the 18th century. Though a figure of fun to some by the time of his death in 1765, as a friend and biographer of Newton he is a significant link between 17th and 18th century approaches to Egyptian history in England (Haycock 2002). In 1718 he became a Fellow of the Royal Society, which was then under Newton's presidency and firm influence, and he first visited Stonehenge and Avebury the following year. Stukeley spent the next two decades working on comprehensive monographs of these sites, in which he developed his theory that both had been built by the British Druids (Ucko *et al.* 1991). We have already seen that Newton had noted the existence of Stonehenge, and had dated it to the most ancient period of the world after the Flood. However, ever since the architect Inigo Jones (1655) had published a book on the subject in 1655, the argument that Stonehenge had been built by the Romans predominated.[7] Newton and Stukeley's redating was, therefore, radical for their day.

At Avebury, Stukeley was inspired by his reading of Athanasius Kircher (Curran Chapter 5, this volume; Iversen 1993: 89–102). He borrowed Kircher's Neo-Platonic notion of hieroglyphics as divine symbols, and interpreted the entire complex of stone circles and avenues at Avebury as the hieroglyphic figure of a winged serpent penetrating a circle (Figure 6:1). On the reverse of a drawing of the termination of the Kennet avenue and temple at Avebury, dated 15 May 1724, he had made a sketch of this glyph, and noted beside it, "this is the representation of god or the great soul of the world among the persian magi[,] the egyptian priests & we find it here among the western Druids doubtless tis of vastest antiquity & borrowd by them all from the post diluvian times". After noting that the Egyptians' doctrines were concealed "in hieroglyphs & symbolical characters" (Stukeley Bodleian Library, Oxford, Gough Maps 231 f. 31), he wrote that he had no doubt "but every part of this & like works has such secret meanings tho' now we have no means left of discovering it". The Avebury symbol, he claimed, was a representation of the Holy Trinity, and proved that the temple's builders, the British Druids, had originally practised the 'true' trinitarian religion of Adam, Noah and Moses (Stukeley 1743). Stukeley talked on a number of occasions with Newton on the subject of Egyptian history, the colonizing of Britain, and the construction of ancient temples, and there is a clear (though possibly

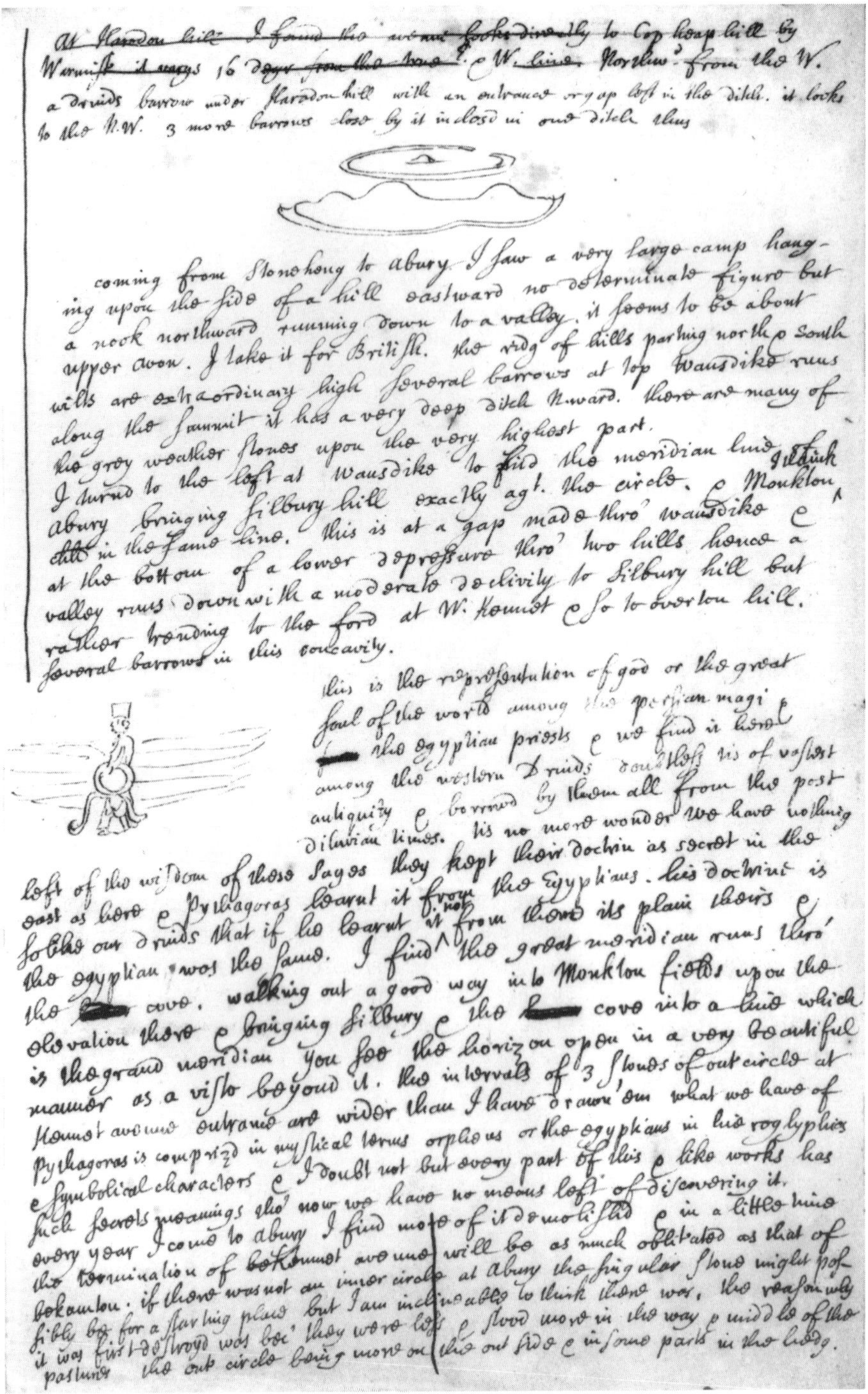

At Harrodon hill I found the avenue looks directly to Cop heap hill by Warwick it runs 16 degrees from the true E. & W. line. Northw'd from the W. a druids barrow under Harrodon hill with an entrance or gap left in the ditch. it looks to the N.W. 3 more barrows close by it inclosd in one ditch thus

coming from Stoneheng to Abury I saw a very large camp hanging upon the side of a hill eastward no determinate figure but a nook northward running down to a valley. it seems to be about upper Avon. I take it for British. the ridg of hills parting north & south hills are extraordinary high several barrows at top Wansdike runs along the summit it has a very deep ditch Nward. there are many of the grey weather stones upon the very highest part. I turnd to the left at Wansdike to find the meridian line which abury bringing Silbury hill exactly agt. the circle. & Monkton still in the same line. this is at a gap made thro' Wansdike & at the bottom of a lower depresure thro' two hills hence a valley runs down with a moderate declivity to Silbury hill but rather trending to the ford at W. Kennet & so to overton hill. several barrows in this concavity.

this is the representation of god or the great soul of the world among the persian magi & the egyptian priests & we find it here among the western Druids doubtless tis of vastest antiquity & borrowd by them all from the post diluvian times. tis no mere wonder we have nothing left of the wisdom of these sages they kept their doctrin as secret in the east as here & Pythagoras learnt it from the Egyptians. his doctrine is so like our druids that if he learnt it from them its plain theirs & the egyptian was the same. I find the great meridian runs thro' the cove. walking out a good way into Monkton fields upon the elevation there & bringing Silbury & the cove into a line which is the grand meridian You see the horizon open in a very beautiful manner as a visto beyond it. the intervals of 3 stones of out circle at Kennet avenue outrance are wider than I have drawn em what we have of Pythagoras is comprizd in mystical terms orpheus or the egyptians in his roglyphics & symbolical characters & I doubt not but every part of this & like works has such secret meanings tho' now we have no means left of discovering it. every year I come to abury I find more of it demolishd & in a little time the termination of Kennet avenue will be as much obliterated as that of Bekamton. if there was not an inner circle at abury the singular stone might possibly be for a staring place but I am inclinable to think there was. the reason why it was first destroyd was bec: they were left & stood more in the way & middle of the pasture the out circle being more on the out side & in some parts in the hedg.

Figure 6:1   William Stukeley's (15 May 1724) representation of the winged serpent penetrating a circle which epitomized the true trinitarian belief of the Druids (Bodleian Library, Oxford, Gough Maps 231 f. 31).

coincidental) relationship between Stukeley's interpretation of Avebury as a hieroglyph of a serpent, and Newton's description of Egyptian temples as hieroglyphs of animals. It is also apparent that Stukeley was, as he declared in his biography of Newton, defending his hero from (in fact quite accurate) accusations of Arianism. As Stukeley confidently but wrongly wrote, "the ch[urch] of England intirely claims him as her son, in faith & in practice" (Stukeley 1752).

Around the time that he gave up medicine and took holy orders in 1729, Stukeley read Samuel Shuckford (1728), who reiterated much of the 17th century 'Cambridge tradition' on the history of ancient philosophy and religion. Shuckford's book enjoyed some success, reaching a fifth edition by 1819. An Anglican clergyman, Shuckford had the same objective as Stukeley: to attack the deistic tenets of natural religion. "If there was no Revelation made to the Men of the first Ages," he asked rhetorically, "how came the Knowledge and Worship of God so early into the World?" (Shuckford 1728: 362–363.) He asserted that what he had taken from reading Phoenician and Egyptian history would "satisfy the judicious Reader, that these ancient Writers, before their Writings were corrupted, left Accounts very agreeable to Moses". He observed that from an examination of these accounts he found that "the ancient Heathen remains ... were clear and true, when left by their Authors, but After-writers corrupted them by the Addition of Fable and false philosophy" (Shuckford 1728: xx–xxi). He reiterated the earlier scholarly tradition that Pythagoras had through his "diligent searches" in Phoenicia, Egypt and Babylon "acquired a great Stock of ancient Truths", and that "*Plato*'s Works are everywhere full of the ancient Traditions" (Shuckford 1728: l–lvi). He (Shuckford 1728: lix–lx) believed that "instead of maintaining the Credit of their Philosophy, they [the Pythagoreans] corrupted it by degrees, made it subtil and unintelligible, until in time they sunk it to nothing". It was only Aristotle, the "last of the ancient Philosophers", whose system was "invented", and by rejecting "the ancient Traditional Knowledge" had advanced a new philosophy "totally distant from Truth" (Shuckford 1728: lx).

Shuckford's reading of ancient writers hinted "that the Egyptians were at first Worshippers of the true God". This seemed to be confirmed by an examination of Egyptian antiquities, as "we may find in their Remains as noble and as true Notions of the Deity, as are to be met with in the Antiquities of any other People". Here "they preserved the Knowledge of the true Religion" until by adding "Speculations of their own, then by degrees they corrupted and lost it" (Shuckford 1728: 312–313). From the example of the Egyptians he continued,

> And thus at first there was a general Agreement about Religion in the World; and if we look into the Particulars of the Heathen Religion, even after they were much corrupted, we may evidently find several Practices, as well as Principles, sufficient to induce us to think that all the ancient Religions in the World were originally the same ...

Shuckford's book thus aimed to counter the rise of atheism by proving the existence of revelation, showing that "there was a Stock of Knowledge in the World, which we cannot see how the Possessors of it could possibly have obtained any other way" (Shuckford 1728: lxiv). This argument, reworked, also formed part of the deistical conviction that God had been knowable in ancient times *without* revelation.

This argument from ancient history, the passing down of ancient knowledge to the present day, appears to have remained a strong historical force in the early decades of 18th century England. It was enshrined in the history of the Freemasons, who emerge into the full light of history in 1717, with the establishment in London of Grand Lodge (Hamill and Mollier 2003). Early members included a number of Royal Society Fellows, and the membership at this date included some of the foremost English scholars. On 29 September 1721 the Grand Master "and the Lodge finding Fault with all the Copies of the *Old Gothic Constitutions*, order'd Brother *James Anderson*, A.M., to digest the same in a new and better Method" (Gould 1893: 138). Anderson's (1723) rewrite of Masonic history contained a 'dedication' by the Newtonian scholar John Theophilus Désagulier, who claimed it contained "a just and exact Account of *Masonry* from the Beginning of the World" to the present day. Anderson began his history with the statement that Masonry's origins lay in geometry, which "ADAM, our first *Parent*, created after the Image of God, *the great Architect of the Universe*" had "written on his Heart" (Anderson 1723: 1). Noah had built the Ark "according to the Rules of Masonry", carrying the geometric and Masonic skills to the postdiluvians, who had used them to build the Tower of Babel. With the subsequent dispersal of nations Masons had "carry'd the mighty Knowledge with them into distant Parts" including Egypt, where they displayed their skills in constructing the pyramids. There the enslaved Israelites had learnt the craft, such that "at their leaving Egypt, [they] were a whole Kingdom of *Masons*, well instructed, under the Conduct of their GRAND MASTER MOSES, who often marshall'd them into a regular and *general Lodge*" (Anderson 1723: 4–5, 8). Subsequently these Jewish Masons had built Solomon's Temple, which was "justly esteemed by far the finest Piece of Masonry upon Earth before or since". They then carried their skills abroad, travelling as far afield as Greece, India and Africa. They had also apparently travelled to Europe, "because some think there are a few *Remains* of good masonry ... in *Europe*, raised by the original Skill that the first Colonies brought with them, as the *Celtic Edifices*, erected by the ancient Gauls, and by the ancient *Britains* too, who were a colony of *Celtes*, long before the *Romans* invaded this Island" (Anderson 1723: 10–13, 27–28).[8] However, this whole biblically-based interpretation of ancient history was increasingly challenged as the 18th century progressed.

The short-lived Egyptian Society first gathered in London in December 1741. There were eight founder members, all of whom had travelled in Egypt, and four of whom subsequently published important travelogues. There were also a number of associate members, who had not travelled to Egypt but had an interest in its history. Among these was Stukeley, who was the only member to make any extensive notes on the Society's activities. As he recorded, under John Montagu, the Earl of Sandwich's presidency, the group's purpose was "the promotion & preserving Egyptian & other antient learning" (Bodleian Library, Oxford, MS Eng. Misc. e. 124 f. 85). Sandwich had included in his Grand Tour itinerary a voyage from Greece and Turkey to Egypt and Malta, and in Istanbul took lessons in Turkish to be better able to understand the customs of the region. Manuscript versions of his book (Montagu 1799) were read by some members of the Egyptian Society. Here, Sandwich recorded the traditional belief that Egypt "Anciently surpassed all others, not only in the fertility of the soil, but also in the learning and knowledge of its inhabitants". Egypt was the origin of all arts and sciences ... and the fountain, whence sprung that religion, which afterwards spread itself abroad in different shapes over the greatest parts of the known world. It was to Ægypt that Greece was beholden, not only for its laws and customs, but also for the greatest part of its inhabitants. The Athenians, who in succeeding ages made so great a figure in the world, owed their original to the Ægyptians; since Attica was peopled by a colony from Ægypt ... they let them [the native Greeks] into the more occult sciences, teaching them the foundations of their religion, communicating to them their knowledge in astronomy, physic, and mathematics; and explaining to them the secrets and mysteries of nature.

(Montagu 1799: 410–411)

At Thebes he recorded how "The temples and palaces in it were innumerable, and the number of obelisks and other public buildings rendered it, according to all authors who have mentioned it, the most splendid city in the universe". But he noted that "Besides many deities ... they also worshipped many ridiculous objects of adoration, collected from among the birds, beasts, aquatic animals, reptiles, plants, and insects" (Montagu 1799: 412). He dismissed hieroglyphs out of hand. They were but an invention "of the priests who composed them ... in that ænigmatical habit purposely to make the common people imagine that some mystery was couched under them" (Montagu 1799: 419). This assured them in their own positions of power, as only they could interpret them, and the same was true of their claims for great antiquity. Altogether, Sandwich's reflections on Egyptian religion were judiciously cautious:

Nothing certainly would afford a more copious subject to an author than the religion of the Ægyptians; as he would have an open field to display both his reading and invention, in the explanation of the many mysteries and ænigmas ... But such an undertaking, however well executed, is liable to the very obvious objection of such an explanation's being the pure invention of the author; whom being sensible that it would not be easy to contradict him, might be concluded to have given an entire scope of his imagination, and explained the difficulties to the suggestion of his own fancy. And such I make no sort of doubt is the foundation, on which all the modern writers have built, who have treated that subject ...

(Montagu 1799: 418–419)

The other chief founding members of the Society were Richard Pococke, Frederick Norden, Charles Perry and William Lethieullier. Pococke, a future bishop in Ireland, had visited Egypt in 1737–1738, ascending the Nile as far as Philae, before travelling on to Palestine, Cyprus, Asia Minor and Greece. His (Pococke 1743–1745) accounts of Egypt, ancient and modern, included numerous illustrations (Figure 6:2). Though of a mixed quality, and revealing no great understanding of architecture, they helped to draw further attention to the architecture of the region. Likewise, the work of Norden (1755, 1757), a Danish naval lieutenant who visited Egypt at the same time as Pococke, was published posthumously with 195 geographical, topographical and archaeological engravings (e.g. Figure 6:3; Wheatcroft 2003: 155–157). Perry (1743) had travelled in the eastern Mediterranean between 1739 and 1741. Lastly, Lethieullier in 1756 bequeathed a collection of Egyptian antiquities, including a mummy, to the British Museum (Gordon 1737). Some 25 of those termed "associates" who had not been to Egypt but were interested in its history were also listed in the Society's minutes. Meetings focused on items brought back from Egypt. Sandwich had returned with two mummies and eight embalmed ibis from the catacombs of

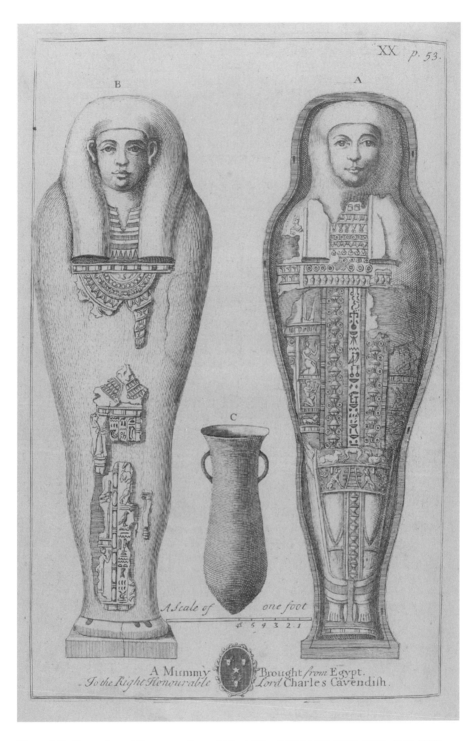

Figure 6:2  Engraving of 'A mummy brought from Egypt' (Pococke 1743–1745, 1: pl. XLVI).

*Tête colossale du Sphynx, vue en face.*

*Elle est au devant de la seconde Pyramide de Memphis.*

XLVI.

Figure 6:3    Norden's 'colossal head of the sphinx' in front of a pyramid at Giza (Norden 1755, 1: pl. XLVI).

Memphis, as well as 50 intaglios and 500 medals. At the Society he showed such things as a mummified ibis, an inscription from Athens, and a Greek bronze. Prints of antiquities were brought to the meetings by Norden, and Pococke delivered an account of the dissection of a human mummy.

In January 1742 Stukeley visited Norden at his London lodgings and saw "his amazing collections of drawings". Stukeley observed how "there are very many intire temples left, of a stupendous grandeur ... many prodigious obelisks set before the temples". Norden, who was a careful and accurate observer, also informed Stukeley that back in Denmark there "are many of the Druids altars left, which they know to be such" (Bodleian Library, Oxford, MS Eng. misc. e. 124, ff. 92–93). For Stukeley, the Druids became a focal point for interpretations of Egyptian antiquities. In the summer of 1741 Pococke had visited him at his home in Stamford, and Stukeley recorded in his diary: "Dr Pocock ... says, when in Ireland, he observ'd a surprizing conformity between the irish & the antient Egyptians" (Stukeley, Bodleian Library, Oxford, MS Eng. misc. e. 125 f. 40; Leerssen 1996). Through the antiquarian writings of John Aubrey, Edward Lhwyd and John Toland, Stukeley was already aware of Irish stone circles and other prehistoric structures such as Newgrange, observing (Stukeley, Bodleian Library, Oxford, MS Eng. misc. c. 323 f. 66) that the locals' "fancy of thos stones coming from the farthest parts of Africa seems to show they were Egyptian colonys". Pococke (Nichols 1817: 808) repeated his belief in 1754, writing to Stukeley from Dublin: "I am sure there was a colony here from Egypt ... I take it, when the Continent was in wars in the 5th and 6th centuries, people came over to study, as to a place of quiet; but I believe the learning was very little."

This kind of information was of profound interest to Stukeley, who had as early as 1723 or 1724 drawn up a list of 13 similarities between the beliefs and practices of Egyptian priests and the Celtic Druids. These included a belief in the immortality of the soul, their division into different 'colleges' and orders, the practice of human sacrifice, "the custom of women reigning" such as Boadicea and Cleopatra, and the "setting up stones of a stupendous size" (Stukeley, Bodleian Library, Oxford, MS Eng. misc. c. 323 f. 240). Even James Macpherson (1773: 233) was writing that "the ideas of the Druids concerning God were certainly the same with those of the eastern philosophers". As odd as this relationship may now strike us, it played an important part in the idea of Egypt and ancient civilizations in the second half of the 18th century.

The belief in a connection between western Europe and the ancient civilizations of the eastern Mediterranean and North Africa had a long legacy. That the Druids of Britain and Gaul had communicated with ancient Greek philosophers, including Pythagoras, had its authority from classical texts. These sources have been the foundation for all subsequent information and speculation regarding the origins of Druidic religion and 'philosophy'. But, as it has been observed, as brief as these passages from the classical and patristic accounts are, they "have possibly never yielded two identical interpretations" (Owen 1962: 1). Posidonius, who travelled widely in the western Mediterranean including Gaul, mentioned the Druids in his *Histories*. Though only fragments of his 52 books on the history of the world survive, his writings on the Druids either influenced or were used by three further writers: the Greek geographer Strabo; the Greek-Sicilian historian Diodorus Siculus; and the

Roman general and dictator Gaius Julius Caesar. According to Diodorus, the Druids were "philosophers and theologians", "skilled in the divine nature" and able to communicate with the gods. Strabo noted their pursuit of natural and moral philosophy, an observation with which Caesar concurred. Caesar (*The Gallic War* VI: 14) wrote that the Druids had "many discussions as touching the stars and their movements, the size of the universe and of the earth, the order of nature, the strength and powers of the immortal gods". Diodorus, Strabo and Caesar all also referred to the opinion that the Celts believed in the immortality of the soul. Diodorus and Ammianus, as well as another Roman historian, Valerius Maximus, associated this notion with the Pythagorean theory of metempsychosis, equating the Celtic doctrine with the "Belief of Pythagoras", and even making the Druids "members of the intimate fellowship of the Pythagorean faith" (Piggott 1975: 113–114). In the third century AD Hippolytus wrote that the Druids had not only "profoundly examined the Pythagorean faith", but had been instructed in it by the mythical Thracian Zalmoxis, said to have been a pupil of Pythagoras himself. And the connection goes further. Also writing in the third century AD, Diogenes Laertius spoke of the Druids, along with the Magi of Persia and the Brahmins of India, as the very originators of the study of philosophy (Owen 1962: 21; Stukeley, Bodleian Library, Oxford, MS Eng. misc. e. 403 f. 14r). It is little wonder then that Stukeley considered those possible links himself, and observed how "from the writings of Caesar, & other classic authors, we learn so much of [the Druids'] theology, astronomy, legislature, & other sublime knoledge as surprizes us, & we earnestly seek to know more of them" (Stukeley n.d.: 1).

By the time of the early Christian period, therefore, the Celtic Druids could not only be written of as wholly Pythagorean, but the very invention of that school of philosophy could be attributed to them. The Greek early Christian writer Clement of Alexandria even wrote that before philosophy came to Greece it had "flourished in antiquity among the barbarians ... First in its ranks were the prophets of the Egyptians, and the Chaldeans among the Assyrians, and the Druids among the Gauls ... and the philosophers among the Celts" (Owen 1962: 90). Stukeley noted that Clement "quotes from the famous Alexander Polyhistor that Pythagoras himself learned both from the Druids & the Brachmans, from the western & from the eastern philosophers". He suggested that the Brachmans or Bramines in turn derived their name from Abraham "as the learned are agreed" (Stukeley, Bodleian Library, Oxford, MS Eng. misc. e. 403 f. 15r and f. 13r). These researches and theorizations by Stukeley and other members of the Egyptian Society were not limited to their own private circle, and Stukeley appears to have discussed them at the highest theological level. At a dinner in December 1741 (Bodleian Library, Oxford, MS Eng. misc. e. 124 f. 90) he recorded that the Archbishop of Canterbury "discoursd with me about the Bramines in the eastern part of the world, who to this day remain of the patriarchal religion, like our Druids".

Stukeley and his Druids, with their apparent Egyptian and patriarchal connections, cannot, however, be taken as totally representative of attitudes to ancient history in mid-18th century England. Jeremiah Milles, who had also been a member of the Egyptian Society, told a mutual friend in 1754 that on the subject of Druid history Stukeley "makes a system out of his own head, and never cares whether he has any authority to support it. There is no imagination so wild that he will not lay down with all solemnity of truth, and treat it as if it were demonstrably certain" (Pool 1986: 13). Warburton also held a counter position to Stukeley on Egyptian history. Stukeley (1980: 116) recorded that he had "very many & warm disputes" with Warburton "upon his notions of the Egyptian antiquitys ... In short we never could agree in our notions about them, about the hieroglyphics, the mysterys, or of antiquitys in general". Warburton (1741: 109–110, 206–207) rejected Kircher, Newton and "the forged Books of *Hermes*", and attacked the Neoplatonic idea, elaborated by Plotinus (*Enneads* V.8.6), that Egyptian hieroglyphs were mystical symbols concealing religious dogmas. Little wonder that he disagreed with Stukeley, whose Avebury thesis was founded on this whole tradition.

Yet Warburton's (1741: 119) study of the subject was, like Stukeley's, totally directed towards countering the freethinking and atheistical trends in England. He argued that Egyptian history was much older than that of the Jews, though this, as he acknowledged, aligned him with the freethinkers, whose "present turn ... is to extol the high antiquity of Egypt, as an advantage to their cause". He also made the important argument that hieroglyphs were a practical device for recording laws, historical events and daily business. His contribution appears to have been one of the most important to the study of the meaning of hieroglyphs prior to the early 1800s. Warburton compared Egyptian hieroglyphs with the 'picture-writing' of China and ancient Mexico, and Iversen (1993: 104) describes his interpretation as being "for their time profoundly original, for he propounded that it was no sacred invention at all, 'made to conceal sacred secrets, as have been hitherto thought', but a practical device made for practical purposes". However, though Warburton's speculations attracted attention, they were not widely adopted. Nevertheless, Perry (1743: 456) of the Egyptian Society described Warburton as "learned, ingenious, and incomparable", treating his subject in "so a masterly Manner" that he deferred to Warburton on the matter of hieroglyphs, even though Warburton had never visited Egypt.

For their reliance on speculation and dubious historical methodology, Shuckford, Stukeley, Warburton and their imitators have tended to be marginalized in histories of later 18th century historiography. Attention has tended to focus instead on 18th century historians such as Henry St John (1752, 1: 6–7), who developed a more rational, 'Enlightened' attitude to the ancient past and attacked most scholars of ancient history: "they have supposed, they have guessed, they have joined disjointed passages of different authors, and broken traditions of uncertain originals, of various people, and of centuries remote from one another as well as from ours. In short, that they might leave no liberty untaken, even a wild similitude of sounds has served to prop up a system". St John complained of "all the learned lumber that fills the head of an antiquary", and showed how the historian of the origins of nations "should touch it lightly, and run swiftly over it", and should rely neither on ancient sources nor biblical texts (St John 1752, 1: 71).

One of the most rational and philosophical approaches to ancient history made in this period was that undertaken by David Hume. But even his measured approach to ancient history remained controversial. The issue centred on Revelation, and just how philosophically and scientifically advanced ancient civilizations had been. As an anonymous reviewer of Hume's (1757) *Four Dissertations* explained,

Mr Hume is of opinion, that if we consider the improvement of human society, from rude beginnings to a state of greater perfection, it will appear, that Polytheism or Idolatry, was, and necessarily must have been, the first and most antient religion of mankind ... In a word, our Author thinks it impossible, that theism could, from reasoning, have been the primary religion of the human race, and have afterwards, by its corruption, given birth to Idolatry, and to all the various superstitions of the heathen world.

(Anon. 1757, in Tweyman 1996: 207–208)

This viewpoint contradicted virtually all the opinions previously proposed by early modern theologians – that monotheism was the original primary religion of most ancient times, and that idolatry and polytheism only appeared later, after a long period of corruption. Obviously Hume's thesis marked a revolution in scholarly opinion, and that it did not meet with popular support is unsurprising. Too much was staked on the traditional interpretation.

Thus, for example, one anonymous critic, 'S. T.', disagreed with Hume's argument that in ancient times all men were necessarily polytheists. In fact, 'S. T.' argued, "mankind were as able to discover the existence of a God in the remotest ages of antiquity, as at present". S. T. could not accept Hume's argument that our ancient ancestors were driven only by emotions of "*fear, revenge,* and *hunger*". Indeed, he suggested, "Why might not a *Bacon, Locke,* or *Newton,* have existed in the remotest times, since human nature hath always been the same from its first creation". And indeed civilizations which did not have the art of letters may even have existed before those recorded by the Greeks. S. T. turned to the evidence of antiquities to contradict Hume's arguments, inviting his reader to "consider the state of mankind in the remotest ages, upon the testimony of the most ancient monuments, and records, and endeavour from thence to form a reasonable idea of their manners and religion". He suggested that the pyramids,

built before the use of letters ... convince us, that its builders compounded the mechanical powers in a manner unknown to us at present; and their situation likewise proves that they were acquainted with astronomy ... If we consider withal the descriptions which [classical] authors have given us of the magnificent cities of Thebes, Babylon, and Memphis; of the temple of Diana at Ephesus ... can we help being astonished at the progress which the ancients had made in the mechanical arts? Is it then reasonable to suppose, with Mr H[ume], that these people were *rude* and *ignorant, and that speculative curiosity was too refined for their gross apprehensions*?

(S. T. in Tweyman 1996: 209)

Noting that many of the ancient philosophers, including Homer, Thales, Pythagoras, and Plato "believed in the existence of a divine being", and that the Egyptians, Ethiopians, Persians and Chinese had all expressed a belief in a superior God, S. T. proceeded to quote from Warburton (1741):

Dr Warburton likewise says, 'It is not only possible that the worship of the first cause of all things was prior to any idol worship, but in the highest degree probable; idol worship having none of the appearances of an original custom, and all the circumstances attending a depraved and corrupted institution'.

(Tweyman 1996: 232)

And lest Warburton's authority be insufficient, the attack on Hume concluded with an extract taken from Newton (1728a):

> The believing that the world was framed by one supreme God, and is governed by him, and the loving and worshipping him, and honouring our parents, and loving our neighbours as ourselves, and being merciful even to brute beasts, is the oldest of all religions.

(Tweyman 1996: 233)

In the following century, arguments of the type advanced by S. T. would continue to be proposed, and it was Hume who, for the time being, was marginalized. This was the time of the voyages of discovery of James Cook, of Tahiti, Hawaii and Easter Island, of the 'noble savage'. These were discoveries which, to some European observers, suggested that ancient civilizations were far more advanced, and far more widespread, than had previously been acknowledged. It was evidence that seemed to contradict Hume's thesis, and added fuel to the idea of a period of ancient skill in sciences such as astronomy, writing and navigation, and a connection between biblical history and the history of the rest of the world.

## Egypt, China and India

In spite of the Earl of Sandwich's cautioning words, the drawing together of archaeological information, both from Egypt and from other more distant nations such as China and India, into a contiguous 'world history' continued to be a popular practice amongst British and European antiquaries, historians and other scholars in the mid- to late 18th century (e.g. Figure 6:4). Since Marco Polo had first visited China in the late 13th century, that nation, like Egypt, played an increasingly important role in the notion of a world religion. In 1697 the French Jesuit missionary Louis Le Comte (quoted in Walker 1972: 199) declared his belief "that the Chinese during 2000 years up to the time of Christ had known the true God, had honoured Him in a way that can serve as an example to Christians, had sacrificed to him in the most ancient temple in the world, had had faith and all the Christian virtues, and of all the nations had been the most favoured by God's grace" (Davis 1983). Le Comte's book was translated and published in England in 1698, and a few years later Bishop Pierre Daniel Huet (1717) argued that the Egyptians were the founders of the civilizations of India and China.

Interest in this subject, which seems to be the dominant one in studies of Egypt in the second half of the 18th century, was revived in England by John Turberville Needham (1761), a Roman Catholic priest and Fellow of both the Royal Society and the Society of Antiquaries. In 1761 he published a treatise in which he attempted to interpret the hieroglyphs on a reputed Egyptian bust from Turin by means of known Chinese characters. According to a review by a Fellow of the Royal Society which was published in the *Philosophical Transactions* (59: 489), Needham's book (which had caught the considerable attention of European scholars) suggested "a supposed connection between the hieroglyphical writing of antient Egypt, and the characteristic writing which is in use at this day, amongst the Chinese". The reviewer considered Needham's "conjecture" to be "pregnant with so many curious consequences" that the Society wrote to Jesuit missionaries in Peking to inquire whether there really was

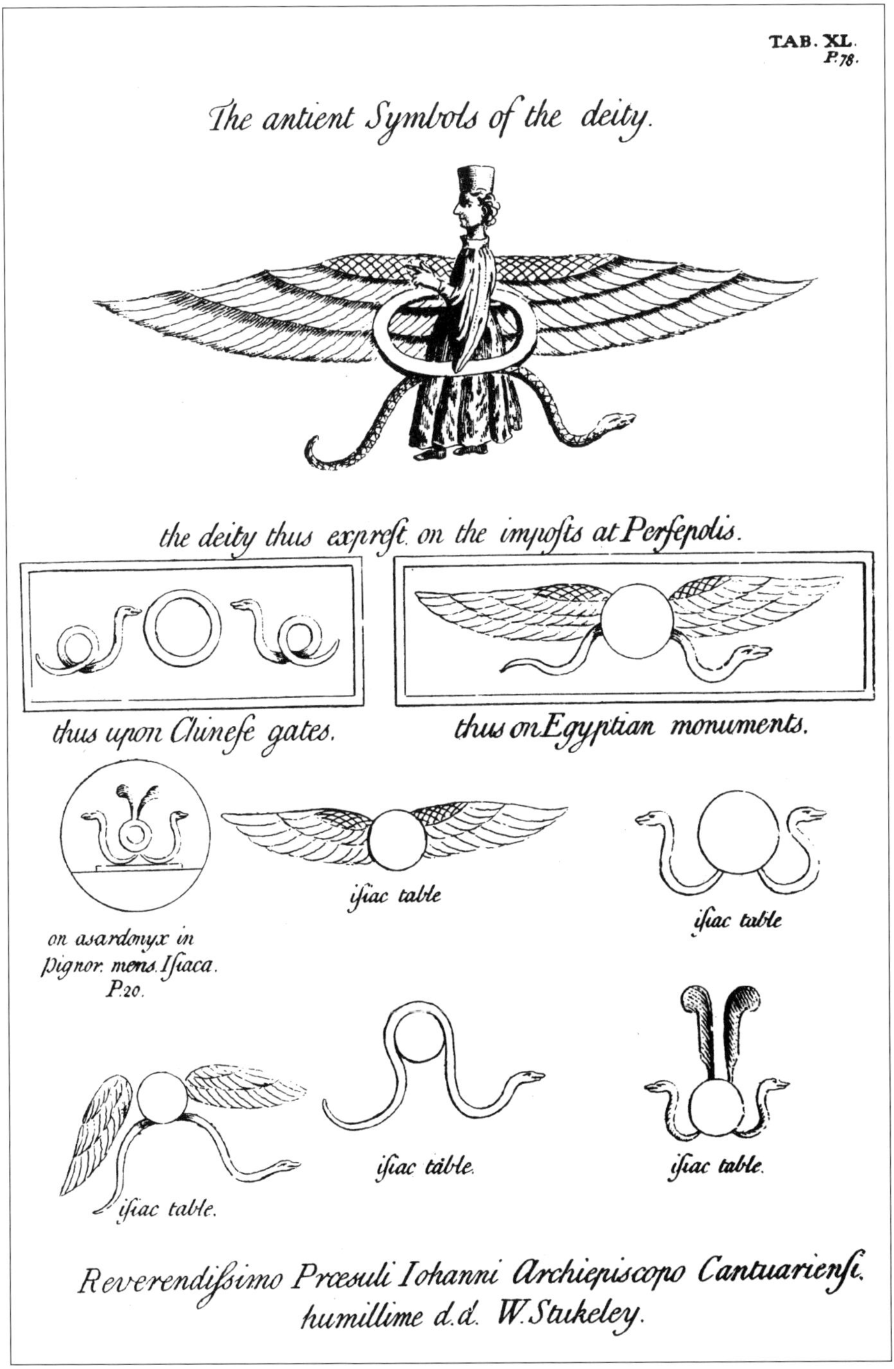

Figure 6:4   William Stukeley's drawing of "Ancient Symbols of the Deity" (Stukeley 1743: pl. XL), which includes a comparison of Chinese with Ancient Egyptian symbols.

any relationship between ancient Egyptian hieroglyphs and modern Chinese writing. It was also asked whether "there are any monuments or customs among the Chinese, which resemble those of the antient Egyptians ...?" (*Philosophical Transactions* 59: 491). An answer was duly received, and a paraphrase of the reply published (*Philosophical Transactions* 59: 493–494). The Jesuit correspondent observed that though both the Chinese and the Egyptians "have subsisted as a nation from the time of the great emigration which followed the confusion of the tongues", and though he believed that writing "was already established in the antediluvian world", he was of the opinion "that there is not the least mark or trace now remaining of any subsequent communication between the Chinese and Egyptians". Furthermore, "any connection between the two modes of writing is hardly discernible at this day".[9]

This supposed but mistaken connection between Chinese and Egyptian scripts that so fascinated scholars in the later 18th century would not, however, be without its benefits. Using a Phoenician inscription that had been published in Pococke (1743–1745), Abbé Jean-Jacques Barthélémy made a comparative study of the Phoenician, Greek and Egyptian languages. He (1761) suggested that the cartouches that appear in Egyptian hieroglyphic inscriptions might contain royal names. Joseph de Guignes (1769), like Needham, also believed that China was an Egyptian colony, and that there should, therefore, be similarities between the writing systems. From his study of Chinese script, Guignes recognized that certain texts contained similar cartouches to give prominence to proper names. From this observation of Chinese writing, like Barthélémy, he concluded that the Egyptian ovals served a similar function, and that they were used for the writing of royal names. Though the historical assumption from which it came was wrong, this nevertheless correct observation would make an important contribution to the final decipherment of Egyptian hieroglyphs in the early 1820s by Jean François Champollion, aided by the work of Thomas Young (Iversen 1993: 107). But the Rosetta Stone did not arrive in England until 1802 (Jeffreys 2003b). With Champollion and the 19th century Egyptologists, the myth of Egypt takes a whole new turn (see Champion Chapter 7, this volume).

As the 17th and 18th century voyages of discovery opened up the world to Europeans, the belief that there was one all-encompassing relationship between human civilizations, from Egypt and China to Britain and Mexico (Medina-González 2003), was increasingly played out and explored. The collection of archaeological and literary material provided additional evidence for scholars which could be used to uphold the same western, Christian interpretation of the history of the world promulgated in the mid-17th century. The eccentric Scottish judge James Burnett (1774–1792: 2, 530–531), speculated that Greek and Sanskrit, the ancient and sacred language of the Indian Hindus, were similar in some "remote analogies and distant relations of things", and drew the conclusion that the Indians and the Greeks had derived their language and other arts from the same parent country, Egypt. Another work executed in a similar vein was by Jacob Bryant (1774–1776, 1: xi–xiii), who attempted to show "that all the rites and mysteries of the Gentiles were only so many memorials of their principal ancestors". Bryant called upon "persons of science" residing abroad, particularly in India and China but also America, to better observe the antiquities around them, which could be used to further embellish and improve his system.

One such was Bryant's acquaintance Sir William Jones (Jones 1799), who observed from his recent study of Sanskrit, and his extensive knowledge of Latin and Greek, that

> no philologer could examine them all three, without believing them to have sprung from some common source, which, perhaps, no longer exists: there is a similar reason, though not quite so forcible, for supposing that both the *Gothick* and the *Celtick*, though blended with a very different idiom, had the same origin with the *Sanscrit*; and the old *Persian* might be added to the same family ...

> (Cannon 1991: 31)

Jones' observation has been credited with sparking the 19th century's interest in the history of linguistics, and he is credited with the first, correct recognition of what are now known as the Indo-European languages (Lamb and Mitchell 1991: 1–8). Jones suggested that "when features of resemblance, too strong to have been accidental, are observable in different systems of polytheism, without fancy or prejudice to colour them and improve the likeness, we can scarce help believing, that some connection has immemorially subsisted between the several nations, who have adopted them" (Jones 1799: 229). As one of the most highly respected scholars of his day, Jones' observations were highly influential, and helped theorists to continue developing a universal, theological human history. This is notable particularly when Jones (1799: 229–230) observed that

> the *Gothick* system, which prevailed in the northern regions of *Europe*, was not merely similar to those of *Greece* and *Italy*, but almost the same in another dress with an embroidery of images apparently *Asiatick*. From all this, if it be satisfactorily proved, we may infer a general union or affinity between the most distinguished inhabitants of the primitive world, at the time when they deviated, as they did too early deviate, from the rational adoration of the only true GOD.

Jones had read Bryant's work and, though cautious of some of its conclusions, he also observed that "we shall, perhaps, agree at last with Mr BRYANT, that Egyptians, Indians, Greeks, and Italians, proceeded originally from one central place, and that the same people carried their religion and sciences into China and Japan: may we not add, even to Mexico and Peru?" (Jones 1799: 274). Even such a cautious antiquary as Richard Gough (1785: xiv–xv) noted how "several respectable literati on the continent" had argued over whether the Chinese were "a colony from Egypt". He himself speculated that "if we may judge from the few representations we have seen of the famous pagoda of Chillambrum on the Coromandel coast, the resemblance approaches near to the Nubian and Egyptian temples".

It is clear that the notion of the communication between cultures in ancient times remained strong, and indeed hardened in the later 18th century. The observations and theories of Jones and other Europeans who travelled abroad helped to complement the speculations of antiquarians back in Europe, and kept Egypt in the forefront of theories of the history of mankind and the history of the world. Yet the biblical foundation on which this study had been founded was, despite the efforts to uphold it, crumbling, and strictly Christian defenders of the faith such as Stukeley and Warburton, who argued endlessly on their respective interpretations of Egyptian history, ended up having their work appropriated by deist writers, who denied the truth of any one religious doctrine. In the end, it would be the theory of Hume that would come to dominate theories of religious development. Clearly, Egypt played a vital role in theological arguments of this era, but these were largely based on an understanding of Egypt that continued to be derived from classical and biblical sources. Egypt itself remained mysterious, distant, misunderstood: a land whose history and reputation still lay hidden behind the tantalizing veil of the hieroglyphs.

## Notes

1   The study of Coptic Gnostic texts since the 1970s has shown parallels between them and the hermetic corpus, once more raising questions concerning their precise dating (Bernal 2001a).

2   Samuel Taylor Coleridge, for example, recorded in his notebook in 1805 (Coburn 1962: 2648): "Man a creature only of some 6000 years: and how much has he not had to do in that time?" His comment reflects both the strength of Ussher's calculation, and its increasing limitation in the face of new knowledge about mankind and the world. Dates alternative to Ussher's were suggested, but they tended to fall within the same chronological arena. By the mid-18th century the French naturalist, Comte de Buffon, was proposing a history of the earth measured in tens of thousands of years, but it remained controversial (Dean 1981).

3   Wilkins (1668) followed Bacon, and rejected Egyptian hieroglyphs as "a slight, imperfect invention, sutable [sic] to those first and ruder Ages". John Locke (1690) rejected the idea that there was any natural connection between words and ideas.

4   But More was criticized by Parker (1666), who considered the Egyptians' theological learning to have been "lamentably frivolous, obscure, fabulous, uncouth, magical and superstitious" (Iliffe 1989: 34).

5   In this manuscript Newton set out his ideas on the origin of idolatry in the postdiluvian world. According to Force and Popkin (1990), it relied heavily, "if not entirely", on a book by Gerard Vossius (1641).

6   This philosophical position appears to have been fairly firmly established in the 17th century. The Book of Common Prayer's "Concerning the service of the church" confirms the weight of this Anglican viewpoint: "There was never any thing by the wit of man so well devised, or so sure established, which in continuance of time had not been corrupted."

7   Counter arguments had been proposed in the 17th century, in particular by John Aubrey, who argued that it had been built by the Druids, and by his colleague Walter Charleton, who claimed that it had been built by the Danes (Ucko et al. 1991). The Romans, however, dominated the argument until Stukeley's 1740 publication (Haycock 2002).

8   This may well be a reference to Stonehenge, and may have been suggested by Stukeley.

9   This was not in fact the Society's first contact with China. In 1760 Stukeley's friend Emanuel Mendes da Costa was involved in attempts by the London Jewish community and the Royal Society to contact Chinese Jews. Keen to hear "what relates to your origin and present condition", the questions enclosed in their letter of contact had included: "Do you know whether there are any congregations or numbers of Israelites in Tartary, or in any countries near or distant from you, and whether they are descendants of the Ten Tribes?" (Katz 1990: 904).

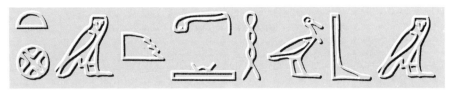

CHAPTER 7

# BEYOND EGYPTOLOGY: EGYPT IN 19th AND 20th CENTURY ARCHAEOLOGY AND ANTHROPOLOGY

*Timothy Champion*

The dawn of the 19th century forms an important milestone in western Europe's knowledge of Egypt. Bonaparte's expedition and short-lived conquest brought Egypt into the sphere of European geopolitics, and made the country more accessible than ever before. Many more western Europeans began to visit Egypt and many more of them began to write about their travels or their discoveries. But it was not only the volume of evidence for Ancient Egypt that was changing. The early decades of the 19th century witnessed the emergence of new disciplines such as ethnology, linguistics, anthropology and archaeology, as well as the reorientation of others, such as history. There was much new information about Egypt, but perhaps more important, there existed new structures of thought with which to analyze that information.

Of all the European countries it was Britain that took the greatest interest in Egypt, not least because of her growing imperial ambitions and Egypt's strategic location. From the beginning of the century Britain took a military, strategic, commercial and cultural interest in Egypt (Sattin 1988), and the British were one of the largest groups of foreign residents there. The opening of the 'overland route' to India via Alexandria and Suez led to a rapid increase in the numbers of people travelling through Egypt and it also became a destination for tourists in its own right; the British were the most prolific producers of tourist guidebooks and travel literature (Reid 2002: 64–92). The campaign to modernize and industrialize Egypt under Mohammed Ali also generated more intense contacts with the more developed nations, especially Britain and the United States.

As the previous chapters have shown, Europe's knowledge of Egypt from the medieval period to the end of the 18th century was drawn almost entirely from biblical and classical texts, though augmented by a small, and only slowly growing, list of accounts by people who had travelled there. Now, however, many new sources of information became available. By far the most common and the most widely read were guidebooks and travel literature; either first-hand through travel or vicariously through reading such works as Alexander Kinglake's (1844) *Eothen* or Harriet Martineau's (1848) *Eastern Life, Past and Present*, western Europeans became more familiar with Egypt, but it was the modern Egypt, not Ancient Egypt (Rees 1995). In contrast to the Egypt known through the classical sources, this was a rural, undeveloped, impoverished, Islamic Egypt, which inspired horror, revulsion and contempt (Barrell 1991; Gregory 1995). Another genre of literature was represented by Edward Lane (1836), who wrote one of the first works of ethnographic description rather than travel. These encounters with modern Egypt underlined how different it was from western Europe, and created a perception of Egypt as alien and exotic. Said (1978: 84) has argued that Egypt was the focal point in the growth of orientalism, and has explored how literary representations and academic disciplines became part of the way in which the East was exoticized and exploited. In a more detailed discussion of the representation of the 'Orient', including Egypt, in art, music and the theatre, MacKenzie (1995) has argued that, although the connotation of such representations may not always have been negative, they did serve to reinforce the sheer 'otherness' of the cultures represented. This exoticism was re-emphasized by other, more popular, representations of Egypt. The exhibition of Egyptian antiquities was not limited to the museums; popular shows in London, such as Belzoni's exhibition in the Egyptian Hall in Piccadilly, London (Werner 2003: Figure 5:5), made them objects of spectacle, in a way that classical antiquities were not, and paraded them alongside the material culture, or even living representatives, of the Americas and sub-Saharan Africa. In all these ways, Egypt was being re-interpreted and re-presented as something alien from the European experience and as something other than the origin of human civilization.

From the later years of the 18th century new disciplines and new sources of evidence appeared to challenge the hitherto unchallenged authority of the written texts. The science of ethnology emerged out of the earlier chronological tradition of universal history (Haycock Chapter 6, this volume), but also drawing its arguments from two new sources, comparative anatomy and historical linguistics; they both promised to cast independent light on the past, but they showed human variability rather than uniformity. The German anatomist, Johann Friedrich Blumenbach (1794), laid the foundations for more than a century of study of the physical difference of the human species; he suggested a classification of all humans into five species (Caucasian, Mongolian, Malay, American and Ethiopian) that dominated most of the later discussions. The place of Ancient Egypt within this scheme was uncertain: it seemed very far from obvious that it belonged with the main group of European (i.e. Caucasian) peoples.

The revolution in philological studies, beginning with the work of Sir William Jones in the late 18th century (see Haycock Chapter 6, this volume), led eventually to the recognition of the Indo-European language family, and the clear linguistic separation of most of Europe from other language groups, especially those of the Near East. At a time when archaeology was still only in its infancy, the history of language still offered the best evidence of the remote past. As the geographical distribution of this large language family became clearer, a search for European origins was focused more on Central Asia than anywhere else. Thus when Prichard (1831) wrote his fundamental work, he was seeking to associate the Celtic languages with the newly recognized Indo-European group and with an origin in Asia, not in the eastern Mediterranean.

Ethnology itself was later transformed, emerging as a cluster of related disciplines including archaeology and anthropology, but at the start of the 19th century one of its major problems was reconciling the traditional narratives and chronologies of the human past with the new evidence from such sources. William Stukeley (see Haycock Chapter 6, this volume) has rightly been recognized as a pioneer in archaeological field recording, and the reaction to his researches and his interpretations was in the short term quite positive. Sir Richard Colt Hoare was one of the more critical and level-headed archaeological writers of the early 19th century in England and his attitude to Stukeley (or "the learned Doctor" as he regularly described him) is instructive. Hoare shows a generally high respect for Stukeley's work, though he could be very critical, especially of his surveying and excavation methods. In this light, it is all the more revealing to see what Hoare (1821: 70) has to say about Stukeley's interpretation of Avebury, which he accepts without demur: "From the winding form of this work, Dr Stukeley has very ingeniously developed the form of a serpent, and distinguished this temple as one of that class called by the ancients Dracontia" (Figure 7:1). Thus, even as late as the 1820s, Stukeley's interpretation of the function and origins of Avebury was accepted by one of the most experienced English antiquarians of the day. Within a short time, however, all such ideas of eastern origins were to be swept away, and with them the role of Egypt in Europe's past. It was not so much a case of new archaeological data suggesting a revised answer to the question; rather the entire intellectual framework of debate and the nature of the questions being asked would change, to the extent that it can now be very difficult to appreciate the rationality or the fervour of the 18th century arguments.

## Egypt and ethnology

The dominant ethnologist of the first half of the 19th century was the Bristol physician, James Cowles Prichard (Augstein 1999). One of the main motivations for his life's work was to reaffirm the essential truth of the biblical account of the human creation in the face of growing evidence of human diversity. His (Prichard 1813) first major work argued that all humans were the product of a single act of creation and indeed the descendants of a single original pair. He attributed human variation, especially in colour, to the effects of civilization, and suggested that the original human population was black: "this leads us to the inference that the primitive stock of men were Negroes, which has every appearance of truth" (Prichard 1813: 233). In an attempt to prove the common derivation of all mankind, he devoted much space to asserting the similarities of the ancient civilizations of Egypt and India and of their populations (Prichard 1813: 318–472). Lengthy discussions of social and religious institutions and chronology were based exclusively on classical and biblical texts, but a brief section on the physical character of the Egyptians used other sources (Prichard 1813: 376–388). In addition to Herodotus, Prichard cited modern travellers such as Norden (1757) and Volney (1792), who described both the Copts, the assumed descendants of the ancient Egyptians (Horbury 2003), and some of the monuments such as the sphinx as displaying a Negro character. Another source of evidence was that of mummies: Prichard drew on work by Blumenbach (1794), who asserted that they showed at least three principal types: one Ethiopian, which Prichard took to be equivalent to the traditional Negro character, one Indian, and one mixed. Thus Prichard (1813: 388) concluded "that the national configuration prevailing in the most ancient times, was nearly the Negro form, with woolly hair ... the general complexion was black, or at

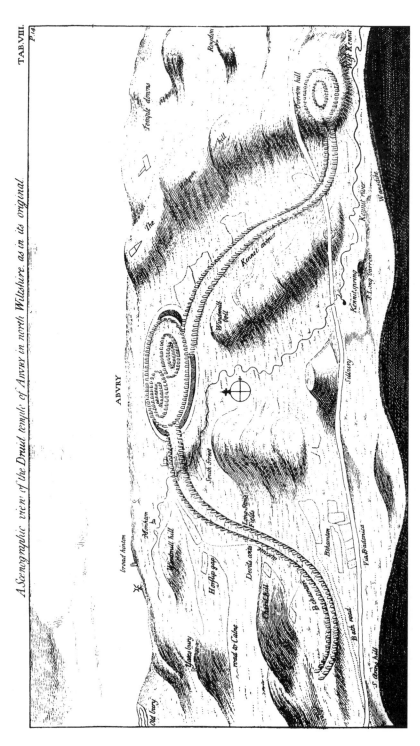

Figure 7:1    William Stukeley's (1743: pl. VII) drawing of a "scenographic view of the druid temple of Avebury in north Wiltshire", in which he interprets the Overton Hill end as the head of a snake, Avebury itself as the snake's coiled body, and the Beckhampton Avenue as its tail.

least a very dusky hue". As a conclusion to his more general argument, he wrote: "lastly in our enquiry into the physical history of the ancient Hindus and Egyptians we found full and sufficient evidence that both these races possessed originally the characters of the genuine Ethiopians or Negroes"; though "it is no longer difficult to imagine them connected in race and origin", Prichard (1813: 471–472) admitted that "as to the quarter whence they first ramified, the cradle perhaps of the human race, we have no data in history".

Prichard (1819) published a further work which dealt at much greater length with the issues that had concerned him in the earlier book. He was again trying to assert a common cultural and physical origin for all humankind, concentrating on reconciling the knowledge of Egypt and India. By now he was familiar with the German literature on historical linguistics, in particular the writings of Friedrich Schlegel (1808), but perhaps because it was dangerous territory for his thesis of a common derivation, he said little about a common linguistic heritage and concentrated on a detailed comparison of Egyptian and Hindu religion (Prichard 1819: 223–298). He appended a lengthy discourse on chronology, based entirely on traditional sources such as Manetho (Tait 2003b: 7; Uphill 2003), in which he arrived at a date of 2357 BC for the first king, Menes, thus being able to assert that although "the historical records of Ancient Egypt have been supposed to claim a degree of antiquity, which far exceeds the duration of the human race, as deduced from the Sacred Scriptures", there was in reality "no want of harmony" (Prichard 1819: vi–vii).

Prichard returned to the same themes yet again in 1826, when he produced a second and greatly enlarged edition of the *Researches*. Although only 13 years after his first edition, there had been a vast increase in the amount of ethnographic literature available, and important advances in comparative anatomy and historical linguistics, all of which were showing a greater extent of human diversity. Prichard still maintained the unity of the human species, but quietly abandoned his belief in descent from a single pair and in the Negro character of the original humans. He restructured and expanded his discussion of Ancient Egypt (Prichard 1826: 316–331), placing greater emphasis on new sources of evidence. He again referred to the classical authors, especially Herodotus, but in contradiction of his earlier assertion, now claimed that their description of the Ancient Egyptians as Negro was not borne out by the verdict of modern travellers. He paid greater attention to the representations on the monuments, citing the *Description* (1809–1828) and Belzoni (1820), and concluding that the Ancient Egyptians had been "a chocolate or red copper" colour. He discussed the evidence of the mummies in more detail: returning to Blumenbach's three types, he correctly argued that this classification was derived more from pictorial representations than from anatomical analyses; on the basis of anatomy and hair type "it does not appear that the Egyptian differed very much from the European" (Prichard 1826: 324). He was by now aware of a larger number of mummy investigations, as William Lawrence's lectures (1819: 344–348) had led him to further researches by Blumenbach's pupil, Soemmering (1794–1801, 1: 70–71), and by Denon (1802, I: 252) and Cuvier (1817: 272–274). In conclusion, Prichard asserted that the Egyptians and the Ethiopians were "nations of the same race" and that "they were not Negroes, such as the Negroes of Guinea, though they bore some resemblance to that description of man, at least when compared with the people of Europe" (Prichard 1826: 328).

Prichard produced a third edition of his *Researches* (1836–1847), though it took 10 years to complete the five volumes of the work, reflecting again the huge amount of ethnographic literature that needed to be synthesized. His main purpose was still to reaffirm his belief in the unity of mankind and a single creation, according to the biblical tradition, despite the growing arguments for multiple creations. A major concern was, as in the earlier editions, to show the similarities between Egyptian and Indian religion and social institutions (Prichard 1836–1847, 2: 196–226), and their equal antiquity. In one remarkable passage, published in 1837, he comes very near to the views of some later archaeologists:

> The cradles or nurseries of the first nations appear to have been extensive plains or valleys traversed by navigable channels and irrigated by perennial and fertilizing streams. Three such regions were the scenes of the most ancient cultivation of the human race, of the first foundation of cities, of the earliest political institutions and of the invention of arts which embellish human life. In one of these, the Semitic nations exchanged the simple habits of wandering shepherds for the splendour of Nineveh and Babylon. In another an Indo-European or Japhetic people brought to its perfection the most elaborate of human dialects, destined to become in later ages under different modifications the mother-tongue of the nations of Europe. In a third, the land of Ham, watered by the Nile, were invented hieroglyphic literature and the arts for which Egypt was celebrated in the earliest ages of history.
>
> (Prichard 1836–1847, 2: 192)

Such speculations were, however, tangential to his main thrust, and he repeated the evidence for the physical history of the Egyptian race, rehearsing once again with more detail the conclusions of mummy investigations and the representations of Ancient Egyptians on the monuments (O'Connor and Quirke 2003: Figure 1:6). The racial identity of the Egyptians was not central to his argument, and he was again content to accept the verdict that anthropology showed them to have been similar to Europeans and the pictures portrayed a variety of types (Prichard 1836–1847, 2: 227–251). At this point, in 1837, Prichard showed no evidence of awareness of progress in Egyptian studies since the publication of Belzoni's travels, and his brief discussion of the Egyptian language is based largely on modern Coptic dialects and gives no indication that he knew of any recent work on the ancient Egyptian language, let alone the progress made by Young and Champollion in deciphering the hieroglyphs (see Haycock Chapter 6, this volume).

Prichard's views on human origins in general and on Egypt's role in particular had changed dramatically in 25 years. He knew the results of the archaeological work that was beginning to be published, and the osteological researches on mummies, but less about linguistic matters. But what induced the change of mind was not so much this new evidence as the changes in the intellectual climate of the times; as the vast range of human diversity began to be better appreciated, theories of multiple origins began to prevail, difference was theorized in terms of race, and races were regarded as unequal. Prichard stuck to his theory of original unity and a single creation, but he gave way on the question of a single ancestral pair of humans, on the idea of the original humans as black, on the possibility that the Egyptians and the Indians represented those original peoples, and on the physical character of the Egyptians and their relationship to the populations of Africa and Europe. In 1813 Egypt had been in the mainstream of human development, in a narrative that was very like Jacob

Bryant's (1774–1776) much earlier theory of civilization spreading by a migration from Babylonia.

By 1837, however, Egypt had slipped to being one among several possible foci for the emergence of human culture. Prichard still worked within the confines of the biblical chronology; he knew nothing of the long time depth that must have lain behind the complex societies and powerful polities seen at the start of the written records in Egypt and elsewhere, and hence was able to reconcile the ethnological and the biblical traditions.

## The Nile of America

A very different vision of the place of Egypt in the human past was soon developed in America. The enthusiasm for all things Egyptian that prevailed in the wake of Bonaparte's expedition was especially strong in the United States (Carrott 1978). Egyptian antiquities began to be imported by amateur collectors, and mummies formed the centrepiece of more commercial shows (Delamaire 2003). Americans were quick to exploit the opportunities for travel to Egypt, and were second only to the British in numbers (Reid 2002: 80). Many of them published accounts of their travels, and works such as William Prime's (1857) *Boat Life in Egypt and Nubia* sold well. Among these travellers and writers were John Stephens and Frederick Catherwood, who were later to be the pioneers of archaeological research on the Maya (Medina-González 2003; Stephens 1837). Before that, however, Catherwood was delivering public lectures on Ancient Egypt to large audiences in the United States. An Egyptian-revival style of architecture was also adopted, especially for major public buildings, and was at its peak in the 1830s and 1840s (Carrott 1978: 47–50; Fazzini and McKercher 2003). But as well as a source of spectacular objects for the public gaze, Egypt was also a fountain of ideological meaning, and in the first half of the 19th century played a central role in a number of important cultural and political debates.

At one level, Egypt was seen as a suitable role model for the newly independent and rapidly developing nation and a valued prototype for its emerging sense of its own future destiny. The use of the Egyptian style for public architecture harnessed the authority of Egyptian civilization to the new nation. The parallel with Egypt took on a new and more precise meaning as European settlement spread westwards from the East Coast. The fertile valley of the Mississippi, Missouri and Ohio rivers recalled that of the Nile, and the Mississippi as well as several of its tributaries were often referred to as the 'Nile of America'. Many of the settlements founded at this time were given names derived from Egypt: names such as Philae, Thebes, Karnak and Luxor, as well as Cairo, Illinois (founded 1818) and Memphis, Tennessee (founded 1819). Egypt was not, however, solely appropriated to the European populations of America. A long-running problem for them had been to account for the origins of the indigenous people of the New World (Willey and Sabloff 1974: 23–36); various solutions were proposed, including descent from the Welsh, the Vikings or a lost tribe of Israel, but by the end of the 18th century there was general agreement that they had migrated at some remote period from Asia. At least one book (Delafield and Lakey 1839) was more specific and claimed that the original inhabitants were Egyptian and had migrated through Asia from the Nile Valley.

Yet another ideological claim on Egypt was made with increasing force from the 1820s (Dain 1993). The campaign for the abolition of slavery had attempted to focus attention on examples of positive achievement by black peoples, and in the early years of the century the spotlight fell on Haiti. Following the successful revolt in 1801 led by Toussaint l'Ouverture, Haiti appeared to offer a good case of a modern, independent, black state, but continuing political unrest and economic decline made it a problematic exemplar. Instead, attention turned to Egypt, and as the abolitionist campaign became more radical in the 1830s, so references to Egypt became more profuse: "Egypt became clearly the most impressive example of black achievement" (Dain 1993: 141). This strategy worked not only because of the increasing prominence of Egypt and Egyptian civilization in public discourse, but also because of the widely accepted view that Egyptians had been black. It may have been based on a similar idea in Volney's (1796) popular translated work. In any case, it was quite simply the unquestioned assumption that prevailed until the mid-1840s.

Thus, by the 1830s Egypt was being invoked on behalf of three different population groups in the United States: as valued precursors for both black and white civilization and as hypothetical ancestors of the Native Americans. As European settlement extended further west, and as the abolition movement became more stridently political in the 1830s, these issues were increasingly addressed in terms of a concept of race. Questions of racial identity, and the fixity or mutability of racial characteristics, were of the utmost cultural and political importance along with topics of scientific inquiry, in the United States and elsewhere (Stepan 1982). These debates were infused with a frequently very explicit belief in the need for racial purity and a fear, or indeed a horror, of racial mixture (Young 1995). In this context a new school of ethnological theory emerged in the late 1830s in the United States that was to hold sway there for the next 20 years, and in which evidence from Egypt played a crucial role.

## The American School of Anthropology

What European scholars came to call the 'American School of Anthropology' (Stanton 1960) grew out of the work of the Philadelphia doctor, Samuel George Morton, whose medical training included a period in Edinburgh, where he would have been exposed to contemporary ethnological thinking. When he returned to Philadelphia he supplemented his practice with a career as a scientific researcher and writer; he held a series of offices in the Academy of Natural Sciences, culminating in the presidency, and became one of America's most highly regarded scientists (Stanton 1960: 24–44). He published early work in palaeontology, but was best known for his researches in physical anthropology, especially craniometry. He started collecting skulls and eventually amassed over 1,000 (Morton 1849). His particular interest was in measuring brain size, and he also pioneered a method of measuring the cavity in the skull by filling it with white pepper seed and later, for greater accuracy, with lead shot. His (Morton 1839) first major work presented the results of his measurements of more than 250 skulls, of which more than half were from the Americas. He performed 13 different measurements on all the skulls and gave full details of the results, but he paid particular attention to the figures for skull capacity. He grouped his skulls into the five races devised by Blumenbach and showed that the average capacity for each of the five showed a decline from Caucasian through Mongolian, Malay, and American to Ethiopian (Negro) at the bottom.

Morton believed that he had demonstrated three important conclusions: that there were significant differences between the races, that the inhabitants of the Americas, with the exception of those in the Arctic regions, were all of one race, and that the prehistoric monuments of North America had been built by the ancestors of the contemporary Native Americans. There had been considerable debate about the attribution of these earthwork mounds, with many authors ascribing them to an extinct tribe of Mound-builders, unrelated to the modern indigenous population, who were deemed incapable of such achievements. Morton thus provided a scientific answer to this question, and a powerful argument for reassessing the capabilities of the Native Americans, but he also showed evidence for the inequality of the races. As in much of his work, he adopted a muted tone appropriate to the reporting of scientific findings, and showed little awareness of the potential religious or political consequences of his work. Thus he scarcely mentioned the problem of the origin of such racial differences and the vexed question of polygeny. His methods showed an awareness of the need for a large sample of data, rather than the description of a single skull or skeleton as representative of the 'type', but his statistical calculations and conclusions have been savagely criticized by Gould (1984).

Morton acquired his skulls through a network of scientific, military, commercial and diplomatic contacts. While working on *Crania Americana* he had appealed for more examples, and on his first visit to the United States in 1837 made contact with a young Englishman, George Robins Gliddon (Stanton 1960: 45–49). Gliddon was the son of an English merchant who had moved to Malta and then Alexandria, where he became the first United States Consul. His son became Vice-Consul in Cairo, and was sent to the United States in 1837 to buy machinery. He promised to procure Egyptian skulls for Morton and in the following years sent more than 100, from sites including Memphis and Thebes.

Morton published the results of his research on 137 Egyptian skulls, 100 of them ancient, in 1844. He "disclaimed all knowledge of hieroglyphic literature", but was aware of the work of Young, Champollion, Rosellini, Wilkinson and Lepsius. Egypt was "the parent of civilization, the cradle of the arts", but the question of the origin of its culture, whether from the north or from the south, was undetermined (Morton 1844: 1–2). Using the same methodology as for the American skulls, he gave details of various measurements, especially cranial capacity. He sought to attribute the skulls to one or other of "the two great races", Caucasian and Negro, and within the Caucasian he distinguished three subdivisions: Pelasgian ("the finest conformation" of the head, compared to the representations of Greek art), Semitic and Egyptian (Morton 1844: 3). No less than 80 per cent of his skulls were deemed to be Caucasian, and he again saw a decline in average internal capacity from Pelasgic through Semitic and Egyptian to Negroid and Negro. He also claimed a corresponding decline in the facial angle, and found further support for his interpretation of the Egyptians as Caucasians in the hairstyles as represented on the monuments illustrated by Rosellini (1832–1844). On the question of the Egyptians' complexion he thought the evidence less conclusive, but was nonetheless dogmatic: "I would, therefore, much more readily believe that the historian [i.e. Herodotus] had never been in Egypt at all, than admit the literal and unqualified interpretation of his words which has been insisted on by some, and which would class the Egyptian with the Negro race." The red and yellow colouring of the figures in the paintings on Egyptian monuments showed that they had been dark like Arabs and other southern Caucasians (Morton 1844: 20–28).

A critical part of Morton's argument was his use of the monumental representations to show that the racial difference that he had inferred from the skull shapes and measurements had existed in the past and had been clearly recognized by the Ancient Egyptians (O'Connor 2003). Though Morton acknowledged that Blumenbach had at an earlier date seen the significance of the monuments, and the English anthropologist Robert Knox (1850: 181) also claimed to have hit on the same idea independently when examining the replica of the tomb of Seti I in Belzoni's exhibition in London in "1822 or 1823" (Werner 2003), Morton's discussion (1844: 33–61) was the first extended exploitation of this evidence.

Morton ended his book with a series of conclusions. Among them were the following:

> The Valley of the Nile, both in Egypt and in Nubia, was originally peopled by a branch of the Caucasian race.

> In their physical character, the Egyptians were intermediate between the Indo-European and the Semitic races.

> Negroes were numerous in Egypt, but their social position in ancient times was the same that it is now, that of servants and slaves.

> The physical or organic characters which distinguish the several races of men, are as old as the oldest records of our species.

Morton's work was delivered in lectures in late 1842 and early 1843, and published in 1844. Meanwhile Gliddon had left Egypt and returned to the United States in early 1842. He spent the following years developing his reputation as a "hieroglyphist" (Figure 7:2). He divided his time between Europe and the United States. In Europe he became personally acquainted with famous Egyptologists such as Samuel Birch of the British Museum (1857) and Richard Lepsius, who led the Prussian expedition to Egypt in 1842–1845 (Lepsius 1849–1858). In the United States he gave public lectures on Egypt to audiences of up to 2,000 people. He acquired a huge landscape of the Nile Valley produced by prominent English painters, including Henry Warren and John Martin (Werner 2003: Figure 5:9), from original drawings by Joseph Bonomi, which had been exhibited at the Egyptian Hall in London (Gliddon 1849; Werner 2003: 95–96). He unrolled this behind him as he lectured surrounded by Egyptian artefacts. He had his lectures printed, and his *Ancient Egypt* (Gliddon 1843), which went through many updated editions, was the first non-specialist account of the decipherment of the hieroglyphics and its impact on recent research in Egypt.

Gliddon was self-taught, but had the advantage of first-hand familiarity with Egypt and with some of the monuments, as well as acquaintance with many of the leading European experts and knowledge of the latest discoveries. He did no original research, but was a highly successful popularizer of the subject. It has been estimated that he lectured to over 100,000 people in seven years and sold more than 24,000 copies

# HAND-BOOK

## AMERICAN

# PANORAMA OF THE NILE,

### Being the Original Transparent Picture

**EXHIBITED IN LONDON, AT EGYPTIAN HALL, PICCADILLY,**

PURCHASED FROM ITS PAINTERS AND PROPRIETORS,

## MESSRS. H. WARREN, J. BONOMI, AND J. FAHEY.

## By GEO. R. GLIDDON.

TRANSLATION.

" Year LXXIV of the *Great Festival*—under General TAYLOR—Commander of the Troops—Powerful Warrior—Victorious like Mentu (*Mars*), Lord of the Upper Region—Ever living—Chief of his country—Head of his land—Chosen by the People—Presiding over America, Western Land enviable and happy—Beloved of Osiris, Protector of the West."

## LONDON:

## JAMES MADDEN, 8, LEADENHALL STREET.

### 1849.

Figure 7:2   Title page of Gliddon 1849 with a hieroglyphic dedication to Zachary Taylor, President of the United States of America.

of his book (Stanton 1960: 49). He was the very opposite of the scholarly, understated scientist Morton. He was a loud and bombastic showman, a chancer with a talent for self-publicity. His lectures were undoubtedly popular, but his written work is polysyllabic pedantry, now almost unreadable. However, his 1841 book, written before he moved to the United States to begin his new career, shows a genuine concern for the destruction of the Egyptian heritage under the forces of 'modernization'.

Gliddon now met and began to collaborate with a man of a very different character, Josiah Clark Nott (Horsman 1987), who had set up in practice at Mobile, Alabama, the centre of the slave trade. He was very much a political animal and an ardent supporter of the social institutions of the South. In later years he would serve as a senior medical officer in the Confederate army during the Civil War. Nott joined the growing debate, partly fuelled by the demographic data of the 1840 Census in the United States, about racial difference and hybridity. His paper (Nott 1843) suggested that the black and white races were distinct, that hybrid offspring of inter-racial unions were less fertile, and that such miscegenation was therefore a threat to the survival of both races. His focus here was on the consequences of racial difference, but in a subsequent publication (Nott 1849), after correspondence with Morton, he openly advocated the theory of the separate creation of the races. Apart from general arguments that the different races had been created for different environments, like many other animal species, Nott relied heavily on evidence from Egypt, through the work of Morton and Gliddon. The latter's summary of the researches of Champollion and Rosellini had pushed the Egyptian chronology firmly back into the third millennium BC, only shortly before or perhaps even beyond the accepted biblical date for the Flood and the population of the earth; these historical facts were to be preferred to the biblical version, and the human races had clearly been on earth much longer than generally allowed. Morton's work had revealed that even at this early date the races were clearly distinct, and Caucasians and Negroes were shown as such on the monuments. Many of the features of Nott's later writing were present: a belief in racial difference, inequality and separate creation, and an abrasively anti-clerical advocacy of science.

Egypt was central to his argument for anthropological and chronological reasons. Through the work of Morton it offered the only scientific study of the physical anthropology of the ancient world then available, and it also provided the longest chronology of human society then known, based on evidence independent of the biblical and classical traditions. Further support for these arguments was found from the work of Ephraim George Squier who, in collaboration with Edwin H. Davis, had published a study of the earthwork monuments of North America based on first-hand observation in the field (Squier and Davis 1848). This work is rightly recognized as the foundation stone of modern archaeology in the region; it showed that the monuments were of great antiquity, though there was no clear way of estimating the date absolutely. Morton's discussion of a skull from one such site, which belonged exactly to his previously defined American racial type, showed that in America, as in Egypt, these racial differences were of a similar antiquity (Stanton 1960: 84). Morton, meanwhile, had returned (Morton 1848) to the question of the racial identity of the Egyptians, asserting that they were not Negroes but the product of an indigenous people in the Nile Valley and conquerors from Asia. Further support came from Peter

Browne (1852), who took a particular interest in the varieties of human hair as a basis for a formal classification. He had examined the hair of a mummy (Browne 1851) and was confident that it came from a woman of the white race.

Nott and Gliddon now planned a major statement of their views. When their massive book, *Types of Mankind* (1854) appeared, it was dedicated to Morton, who had died in 1851 but whose cranial research was fundamental to it. The book is a collection of disparate sections by the major authors and others; over half of it is given over to Gliddon's display of biblical scholarship, but there are long sections on monumental representations of racial types and on Egypt (Figure 7:3; Nott and Gliddon 1854: 141–179, 210–245), which develop the arguments of Morton's *Crania Aegyptiaca* at much greater length. The messages are clearly and repetitively propounded. Egypt provided the proof of the permanence of racial difference:

Figure 7:3   Profiles of pharaonic portraits used to demonstrate the Caucasian identity of the Ancient Egyptians (Nott and Gliddon 1854: figs. 44–47).

It is clear and positive that, at that early day (14th or 15th centuries BC), the Egyptians not only recognized, and faithfully represented on their monuments, many distinct races, but that they possessed their own ethnographic systems, and had already classified humanity, as known to them, accordingly.

(Nott and Gliddon 1854: 84)

Egyptian monuments, considered ethnologically, are not only inestimable as presenting us two types of mankind at this early period, but they display other contemporary races equally marked – thus affording proof that humanity, in its infinite variety, has existed much longer upon earth than we have been taught: and that physical causes have not, and cannot transform races from one type into another.

(Nott and Gliddon 1854: 211)

On the theme of the racial identity of the Egyptians, Gliddon quoted from a letter of his to Morton in 1841:

I am hostile to the opinion of the African origin of the Egyptians – I mean the high caste – kings, priests and military ... Monumental evidence appears to overthrow the African theory. Look at the portraits of the kings of Egypt ... Look at the Ramses family – their men are quite Caucasian – their women are white, or only yellowish, but I can see nothing African.

(Nott and Gliddon 1854: xxxvi–xxxviii)

Nott took an identical line, but with a more overt political tone: "The monuments of Egypt prove, that the Negro races have not, during 4000 years at least, been able to make one solitary step, in Negro-land, from their savage state" (Nott and Gliddon 1854: 95–96).

*Types of Mankind* was immediately successful and went through many editions, remaining the standard American introduction to ethnology for several decades. Nott and Gliddon (Nott *et al.* 1857) collaborated on a further volume with other authors, a work ranging much wider, with chapters on language and racial iconography, but it was too diffuse and had much less impact on the public.

The 1850s marked the zenith of the American polygenist school. Gliddon continued his lecturing with varying success and survived a public humiliation when a mummy that he was opening in front of a large audience and which he had confidently asserted was a female, turned out to be very obviously male. In 1857, under increasing financial pressure, he went to the jungles of Honduras to promote Squier's scheme for a trans-continental railway, but died within six months from an overdose of opium (Stanton 1960: 180–181). Nott continued to practise as a doctor, but after the Civil War moved from the south to New York, and re-established himself with a new reputation in obstetrics, taking little further part in political or scientific debates until his eventual death in 1873.

The supposed evidence from Egypt had been central to the debates of the previous decades, though the main arguments had been about other issues: the notion of race, racial difference and racial inequality, racial inter-mixture, the growing conflict of science and religion, the politics of slavery and the antagonism of North and South. What Egypt provided was a uniquely valuable body of evidence, drawing on the advances made in physical anthropology and Egyptology and the esteem in which those disciplines were held at the time. Egypt was the only source of ancient skeletal material available then: the catalogue of Morton's collection, the largest in America and left to the Academy of Natural Sciences, shows that apart from the Egyptian material the vast majority of the specimens were recent. Advances in Egyptology were also confirming the chronology: though there were, and still are, disputes over matters of detail, an outline chronology of the historic period back to about 3000 BC was becoming ever more certain.

Some of Nott and Gliddon's opponents certainly tried to dispute the chronological evidence. A review of *Types of Mankind* in the *Presbyterian Quarterly Review* (quoted by Stanton 1960: 167) argued that the chronology depended on as yet unproven assumptions about the hieroglyphic inscriptions: that the new readings were correct, that the authors were well-informed and truthful, and that the dynasties were consecutive and not concurrent. Thomas Smyth (1850) adopted a different line of attack in his book on *The Unity of Mankind*: he developed a theoretical argument to support the possibility and the reality of black civilization, and he also criticized the validity of Morton's conclusions. He questioned the dating of the examples that Gliddon had collected, arguing that the tombs had been often reused and that the skulls could be hellenistic or even more recent (Smyth 1850: 362).

The chronology of Egyptian civilization and of the anthropological evidence was vital to the polygenists to be able to assert, on the basis of the skulls and the monumental representations, the long-lasting nature of racial differences, but to go further and to argue that they were permanent required a recourse to the accepted biblical chronology. Nott and Gliddon took great delight in arguing that the scientific evidence was incompatible with, and disproved, the biblical tradition of the Flood, yet it was only the biblical chronology of a creation about 4000 BC and a flood about 2700 BC that allowed them to argue that there was insufficient time for climate, environment or other factors to have produced the racial differences observed in the earliest Egyptian evidence.

By the 1860s, the political and intellectual climate had changed. The defeat of the South and the abolition of slavery completely altered the context in which the previous arguments had been conducted, and made polygenism both less acceptable and less necessary. The publication of Darwin's *Origin of Species* in 1859 similarly redefined the intellectual argument. Nott's initial response to Darwin was negative: "the man is clearly crazy, but it is a capital dig into the parsons" (in a letter to Squier quoted in Stanton (1960: 183)). In time, however, he came to accept the fundamental principle of evolution, which presented major problems for polygenist theories. He and Gliddon (Nott *et al.* 1854: 360) had already been aware of advances made in palaeolithic archaeology in Europe, especially the work of Boucher de Perthes (1847–1864) in France, and the vastly longer timescales now opened up for the origin of the human species totally undermined the argument for racial permanence derived from Egypt.

## The end of ethnology

Political and social circumstances were very different in Europe, and so were the emphases in anthropological debate: the permanence of racial difference and the possibility of a black civilization, for which the Egyptian evidence had been so critical in the United States, were certainly important issues, but less so than racial inequality and hybridity. Responses to the work of Morton, Nott and Gliddon varied accordingly.

In the middle of the long task of producing the extended third edition of the *Researches*, Prichard (1843) published another book, aimed at a rather more popular readership, and reflecting popular racial prejudices more than his earlier work, but repeating the main points of his current beliefs. He repeated his idea of human development in three contiguous areas, and rehearsed the evidence of classical texts and mummy investigations for the physical character of the Egyptians, who "showed many tokens of relationship to the people of Africa" (Prichard 1843: 161). In the second edition (Prichard 1845), he added an appendix dealing with the ethnography of the Ancient Egyptians, which was a summary and critique of Morton's cranial data. Prichard recognized it as "a most interesting and really important addition" to knowledge of the Ancient Egyptians, but had major reservations. He reasserted Blumenbach's identification of Negro-like features among the Egyptian representations, and questioned the identity of the group Morton had described as Egyptian and assigned to the Caucasian category. Prichard argued that these were a common African type. This was Prichard's only response to Morton's craniometry; the appendix was repeated in the third and fourth (posthumous, since Prichard died in 1848) editions, but without alteration.

When the fifth and final volume of the third edition of Prichard's *Researches* was published in 1847, he added a long note on biblical chronology, in which he wrote:

> It has been observed that one of the greatest difficulties connected with the opinion that all mankind are descended from one primitive stock arises from the shortness of the period of time allowed, by the received chronology, for the developement [*sic*] of those physical varieties, which distinguish the different races of men ... It has been said with reference to this subject that Egyptian paintings which may be dated at 1000 or 1500 years before the Christian era display the forms and complexions of the Negro and the Egyptian and of some Asiatic nations distinctly marked.

> (Prichard 1836–1847, 5: 557)

This is Prichard's only allusion to the debate about permanence, but it is not clear precisely whose observations he was referring to, since the only citation he offered was to Kenrick's (1846) *Primeval History*, but the only comment there is that: "The Negro, with all his peculiarities of form, colour and hair, appears just the same in the paintings of the age of Thothmes [Tuthmosis] III, fifteen centuries before the Christian era, as he is now seen in the interior of Africa" (Kenrick 1846: 16).

Prichard may well have been more familiar with the arguments over the cranial evidence and the monumental representations than his discussion and stated sources reveal, but his main concern was not Egypt but chronology and origins. Even the question of the colour of the Ancient Egyptians, which had been answered very forcefully in the United States, was less important in England and answers continued to be ambivalent. The idea that the Egyptian population was very mixed in its origin, and may therefore have been very diverse in complexion as well as anatomically, had been debated since the researches of Blumenbach and had been supported by Prichard's later writings. Knox could be inconsistent: he used the evidence of the monumental representations to argue for the diversity of the Egyptian population: "on the tombs of Egypt, the most valuable of all existing records, there stands the Negro, the Jew, the Copt, the Persian, the Sarmatian, nearly as we find them now" (Knox 1850: 98–99). He took this to refute Herodotus' account of them, but a few pages later he argued that "the race [i.e. the Egyptians] was quite peculiar, and was, I think, African, or at least allied to the African races. The mouth and the lips all but prove this" (Knox 1850: 186). John Stuart Mill (1850) could be dogmatic: "The earliest known civilization was, we have the strongest reason to believe, a negro civilization. The original Egyptians are inferred, from the evidence of their sculptures, to have been a negro race; it was from the negroes, therefore, that the Greeks learnt their first lessons in civilization." The question does not seem to have been of central importance in academic debate, though it had a polemic and political significance.

What was important was chronology. In order to maintain a belief in a single creation in the face of the growing evidence for diversity and for the antiquity of the human species, Prichard was ultimately persuaded to allow a longer chronology than that traditionally derived from the Bible. This solution had already been suggested by Kenrick (1846: xii): "history cannot be confined within the narrow limits which the common chronology allows." Prichard (1836–1847, 5: 559–561) follows a similar line: "the compilations are wrong" but there is still "true history to be discerned"; he dismisses the first part of Genesis as a compilation of fragments, not a true chronological narrative.

One important factor pointing various scholars in this direction was the realization that the historical chronology of the Egyptian dynasties, whatever absolute dates were assigned to it, did not indicate the beginning of human settlement in Egypt or of the evolution of distinct human cultures. Baron Bunsen, a friend of Prichard, published a massively learned, five-volume study of Egyptian chronology (1845–1867), translated into English (1848–1867), in which he recognized that there had been a long period when "the world must have been differently constituted, before national bodies, possessing languages and religious systems, could appear on the stage of history" (Bunsen 1848–1867, 1: xxxii). He eventually suggested a date of around 20000 BC for the origin of the human species in Central Asia and a period of about 15000 to 9500 BC for the formation of language (Bunsen 1848–1867, 4: 55, 477–480, 557). E. B. Tylor followed a similar line, accepting that the known chronologies extended back about 5,000 years in respect of "traces of comparatively high civilization"; Bunsen had been correct, even if the precise dates were uncertain: "Here [viz. in the nineteenth Dynasty], before classic culture had arisen, the culture of Egypt culminated, and behind this time lies the somewhat less advanced age of the Pyramid kings, and behind this again the indefinite lapse of ages which such a civilization required for its production" (Tylor 1871, 1: 49). Such an extended chronology could also be accepted by those who sought to defend the permanent inequality of races. The Duke of Argyll (1869: 97), arguing against the possibility of some races improving without external influence, was happy to accept the longer chronology, since "the question is not the rise of kingdoms, but the origin of races".

The evidence for human diversity and the much longer chronology now required made the traditional narratives of human development untenable, and in as much as Ancient Egypt's importance was derived from that story, the decline of the grand narrative meant the decline of Egypt. The evidence from Mesopotamia and India, and the possibility of multiple foci for human development, diminished the uniqueness and significance of Ancient Egypt. The limitation of the Egyptian evidence to the historical period of the recorded dynasties also excluded it from any significant role in the growing debates about the nature of primitive human society.

The changing nature of the evidence and the chronology of human social development also led to a restructuring of the disciplines addressing these questions. New areas of study such as historical linguistics and archaeology emerged out of the tradition of ethnology and soon became recognized as academic specialisms in their own right. Ethnology itself was transformed and re-emerged as anthropology.

## Egypt and the new disciplinary formations

In the changed structure of academic disciplines after the middle of the 19th century, Egypt played an ambivalent role. The anthropology that developed in Britain was predominantly evolutionary. It was concerned with the evolution of the cultural forms of human life at a general level, not with narrative of the particular great nations of the past. Thus in one of the first major works of the new tradition, Tylor cited Egypt only twice: once as an example in the history of the development of writing, and once in a passing reference to the decline of culture (Tylor 1865: 97–98, 181). It was not just that the new discipline paid less attention to any individual society: its main focus was on the earlier and less developed societies, and it had become increasingly obvious that the evidence from Egypt represented a comparatively late phase of human development. The questions that now figured high on the agenda for the new evolutionary anthropology were not ones for which the evidence from Ancient Egypt was centrally relevant.

In Germany, on the other hand, anthropology adopted a far less evolutionary method (Zimmerman 2001). Culminating in the work of Franz Boas (1896), it emphasized the distinctiveness of individual human societies and valued detailed description and particular understanding, rather than general theorizing. With its focus on contemporary societies and little interest in diachronic development, there was little scope for Egypt. On the other hand, anthropology was sometimes seen as a counterbalance to a vision of the past created by the discipline of history, which was increasingly focused on the growth of the successful and progressive nations; Europe was celebrated in history, while the oppressive and stagnant societies of the Orient were excluded and the less developed societies of the past had no history at all. This approach is typified by Leopold von Ranke (1881–1886), and starts 'real history' with the Greeks.

Egypt was not totally absent from the anthropological literature, however, but it served as only one example among many of the cultural and social practices of the more advanced societies of the past, albeit at that time one of the best documented and dated. It provided evidence for complex political organization and social differentiation. Thus, the American anthropologist Lewis Henry Morgan (1877) cited Egypt in his study of the evolution of social complexity. Similarly, Weber (1976, originally published in German in 1896 and 1909) used Egypt as one case study to explore the social formations of pre-industrial agrarian civilizations, alongside Mesopotamia, Israel, classical and hellenistic Greece and republican and imperial Rome. For those anthropologists more interested in the history of human religion, Egypt also seemed to offer a wealth of evidence, although not for the earliest periods of human evolution. Tylor, however, found fault with the type of evidence available from Egypt: "the religion of Ancient Egypt is one of which we know much, yet little – much of its temples, rites, names of deities, liturgical formulas, but little of the esoteric religious ideas which lay hidden within these outer manifestations" (Tylor 1871, 2: 267). Frazer, inspired by Tylor's work, also drew on the Egyptian evidence, but very selectively. In his omnivorous accumulation of ethnographic and historical examples, he picked on Osiris as a further case of the dying and regenerated god; this was already present in the first edition of *The Golden Bough* (1890), but grew to take a dominant role in later editions. Frazer's work, especially on totemism (1910), in turn inspired Freud. He was an avid collector of antiquities (Gamwell and Wells 1989) with a considerable knowledge of archaeology including Egypt and Egyptology (Ucko 2001), but the comparatively advanced nature of Egyptian society would have made the evidence from there of little relevance to his theories of the correspondence of the psychology of primitive peoples and of neurotics.

Another strand of anthropological research continued to work with the notion of race. Although this was a politically and socially emotive set of ideas, in intellectual terms it became increasingly contorted, as scholars wrestled with the obvious diversity of the human form and tried to draw ever more fine-grained distinctions between race, language and culture. Though most of this work was addressed to the races of the contemporary world, it inevitably had an interest in the past. The Italian anthropologist Giuseppe Sergi (1897) confirmed that the Egyptian race had remained unchanged from the past to the present, but also attributed the Ancient Egyptians to a larger Mediterranean racial grouping, linking them to Europe and western Asia rather than to Africa (Sergi 1904).

If Ancient Egypt's place in anthropology and history was uncertain, its role in archaeology should have been guaranteed. In a sense it was, but some of the major developments in the history of archaeology in Europe marginalized it. Some of the main intellectual approaches in the later 19th century to the study of the past through its physical remains were evolutionary, culture historical and nationalistic. The latter two stressed cultural and historical continuity and emphasized the archaeology of the homeland or the ancestors of the European nations. Clearly Egypt had little or no role in this sort of archaeology, except for the Egyptians themselves, and they were largely excluded form the subject (El Daly Chapter 3: 62, this volume; Haikal 2003: 123–127; Reid 2002: 21–63).

In fact, the archaeology of Egypt, or Egyptology, developed as a very separate and distinct area of intellectual activity and practice (Jeffreys 2003b). In view of the decline of the eastern model for the origin of classical civilization, it is understandable that the study of the history and archaeology of Egypt and of the Greek and Roman worlds should have gone their separate ways. Nevertheless, the subsequent development of Egyptology seems quite close to that of classical archaeology, in its disciplinary priorities, its regional particularism and its emphasis on the historically recorded periods. It is certainly different from the growth of prehistory, and indeed the two fields have been subject to very different influences in their development this century. This has often discouraged academic interchange on themes which with hindsight might now seem fruitful (Jeffreys 2003a).

The word 'Egyptologist' is attested from 1859 and 'Egyptology' from 1862; in America before that, Gliddon (1843) had used the terms 'hierology' and 'hieroglyphicist'. These terms undoubtedly indicate the recognition of this subject area as distinct and a specialism in that field as an appropriate way of identifying an individual. This disciplinary distinctiveness was perhaps due to three related factors: the decipherment of the hieroglyphs, the emphasis placed on the documentary record, and the almost total concentration on the archaeology of the dynastic period. By the 1870s most accounts of Egypt were rooted firmly in the deciphered literary tradition, and a knowledge of the language now played a major role in the discipline. In addition to the rapidly growing body of evidence concerning material culture, especially art and architecture, a knowledge of the symbol system and the language was now required, and possession of such esoteric knowledge was clearly a mark of distinction.

The development of more formal academic and professional structures for archaeology also served to isolate the study of Egypt from that of other regions. In Britain, the creation of academic posts specifically in Egyptology at the universities of London (1892), Oxford (1901), Liverpool (1906) and Manchester (1913) both recognized and reinforced its emergence as a distinct discipline. The Egypt Exploration Fund, established in 1882 (Hassan 2003; Jeffreys 2003b: 8), was a very early forerunner of modern research funding authorities, and provided financial support and employment opportunities for Egyptologists in a way that was rare for archaeologists elsewhere, outside the British Schools in Athens and Rome. With its own disciplinary jargon, its own geographically and culturally defined content, its own specialized publications and its own pattern of research and employment opportunities, Egyptology had clearly emerged as a separate discipline well before the end of the 19th century. In this, it lagged little if at all behind classical archaeology, and was well ahead of other specialisms such as prehistory or Romano-British archaeology. It is revealing that T. E. Peet, who held posts at Manchester and Liverpool before acceding briefly to the newly upgraded Chair of Egyptology at Oxford, had originally specialized in the prehistory of Italy (Peet 1909), but had been persuaded to switch to Egyptology because it offered a more secure opportunity for earning a living (Gunn 1949).

Most of the British archaeologists who worked in Egypt in the 19th and 20th centuries had little experience of the past of any other region, especially outside the east Mediterranean (Levine 1986: 32); the Egypt Exploration Fund and the Society for Biblical Archaeology provided them with a disciplinary home. It is true that Sir Flinders Petrie surveyed prehistoric monuments in Britain with his father, but this was very much a training run before pursuing his real mission; subsequently he worked exclusively in Egypt and Palestine. It is also true that two of Britain's leading prehistorians, Lubbock and Pitt Rivers, both worked in Egypt, but these were little more than brief diversions while on holiday, and in any case were concerned with prehistory, not the dynastic period. On the basis of a little time spent collecting surface flints in 1873, Sir John Lubbock (1875) added to the then ongoing debate about the date of flint tools in Egypt, while General Pitt Rivers (1881) was much more thorough in undertaking a brief excavation which produced conclusive evidence of such flints stratified in river deposits and hence of their early date. Ironically, when Pitt Rivers met Petrie in the field in 1881, they failed initially to recognize each other (Burleigh and Clutton-Brock 1982).

The growth of disciplinary specialisms can also be traced in the progressive break-up of the original Department of Antiquities at the British Museum. In 1861 two specialist areas, Coins and Medals and Greek and Roman Antiquities, were hived off into separate departments, leaving a remnant Department of Oriental, British and Medieval Antiquities. This ragbag was further divided in 1866, separating Egyptian and Oriental Antiquities from the rest. Though there was a series of subsequent changes, Egyptian and Assyrian archaeology had started to establish their own disciplinary identity within the museum.

This fragmentation at the level of the academic discipline was mirrored elsewhere in educational structures. The German tradition of *Altertumswissenschaft*, imported into England as classics, formed the backbone of most education until well into the 20th century. Egypt was excluded from the canon of 19th century education. Egyptian never played the same role in education even as Hebrew, let alone Greek and Latin, and in consequence the learning of hieroglyphs and ancient Egyptian remained a minority specialism, alongside other languages such as Akkadian.

## Evolutionary archaeology

For European archaeologists operating within a culture-historical or nationalistic paradigm, Egypt had little importance. Evolutionary archaeology was different, however; it was a generalizing discipline, rather than one concerned with regional specialization, and it often used an explicitly comparative methodology. For evolutionary archaeology, as for evolutionary anthropology, Egypt became just one example of more general processes such as the evolution of writing, religion, agriculture or metalworking. Nevertheless, despite the fact that Egypt offered one of the fastest growing bodies of archaeological evidence, as well as one of the longest and best dated cultural sequences, evidence from Egypt was seldom, if ever, cited. One reason for this has already been discussed: the disciplinary isolation of Egyptology as a specialist area of archaeological research, and its narrow focus on the period after about 3000 BC, thus excluding the long periods of prehistory that would have been of interest to a comparative methodology. Closely related to this narrow concentration on the dynastic period was the real lack, until a comparatively late date, of any substantial evidence for the predynastic period. This was almost completely unknown until work at Ballas, Naqada, Hierakonpolis and other sites in the 1890s. Another reason is to be found within evolutionary archaeology itself, in the ideas and concepts that shaped the questions it posed and determined its agenda. It was primarily concerned with economic or technological advances, mostly seen as separate items rather than as components of a particular mode of social organization; questions of the evolution of social institutions, such as would now be called the emergence of complex societies, were scarcely posed in their modern formulation and had not yet emerged as the central issues.

The nature of evolutionary archaeology can be exemplified by the work of one of its leading exponents, Sir John Lubbock. His book *Pre-historic Times*, first published in 1865, began as a collection of separate articles rather than as a coherent treatment of prehistory, but it was greatly expanded in its successive editions and remained an influential text for much of the century. Lubbock (1869: 2–3) had invented the term 'neolithic' to describe the second of his four epochs of prehistoric archaeology: "The later or polished stone age; a period characterized by beautiful weapons and instruments made of flint and other kinds of stone; in which, however, we find no trace of the knowledge of any metal, excepting gold, which seems to have been sometimes used for ornaments. This we may call the 'Neolithic' period." The period is clearly defined as one of technical progress, rather than as one of transformation of social and domestic institutions. Lubbock does sporadically mention agriculture and domestic animals, but there is no consistent treatment of these as critical themes in the development of human society. It is as though archaeological methodology had not yet reached a point where these questions could be addressed; yet Lubbock's (1869: 183–203) discussion of the animal bones from the Swiss lake dwellings showed an ability to recognize domesticated and wild species, and he (Lubbock 1869: 203–205) used the discovery of carbonized seed remains, some of domesticated cereal species, to prove the presence of agriculture.

It is therefore easy to understand why Egypt is mentioned only twice in the book: one is a casual reference to the high civilization there as evidenced by the Bible, and the other is an attempt to date the build-up of the deposits in the Nile Delta (Lubbock 1869: 67, 385). Egypt was not included in his discussion partly because at the time there was no usable evidence for the origins of agriculture or any other important innovations of the prehistoric period. Similarly, the later phases of Egyptian archaeology were not included partly because they would not have been considered as prehistoric, and partly because questions of the origin of complex political organization were not yet formulated in that way as a key concern for prehistoric archaeology.

With the general acceptance of a model of Greek, and more generally European, civilization derived from the Indo-Europeans, the archaeology of the Near East and Egypt played a minor role in its past. Though some archaeologists, such as Oscar Montelius (1899), argued that Europe was but a pale reflection of the oriental precursors on which it relied for its entire cultural development, others, such as Salomon Reinach (1893), maintained that the idea of oriental influence was a mirage. There were few attempts to provide an account of the prehistoric past which re-integrated Egypt and the Near East with Europe. One such was Sir John Myres (1911), who, like Prichard in 1837, saw a connection between major river valleys and the emergence of civilization, and clearly believed in the multiple independent origins of such developments, which in turn became the centres of further diffusion. For him (Myres 1911: 15–30), sedentism was the critical step that preceded agriculture and was a necessary precondition for its development: "the first stage is one in which the centres of advancement are provided and defined, by great river valleys, with alluvial irrigable soil ... the common character of what historians group together as the Ancient East, is that of detached, riparian, essentially agricultural civilizations, in recurrent peril from the men of the grassland and the mountain, and only in intermittent touch with each other." One such focus was the Nile Valley: "Egypt is the gift of the Nile" (Myres 1911: 45). Like Lubbock before him, he emphasized technical and intellectual evolution, but Egypt was not the innovator of crafts such as pottery, which were introduced from elsewhere; Egypt and Babylonia were two independent areas developing in ways that were generally similar though very different in detail. Together they formed a core area from which civilization was diffused to the West via Crete, Cyprus and Greece.

From 1911 to the 1930s, Egypt enjoyed a brief period of fame, or notoriety, as the origin of all world civilizations. Grafton Elliot Smith, who had worked on Ancient Egyptian skeletons while Professor of Anatomy at Cairo, argued (Smith 1911, 1915) that the techniques of tomb building and mummification were so complex that they could only have been invented once – in Egypt (Champion 2003). In collaboration with William Perry, he elaborated the ideas into a theory of diffusion of these and many other cultural traits from Egypt around the world. These 'hyperdiffusionist' views were very widely publicized in popular media, but enjoyed little academic support, either from Egyptologists or prehistorians, and faded rapidly in the 1930s, to the point where they are now regarded as an embarrassing episode in the history of the discipline.

Gordon Childe (1951: 22) developed a view of prehistory that attached more importance to economic factors, especially the mode of food procurement. He credited Elliot Smith with recognizing the importance of agriculture in prehistoric social development, but adopted a very much modified and less extreme form of diffusionism. At the time when Childe (1928) wrote his first review of the evidence for the Near Eastern background to European prehistory, it was not clear whether Egypt or Mesopotamia had chronological priority in the development of agriculture, and he treated them as possibly contemporary. Like Prichard and Myres before him, he emphasized the importance of the major river valleys of the Near East, the Nile, the Tigris and Euphrates and the Indus, as the probable location of the origins of sedentism and agriculture, but stressed the very different nature of the societies that had developed there. Egypt was not the origin of these processes, but one of perhaps three areas where broadly similar developments had taken place. Frankfort (1951) likewise viewed Egypt and Mesopotamia as very different social developments on a similar agricultural basis. By the time of a second edition of Childe's book (1934), it was already becoming clearer that farming had developed earlier in Mesopotamia, and Egypt played a correspondingly reduced role in his narrative. By the middle of the century, further work in Mesopotamia, especially that by Braidwood (1966) at Jarmo, and application of the new radiocarbon dating method, were making this sequence even more firmly based. Egypt's claim to a unique place in the story of the development of civilization in western Asia and Europe as the origin of sedentism, agriculture or political centralization was finally discredited, though in recent years Bernal (1987, 1991, 2003) has attempted to restore the balance in Egypt's favour on other grounds.

## Egypt in context?

In the last third of the 20th century the so-called 'New Archaeology' that dominated much of Anglo-American prehistoric archaeology and had an effect on other areas of archaeological study re-introduced a comparative approach as well as an evolutionary agenda. In contrast to the evolutionary archaeology and anthropology of the later 19th century, it had extended its range to include the development of larger-scale sedentary societies and the origin of complex social organizations including states and empires. Although the wealth of evidence from Egypt might suggest that it should have been an obvious choice as a case study for such a programme, it is remarkable how little Egypt features in such literature.

Some of the most important advances were made in the predynastic and even more remote periods of Egypt's past. Building on the earlier geological work of Sandford and Arkell (1933, 1939) in the 1920s and 1930s, further research (e.g. Arkell 1975; Wendorf *et al.* 1976) began to clarify the environmental history of Egypt and of the Nile Valley in particular, and the palaeolithic and neolithic cultural sequences there. Much of the impact of these studies was to enable Egypt to be placed in its proper regional context, or was specific to the development of human societies in Egypt (Hoffman 1979). Some of the work done on predynastic Egypt, however, has had an impact well outside the regional research world (for example, Butzer's (1976) study of early agriculture in the Nile Valley) or has been published in an explicitly comparative framework (for example, contributions to Krzyzaniak and Kobusiewicz 1984). By contrast, it is remarkable how small a role Egypt still plays in comparative studies of more complex societies. There have been important studies of the development of state societies in Egypt using the same theoretical and methodological approach as elsewhere (Kemp 1989), but the one explicitly comparative study of the development of Egyptian civilization is by Trigger (1993). Egypt is absent, for example, from classic studies of ancient civilization and trade (Sabloff and Lamberg-Karlovsky 1975) and social evolution (Johnson and Earle 1987), but has appeared in a volume of comparative studies of empires (Alcock *et al.* 2001). Intriguingly, despite Tylor's use of Egypt as the prime example of the decline of a culture, Egypt scarcely figures in two important books on this theme: it is absent from Yoffee and Cowgill (1988), and cited only sporadically by Tainter (1988). Egypt has a remarkably, and possibly uniquely, long history of more or less continuous urban settlement and centralized polities in a restricted geographical zone, despite the rise and fall of individual ruling groups; other areas, such as the Valley of Mexico, have shorter sequences or, like Mesopotamia, much more geographically dispersed occupation. It thus has an unparalleled set of data for studies of settlement power structures, which does not seem to have been exploited.

Egypt has figured more prominently in comparative works by recent anthropologists and historical sociologists. There is a section devoted to it in Service (1975: 225–237), it figures intermittently in Mann (1986), and more briefly in works by Parsons (1966), Krader (1968) and Sanderson (1995: 60–62). It is also one of the case studies in Eisenstadt's (1963) classic study of empires and their political organization, though considered more briefly than some other examples.

It is interesting to note how few of these contributions to a wider, comparative view of the past have been made by Egyptologists. As Egypt's claim to a unique role in the human past has gradually been reassessed during the 19th and 20th centuries, so it has played a less central role in the grand narratives. Other disciplines have taken note of Egypt, increasingly in the context of a comparative study of complex societies, but Egyptology has only slowly begun to counter Redford's (1979: 10–12) or Jeffreys' (2003b: 5–6) criticism of its 'insularity'.

# References

Note: references to chapters and books in the *Encounters with Ancient Egypt* series are denoted in bold type.

'Abdeen, 'A. 1964, Lamahat mn tarikh al-haya al-fikriya al-misriya qabl al-fatih al-'arabi wa ba'duh. Cairo: Al-Shubukshi

Abu Lughod, J. L. 1989, *Before European Hegemony: The World System AD 1250–1350*. New York: OUP

Adlington, W. (ed.) 1915, *Apuleius. Golden Ass (Metamorphoses)*. Cambridge, Mass: Harvard UP

Agapius, Ibn Qustantin (Agapius Episcopus Mabbugensis) 1954, *Al-'Unwan*. L. Cheikho (ed.). Louvain: Imprimerie Orientalist

Aharoni, Y. 1966, The Use of Hieratic Numerals in Hebrew Ostraca and the Shekel Weights. *Bulletin of the American Schools of Oriental Research* 184, 13–19

Alberti, L. B. 1485, *De re Aedificatoria VIII*. Florence

Alcock, S. E., T. N. D'Altroy, K. D. Morrison and C. Sinopoli 2001, *Empires: Perspectives from Archaeology and History*. Cambridge: CUP

Allen, D. C. 1960, The Predecessors of Champollion. *Proceedings of the American Philosophical Society* 105, 527–547

Allen, D. C. 1979, *Mysteriously Meant: The Rediscovery of Pagan Symbolism and Allegorical Interpretation in the Renaissance*. Baltimore: Johns Hopkins UP

**Allen, J. P. 2003, The Egyptian Concept of the World, in D. O'Connor and S. Quirke (eds), *Mysterious Lands*, 23–30. London: UCL Press**

Allen, M. J. B. 1990, Marsilio Ficino, Hermes Trismegistus and the Corpus Hermeticum, in J. Henry and S. Hutton (eds), *New Perspectives on Renaissance Thought*, 38–47. London: Duckworth

Amari, M. 1863, *I Diplomi Arabi del R. Archivio Fiorentino*. Florence: Archivio di Stato

Amélineau, M. 1888, *Contes et Romans de l'Égypte Chrétienne*. Paris: Ernst Leroux

Anderson, J. 1723, *The Constitutions of the Free Masons. Containing the History, Charges, Regulations etc. of that most Ancient and Right Worshipful Fraternity*. London: William Hunter, for John Senex and John Hooke

Angeleri, C. 1955, *De Honesta Disciplina: Pietro Crinito*. Rome: Bocca

Annius of Viterbo 1498, *Commentaria Fratris Ioannis Annii Viterbensis Ordinis Praedicator, Theologiae Professoris Super Opera Diversorum Auctorum de Antiquitatibus Loquentorum*. Rome: E. Silber

Argyll, Duke of 1869, *Primeval Man: an Examination of Some Recent Speculations*. London: Strahan

Arkell, A. J. 1975, *The Prehistory of the Nile Valley*. Leiden: Brill

Armayor, O. K. 1985, *Herodotus' Autopsy of the Fayoum: Lake Moeris and the Labyrinth of Egypt*. Amsterdam: Gieben

Artin, Y. 1889, Trois différentes armoiries de Kait Bay. *Bulletin de l'Institut Egyptien* 9, 67–77

Aslanov, C. 2002, Languages in Contact in the Frankish Levant. *Crusades: The Journal of the Society for the Study of the Crusades and the Latin East* 1, 155–181

Assmann, J. 1997, *Moses the Egyptian. The Memory of Egypt in Western Monotheism*. Cambridge, Mass: Harvard UP

Assmann, J. 2000, *Weisheit und Mysterium. Das Bild der Griechen von Ägypten*. Munich: Beck

Atiya, A. 1986, KIBT, in *Encyclopedia of Islam* 5, 89–95. 2nd edition, Leiden: Brill

Aufrère, S. H. 1990, *La Momie et la tempête: Nicholas-Claude Fabri de Peiresc et la curiositée Egyptienne en Provence au début du XVIIe siècle*. Avignon: Editions A. Barthélemy

Augstein, H. F. 1999, *James Cowles Prichard's Anthropology: Remaking the Science of Man in Early Nineteenth-Century*. Amsterdam: Rodopi

Ayub ibn Masalama (attributed), *K. aqlam al-mutaqadimeen*. (Book of the Scripts of the Ancients) MS 10244 Al-Asad Library, Damascus, Syria


Bacon, F. 1620, *The New Organon*. London: John Bill

Bacon, F. 1701, *The Essays, Or Councils, Civil and Moral, of Sir Francis Bacon, Lord Verulam, Viscount of St Albans. With a Table of the Colours of Good and Evil. And a Discourse of the Wisdom of the Ancients*. London: E. Holt, for Henry Henningham

Badawi, A. 1965, *Al-athar al-misriyah fi al-adab al-'arabi*. Cairo: Dar Al-Qalam

Al-Baghdadi, 'Abd Al-Latif 1985, *K. Al-ifadah wa al-i'tibar fi al-amour al-mushahadh wa al-hawadith al-mu'ayanah biard Misr*. B. Ghalioungui (ed.). Cairo: Egyptian General Book Orgainisation

Baines, J. 1990, Restricted Knowledge, Hierarchy, and Decorum: Modern Perceptions and Ancient Institutions. *Journal of the American Research Center in Egypt* 27, 1–23

Baines, J. and C. J. Eyre 1983, Four Notes on Literacy. *Göttinger Miszellen* 61, 65–96

Al-Balawi, Abu Muhammad 'Abd-Allah 1939, *Sirat Ahmad Ibn Tulun*. M. K. 'Ali (ed.). Damascus: Al-Maktabah Al-'Arabiyah

Baldwin, B. 1973, *Studies in Lucian*. Toronto: Hakkert

Barker, N. 2000, in A. Weston-Lewis (ed.), *'A Poet in Paradise': Lord Lindsay and Christian Art*, 148–149. Edinburgh: Trustees of the National Galleries of Scotland

Barrell, J. 1991, Death on the Nile: Fantasy and the Literature of Tourism 1840–1860. *Essays in Criticism* 41, 97–127

Barthélémy, J-J. 1761, Explication d'une bas-relief Egyptienne et d'une inscription Phénicienne qui l'accompagne. *Mémoires de l'Académie des Inscriptions*, 32

Bashear, S. 1997, *Arabs and Others in Early Islam*. New Jersey: Darwin

Bauer, G. 1972, *Athnasius von Qus: Qiladat at-tahrir fi 'ilm at-tafsir. Eine koptische Grammatik in arabischer Sprache aus dem 13/14 Jahrhundert*. Freiburg im Breisgau: Klaus Schwarz

Bean, J. 1960, *Inventaire général des dessins des musées de province Bayonne, Vol. IV: Les Dessins Italiens de la Collection Bonnat*. Paris: Presses Artistiques

Bedini, S. A. 1986, Citadels of Learning, in M. Casciato, M. G. Ianiello and M. Vitale (eds), *Enciclopedismo in Roma Barocca: Athanasius Kircher e il Museo del Collegio Romano tra Wunderkammer e Museo Scientifico*, 249–267. Venice: Marsilio

Behlmer, H. 1996, Ancient Egyptian Survivals in Coptic Literature: An Overview, in A. Loprieno (ed.), *Ancient Egyptian Literature: History and Forms*, 567–590. Leiden: Brill

Beinlich, H. 1991, *Das Buch vom Fayum: Zum Religiösen Eigenverständnis einer Ägyptischen Landschaft*. Wiesbaden: Harrassowitz

Belzoni, G. B. 1820, *Narrative of the Operations and Recent Discoveries Within the Pyramids, Temples, Tombs and Excavations in Egypt and Nubia, and of a Journey to the Red Sea, in search of the Ancient Berenice, and Another to the Oasis of Jupiter Ammon*. London: John Murray

Bergmeister, H-J. (ed.) 1975, *Die Historia de Preliis Alexandri Magni (Der Lateinische Alexanderroman des Mittelalters)*. Meisenheim am Glan: Hain

Berlinerblau, J. 1999, *Heresy in the University: The Black Athena Controversy and the Responsibilities of American Intellectuals*. New Brunswick, NJ: Rutgers UP

Bernal, M. 1987, *Black Athena: the Afroasiatic Roots of Classical Civilization. Vol. 1, The Fabrication of Ancient Greece, 1785–1985*. London: Free Association Books

Bernal, M. 1991, *Black Athena: the Afroasiatic Roots of Classical Civilization. Vol. 2, The Archaeological and Documentary Evidence*. New Brunswick, NJ: Rutgers UP

Bernal, M. 2001a, Black Athena is the Ancient Model. *Times Literary Supplement*, 11 May

Bernal, M. 2001b, *Black Athena Writes Back: Martin Bernal Responds to his Critics*. Durham, NC: Duke UP

**Bernal, M. 2003, Afrocentrism and Historical Models for the Foundation of Ancient Greece, in D. O'Connor and A. Reid (eds), *Ancient Egypt in Africa*, 23–30. London: UCL Press**

Bilabel, F., A. Grohmann and G. Graf 1934. *Griechische, Koptische und Arabische Texte zur religion und Religiösen Literatur in Ägypten Spätzeit*. Heidelberg: Universitätes Bibliothek

Al-Biruni, Abu Al-Rihan Muhammad ibn Ahmad 1923, *Al-athar al-baqiya 'an al-qrun al-khaliya*. E. Sachau (ed.). Wiesbaden: Harrassowitz

Bischoff, B. 1967, The Study of Foreign Languages in the Middle Ages, in B. Bischoff, *Mittelalterliche Studien Vol. II*, 227–245. Stuttgart: Hiersemann

Blackman, A. and W. Davies 1988, *The Story of King Kheops and the Magicians. Transcribed from Papyrus Westcar (Berlin Papyrus 3033)*. Reading: J. V. Books

Bloch, H. 1986, *Monte Cassino in the Middle Ages*. Rome: Edizioni di Storia e Letteratura

Blochet, E. 1907, Peintures de Manuscrits Arabes. Types Byzantins. *Revue Archéologique* 9, 193–223

Blount, H. 1636, *A Voyage into the Levant*. London: Andrew Cooke

Blumenbach, J. F. 1794, Observations on Some Egyptian Mummies Opened in London. *Philosophical Transactions of the Royal Society of London* 84, 177–195

Boas, F. 1896, The limitations of the comparative method of anthropology. *Science* 4, 901–908

Boas, G. 1950, *The Hieroglyphics of Horapollo* (reprinted 1993). New York: Pantheon

Bober, H. 1980, The Eclipse of the Pyramids in the Middle Ages, in P. Berg and M. Jones (eds), *Pyramidal Influence in Art*, 5–18. Dayton, Ohio: Fine Arts Gallery

Bohak, G. 1999, Greek, Coptic, and Jewish Magic in the Cairo Genizah. *Bulletin of the American Society of Papyrologists* 36, 27–44

Boll, F. 1903, *Sphaera*. Leipzig: Teubner

Boll, F. 1950, *Kleine Schriften zur Sternkunde des Altertums*. Leipzig: Koehler and Amelang

Boncompagni, B. 1857–1862, *Scritti di Leonardo Pisano del Secolo Decimoterzo*. Rome: Tipografia delle Scienze Matematiche e Fisiche

Bonnardot, F. and A. Longnon (eds) 1878, *Le Saint voyage de Jherusalem du Seigneur d'Anglure*. Paris: Librairie de Firmin Didot

Bouché-Leclercq, A. 1899: *L'Astrologie Grecque*. Paris: Leroux

Boucher de Perthes, J. 1847–1864. *Antiquités Celtiques et Antédiluviennes: mémoire sur l'industrie primitive et les arts à leur origine*. Paris: Treuttel and Wurtz

Bourbon, F. 1996, *Egypt Yesterday and Today. Lithographs and Diaries by David Roberts, R. A.* New York: Stewart Tabori & Chang

Bourdieu, P. and A. Darbel 1966, *L'Amour de l'art: les musées et leur public*. Paris: Editions de Minuit

Braidwood, R. J. and B. Howe 1966, *Prehistoric Investigations in Iraqi Kurdistan*. Chicago: University of Chicago Press

Braudel, F. 1972, *The Mediterranean and the Mediterranean World in the Age of Philip II*. London: Collins

Braun, T. F. R. G. 1982, The Greeks in Egypt, in *The Cambridge Ancient History, Vol. 3*, 32–56. Cambridge: CUP

Broadhurst, R. 1952, *The Travels of Ibn Jubayer*. London: Jonathan Cape

Browne, P. A. 1851, Examination of the Hair of the Head of a Mummy, Unrolled in Philadelphia, in Jan., 1851. *Charleston Medical Journal* 6, 371–372

Browne, P. A. 1852, *The Classification of Mankind by the Hair and Wool of their Heads*. Philadelphia: J.H. Jones

Browne, Sir T. 1643, *Religio Medici*. London

[Browne, Sir T.] 1931, Fragment on Mummies, in G. Keynes (ed.), *The Miscellaneous Writings of Sir Thomas Browne*, 459–463. London: Faber and Faber

Brugsch, H. 1902, *Egypt under the Pharaohs: A History Derived Entirely from the Monuments*. 3rd edition, London: John Murray

Brunner, H. 1957, *Altägyptische Erziehung*. Wiesbaden: Harrassowitz

Brunon, C-F. 1981, Signe, figure, langage: les 'hieroglyphica' d'Horapollon, in Y. Giraud (ed.), *L'Emblème à la Renaissance*, 29–47. Paris: Société d'Édition d'Enseignement Supérieur

Bryant, J. 1774–1776, *A New System, Or, An Analysis of Ancient Mythology: Wherein an Attempt is Made to Divest Tradition of Fable; And to Reduce the Truth to its Original Purity*. London: Payne, Elmsley, White and Walker

Bubnov, N. 1899, *Gerberti postea Silvestri II papae Opera mathematica (972–1003)*. Berlin: Friedländer

Budge, E. A. W. 1928, *The Divine Origin of the Craft of the Herbalist*. London: Society of Herbalists

Budge, E. A. W. 1929, *The Rosetta Stone*. London. Dover

Bull, G. (ed.) 1989, *The Pilgrim: The Travels of Pietro della Valle*. London and Sydney: Hutchinson

Bunsen, C. J. K. 1845–1867, *Aegyptens Stelle in der Weltgeschichte*. Hamburg: Perthes

Bunsen, C. J. K. 1848–1867, *Egypt's Place in Universal History*. London: Longman, Brown, Green and Longman

Burleigh, R. and J. Clutton-Brock 1982, Pitt Rivers and Petrie in Egypt. *Antiquity* 56, 208–209

Burnet, T. 1684. *The Sacred Theory of the Earth*. London: R. Norton, for Walter Kettilby

Burnet, T. 1692, *Archaeologiae Philosophicae sive Doctrina Antiqua de Rerum Originibus*. London: R. Norton, for Walter Kettilby

Burnet, T. 1736, *Archaeologiae Philosophicae sive Doctrina Antiqua de Rerum Originibus*. London: E. Curll

Burnett, C. 1976, The Legend of the Three Hermes and Abū Ma'shar's Kitāb al-Uluf in the Latin Middle Ages. *Journal of the Warburg and Courtauld Institutes* 39, 231–234

Burnett, C. 1977, A Group of Arabic-Latin Translators Working in Northern Spain in the Mid-twelfth Century. *Journal of the Royal Asiatic Society*, 62–108

Burnett, C. 1981, Hermann of Carinthia and the Kitāb al-Istamatis: Further Evidence for the Transmission of Hermetic Magic. *Journal of the Warburg and Courtauld Institutes* 44, 167–169

Burnett, C. (ed.) 1982, *Hermann of Carinthia, De Essentiis*. Leiden: Brill

Burnett, C. 1994. The Chapter on the Spirits in the *Pantegni* of Constantine the African, in C. Burnett and D. Jacquart (eds), *Constantine the African and 'Ali ibn al-'Abbas al-Majusi: The Pantegni and Related Texts*, 99–120. Leiden: Brill

Burnett, C. 1997, The Works of Petrus Alfonsi: Questions of Authenticity. *Medium Ævum* 66, 42–79

Burnett, C. 1998, King Ptolemy and Alchandreus the Philosopher: The Earliest Texts on the Astrolabe and Arabic Astrology at Fleury, Micy and Chartres. *Annals of Science* 55, 329–368

Burnett, C. 2001a, The Establishment of Medieval Hermeticism, in P. Linehan and J. L. Nelson (eds), *The Medieval World*, 111–130. London: Routledge

Burnett, C. 2001b, The Coherence of the Arabic-Latin Translation Programme in Toledo in the Twelfth Century. *Science in Context* 14, 249–288

Burnett, C. 2001c, Bartholomeus Parmensis, *Tractatus spere*, pars tercia, in P. Battistini, F. Bònoli, A. Braccesi and D. Buzzetti, *Seventh Centenary of the Teaching of Astronomy in Bologna 1297–1997*, 151–212. Bologna: CLUEB

Burnett, C. forthcoming, Thabit ibn Qurra the Harranian on Talismans and the Spirits of the Planets, in R. Rashed and R. Morelon (eds), *The Proceedings of the al-Furqan Conference on the Ninth Centenary of the Death of Thabit ibn Qurra*

Burnett, C. and E. Poulle forthcoming, Raymond of Marseille, *Liber Cursuum*

Burnett, C., K. Yamamoto and M. Yano (eds) 1994, *Abu Ma'sar, The Abbreviation of the Introduction to Astrology Together with the Medieval Latin Translation of Adelard of Bath*. Leiden: Brill

Burnett, C. and K. Yamamoto 2000, *Abu Ma šar on Historical Astrology*. Leiden: Brill

Burnett, C., K. Yamamoto and M. Yano (eds) forthcoming, *The Arabic and Latin texts of al-Qabitaci (Alcabitius), Introduction to Astrology ('Introductorius')*

Burnett, J. 1774–1792, *Of the Origin and Progress of Language*. Edinburgh: A. Kincaid and W. Kreech, for T. Cadell

Burri, C. and S. Sergeron (eds) 1971, *Voyages en Égypte des années 1589, 1590, et 1591*. Cairo: Institut Français d'Archéologie Orientale

Busard, H. L. L. (ed.) 2001, *Johannes de Tinemue's Redaction of Euclid's Elements, the So-Called Adelard III Version*. Stuttgart: Franz Steiner

Butler, A. 1978, *The Arab Conquest of Egypt and the Last Thirty Years of the Roman Dominion*. 2nd edition, Oxford: Clarendon

**Butler, B. J. 2003, 'Egyptianizing' the Alexandrina: The Contemporary Revival of the Ancient Mouseion/Library, in J-M. Humbert and C. Price (eds), *Imhotep Today: Egyptianizing architecture*, 257–282. London: UCL Press**

Buttimer, C. H. (ed.) 1939, *Hugh of St Victor, Didascalicon*. Washington, DC: Catholic University of America Press

Butzer, K. 1976, *Early Hydraulic Civilization in Egypt: a Study in Cultural Ecology*. Chicago: University of Chicago Press

Calvesi, M. 1980, *Il Sogno di Poliphilo Prenestino*. Rome: Officina

Calvesi, M. 1996, *La 'Pugna d'Amore in Sogno' di Francesco Colonna Romano*. Rome: Lithos editrice

Camille, M. 1999, The Corpse in the Garden: *mummia* in Medieval Herbal Illustrations. *Micrologus* 7, 296–318

Cannon, G. 1991, Jones's "sprung from some common source": 1786–1986, in S. M. Lamb and E. D. Mitchell (eds), *Sprung from Some Common Source: Investigations into the Prehistory of Languages*, 23–47. Stanford: Stanford UP

Cannuyer, C. 1984a, Une Description méconnue de l'Egypte au XIIe siècle. *Göttinger Miszellen* 70, 13–18

Cannuyer, C. 1984b, Les Pyramides d'Egypte dans la littérature médio-latine. *Revue Belge de philologie et d'histoire* 162, 673–681

Cannuyer, C. 1985, Hieroglyphica Thevetana. *Discussions in Egyptology* 3, 7–20

Carozzi, C. (ed.) 1979, *Poème au Roi Robert*. Paris: Belles Lettres

Carra de Vaux 1898, *L'Abregé des merveilles*. Paris: Société Philologique

Carrott, R. G. 1978, *The Egyptian Revival: Its Sources, Monuments, and Meaning, 1808–1858*. Berkeley: University of California Press

Cartari, V. 1615, *Le Vere e Nove Imagini Degli dei Degli Antichi*. Padua: Tozzi

Casaubon, I. 1614, *De rebus sacris et ecclesiasticis execritationes XVI*. London: Norton

Casini, P. 1984, Newton: The Classical Scholia. *History of Science* 22, 1–58

Casini, P. 1988, Newton's *Principia* and the Philosophers of the Enlightenment. *Notes and Records of the Royal Society* 42, 35–53

Casson, L. 2001, *Libraries in the Ancient World*. New Haven: Yale UP

Caussin, N. 1631, *De Symbolica Aegyptorium Sapientia*. Cologne: I. Kinckium

Černý, J. 1976, *A Coptic Etymological Dictionary*. Cambridge: CUP

**Champion, T. 2003, Egypt and the Diffusion of Culture, in D. Jeffreys (ed.), *Views of Egypt since Napoleon Bonaparte: imperialism, colonialism and modern appropriations*, 127–146. London: UCL Press**

Chaudhuri, K. N. 1985, *Trade and Civilisation in the Indian Ocean: An Economic History from the Rise of Islam to 1750.* Cambridge: CUP

Chaudhuri, K. N. 1990, *Asia before Europe: Economy and Civilisation of the Indian Ocean from the Rise of Islam to 1750.* Cambridge: CUP

Chauveau, M. 1991, P. Carlsberg 301: le manuel juridique de Tebtynis, in P. J. Frandsen (ed.), *The Carlsberg Papyri 1: Demotic Texts from the Collection*, 103–123. Copenhagen: Museum Tusculanum Press

Childe, V. G. 1928, *The Most Ancient East: the Oriental Prelude to European Prehistory.* London: Kegan Paul

Childe, V. G. 1934, *New Light on the Most Ancient East: the Oriental Prelude to European Prehistory.* London: Kegan Paul

Childe, V. G. 1951, *Social Evolution.* London: Watts

Christides, V. 2000, The Tomb of Alexander the Great in Arabic Sources, in I. Netton (ed.), *Studies in Honour of C. E. Bosworth*, 165–173. Leiden: Brill

Churchill, A. and J. Churchill 1744–1746, *A Collection of Voyages and Travels, some now first printed from original manuscripts, others now first published in English.* London: H. Lintot and J. Osborn

Cipriani, G. 1993, *Gli Obelischi Egizi: Politica e Cultura Nella Roma Barocca.* Florence: Olschki

Coburn, K. (ed.) 1962, *The Notebooks of Samuel Taylor Coleridge, Vol. 2: 1804–1808.* London: Routledge and Kegan Paul

Coles, R. 1981, A Quadrilingual Curiosity in the Bodleian Library in Oxford. *Proceedings of the XVI International Congress of Papyrology*, 193–197

Collins, A. 2000, Renaissance Epigraphy and its Legitimating Potential: Annius of Viterbo, Etruscan Inscriptions, and the Origins of Civilization, in A. E. Cooley (ed.), *The Afterlife of Inscriptions: Reusing, Rediscovering, Reinventing, and Revitalizing Ancient Inscriptions*, 57–76. London: Institute of Classical Studies

Colonna, F. 1499 [1999], *Hypnerotomachia Poliphili.* Venice

Cook, M. 1983, Pharaonic History in Medieval Egypt. *Studia Islamica* 57, 67–103

Copenhaver, B. P. 1992, *Hermetica: The Greek Corpus Hermeticum and the Latin Asclepius in a New English Translation, with Notes and Introduction.* Cambridge: CUP

Copernicus, 1543, *De Revolutionibus Orbium Coelestium.*

Corbin, H. 1986, *Temple and Contemplation.* London: Kegan Paul

Crone, P. and M. Cook 1977, *Haggarism: The Making of the Islamic World.* Cambridge: CUP

Cudworth, R. 1678, *The True Intellectual System of the Universe.* London: Richard Royston

Curran, B. 1998, The 'Hypnerotomachia Poliphili' and Renaissance Egyptology. *Word and Image* 14, 156–185

Curran, B. 2000, De Sacrarum Litterarum Aegyptiorum Interpretatione: Reticence and Hubris in Hieroglyphic Studies of the Renaissance: Pierio Valeriano and Annius of Viterbo. *Memoirs of the American Academy in Rome* 43/44, 139–182

Curran. B. forthcoming, The Sphinx in the City: Egyptian Monuments and Urban Spaces in Renaissance Rome, in S. J. Milner and S. J. Campbell (eds), *Italian Renaissance Cities: Artistic Exchange and Cultural Translation.* Cambridge: CUP

Curran, B. and A. Grafton 1995, A Fifteenth-Century Site Report on the Vatican Obelisk. *Journal of the Warburg and Courtauld Institutes* 58, 234–248

Curran, B. and G. Periti forthcoming, Epigraphic Hieroglyphic Drawings from Michele Fabrizio Ferrarini's Antiquarium

Cuvier, G. 1817, Extrait d'Observations faites sur le cadaver d'une femme connue à Paris et à Londres sous le nom de Vénus Hottentotte. *Mémoires de Muséum d'Histoire Naturelle* 3, 259–274

Cyriacus of Ancona 1742, *Kyriaci Anconitani Itinerarium nunc Primum ex ms. cod. in Lucem Erutum ex Bibl. Illus. Clarissimique Baronis Philippi Stosch.* Florence: Laurentius Mehus

Dain, B. 1993, Haiti and Egypt in Early Black Racial Discourse in the United States. *Slavery and Abolition* 14, 139–161

Dannenfeldt, K. 1959, Egypt and Egyptian Antiquities in the Renaissance. *Studies in the Renaissance* 6, 7–27

Darwin, C. 1859, *On the Origin of Species by Means of Natural Selection.* London: J. Murray

David, R. 1993, *Discovering Ancient Egypt.* London: Michael O'Mara

Davis, W. W. 1983, China, the Confucian Ideal, and the European Age of Enlightenment. *Journal of the History of Ideas* 44, 523–548

Ibn Al-Dawadari 1981, *Kanz al-durar wa jami 'al-ghurar, Vol. 3.* M. A. Gamal Ad-Din (ed.). Cairo and Wiesbaden: Steiner

Dean, D. R. 1981, The Age of the Earth Controversy: Beginnings to Hutton. *Annals of Science* 38, 435–456

Dear, P. 2001, *Revolutionizing the Sciences: European Knowledge and its Ambitions, 1500–1700.* Basingstoke: Palgrave

Delafield, J. and J. Lakey 1839, *An Inquiry into the Origin of the Antiquities of America.* Cincinnati: Burgess

**Delamaire, M-S. 2003, Searching for Egypt: Egypt in 19th Century American World Exhibitions, in. J-M. Humbert and C. Price (eds), *Imhotep Today: Egyptianizing architecture*, 123–134. London: UCL Press**

Deluz, C. 1972, Liber de Quibusdam Ultramarinis Partibus et Praecipue de Terra Sancta de Guillaume de Boldensele 1336 Suivi de la Traduction de Frère Jean le Long 1351, unpublished PhD thesis, Sorbonne University, Paris

Denon, V. 1802 [1990], *Voyage dans la basse et la haute Égypte: pendant les campagnes du Général Bonaparte.* Paris: P. Didot, and Cairo: Institut Français d'Archéologie Orientale

Derchain, P. 1999, Mendes et les Femmes. *Enchoria* 25, 20–23

*Description* 1809–1828, *Description de l'Égypte, ou Recueil des observations et des recherches qui ont été faites en Égypte pendant l'expédition de l'Armée française.* Paris: Imprimerie Impériale

Diab, A. 1998, *Tarikh Al-Aqpat of Al-Maqrizi.* Cairo: Dar Al-Fadilah

Dieckmann, L. 1970, *Hieroglyphics: The History of a Literary Symbol.* St Louis, MI: Washington UP

Dodge, B. 1970, *The Fihrist of al-Nadim.* New York: Columbia UP

Donadoni, S., S. Curto and A. M. Donadoni Roveri 1990, *Egypt from Myth to Egyptology.* Milan: Fabbri

Donadoni, S., L. Rowland, E. Leospo and C. Mazza 2001, 'I geroglifici di Athanasius Kircher' (Donadoni); 'Kircher Trismegisto' (Rowland); 'La Collezione del Museo Kircheriano' (Leospo); 'Le antichità imperiale e I culti orientali: L'Iseo Campense' (C. Mazza), in E. Lo Sardo (ed.), *Athanasius Kircher: Il Museo del Mondo*, 101–141. Rome: De Luca

Donker van Heel, K. 1990, *The Legal Manual of Hermopolis (P. Mattha): Text and Translation.* Leiden: Het Leids Papyrologisch Instituut

Donner, H. 1995, *Isis in Petra.* Leipzig: University of Leipzig

Donner, M. 1998, *The Narratives of Islamic Origins.* New Jersey: Darwin

Doxiadis, E. 1995, *The Mysterious Fayum Portraits: Faces from Ancient Egypt.* New York: Harry N. Abrams

Dronke, P. 1990, *Hermes and the Sibyls: Continuations and Creations.* Cambridge: CUP

Drower, E. S. 1937, *The Mandaeans of Iraq and Iran.* Oxford: Clarendon

Drower, E. S. 1956, *Water into Wine: A Study of Ritual Idiom in the Middle East.* London: John Murray

Dryden, J. 1693, *The Satires of D. J. Juvenalis.* London

DuQuesne, T. 1999, Egypt's Image in the European Enlightenment. *Seshat* 3, 32–51

DuQuesne, T. 2001, Concealing and Revealing: The Problem of Ritual Masking in Ancient Egypt. *Discussions in Egyptology* 51, 5–31

Eisenstadt, S. N. 1963, *The Political Systems of Empires*. London: Free Press of Glencoe

El Daly, O. 2000, Mummies as Medicine. *Discussions in Egyptology* 48, 49–65

**El Daly, O. 2003a, What do Tourists Learn of Egypt?, in S. MacDonald and M. Rice (eds), Consuming Ancient Egypt, 139–150. London: UCL Press**

El Daly, O. 2003b, *"The Virtuous Scholar": Queen Cleopatra in Medieval Moslim/Arab Writings*, in S. Walker and S-A. Ashton (eds), *Cleopatra Re-assessed*. London: British Museum Occasional Papers

Elliott, R. W. V. 1957, Issac Newton's "Of An Universall Language". *Modern Language Review* 52, 1–18

El-Shayyal, G. 1962, *A History of Egyptian Historiography in the Nineteenth Century*. Alexandria: Alexandria UP

Emiliozzi, A. 1986, *Il Museo Civico di Viterbo: Storia delle Raccolte Archeologiche*. Rome: Musei e Collezioni d'Etruria

Empereur, J-Y. 1998, *Alexandria Rediscovered*. London: British Museum Press

Enan, M. 1969, *Misr-ul-islamieh*. Cairo: Lajnat-ul-Taalif

Evans, R. J. W. 1979, *The Making of the Habsburg Monarchy 1550–1700*. Oxford: Clarendon

Ibn Al-Faqih Al-Hamadhani, Abu Bakra Ahmed Ibn Muhammad Ibn Ishaq 1996, Kitāb Al-Buldan. Y. Al-Hadi (ed.). Beirut: 'Alam Al-Kutub

Faris, A. 1938, *The Antiquities of South Arabia*. Oxford: OUP

Ibn Fatik, Abu Al-Wafaa Al-Mubashir 1958, *Mukhtar al-hikam wa mahasin al-kalim*. 'Abdurrahman Badawi (ed.). Madrid: Instituto Egipcio de Estudios Islamicos

**Fazzini, R. A. and M. E. McKercher 2003, 'Egyptomania' and American Architecture, in J-M. Humbert and C. Price (eds), Imhotep Today: Egyptianizing architecture, 135–160. London: UCL Press**

Ferro, M. 1984. *The Use and Abuse of History or How the Past is Taught*. London: Routledge and Kegan Paul

Ficino, M. 1474, *De Christiana Religione*. Florence

Ficino, M. 1576, *Opera Omnia*. Reprinted 1959, Turin: Bottega d'Erasmo

Findlen, P. 1994, *Possessing Nature: Museums, Collecting, and Scientific Culture in Early Modern Italy*. Berkeley: University of California Press

Finzi, C. 1991, Leon Battista Alberti: Geroglifiche e Gloria, in C. M. Govi, S. Curto and S. Pernigotti (eds), *L'Egitto fuori dell'Egitto: Dalla riscoperta all'Egittologia*, 205–208. Bologna: CLUEB

Fletcher, J. and D. Montserrat 1998, The Human Hair in the Tomb of Tutankhamun: A Re-Evaluation, in C. Eyre (ed.), *Proceedings of the Seventh International Congress of Egyptologists. Cambridge, 3–9 September 1995*, 401–407 Leuven: Peeters

Fodor, A. and L. Foti 1976, *Haram* and Hermes: Origin of the Arabic Word *Haram* Meaning Pyramid. *Studia Aegyptiaca* 2, 157–167

Fontana, D. 1590, *Della Trasportatione dell' Obelisco Vaticano*. Reprinted 1978, A. Carugo (ed.). Milan: Il Polifilo

Force, J. E. and R. H. Popkin 1990, *Essays on the Context, Nature and Influence of Isaac Newton's Theology*. Dordrecht: Kluwer

Fowden, G. 1982, The Pagan Holy Man in Late Antique Society. *Journal of Hellenic Studies* 102, 33–59

Fowden, G. 1986, *The Egyptian Hermes. A Historical Approach to the Late Pagan Mind*. Princeton: Princeton UP

Frankfort, H. 1951, *The Birth of Civilization in the Near East*. London: Benn

Fraser, P. M. 1972, *Ptolemaic Alexandria*. Oxford: OUP

Frazer, J. G. 1890, *The Golden Bough*. London: Macmillan

Frazer, J. G. 1910, *Totemism and Exogamy: a Treatise on Certain Early Forms of Superstition and Society*. London: Macmillan

Froidefond, C. 1971, *Le Mirage Égyptien dans la littérature Grecque d'Homère à Aristote*. Aix-en-Provence: Ophrys

Frommel, C. 1991–1992, Peruzzi's Römische Anfänge: von der 'Pseudo-Cronaca-Gruppe' zu Bramante. *Römisches Jahrbuch der Bibliotheca Hertziana* 27, 139–180


Gale, T. 1669, *The Court of the Gentiles: Or, A Discourse touching the Original of Human Literature, both Philologie and Philosophie, from the Scriptures and Jewish Church. Part I*. Oxford

Galen 1542, *Opera*. Basle: Hier Frobenius and Nic. Episcopium

Gamwell, L. and Wells, R. (eds) 1989, *Sigmund Freud and Art: His Personal Collection of Antiquities*. London: Thames and Hudson

Gardiner, A. 1916, The Egyptian Origin of the Semitic Alphabet. *Journal of Egyptian Archaeology* 3, 1–16

Gascoigne, J. 1991, The Wisdom of the Egyptians and the Secularisation of History in the Age of Newton, in S. Gaukroger (ed.), *The Uses of Antiquity. The Scientific Revolution and the Classical Tradition*, 171–212. Dordrecht: Kluwer

Gershoni, I. and J. Jankowski 1986, *Egypt, Islam and the Arabs: The Search for Egyptian Nationhood, 1900–1930*. New York: OUP

Al-Gharnati, Abu Hamid 'Abd Al-Rahim ibn Soliman 1993, *Tuhfat al-albab wa nukhbat al-il'jab*. Isma'il Al-'Arabi (ed.). Casablanca: Dar Al-Afaq Al-Jadidah

Giehlow, K. 1915, Die Hieroglyphenkunde des Humanismus in der Allegorie der Renaissance. *Jahrbuch der Kunsthistorisches Sammlungen des Allerhöchsten Kaiserhauses* 32, 1–229

Gliddon, G. R. 1841, *An Appeal to the Antiquaries of Europe on the Destruction of the Monuments of Egypt*. London: J. Madden

Gliddon, G. R. 1843, *Ancient Egypt: A Series of Chapters on Early Egyptian History, Archaeology, and other Subjects Connected with Hieroglyphical Literature*. New York: J. Winchester

Gliddon, G. R. 1849, *Hand-book to the American Panorama of the Nile. Being the Original transparent Picture exhibited in London, at Egyptian Hall, Piccadilly*. London: James Madden

*Glossa ordinaria* 1992, facsimile of ed. Strassburg 1480/1, introduced by K. Froehlich and M. T. Gibson. Turnhout: Brepols

Golenischeff, W. 1906, Le Papyrus No 1115 de L'Ermitage Impérial De Saint-Petersbourg. *Recueil de Travaux* 28, 1–40

Gordon, A. 1737, *Essay Towards Explaining the Hieroglyphical Figures on the Coffin of the Ancient Mummy Belonging to Captain W. Lethieullier*. London: A. Gordon

van Gorp, J. B. 1580, Hieroglyphica, in J. B. van Gorp, *Opera Ioan. Coropi Becani*, 106–110. Antwerp: C. Plantinus

Gough, R. 1785, *A Comparative View of the Antient Monuments of India*. London: John Nichols

Gould, R. F. 1893, Masonic Celebrities, No. 5 – The Rev. William Stukeley, MD. *Ars Quatuor Coronatorum* 6, 127–145

Gould, S. J. 1984. *The Mismeasure of Man*. Harmondsworth: Penguin

Gousset, M-T. and J-P. Verdet 1989, *Georgius Zothorus Zaparus Fendulus, Liber Astrologiae*. Paris: Herscher

Graefe, E. 1984, Der Pyramidenbesuch des Guilielmus de Boldensele in Jahre 1335 mit einem Anhang: Der Zeitpunkt des Aufbrechens der Chefrenpyramide im Mittelalter. *Studien zur altägyptischen Kultur* 11, 569–584

Graefe, E. 1990, A Propos de Pyramidenbeschribung des Wilhelm von Boldeusche aus dem Jahre 1335 (II), in E. Hornung (ed.), *Zum Bild Ägyptens im Mittelalter und in der Renaissance,* 9–28. Freiburg: Universitätsverlag Freiburg Schweiz

Grafton, A. 1983, Protestant Versus Prophet: Isaac Casaubon on Hermes Trismegistus. *Journal of the Warburg and Courtauld Institutes* 46, 78–93

Grafton, A. 2000, *Leon Battista Alberti: Master Builder of the Italian Renaissance.* London: Allen Lane

Grapow, H. 1959, *Von den Medizinischen Texten.* Berlin: Akademie

Gratwick, A. S. 1995, Alexandria, Syene, Meroe: Symmetry in Eratosthenes' *Measurement of the World,* in L. Ayres (ed.), *The Passionate Intellect: Essays on the Transformation of Classical Traditions Presented to Professor I. G. Kidd,* 177–200. New Brunswick: Transaction

Grayson, C. 1960, The Composition of L. B. Alberti's 'Decem libri de re aedificatoria'. *Münchner Jahrbuch der Bildenden Kunst* 11, 152–161

Greaves, J. 1646, *Pyramidographia: or a Description of the Pyramids in Ægypt.* London: G. Badger

Green, T. 1992, *The City of the Moon God. Religious Traditions in Harran.* Leiden: Brill

Greener, L. 1967, *The Discovery of Egypt.* New York: Viking

Greenhill, T. 1705, *Nekrokedeia: Or the Art of Embalming.* London: T. Greenhill

Gregory, D. 1715, *The Elements of Astronomy, Physical and Geometrical.* London: John Morphew

Gregory, D. 1995, Between the Book and the Lamp: Imaginative Geographies of Egypt, 1849–50. *Transactions of the Institute of British Geographers* 20, 29–57

Grelot, P. 1972, *Documents Araméens d'Égypte.* Paris: Editions du Cerf

Griffith, J. G. 1980, Interpretatio Graeca, in W. Helck and E. Otto (eds), *Lexikon der Ägyptologie, 3,* 167–172, Wiesbaden: Harrassowitz

Gril, D. 1978, Le Personage coranique de Pharaon d'après l'interprétation d'Ibn Arabi. *Annales Islamalogiques* 14, 37–57

Grotefend, C. L. 1855, Des Edelherrn Wilhelm von Boldensele Reise nach dem gelobten Lande. *Zeitschrift des historischen Vereins für Niedersachsen,* 209–286

Grube, E. 1962, Studies in the Survival and Continuity of Pre-Muslim Traditions in Egyptian Islamic Art. *Journal of the American Research Center in Egypt* 1, 75–97

Guérin-Dalle Mese, J. 1991, *Égypte: la mémoire et le rêve: itinéraires d'un voyage, 1320–1601.* Florence: Olschki

de Guignes, J. 1769, *Mémoires dans lequel on prouve que les Chinois sont une colonie Egyptienne.* Paris

Gunn, B. 1949, Peet, Thomas Eric, in *Dictionary of National Biography 1931–1940,* 685–686. Oxford: OUP

Haarmann, U. 1978, Die Sphinx. *Saeculum* 29, 367–384

Haarmann, U. 1980, Regional Sentiment in Medieval Islamic Egypt. *Bulletin of the School of Oriental and African Studies* 43, 55–66

Haarmann, U. 1982, Quellen zur Geschichte des islamischen Ägypten. *Mitteilungen des Deutchen Archäologischen Instituts, Abteilung Kairo* 38, 201–210

Haarmann, U. 1990, Das Pharaonische Ägypten bei Islamischen Autoren des Mittelalters, in E. Hornung (ed.), *Zum Bild Ägyptens im Mittelalter und in der Renaissance,* 29–57. Freiburg: Universitätsverlag Freiburg Schweiz

Haarmann, U. 1996, Medieval Muslim Perceptions of Pharaonic Egypt, in A. Loprieno (ed.), *Ancient Egyptian Literature: History and Forms,* 605–627. Leiden: Brill

Haarmann, U. 2001, Islam and Ancient Egypt, in D. Redford (ed), *The Oxford Encyclopaedia of Ancient Egypt Vol II,* 191–194. Oxford: OUP

Haig Gaisser, J. 1993, *Catullus and his Renaissance Readers*. Oxford: Clarendon

**Haikal, F. 2003, Egypt's Past Regenerated by its Own People, in S. MacDonald and M. Rice (eds), *Consuming Ancient Egypt*, 123–138. London: UCL Press**

Ibn 'Abd Al-Hakam, Abu Al-Qusim 'Abd Al-Rahman 1922, *Futuh Misr*. Ch. Torrey (ed.). Newhaven: Yale Oriental Research Series

Hale, M. 1677, Preface to the Reader, in *The Primitive Origination of Mankind, Considered and Examined According to the Light of Nature*. London: William Godbid, for William Shrowsbery

Hall, E. 1989, *Inventing the Barbarian. Greek Self-Definition Through Tragedy*. Oxford: OUP

Hall, J. M. 1981, *Lucian's Satire*. New York: Arno

Hall, J. M. 1997, *Ethnic Identity in Greek Antiquity*. Cambridge: CUP

Al-Hamadani, Al-Hasan ibn Ahmad ibn Ya'qub. 1974. *Sifat jazirat al-'arab*. M. A. Al-Akwa 'Al-Hawali (ed.). Riyadh

Hamarneh, S. 1971, The Ancient Monuments of Alexandria According to Accounts by Medieval Arab Authors (IX–XV century). *Folia Orientalia* 13, 77–110

**Hamill, J. and P. Mollier 2003, Rebuilding the Sanctuaries of Memphis: Egypt in Masonic Iconography and Architecture, in J-M. Humbert and C. Price (eds), *Imhotep Today: Egyptianizing architecture*, 207–220. London: UCL Press**

Hanson, A. 1992, Egyptians, Greeks, Romans, Arabs, and *IOUDAIOI* in the first century A.D. Tax Archive from Philadelphia: P. Mich, inv. 880 Recto and P. Princ. III 152 Revised, in J. Johnson (ed.), *Life in a Multi-Cultural Society*, 133–145. Chicago: Oriental Institute

Harley, J. B. and D. Woodward (eds) 1987, *The History of Cartography. Vol 1, Cartography in Prehistoric, Ancient and Medieval Europe and the Mediterranean*. Chicago: University of Chicago Press

Harris, J. R. 1971, Medicine, in J. R. Harris (ed.), *The Legacy of Egypt*, 112–137. Oxford: Clarendon

Harrison, P. 1990, *'Religion' and the Religions in the English Enlightenment*. Cambridge: CUP

**Harrison, T. 2003, Upside Down and Back to Front: Herodotus and the Greek Encounter with Egypt, in R. Matthews and C. Roemer (eds), *Ancient Perspectives on Egypt*, 145–156. London: UCL Press**

Hart, V. and P. Hicks 1996, *Sebastiano Serlio on Architecture, Vol. I: Books I–V of 'Tutte l'opere d'architettura et prospettiva' by Sebastiano Serlio*. New Haven: Yale UP

Hartog, F. 1986, Les Grecs Égyptologues. *Annales: economies, sociétés, civilisations* 41, 953–967

Hartog, F. 1988, *The Mirror of Herodotus with a Representation of the Other in the Writing of History* (trans. J. Lloyd). Berkeley: University of California Press

Hassan, F. A. 1998, Memorabilia: Archaeological Materiality and National Identity in Egypt, in L. Meskell (ed.), *Archaeology Under Fire: Nationalism, Politics and Heritage in the Eastern Mediterranean and the Middle East*, 200–216. London: Routledge

**Hassan, F. A. 2003, Imperialist Appropriations of Egyptian Obelisks, in D. Jeffreys (ed.), *Views of Ancient Egypt since Napoleon Bonaparte: imperialism, colonialism and modern appropriations*, 19–68. London: UCL Press**

Hassan, S. 1951, *Le Sphinx: son histoire à la lumière des fouilles récentes*. Cairo: Misr

Hay, D. 1968, *Europe: The Emergence of an Idea*. Edinburgh: Edinburgh UP

Haycock, D. B. 2002, *Dr William Stukeley: Science, Archaeology and Religion in Eighteenth-Century England*. Woodbridge: Boydell

Hearne, T. 1732, *Collections* 11, 100–101

Heckscher, W. S. 1947, Bernini's Elephant and Obelisk. *Art Bulletin* 29, 155–182

Hedegård, G. (ed.) 2002, *Liber Iuratus Honorii*. Stockholm: Almqvist and Wiksell International

Henein, N. and T. Bianquis 1975, *La Magie par les psaumes*. Cairo: Institut Français d'Archéologie Orientale

Herwart von Hohenburg, J. F. 1623, *Admiranda Ethicae Theologiae Mysteria Propalata*. Ingolstadt: Nicolai Henrici

Higgins, I. M. 1997, *Writing East: The "Travels" of Sir John Mandeville*. Philadelphia: University of Pennsylvania Press

Highet, G. 1954, *Juvenal the Satyrist: A Study*. Oxford: Clarendon

Hitchens, C. 1997, *The Elgin Marbles: Should They Be Returned To Greece?* 2nd edition, London: Verso

Hitti, P. 1970, *History of the Arabs*. London: Macmillan

Hoare, R. C. 1821, *The History of Ancient Wiltshire, Vol. 2*. London: Lackington, Hughes, Harding, Mavor and Lepard

Hoch, J. 1994, *Semitic Words in Egyptian Texts of the New Kingdom and Third Intermediate Period*. Princeton: Princeton UP

Hoffman, M. A., 1979, *Egypt before the Pharaohs: the Prehistoric Foundations of Egyptian Civilization*. New York: Knopf

Hopfner, T. 1922–1925, *Fontes Historiae Religionis Aegyptiacae*. Bonn: Marc & Weber

**Horbury, M. 2003, The British and the Copts, in D. Jeffreys (ed.), *Views of Ancient Egypt since Napoleon Bonaparte: imperialism, colonialism and modern appropriations*, 153–170. London: UCL Press**

Horden, P. and N. Purcell 2000, *The Corrupting Sea: A Study of Mediterranean History*. Oxford: Blackwell

Hornung, E. 1982, *Conceptions of God in Ancient Egypt* (trans. J. Baines). Ithaca: Cornell UP

Hornung, E. (ed.) 1990, *Zum Bild Ägyptens im Mittelalter und in der Renaissance*. Freiburg: Universitätsverlag Freiburg Schweiz

Hornung, E. 2001, *The Secret Lore of Egypt: its Impact on the West*. Ithaca: Cornell UP

Horsman, R. 1987, *Josiah Nott of Mobile: Southerner, Physician, and Racial Theorist*. Baton Rouge: Louisiana State UP

Howald, E. and H. E. Sigerist 1927, Liber Pseudoapulei Herbarius, in *Corpus Medicorum Latinorum Vol. IV*, 13–225. Leipzig and Berlin: Teubner

Hoyland, R. 2001, *Arabia and the Arabs from the Bronze Age to the Coming of Islam*. London: Routledge

Huet, P. D. 1717, *History of the Commerce and Navigations of the Ancients*. London: B. Lintot and W. Mears

Hülsen, C. 1910, *Il Libro di Giuliano da Sangallo. Codice Vaticano Barberiniano Latina 4424*. Leipzig

**Humbert, J-M. 2003, The Egyptianizing Pyramid from the 18th to the 20th Century, in J-M. Humbert and C. Price (eds), *Imhotep Today: Egyptianizing architecture*, 25–40. London: UCL Press**

**Humbert, J-M. and C. Price 2003, *Imhotep Today: Egyptianizing architecture*. London: UCL Press**

Hume, D. 1757, *Four Dissertations*. London: A. Millar

Humphries, R. 1958, *Juvenal, Satires*. Bloomington: Indiana UP

Hunter, M. 1990, Science and Heterodoxy: An Early Modern Problem Reconsidered, in D. C. Lindberg and R. S. Westman (eds), *Reappraisals of the Scientific Revolution*, 437–460. Cambridge: CUP

Husayn, T. 1938, *Mustaqbal al-thaqafah fi Misr*. Cairo: Dar Al-Ma^carif

Huygens, R. B. C. (ed.) 1986, *William of Tyre, Chronicon, Corpus Christianorum Continuatio Mediaevalis*. Turnhout: Brepols

Huygens, R. B. C. 2000, *Serta Mediaevalia, Textus Varii Saeculorum x–xiii*. Turnhout: Brepols

Al-Idrisi, Abu Ja'far Muhammad ibn 'Abd Al-'Aziz 1991, *Anwar 'ulwiyy al-ajram fi al- kashf 'an asrar al-ahram*. U. Haarmann (ed.). Stuttgart: Steiner

Iliffe, J. 1995, *Africans: the History of a Continent*. Cambridge: CUP

Iliffe, R. 1989, "The Idols of the Temple": Isaac Newton and the Private Life of Anti-Idolatry, unpublished PhD thesis, University of Cambridge

Al-Isfahani, El-Emad Al-Katib 1979, *Sana al-barq al-shami*. F. Al-Nabarawi (ed.). Cairo: Al-Khangi

Iversen, E. 1961, *The Myth of Egypt and its Hieroglyphs in European Tradition*. Copenhagen: Gad

Iversen, E. 1968, *Obelisks in Exile, 1*. Copenhagen: Gad

Iversen, E. 1993 *The Myth of Egypt and its Hieroglyphs in European Tradition*. 2nd edition, Princeton: Princeton UP

Ibn Iyas, Abu Al-Barakat Muhammad ibn Ahmad 1982–1984, *Badai 'al-zuhur fi waqai al- duhur*. Muhammad Mustafa (ed.). Cairo: Al-Hay'ah Al-Misriyah Al-'Amah l-Al-Kitab


Jaeger, B. 1991, L'Antico Egitto alla corte dei Gonzaga, in C. Morigi, S. Curto and S. Pernigotti (eds), *L'Egitto fuori dell'Egitto. Dalla riscoperta all'Egittologia*, 233–253. Bologna: CLUEB

Jaeger, B. 1994. La Loggia delle Muse nel Palazzo Te e la reviviscenza dell'Egitto antico nel Rinascimento, in *Mantova e l'Antico Egitto da Giuliano Romano a Giuseppe Acerbi*, 21–39. Florence: L-S. Olschki

James, M. R. 1921, *A Descriptive Catalogue of the Latin Manuscripts in the John Rylands Library at Manchester*. Manchester: Manchester UP

Jardine, L. and M. Silverthorne (eds) 2000, *Francis Bacon, The New Organon*. Cambridge: CUP

Jasnow, R. 1997, The Greek Alexander Romance and Demotic Egyptian Literature. *Journal of Near Eastern Studies* 56, 95–103

Jeffreys, D. 1985, *The Survey of Memphis Part I*. London: Egypt Exploration Society

**Jeffreys, D. 2003a, *Views of Ancient Egypt since Napoleon Bonaparte: imperialism, colonialism and modern appropriations*. London: UCL Press**

**Jeffreys, D. 2003b, Introduction: Two Hundred Years of Ancient Egypt: Modern History and Ancient Archaeology, in D. Jeffreys (ed.), *Views of Ancient Egypt since Napoleon Bonaparte: imperialism, colonialism and modern appropriations*, 1–18. London: UCL Press**

Al-Jobry, 'Abd Al-Rahim 1992, *Al-Mukhatar fi Kashf Al-Asrar wa Hatk Al-Astar*. 'Isam Shaparo (ed.). Beirut: Dar Al-Tadamun

Johnson, A. and T. Earle 1987, *The Evolution of Human Societies: from Foraging Group to Agrarian State*. Stanford, Cal: Stanford UP

Jones, C. W. 1934. Polemius Silvius, Bede and the Names of the Months. *Speculum* 9, 50–56

Jones, I. 1655, *The Most Notable Antiquity of Great Britain, Vulgarly called Stone-Heng on Salisbury Plain, Restored*. London

Jones, W. 1799, *The Works of Sir William Jones*. London

Junger, F. with H. Belhmer 2001, Language, in D. B. Redford (ed.), *The Oxford Encyclopedia of Ancient Egypt Vol II*, 258–267. Oxford: OUP


Kákosy, L. 1989, Survival of Ancient Egypt and Religion. Other Domains of Culture. Egyptian Influence on Gnosticism and Hermetism: A Brief Survey. *Studia Aegyptiaca* XII, 263–287

Kákosy, L. 1999, *Egyptian Healing Statues in Three Museums in Italy: Turin, Florence, Naples*. Turin: Museo Egizio

Kamal, A. 1902, Les Idols Arabes et les divinités Egyptiennes. *Recueil de Travaux* 24, 11–24

Kamal, A. 1917, Le Procédé graphique chez les anciens Egyptiens, l'origine du mot Égypte, les noms géographiques désignant cette contrée et ses primitives. *Bulletin de l'Institut Égyptien* 5, 325–338

Katz, D. S. 1990, The Chinese Jews and the Problem of Biblical Authority in Eighteenth- and Nineteenth-Century England. *English Historical Review* 105, 893–919

Kemp, B. J. 1989, *Ancient Egypt: anatomy of a civilization*. London: Routledge

Kenrick, J. 1846, *An Essay on Primeval History*. London: B. Fellowes

Ibn Khaldun, 'Abd Al-Rahman ibn Muhammad 1967, *The Muqaddima: An Introduction to History* (trans. F. Rosenthal). Princeton: Princeton UP

Khourshid, F. 2002, *Adeeb al-ustourah 'ind al-'arab*. Kuwait: 'Alam Al-Ma'rifah

Kinglake, A. W. 1844. *Eothen, or Traces of Travel Brought Home from the East*. London: J. Ollivier

Kircher, A. 1636, *Prodromus Coptus Sive Aegyptiacus*. Rome: 5, Cong-de Propoganda Fide

Kircher, A. 1646, *Lingua Aegyptiaca Restituta*. Rome: Herman Elliot

Kircher, A. 1650, *Obeliscus Pamphilius*. Rome: L. Grignani

Kircher, A. 1652–1654, *Oedipus Aegyptiacus*. Rome: Vitalis Mascardi

Kircher, A. 1666, *Ad Alexandrum VIII Obelisci Aegyptiaci Nuper inter Isaei Romani Effossi Interpretatio Hieroglyphica*. Rome: Varesij

Kircher, A. 1676, *Sphinx Mystagoga*. Amsterdam: Officina Jansonnio-Waesbergiani

Kitchen, K. A. 1999, Further Thoughts on Punt and its Neighbours, in A. Leahy and J. Tait (eds), *Studies on Ancient Egypt in honour of H. S. Smith*, 173–178. London: Egypt Exploration Society

Klibansky, R. 1941–1943, The Rock of Parmenides: Mediaeval Views on the Origin of Dialectic. *Medieval and Renaissance Studies* 1, 178–186

Knox, R. 1850, *The Races of Men: a Fragment*. London: H. Renshaw

Krader, L. 1968, *Foundation of the State*. London: Prentice-Hall

Krause, M. 1985, Zum Fortwirken Altägyptischer Elemente im Koptischen Ägypten, in *Ägypten: Dauer und Wandel*, 115–122. Cairo: Mitteilungen des Deutschen Archäologischen Instituts, Abteilung Kairo

Krzyzaniak, L. and M. Kobusiewicz (eds) 1984, *Origin and Early Development of Food-Producing Cultures in North-Eastern Africa*. Poznan: Polish Academy of Sciences

Kunitzsch, P. 1970, Das Abū Ma'sar-Zitat im Rosenroman. *Romanische Forschungen* 82, 102–111

La'da, C. 2003, Encounters with Ancient Egypt: The Hellenistic Greek Experience, in R. Matthews and C. Roemer (eds), *Ancient Perspectives on Egypt*, 157–170. London: UCL Press

Lamb, S. M. and E. D. Mitchell (eds) 1991, *Sprung from Some Common Source: Investigations into the Prehistory of Languages*. Stanford: Stanford UP

Lane, E. W. 1836, *An Account of the Manners and Customs of the Modern Egyptians*. London: Charles Knight

van Lantschoot, A. 1948, *Un précurseur d'Athanase Kircher*. Louvain: Bibliothèque du Muséon

Lapp, G. 1997, *The Papyrus of Nu*. London: British Museum Press

Lappenbeerg, J. M. 1869, Arnoldi Abbatis Lubecensis Chronica, in *Monumenta Germaniae Historica*, 21. Hannover: Hahnsche Buchhandlung

Lauro, P. 1550, *I cinque libri de la antichità de Beroso ... con lo commento di Giovanni Annio da Viterbo*. 2nd edition, Venice: Baldisiera Constantini

Lawrence, W. 1819, *Lectures on the Physiology, Zoology and Natural History of Man*. London: J. Callow

Leerssen, J. 1996, *Mere Irish and Fíor-Ghael: Studies in the Idea of Irish Nationality, its Development and Literary Expression Prior to the Nineteenth Century*. Cork: Cork UP

Lefebvre, G. 1956, *Essai sur la médecine Égyptienne de l'époque pharaonique*. Paris: Presses Universitaires de France

Lefkowitz, M. and G. M. Rogers (eds) 1996, *Black Athena Revisited*. Chapel Hill: University of North Carolina Press

Lehmann, P. W. 1977, *Cyriacus of Ancona's Egyptian Visit and its Reflections in Gentile Bellini and Hieronymus Bosch*. New York: J. J. Augustin

Lemay, R. 1978, Origin and Success of *Kitab [al-]Thamara* of Abu Ja'far Ahmad ibn Yusuf ibn Ibrahim, in *Proceedings of the First International Symposium for the History of Arabic Science, Vol II*, 91–107. Aleppo: Ministry of Science and Technology

Lemay, R. 1995–1996, *Abu Ma'sar al-Balkhi, Kitab al-mudkhal al-kabir ila 'ilm ahkam an-nujum, Liber introductorii maioris ad scientiam judiciorum astrorum*. Naples: Istituto Universitario Orientale

Lembke, K. 1992, Alcune osservazioni sull'obelisco di Urbino. *Xenia Antiqua* I, 13–20

Lembke, K. 1994. *Das Iseum Campense in Rom. Studie über der Isiskult unter Domitian*. Heidelberg: Verlag Archäologie und Geschichte

Leospo, E. 1978, *La Mensa Isiaca di Torino*. Leiden: Brill

Lepsius, C. R. 1849–1858, *Denkmäler aus Aegypten und Aethiopien*. Berlin: Nicolaische Buchhandlung

Levine, P. 1986, *The Amateur and the Professional: Antiquarians, Historians and Archaeologists in Victorian England, 1838–1886*. Cambridge: CUP

Lichtheim, M. 1975, *Ancient Egyptian Literature, Vol. 1: The Old and Middle Kingdoms*. Berkeley: University of California Press

Lichtheim, M. 1980, *Ancient Egyptian Literature, Vol. 3: The Late Period*. Berkeley: University of California Press

Lichtheim, M. 1983, *Late Egyptian Wisdom Literature in the International Context*. Freiburg-Göttingen: Vandenhoeck and Rupprecht

Lloyd, A. B. 1975, *Herodotus: Book II, introduction*. Leiden: Brill

Lloyd, A. B. 1983, The Late Period, in B. G. Trigger, B. J. Kemp, D. O'Connor and A. B. Lloyd (eds), *Ancient Egypt: A Social History*, 279–348. Cambridge: CUP

Locke, J. 1690, *Essay Concerning Human Understanding*. London: Elizabeth Holt, for Thomas Bassett

Lubbock, J. 1869, *Pre-historic Times, as Illustrated by Ancient Remains, and the Manners and Customs of Modern Savages*. 2nd edition, London: Williams and Norgate

Lubbock, J. 1875, Notes on the Discovery of Stone Implements in Egypt. *Journal of the Anthropological Institute* 4, 215–222

Lucentini, P. and V. Perrone-Compagni 2001, *I Testi e i Codici di Esmate nel Medioevo*. Florence: Edizione Polistampo

Lumbroso, G. 1879, Descrittori Italiani dell'Egitto e di Alessandria. *Atti della Reale Accademia dei Lincei, Rendiconti, Memorie, Classe di Scienze Morali, Storiche, e Filologiche* 3, 429–503

**Lupton, C. 2003, 'Mummymania' for the Masses – is Egyptology Cursed by the Mummy's Curse?, in S. MacDonald and M. Rice (eds), *Consuming Ancient Egypt*, 23–46. London: UCL Press**

Lutfi, H. 1998, Coptic festivals of the Nile: Abberrations of the Past, in T. Philipp and U. Haarmann (eds), *The Mamluks in Egyptian Politics and Society*, 254–282. Cambridge: CUP

Lutz, C. E. 1956, Remigius' Ideas on the Origin of the Seven Liberal Arts. *Mediaevalia et humanistica* 10, 32–49

**MacDonald, K. C. 2003, Cheikh Anta Diop and Ancient Egypt in Africa, in D. O'Connor and A. Reid (eds), *Ancient Egypt in Africa*, 93–106. London: UCL Press**

**MacDonald, S. and M. Rice (eds) 2003, *Consuming Ancient Egypt*. London: UCL Press**

MacKenzie, J. 1995, *Orientalism. History, Theory and the Arts*. Manchester: Manchester UP

Macpherson, J. 1773, *An Introduction to the History of Great Britain and Ireland*. London: Becket and De Hondt

**Maehler, H. 2003, Roman Poets on Egypt, in R. Matthews and C. Roemer (eds), *Ancient Perspectives on Egypt*, 213–216. London: UCL Press**

Magnuson, T. 1954. The Project of Nicholas V for Rebuilding the Borgo Leonino in Rome. *Art Bulletin* 36, 89–115

Mallon, A. 1906, Une École de savants Egyptiens au moyen age. *Mélanges de la Faculté Orientale de l'Université Saint-Joseph de Beyrouth* 1, 109–131

Mallon, A. 1907, Une École de savants Egyptiens au moyen age. *Mélanges de la Faculté Orientale de l'Université Saint-Joseph de Beyrouth* 2, 213–264

Mandeville, Sir J. 1900, *The Travels of Sir John Mandeville. The Version of the Cotton Manuscript in Modern Spelling*. A. W. Pollard and I. Macleod (eds). London: Macmillan

Manetti, G. 1734. Vita Nicholai Summa Pontificis (ca. 1455), in L. Muratori (ed.), *Rerum Italicarum Scriptores Vol. III*. Milan: Societa Palatina

Mann, M. 1986, *Sources of Social Power, Vol. I. A History of Power from the Beginning to AD 1760*. Cambridge: CUP

Manuel, F. E. 1974, *The Religion of Isaac Newton*. Oxford: Clarendon

Al-Maqrizi, Abu Al-'Abas Ahmed ibn 'Abd-Allah 2002, *Al-mawa'iz wa al-i'tbar fi dhikr al-khitat wa al-athar*. A. F. Sayed (ed.). London: Al-Furqan

Marcanova, G. 1465, Quaedam Antiquitatum Fragmenta (Padua). Princeton University Library MS Garrett 158, fol. 6v

Marsham, Sir J. 1672, *Chronicus Canon Ægyptiacus, Ebraicus, Graecus*. London: T. Roycroft

Martin, L. C. (ed.) 1964. *Sir Thomas Browne: Religio Medici and Other Works*. Oxford: Clarendon

Martineau, H. 1848, *Eastern Life, Past and Present*. London: Moxon

Al-Mas'udi, Abu Al-Hasan 'Ali ibn Al-Husain 1988, *Muruj al-dhahab wa ma'adin al- Jawhar*. M. 'Abd Al-Hamid (ed.). Beirut: Al-Maktabah Al-'asriyah

Maspero, J. 1914, Horapollon et la fin du paganisme Égyptien. *Bulletin de l'Institut Française d'Archéologie Orientale du Caire* 11, 164–195

Masson, J. (ed.) 1975, *Le Voyage en Égypte de Felix Fabri, 1483*, Cairo: Institut Français d'Archéologie Orientale

Mattha, G. 1975, *The Demotic Legal Code of Hermopolis West*. Cairo: Institut Français d'Archéologie Orientale

**Matthews, R. and C. Roemer (eds) 2003a, *Ancient Perspectives on Egypt*. London: UCL Press**

**Matthews, R. and C. Roemer 2003b, Introduction: The Worlds of Ancient Egypt – Aspects, Sources, Interactions, in R. Matthews and C. Roemer (eds), *Ancient Perspectives on Egypt*, 1–20. London: UCL Press**

Matthiae, G. S. 2000, *L'Idea del Bello: Viaggio per Roma nel Seicento con Giovan Pietro Bellori*. Rome: Edizioni de Luca

Mattiangeli, P. 1981, Annio de Viterbo Inspiratore di Cicli Pittorici, in G. Baffioni and P. Mattiangeli, *Annio da Viterbo: Documenti e ricerche Vol. I*, 257–303. Rome: CNR

Maurach, G. 1979, Daniel von Morley "Philosophi". *Mittellateinisches Jahrbuch* 14, 204–254

Mazrui, A. A. 1986, *The Africans: a Triple Heritage*. London: BBC

Mazzaoui, M. 1991, Alexander the Great and the Arab Historians. *Graeco-Aribica* 4, 33–43

McCullough, W. 1967, *Jewish and Mandaean Incantation Bowls in the Royal Ontario Museum*. Toronto: University of Toronto Press

McDowell, A. G. 1995, Patterns of Instruction in the New Kingdom, in C. J. Eyre (ed.), *Seventh International Congress of Egyptologists. Cambridge, 3–9 September 1995: Abstracts of Papers*, 123. Cambridge: International Association of Egyptologists

McDowell, A. G. 1999, *Village Life in Ancient Egypt: Laundry Lists and Love Songs*. Oxford: OUP

McGrath, R. L. 1963, The Old and New Illustrations for Cartari's 'Imagini dei dei degli antichi': A Study of 'Paper Archaeology' in the Italian Renaissance. *Gazette des Beaux-Arts* 6.59, 213–226

McGuire, J. E. 1977, Neoplatonism and Active Principles: Newton and the Corpus Hermeticum, in R. S. Westman and J. E. McGuire, *Hermeticism and the Scientific Revolution*. Los Angeles: University of California Press

McGuire, J. E. and P. M. Rattansi 1966, Newton and the "Pipes of Pan". *Notes and Records of the Royal Society* 21, 108–143

McLachlan, H. (ed.) 1950, *Sir Isaac Newton: Theological Manuscripts*. Liverpool: Liverpool UP

**Medina-González, I. 2003, 'Trans-Atlantic Pyramidology', Orientalism and Empire: Ancient Egypt and the 19th Century Archaeological Experience of Mesoamerica, in D. Jeffreys (ed.), *Views of Ancient Egypt since Napoleon Bonaparte: imperialism, colonialism and modern appropriations*, 107–126. London: UCL Press**

Meinecke-Berg, V. 1985, Spoilen in der Mittelalterlichen Architekture von Kairo, in *Ägypten: Dauer und Wandel*, 131–142. Cairo: Mitteilungen des Deutschen Archäologischen Instituts, Abteilung Kairo

Mercati, M. 1589, *Degli Obelischi di Roma*. Rome

Merkelbach, R. 1977, *Die Quellen des Griechischen Alexanderromans*. Munich: Beck

Meyer, M. and R. Smith 1994, *Ancient Christian Magic*. San Francisco: Harper

Mill, J. S. 1850, On the Negro Question. *Fraser's Magazine*, January

Millàs Vallicrosa, J-M. 1931, *Assagia d'Historia de les Idees Físiques i Matemàtiques a la Catalunya Medieval*. Barcelona: Institució Patxot

Al-Minufi, Ahmad ibn 'Abd Al-Salam, *Al-Fayd al-madid bi-akhbar Al-Nil al-sa'eed*. MS (1639) 48076, Marseille: Bibliotheque Municipale

Mitchell, C. 1960, Archaeology and Romance in Renaissance Italy, in E. F. Jacob (ed.), *Italian Renaissance Studies*, 455–483. London: Faber and Faber

Montagu, J. 1799, *A Voyage performed by the late Earl of Sandwich round the Mediterranean in the years 1738 and 1739*. London: T. Cadell and W. Davies

Montelius, O. 1899, *Der Orient und Europa*. Stockholm: Königlich Akademie der schönen Wissenschaften, Geschichte und Alterthumskunde

Montfaucon, B. de. 1719–1724, *L'Antiquité expliquée et representée en figures*, II. Paris: F. Delaune

More, H. 1653, *Conjectura Cabbalistica*. London: J. Flesher

Morgan, L. H. 1877, *Ancient Society*. London: Macmillan

Morienus 1564, Morieni Romani … *Liber de re metallioa*. Paris

Morton, S. G. 1839, *Crania Americana, or, a Comparative View of the Skulls of Various Aboriginal Nations of North and South America: to Which is Prefixed an Essay on the Varieties of the Human Species*. Philadelphia: J. Dobson

Morton, S. G. 1844, *Crania Aegyptiaca, or, Observations on Egyptian Ethnography, Derived from Anatomy, History and the Monuments*. Philadelphia: John Penington

Morton, S. G. 1848, Account of a Craniological Collection with Remarks on the Classification of Some Families of the Human Race. *Transactions of the American Ethnological Society* 2, 215–222

Morton, S. G. 1849, *Catalogue of Skulls of Man and the Inferior Animals, in the Collection of Samuel George Morton*. Philadelphia: Merrihew and Thompson

Moyer, I. S. 2002, Herodotus and an Egyptian Mirage: The Genealogies of the Theban Priests. *Journal of Hellenic Studies* 122, 70–90

Mugnos, F. 1658, *Historia della Augustissima Famiglia Colonna*. Venice: Turrini

Muhammad, M. 'A. 1977, Al-'ilaqat al-misryah al-'arabyah fi al-'usur al-qadima: masadir wa drasat, in A. M. Abdalla, S. Al-Sakkar and R. T. Mortel (eds), *Studies in the History of Arabia Vol I*, 13–38. Riyadh: University of Riyadh

Murnane, W. J. 2000, Imperial Egypt and the Limits of Power, in R. Cohen and R. Westbrook (eds), *Amarna Diplomacy*, 101–111. Baltimore: Johns Hopkins UP

Murray, G. W. 1956, Felix Fabri's Pilgrimage from Gaza to Mount Sinai and Cairo, AD 1483. *The Geographical Journal* 122, 335–342

Myres, J. L. 1911, *The Dawn of History*. London: Williams and Norgate


Ibn Al-Nadim, Abu Al-Faraj Muhammed 1988, *Al-fihrist*. Rida Tajaddud (ed.). Tehran: Dar Al-Masirah

Nasr, S. 1968, *Science and Civilization in Islam*. Cambridge, Mass: Harvard UP

Neuerburg, N. 1969, Greek and Roman Pyramids. *Archaeology* 22, 106–115

Neugebauer, O. 1962, *The Astronomical Tables of al-Khwarizimi*. Copenhagen: Munsgaard

Newton, I. 1721, *Opticks: or, A Treatise of the Reflection, Refractions, Inflections and Colours of Light*. 3rd edition, London: William and John Innys

Newton, I. 1728a, *The Chronology of Ancient Kingdoms Amended*. London: J. Tonson, J. Osborn and T. Longman

Newton, I. 1728b, *A Treatise of the System of the World*. London: F. Fayram

Newton, I. 1733, *Observations Upon the Prophecies of Daniel, and the Apocalypse of St John*. London: J. Darby and T. Browne

Nichols, F. M. 1889, *Mirabilia Urbis Romae. The Marvels of Rome, or a picture of the Golden City*. London: Ellis and Elvey

Nichols, J. 1817, *Illustrations of the Literary History of the 18th Century, Vol. II*. London: J. Nicols

Norden, F. L. 1755, *Voyage d'Égypte et de Nubie*. Copenhagen: Imprimerie de la Maison Royale

Norden, F. L. 1757, *Travels in Egypt and Nubia*. London: L. Davis and C. Reymers

Nott, J. C. 1843, The Mulatto a Hybrid: Probable Extermination of the Two Races if the Whites and Blacks are Allowed to Intermarry. *American Journal of the Medical Sciences* 6, 252–256

Nott, J. C. 1849, *Two Lectures on the Connection Between the Biblical and Physical History of Man. Delivered by Invitation from the Chair of Political Economy, etc., of the Louisiana University, in December 1848*. New York: Bartlett and Welford

Nott, J. C. and G. R. Gliddon 1854, *Types of Mankind or, Ethnological Researches: Based upon the Ancient Monuments, Paintings, Sculptures, and Crania of Races, and Upon their Natural, Geographical, Philological and Biblical History*. Philadelphia: Lippincott Grambo

Nott, J. C., L. F. A. Maury, G. R. Gliddon, F. A. Pulszky and J. A. Meigs 1857, *Indigenous Races of the Earth; or, New Chapters of Ethnology Inquiry: Including Monographs on Special Departments*. Philadelphia: J. B. Lippincott

Nunn, J. F. 1996, *Ancient Egyptian Medicine*. London: British Museum Press


O'Connor, D. 2003, Egypt's Views of 'Others', in J. Tait (ed.), *'Never had the like occurred': Egypt's view of its past*, 155–186. London: UCL Press

O'Connor, D. and A. Reid 2003a, *Ancient Egypt in Africa*. London: UCL Press

O'Connor, D. and A. Reid 2003b, Introduction – Locating Ancient Egypt in Africa: Modern Theories, Past Realities, in D. O'Connor and A. Reid (eds), *Ancient Egypt in Africa*, 1–22. London: UCL Press

O'Connor, D. and S. Quirke 2003, Introduction: Mapping the Unknown in Ancient Egypt, in D. O'Connor and S. Quirke (eds), *Mysterious Lands*, 1–22. London: UCL Press

Omont, H. 1882, Les Sept merveilles du monde au moyen age. *Bibliothèque de l'Ecole des Chartes* 43, 40–60

D'Onofrio, C. (ed.) 1989, *Visitiamo Roma nel Quattrocento: La città degli Umanisti*. Rome: Romana

D'Onofrio, C. 1992, *Gli Obelischi di Roma: Storia e Urbanistica di una Città dall' età Antica al XX Secolo.* 3rd edition, Rome: Romana

Oppenheim, A. L. 1956, The Interpretation of Dreams in the Ancient Near East. *Transactions of the American Philosophical Society* 45, 179–373

Orbaan, J. A. F. 1910, *Sixtine Rome.* London: Constable

Osborne, J. L. (ed.) 1987, *Master Gregorius, The Marvels of Rome.* Leiden: Brill

Osborne, J. L. 1986, Peter's Grain Heap: A Medieval View of the *Meta Romuli. Echos du Monde Classique/Classical Views* 30, 111–118

Osing, J. 1998, *The Carlsberg Papyri 2: Hieratische Papyri aus Tebtunis.* Copenhagen: Museum Tusculanum Press

Owen, A. L. 1962, *The Famous Druids: A Survey of Three Centuries of English Literature on the Druids.* Oxford: OUP


Pahta, P. 1998, *Medieval Embryology in the Vernacular: the Case of 'De spermata'.* Helsinki: Société Néophilologique

Panofsky, E. 1961, Canopus Deus: The Iconography of a Non-Existent God. *Gazette des Beaux-Arts* 6.57, 193–216

Parker, R. A. 1959, *A Vienna Demotic Papyrus on Eclipse-And Lunar-Omina.* Providence, RI: Brown UP

Parker, R. A. 1972, *Demotic Mathematical Papyri.* Providence, RI: Brown UP

Parker, S. 1666, *A Free and Impartial Censure of the Platonick Philosophie.* Oxford: W. Hall, for Richard Davis

Parkinson, R. B. 1999, *Cracking Codes: The Rosetta Stone and Decipherment.* London: British Museum Press

Parks, N. R. 1979, On the Meaning of Pinturicchio's Sala dei Santi. *Art History* 2, 291–317

Parsons, T. 1966, *Societies; Evolutionary and Comparative Perspectives.* Englewood Cliffs, NJ: Prentice-Hall

Patrides, C. A. 1969, *The Cambridge Platonists.* London: Edward Arnold

Paulus, A. and B. Van den Abeele 2000, *Frédéric II de Hohenstaufen, L'Art de chasser avec les oiseaux.* Nogent-le-Roi: Jaques Laget

Peebles, B. M. 1936, La Meta Romuli e una Lettera di Michele Ferno. *Rendiconti della Pontificia Accademia di Archeologia Romana* 12, 21–36

Peet, T. E. 1909, *The Stone and Bronze Ages in Italy and Sicily.* Oxford: Clarendon

Peet, T. E. 1923, *The Rhind Mathematical Papyrus.* London: British Museum Press

Pernigotti, S. 1996, Les Rapports entre les Grecs et l'Égypte à l'époque Saïte: les aspects juridiques et institutionnels. *Méditerranées* 6/7, 87–101

Perry, C. 1743, *A View of the Levant: Particularly of Constantinople, Syria, Egypt and Greece.* London: T. Woodward, C. Davis and J. Shuckburgh

Pevsner, N. and S. Lang 1968, The Egyptian Revival, in N. Pevsner (ed.), *Studies in Art, Architecture and Design Vol. 1, From Mannerism to Romanticism,* 212–235. London: Thames and Hudson

Piggott, S. 1975, *The Druids.* London: Thames and Hudson

Pignoria, L. 1670, *Mensa Isiaca, qua Sacrorum Apud Aegyptios Ratio et Simulacra, Subjectis Tabulis aeneis Exhibentur et Explicantur* (1st edition 1605, Venice). Amsterdam: Sumptibus Andreae Frisii

Pingree, D. (ed.) 1978, *The Yavanjataka of Sphujidhvaja.* Cambridge, Mass: Harvard UP

Pingree, D. (ed.) 1986, *Picatrix. The Latin version of the Ghayat Al-Hakim.* London: Warburg Institute

Pingree, D. 1963, The Indian Iconography of the Decans and Horâs. *Journal of the Warburg and Courtauld Institutes* 26, 223–54

Pitt Rivers, A. H. 1881, On the Discovery of Chert Implements in Stratified Gravel in the Nile Valley near Thebes. *Journal of the Anthropological Institute* 11, 382–400

Pococke, R. 1743–1745, *A Description of the East, and Some Other Countries*. London: J. and R. Knapton

Pollès, R. 2001, *La Momie de Khéops à Hollywood: généalogie d'un mythe*. Paris: Editions de l'Amateur

Pool, P. A. S. 1986, *William Borlase*. Truro: Royal Institute of Cornwall

Pope, M. 1999, *The Story of Decipherment*. London: Thames and Hudson

Porreca, D. 2001, The Influence of Hermetic Texts on Western European Philosophers and Theologians (1160–1300), unpublished PhD thesis, University of London

Porten, B. 1992, Aramaic-Demotic Equivalents: Who is the Borrower and Who is the Lender?, in J. Johnson (ed.), *Life in a Multi-Cultural Society*, 259–264. Chicago: University of Chicago Press

Porter, B. and R. Moss 1974, *Topographical Bibliography of Ancient Egyptian Hieroglyphic Texts, Reliefs, and Paintings, Vol 2, Theban Temples*. 2nd edition, Oxford: Clarendon

Posener, G. 1957, Les Asiatiques en Egypte sous les XIIe et XIIIe dynasties. *Syria* 34, 145–163

Preimesberger, R. 1974, Obeliscus Pamphilius: Beiträge zu Vorgeschichte und Ikonographie des Vierströmebrunnes auf Piazza Navona. *Münchner Jahrbuch der Bildenden Kunst* 25, 77–162

Prescott, H. F. M. 1950, *Friar Felix at Large: A Fifteenth-Century Pilgrimage to the Holy Land*. New Haven: Yale UP

Prichard, J. C. 1813, *Researches into the Physical History of Man*. London: John and Arthur Arch

Prichard, J. C. 1819, *An Analysis of the Egyptian Mythology, to Which is Subjoined a Critical Examination of the Egyptian Chronology*. London: John and Arthur Arch

Prichard, J. C. 1826, *Researches into the Physical History of Mankind*. 2nd edition, London: John and Arthur Arch

Prichard, J. C. 1831, *The Eastern Origin of the Celtic Nations*. London: John and Arthur Arch

Prichard, J. C. 1836–1847, *Researches into the Physical History of Mankind*. 3rd edition, London: Sherwood, Gilbert and Piper

Prichard, J. C. 1843, *The Natural History of Man, Comprising Inquiries into the Modifying Influence of Physical and Moral Agencies on the Different Tribes of the Human Family*. London: H. Baillière

Prichard, J. C. 1845, *The Natural History of Man, Comprising Inquiries into the Modifying Influence of Physical and Moral Agencies on the Different Tribes of the Human Family*. 2nd edition, London: H. Baillière

Prime, W. C. 1857, *Boat Life in Egypt and Nubia*. New York: Harper

Pritchard, R. T. 1992, *The History of Alexander's Battles: Historia de Preliis – the J¹ Version*. Toronto: Pontifical Institute of Mediaeval Studies

Ptolemy 1519a, *Tetrabiblos*, in *Liber Quadripartiti Ptholomei …* Venice: Octavianus Scotus

Ptolemy 1519b, *Centiloquium*, in *Liber Quadripartiti Ptholomei …* Venice: Octavianus Scotus

Ptolemy 1528, *Almagest*. Venice: Giunta

Ptolemy 1540, *Geography*, in S. Münster (ed.), Basle: Henricus Petrus (facsimile reprint 1966)


Ibn Qadi Shuhba 1977–1997, *Tarikh ibn Qadi Shuhba*. A. Darwich (ed.). Damascus: Institut Français de Damas

Al-Qalqashandi, Shihab Al-Din Abu Al-ʿAbas ibn Ahmed Al-Misri 1913–1919, *Kitab Subh al-aʿsha fi sina ʿat al-insha*. Beirut, Dar Al-Fikr

Al-Qazwini, Zakaria ibn Muhammad 1960, *Athar al-bilad wa akhbar al-ʿibad*. Beirut: Dar Sader

Quirke, S. 2001, *The Cult of Ra: Sun-Worship in Ancient Egypt*. London: Thames and Hudson

Rabie, H. 1972, *The Financial System of Egypt*. Oxford: OUP

Ramos, A. 1990, *Tuhafa Al-Albab*. Madrid: Instituto de Cooperación con el Mundo Arabel

Ramusio, G. B. 1978, *Navigazioni e Viaggi nel qual si Contiene la Descrittione dell'Africa Vol. I*. Turin: Einaudi

Ranke, L. von 1881–1886, *Weltgeschichte*. Leipzig: Duncker and Humblot

Ray, J. 1994, Osiris in Medieval Egypt, in C. Eyre, A. Leahy and L. Montagno Leahy (eds), *The Unbroken Reed. Studies in the Cultural and Heritage of Ancient Egypt in Honour of A. F. Shore*, 273–280. London: Egypt Exploration Society

Rea, J. R. 1978, *The Oxyrhynchus Papyri, 46*. London: Egypt Exploration Society

Redford, D. B. 1979, The Historiography of Ancient Egypt, in K. Weeks (ed.), *Egyptology and the Social Sciences*, 3–20. Cairo: American University in Cairo Press

Redwood, J. 1996, *Reason, Ridicule and Religion: The Age of Enlightenment in England, 1660–1750*. London: Thames and Hudson

Rees, J. 1995, *Writings on the Nile: Harriet Martineau, Florence Nightingale, Amelia Edwards*. London: Rubicon

Reid, D. M. 1985, Indigenous Egyptology: The Decolonization of a Profession? *Journal of the American Oriental Society* 105, 233–246

Reid, D. M. 1990, *Cairo University and the Making of Modern Egypt*. Cambridge: CUP

Reid, D. M. 2002, *Whose Pharaohs? Archaeology, Museums, and Egyptian National Identity from Napoleon to World War I*. Berkeley, LA: University of California Press

Reinach, S. 1893, *Le Mirage Oriental*. Paris: Masson

**Rice, M. and S. MacDonald 2003, Introduction – Tea with a Mummy: The Consumer's View of Egypt's Immemorial Appeal, in S. MacDonald and M. Rice (eds), *Consuming Ancient Egypt*, 1–22. London: UCL Press**

Riess, E. 1892, Nechepsonis et Petosiridis fragmenta magica. *Philologus* 6 Supplement, 325–394

Ritner, R. K. 1992, Egyptian Magic: Questions of Legitimacy, Religious Orthodoxy and Social Deviance, in A. Lloyd (ed.), *Studies in Pharaonic Religion and Society in Honour of J. Gwyn Griffiths*, 189–200. London: Egypt Exploration Society

Ritner, R. K. 1993, *The Mechanics of Ancient Egyptian Magical Practice*. Chicago: University of Chicago Press

Ritner, R. K. 2001, Medicine, in D. B. Redford (ed.), *The Oxford Encyclopedia of Ancient Egypt Vol II*, 353–356. Oxford: OUP

Ritter, H. 1933, *Pseudo-Majriti, Das Ziel des Weisen 1*. Leipzig: Teubner

Robbins, F. E. (ed.) 1971, *Ptolemy, Tetrabiblos*. Cambridge, Mass: Harvard UP

Roberts, D. 1855, *The Holy Land. Syria, Idumea, Arabia, Egypt and Nubia. After Lithographs by Louis Haghe From Drawings made on the spot by David Roberts Vols I-III*. London: Day and Son

Robins, G. and C. Shute 1987, *The Rhind Mathematical Papyrus*. London: British Museum Press

Robinson, J. (ed.) 1996, *The Nag Hamadi Library in English*. 4th edition, Leiden: Brill

Ronca, I. 1995, "Senior de Chemia": A Reassessment of the Medieval Latin Translation of Ibn Umayl's al-maʿ al-waraqī wa l-ard al-najmiya. *Bulletin de Philosophie Médiévale* 37, 9–31

Rosa, G. 1986, Dalle Fosse, Giovanni Pietro (Pierio Valeriano). *Dizionario Biografico degli Italiani* 32, 85–88

Rosellini, I. 1832–1844, *I monumenti dell'Egitto e della Nubia*. Pisa: N. Capurro

Ross, D. J. 1963, *Alexander Historiatus: A Guide to Medieval Illustrated Alexander Literature*. London: Warburg Institute

Ross, D. J. 1985, *Studies in the Alexander Romance*. London: Pindar

Rossi, P. 1984, *The Dark Abyss of Time: The History of the Earth and the History of Nations from Hooke to Vico*. Chicago: University of Chicago Press

Rowland, I. D. 2000, *The Ecstatic Journey: Athanasius Kircher in Baroque Rome*. Chicago: University of Chicago Press

Rusche, P. G. 1996, The Cleopatra Glossaries: An Edition and Commentary on the Glosses and their Sources, unpublished PhD thesis, Yale University

Ruska, J. 1926, *Tabula Smaragdina*. Heidelberg: Carl Winter

Ruska, J. 1928, Zwei Bücher de compositione alchemiae und ihre Vorreden. *Archiv für Geschichte der Mathematik, der Naturwissenschaft und der Technik (Sudhoffs Archiv)* 11, 28–37

Ruska, J. 1934. Der Urtext der *Tabula chemica*. *Archeion* 16, 273–283

Ruska, J. 1935, Studien zu Muhammad ibn Umail. *Isis*, 24, 310–342

Russell, D. 1986, Emblems and Hieroglyphics: Some Observations on the Beginnings and Nature of Emblematic Forms. *Emblematica* 1, 227–239

Ryholt, K. 1998, A Demotic Version of Nectanebo's Dream (P. Carlsberg 562). *Zeitschrift für Papyrologie und Epigraphik* 122, 196–200

Ryholt, K. 2002, Nectanebo's Dream, or the Prophecy of Petesis, in A. Blasius and B. U. Schipper (eds), *Apokalyptik und Ägypten: ein kritische Analyse der relevanten Texte aus dem griecisch-römischen Ägypten*, 221–241. Leuven: Peeters


Sabloff, J. A. and C. C. Lamberg-Karlovsky (eds) 1975, *Ancient Civilization and Trade*. Albuquerque: University of New Mexico Press

Sachau, E. 1879, *The Chronology of the Ancient Nations*. London: W. H. Allen

Said, E. 1978, *Orientalism*. London: Routledge and Kegan Paul

Said, L. 1999, 'ilm al misriyat: mata uisbih misriyan? *Ahwal Misriya* 5, 170–176

Sailor, D. B. 1988, Newton's Debt to Cudworth. *Journal of the History of Ideas* 49, 511–518

Sanderson, S. K. 1995, *Social Transformations: a General Theory of Historical Development*. Oxford: Blackwell

Sandford, K. S. and W. J. Arkell 1933, *Paleolithic Man and the Nile Valley in Nubia and Upper Egypt: A Study of the Region during Pliocene and Pleistocene Times*. Chicago: University of Chicago Press

Sandford, K. S. and W. J. Arkell 1939, *Paleolithic Man and the Nile Valley in Lower Egypt, with some notes upon a part of the Red Sea Littoral: A Study of the Regions during Pliocene and Pleistocene Times*. Chicago: University of Chicago Press

Sattin, A. 1988, *Lifting the Veil: British Society in Egypt 1768–1956*. London: Dent

Sauneron, S. 1952, Le Temple D'Akhmim décrit par Ibn Jobair. *Bulletin de l'Institut Français d'Archéologie Orientale du Caire* 51, 123–135

Sauneron, S. 1996, *Un Traité Égyptien d'Ophiologie: Papyrus du Brooklyn Museum no. 47.218.48 et .85*. Cairo: Institut Français d'Archéologie Orientale

Al-Sawi, A. (ed.) 1938, *Akhbar al-zaman*. Cairo: 'Abd Al-Hamid Hanafi

Saxl, F. 1957, The Appartamento Borgia, in F. Saxl, *Lectures* 1, 174–188. London: Warburg Institute

Al-Sayar, N. 1995, *Qudma 'al-misreen awal al-muahdeen*. Cairo

Scafi, A. 1999, The Earthly Paradise, unpublished PhD thesis, University of London

Scafi, A. 2003, *Mapping Paradise. A History of Heaven on Earth*. London: British Library

Scamuzzi, E. 1939, *La Mensa Isiaca del Regio Museo di Antichità di Torino*. Rome: Museo di Torino

Schiaparelli, C. 1861, *Vocabulista in Arabico*. Florence: Tipografia dei successori le Monnier

Schlegel, F. v. 1808, *Ueber die Sprache und Weisheit der Indier. Ein Beitrag zur Begrundung der Alterthumskunde*. Heidelberg: Mohr und Zimmer

Schnapp, A. 1996, *The Discovery of the Past: The Origins of Archaeology.* London: British Museum Press

Schneider, L. 1990, Leon Battista Alberti: Some Biographical Implications of the Winged Eye. *Art Bulletin* 72, 261–270

Scott, W. 1985, *Hermetica.* Boston: Shambhala

Sears, J. 1985, *Commentary on a Canzone of Beniveni by Giovanni Pico della Mirandola.* New York: P. Lang

Sergi, G. 1897, *Africa: Antropologia Della Stirpe Camitica (Specie Euroafricana).* Turin: Fratelli Bocca

Sergi, G. 1904. *The Mediterranean Race: a Study of the Origin of European Peoples.* London: Walter Scott

Serlio, S. 1540, *Terzo Libro d'Architettura,* in S. Serlio 1619, *Tutte le Opere d'Architettura et Prospetiva di Sebastiano Serlio Bolognese, Vol 3.* Venice: G. de Franceschi

Serlio, S. 1619, *Tutte le Opere d'Architettura et Prospetiva di Sebastiano Serlio Bolognese.* Venice: G. de Franceschi

Service, E. R. 1975, *Origins of the State and Civilization.* New York: W. W. Norton

**Sevilla Cueva, C. 2003, Vicent Lleó's Operetta: *La Corte de Faraón,* in S. MacDonald and M. Rice (eds), *Consuming Ancient Egypt,* 63–76. London: UCL Press**

Sezgin, F. 1967, *Geschichte des Arabischen Schrifitums, Vol 1.* Leiden: Brill

Seznec, J. 1931, Un Essai de mythologie compareé au début du XVII$^e$ siècle. *Mélanges d'Archéologie et d'Histoire* 48, 268

Seznec, J. 1953, *The Survival of the Pagan Gods.* New York: Pantheon

Al-Shahrastani, Abu Al-Fath Muhammad ibn 'Abd Al-Kareem 1948, *Al-milal wa al-nihal.* A. F. Muhammad (ed.). Beirut: Dar Al-Surur

Shaw, J. B. 1976, *Drawings by Old Masters at Christ Church, Oxford.* Oxford: Clarendon

Shelley, M. 1826, *The Last Man.* London: H. Colburn

Shuckford, S. 1728, *The Sacred and Profane History of the World Connected, From the Creation of the World to the Dissolution of the Assyrian Empire.* London: R. Knaplock and J. Tomson

Al-Shurbagi, A. 1994. Ru'yat al-rahala al-moslemin li-ahwal misr al-iqtisadyah fi al-'asr al-fatimi. Cairo: Egyptian General Book Organisation

Sider, S. 1986, Horapollo, in F. E. Cranz, V. Brown and O. Kristeller (eds), *Catalogus Translationum Vol. VI,* 15–29, Washington, DC: Catholic University of America Press

Silverstein, T. 1955, Liber Hermetis Mercurii Triplicis de VI rerum principiis. *Archives d'histoire doctrinale et littéraire du moyen age* 30, 217–301

Singer, T. C. 1989, Hieroglyphs, Real Characters, and the Idea of Natural Language in English Seventeenth-Century Thought. *Journal of the History of Ideas* 50, 49–70

Skeat, T. and E. Turner 1968, An Oracle of Hermes Trismegistos at Saqqara. *Journal of Egyptian Archaeology* 54, 199–208

Skelton, R. A. 1966, *Claudius Ptolemaeus Geography.* Amsterdam: Theatrum Orbis Terrarum

Sladek, M. 1988, Mercurius Triplex, Mercurius termaximus et les "trois Hermès", in A. Faivre (ed.), *Présence d'Hermès Trismegiste,* 88–99. Paris: Albin Michel

Smith, G. E. 1911, *The Ancient Egyptians and their Influence on the Civilization of Europe.* London: Harper

Smith, G. E. 1915, *The Migrations of Early Culture.* Manchester: Manchester UP

Smith, H. S. and H. M. Stewart 1984, The Gurob Shrine Papyrus. *Journal of Egyptian Archaeology* 70, 54–64

Smyth, T. 1850, *The Unity of Mankind Proved to be the Doctrine of Scripture, Reason, and Science, With a Review of the Present Position and Theory of Professor Agassiz.* New York: Putnam

Snape, S. 2003, The Emergence of Libya on the Horizon of Egypt, in D. O'Connor and S. Quirke (eds), *Mysterious Lands*, 93–106. London: UCL Press

Snobelen, S. D. 1999, Isaac Newton, Heretic: The Strategies of a Nicodemite. *British Journal for the History of Science* 32, 381–419

Soemmering, S. T. von 1794–1801, *De corporis humani fabrica*. Frankfurt

Solé, R. and D. Valbelle 1999, *La Pierre de Rosette*. Paris: Edition du Seuil

Soliman, A. M. 1985, *Scientific Trends in the Quran*. London: Taha

Spencer, J. 1685, *De Legibus Hebraeorum Earum Rationibus*. Cambridge: Jonathon Haynes

Spiegelberg, W. 1906–1908, *Die Demotischen Denkmäler 30601–31270, 50001–50022: Die Demotischen Papyrus, Vol. 1, Plates*. Leipzig: Fischbach (Hiersman)

Spiegelberg, W. 1927, *The Credibility of Herodotus' Account of Egypt in the Light of the Egyptian Monuments* (trans. A. M. Blackman). Oxford: Blackwell

Sprat, T. 1667, *The History of the Royal Society of London for Improving of Natural Knowledge*. London: J. Martyn

Squier, E. G. and E. H. Davis 1848, *Ancient Monuments of the Mississippi Valley: Comprising the Results of Extensive Original Surveys and Explorations*. Washington, DC: Smithsonian Institution

St John, H. 1752, *Letters on the Study and Use of History*. London: A. Miller

Stanton, W. 1960, *The Leopard's Spots: Scientific Attitudes Towards Race in America 1815–59*. Chicago: University of Chicago Press

Stapleton *et al.* 1933, Three Arabic Treatises on Alchemy by Muhammad Bin Umail (10th century AD). *Memoirs of the Asiatic Society of Bengal* 12:1, 1–213

Stavenhagen, L. 1974. *A Testament of Alchemy, Being the Revelations of Morienus*. Hanover, New Hampshire: University Press of New England

Steele, R. 1919, Dies Egyptiaci. *Proceedings of the Royal Society of Medicine* 13, 109–121

Stepan, N. 1982, *The Idea of Race in Science: Great Britain 1800–1960*. London: Macmillan

Stephens, J. 1837, *Incidents of Travel in Egypt, Arabia, Petraea, and the Holy Land*. New York: Harper

Stephens, W. 1989, *Giants in Those Days: Folklore, Ancient History, and Nationalism*. Lincoln: University of Nebraska Press

Stewart, L. 1996, Seeing through the Scholium: Religion and Reading Newton in the Eighteenth Century. *History of Science* 34, 123–165

Stolzenberg, D. (ed.) 2001, *The Great Art of Knowing: The Baroque Encyclopedia of Athanasius Kircher*. Stanford: Stanford University Libraries

Strasser, G. F. 1988, La Contribution d'Athanasius Kircher à la tradition humaniste hiéroglyphique. *XVIIe Siècle* 40, 79–82

Stricker, B. H. 1943, La Prison de Joseph. *Acta Orientalia* 19, 100–137

Stukeley, W. 1727, *Letter to John Conduitt, 26 June–22 July 1727*. Keynes MS 136

Stukeley, W. 1743, *Abury: a Temple of the British Druids*. London: W. Innys, R. Manby, B. Dod and J. Brindley

Stukeley, W. 1752, *Palaeographia Britannica: Or, Discourses on Antiquities in Britain, Number III*. London

Stukeley, W. 1980, *The Commentarys, Diary, and Common-Place Book of William Stukeley*. London: Doppler

Stukeley, W. n. d. *A Catalogue of Druids*. Wellcome Institute Library, London, MS 4720, f. 1

Suter, H. 1922, Beiträge zur Gechichte der Mathematik bei den Griechen und Arabern. *Abhandlungen zur Geschichte der Naturwissenschften und der Medizin* 4. Erlangen: M. Mencke

Syndram, D. 1989, Das Erbe der Pharaonen zur Ikonographie ägyptens in Europa, in G. Sievernich and H. Budde (eds), *Europa und der Orient*, 18–57. Berlin: Bertelsmann Lexikon

Tainter, J. A. 1988, *The Collapse of Complex Societies*. Cambridge: CUP

Tait, J. 1991a, P. Carlsberg 230: Eleven Fragments from a Demotic Herbal, in P. J. Frandsen (ed.), *The Carlsberg Papyri 1: Demotic Texts from the Collection*, 47–92. Copenhagen: Museum Tusculanum Press

Tait, J. 1991b, P. Carlsberg 36: Another Fragment of a Demotic Legal Manual, in P. J. Frandsen (ed.), *The Carlsberg Papyri 1: Demotic Texts from the Collection*, 93–99. Copenhagen: Museum Tusculanum Press

Tait, J. 1992, Demotic Literature and Egyptian Society, in J. H. Johnson (ed.), *Life in a Multi-Cultural Society: Egypt from Cambyses to Constantine and Beyond*, 303–310. Chicago: University of Chicago Press

Tait, J. 2000, P. Carlsberg 450–5: Fragments of Demotic Word-Lists, in P. J. Frandsen and K. Ryholt (eds), *The Carlsberg Papyri 3: A Miscellany of Demotic Texts and Studies*, 83–93. Copenhagen: Museum Tusculanum Press

**Tait, J. 2003a, The 'Book of the Fayum': Mystery in a Known Landscape, in D. O'Connor and S. Quirke (eds), *Mysterious Lands*, 183–202. London: UCL Press**

**Tait, J. 2003b, Introduction – '… since the time of the Gods', in J. Tait (ed.), *'Never had the like occurred': Egypt's view of its past*, 1–14. London: UCL Press**

**Tanner, J. 2003, Finding the Egyptian in Early Greek Art, in. R. Matthews and C. Roemer (eds), *Ancient Perspectives on Egypt*, 115–144. London: UCL Press**

Tardieu, M. 1986, Sabiens Coranique et "Sabiens" de Harran. *Journal Asiatique* 274, 1–44

Taylor, J. 1961, *The Didascalicon of Hugh of St Victor*. New York: Columbia UP

Teeter Dobbs, B. J. 1991, *The Janus Face of Genius: The Role of Alchemy in Newton's Thought*. Cambridge: CUP

Tezmen-Siegel, J. 1985, *Die Darstellungen der Septem Artes Liberales in der Bildenden Kunst als Rezeption der Lehrplangeschichte*. Munich: Tuduv-Verlagsgesellschaft

Thevet, A. 1556, *Cosmographie de Levant par F. André Thevet d'Angoulesme*. Lyon: Jan de Tournes and Guillaume Gazeau

Thissen, H. J. 1977, Graeco-ägyptische Literatur, in W. Helck and E. Otto (eds), *Lexikon der Ägyptologie* 2, 873–878. Wiesbaden: Harrassowitz

Thissen, H. J. 1984. *Die Lehre des Anchscheschonqi (P. BM 10508): Einleitung, Übersezung, Indices*. Bonn: Habelt

Thomas, R. 2000, *Herodotus in Context. Ethnography, Science and the Art of Persuasion*. Cambridge: CUP

Thorndike, L. 1934–1958, *A History of Magic and Experimental Science*. New York: Columbia UP

Tindal, M. 1730, *Christianity as Old as the Creation: Or, the Gospel a Republication of the Religion of Nature*. London

Toland, J. 1720, *Tetradymus. Containing: I. Hodegus … II. Clidophorus … III. Hypatia … IV. Mangoneutes*. London: J. Brotherton and W. Meadows, J. Roberts, W. Meres, W. Chetwood, S. Chapman and J. Graves

Trigger, B. G. 1989, *A History of Archaeological Thought*. Cambridge: CUP

Trigger, B. G. 1993, *Early Civilizations. Ancient Egypt in Context*. Cairo: American University in Cairo Press

Turberville Needham, J. 1761, *De inscriptione quadam Ægyptiaca Taurini inventa et characteribus Ægyptiis olim et Sinia communibus exarata idolo cuidam antiquo in Regia Universitate servato: ad utrasque academias Londinensem et Parisiensem rerum antiquarum investigationi et studio praepositas data epistola*. Rome: Ex typographia Palladis

Turnbull, H. W. 1959–1977, *The Correspondence of Sir Isaac Newton*. Cambridge: CUP

Tweyman, S. 1996, *Hume on Natural Religion*. Bristol: Thoemmes

Tylor, E. B. 1865, *Researches into the Early History of Mankind and the Development of Civilization*. London: John Murray

Tylor, E. B. 1871, *Primitive Culture: Researches into the Development of Mythology, Philosophy, Religion, Art and Custom*. London: John Murray

Ucko, P. J. 2001, Unprovenanced Material Culture and Freud's Collection of Antiquities. *Journal of Material Culture* 6, 269–322

Ucko, P. J., M. Hunter, A. J. Clark and A. David 1991, *Avebury Reconsidered. From the 1660s to the 1990s*. London: Unwin-Hyman

Ullmann, M. 1972a, *Die Natur und Geheimwissenschaften im Islam*. Leiden: Brill

Ullmann, M. 1972b, Kleopatra in einer arabischen alchemistischen Disputation. *Wiener Zeitschrift für die Kunde des Morgenlandes* 63/4, 158–175

Ibn Umail, Muhammad, *MS Sharh al-siwar wa al-ashkal*. Paris: Arabe 2609, Bibliothèque Nationale

**Uphill, E. P. 2003, The Ancient Egyptian View of World History, in J. Tait (ed.), 'Never had the like occurred': Egypt's view of its past, 15–30. London: UCL Press**

Ibn Abi Usaiybi'ah Muwafaq Al-Din Abi Al-'Abas Ahmad ibn Al-Qasim 1998, *Kitab fun al-anbaa fi tabaqat al-atibaa*. Beirut: Dar al-Kotob al-'Ilmiyah

Ussher, J. 1658, *The Annals of the World*. London: E. Tyler, for J. Crook; first published in Latin, 1650


Vachala, B. and F. Ondráš 2000, An Arabic Inscription on the Pyramid of Neferfra, in M. Bárta and J. Krejčí (eds), *Abusir and Saqqara in the Year 2000*, 73–76. Prague: Academy of Science of the Czech Republic

Valeriano, G. P. 1602, *Hieroglyphica*. Lyon: P. Frelon; reprinted 1976, New York: Garland

Valle, P. della 1672, *Viaggi di Pietro della Valle il Pellegrino: Descritti da Lui Medesimo Lettere Familiari: all'erudito suo Amico Mario Schipano*. Bologna: Gioseffo Longhi

Vallone, G. A. 1576, *Le Oscurissime Satire di Perseo con la Chiarissima Spositione di Giovanni'Antonio Vallone di Castelmonardo, con Diversi Capitoli Interposi, e con la Vera Origine di due Case Illustrissime Colonna, e Pignatello*. Naples: G. Cacchio

Van der Horst, P. W. 1982, The Secret Hieroglyphs in Classical Literature, in J. den Boeft and A. H. M. Kessels (eds), *Actus: Studies in Honour of H. L. W. Nelson*, 115–123. Utrecht: Institut voor Klassieke Talen

Van Essen, C. C. 1958, Cyriaque d'Ancona en Égypte. *Mededelingen der Koninkijke Nederlandse Akademie van Wetenschappen, Afdelins Letterkunde* 21, 293–306

Vasari, G. B. 1568, *Le Vite de' Più Eccellenti Pittori, Scultori ed Architettori*, in G. Milanesi (ed.) 1906, *Le Opere di Giorgio Vasari*. Florence: Sansoni

Vergote, J. 1964. L'Etymologie de Égypte. *r³-pr*. Copte *rpe*. ar. *birba*. *Zeitschrift für Ägyptische Sprache und Altertumskunde* 91, 135–137

Vincent of Beauvais 1624: *Speculum Quadripartitum*. Douai: Baltazar Beller (reprinted Graz: Akademische Druck u. Verlagsanstalt)

Vittmann, G. 1998, Beobachtungen und Überlegungen zu fremden und Helleisierten Ägyptern im Dienste einheimischer Kulte, in J. Quaegebeur, W. Clarysse, A. Schoors and H. Willems (eds), *Egyptian Religion: The Last Thousand Years Vol. II*, 1,231–1,250. Leuven: Orientalia Lovaniensia Analecta

Vodraska, S. L. 1969, 'Pseudo-Aristotle, De Causis Proprietatum et Elementorum', a Critical Edition and Study, unpublished PhD thesis, University of London

Volkmann, L. 1923, *Bilderschriften der Renaissance: Hieroglyphik und Emblematik in ihren Beziehungen und Fortwirkung*. Leipzig: Veröffentlichungen des deutschen Vereins für Buchwesen und Schrifttum

Volney, C. F. 1792, *Voyage en Syrie et en Egypte, pendant les années 1783, 1784 et 1785*. Paris: Volland

Volney, C. F. 1796, *The Ruins: or A Survey of the Revolutions of Empires*. New York: E. Duyckink

Volpi, C. 1997, Le fonti delle Immagini degli dei degli antichi di Vincenzo Cartari, in F. Cappelletti and G. Huber-Rebenich (eds), *Antike Mythos und Europa: Texte und Bilder von der Antike bis ins 20, Jahrhundert*, 58–73, 238. Berlin: Mann

Volten, A. 1942, *Demotische Traumdeutung (Pap. Carlsberg XIII und XIV Verso)*. Copenhagen: Munksgaard

Vossius, G. 1641, *De Theologia Gentili et Physiologia Christiana*. Amsterdam: John and Cornelius Blaeu

Vycichl, W. 1991a, Magic, in A. Atiya (ed.), *The Coptic Encyclopedia Vol 5*, 1,499–1,509. New York: Macmillan

Vycichl, W. 1991b, Vocabulary, Copto-Arabic, in A. Atiya (ed.), *The Coptic Encyclopedia Vol 8*, 215. New York: Macmillan

Ibn Wahshiyah, Abu Bakr Ahmad Ibn 'Ali ibn Qys Al-Kasandi. *Kitab Shauq Al-mustaham fi ma 'irfat rumuz al-aqlam*. Paris: Bibliothèque Nationale (MS Arabe 6805)

Walker, D. P. 1972, *The Ancient Theology: Studies in Christian Platonism from the Fifteenth to the Eighteenth Centuries*. London: Duckworth

**Walker, S. 2003, Carry-on at Canopus: the Nilotic Mosaic from Palestrina and Roman Attitudes to Egypt, in R. Matthews and C. Roemer (eds), *Ancient Perspectives on Egypt*, 191–202. London: UCL Press**

Wallis, F. 1999, *Bede, The Reckoning of Time [De temporum ratione], with Introduction, Notes and Commentary*. Liverpool: Liverpool UP

**Warburton, D. 2003, Love and War in the Late Bronze Age: Egypt and Hatti, in R. Matthews and C. Roemer (eds), *Ancient Perspectives on Egypt*, 75–100. London: UCL Press**

**Warburton, D. and R. Matthews 2003, Egypt and Mesopotamia in the Late Bronze and Iron Ages, in R. Matthews and C. Roemer (eds), *Ancient Perspectives on Egypt*, 101–114. London: UCL Press**

Warburton, W. 1741, *The Divine Legation of Moses Demonstrated, On the Principles of a Religious Deist, From the Omission of the Doctrine of a Future State of Reward and Punishment in the Jewish Dispensation*. London: Fletcher and Gyles

Watkins, R. 1960, L. B. Alberti's Emblem, the Winged Eye, and his Name, Leo. *Mitteilungen des Kunsthistorischen Instituts in Florenz 9*, 256–258

Weber, M. 1976, *The Agrarian Sociology of Ancient Civilizations*. London: New Left Books

Weiss, R. 1962, An Unknown Epigraphic Tract by Annius of Viterbo, in C. P. Brand, K. Foster and U. Limentani (eds), *Italian Studies Presented to E. R. Vincent*, 101–120. Cambridge: Heffer and Sons

Weiss, R. 1969, *The Renaissance Discovery of Classical Antiquity*. Oxford: Basil Blackwell

Wendorf, F., R. Schild and B. Issawi 1976, *Prehistory of the Nile Valley*. New York: Academic Press

**Wengrow, D. 2003, Forgetting the *Ancien Régime*: Republican Values and the Study of the Ancient Orient, in D. Jeffreys (ed.), *Views of Ancient Egypt since Napoleon Bonaparte: imperialism, colonialism and modern appropriations*, 179–194. London: UCL Press**

**Werner, A. 2003, Egypt in London – Public and Private Displays in the 19th Century Metropolis, in J-M. Humbert and C. Price (eds), *Imhotep Today: Egyptianizing architecture*, 75–104. London: UCL Press**

Westendorf, W. 1980, Medizin, in W. Helck and E. Otto (eds), *Lexikon der Ägyptologie, 3*, 1,273–1,276. Wiesbaden: Harrassowitz

Westendorf, W. 1999, *Handbuch der Altägptischen Medizin*. Leiden: Brill

Westfall, R. 1982, Isaac Newton's *Theologiae Gentilis Origines Philisophicae*, in W. W. Wagar (ed.), *The Secular Mind: Transformations of Faith in Modern Europe*, 15–34. New York: Holmes and Meyer

Westrem, S. 2001, *The Hereford Map*. Turnhout: Brepols

Wetherbee, W. (ed.) 1994, *Johannes de Hauvilla, Architrenius*. Cambridge: CUP

**Wheatcroft, A. 2003, 'Wonderful Things': Publishing Egypt in Word and Image, in S. MacDonald and M. Rice (eds), *Consuming Ancient Egypt*, 151–164. London: UCL Press**

Whitehouse, H. 1989, Egyptology and Forgery in the Seventeenth Century: The Case of the Bodleian Shabti. *Journal of the History of Collections* 1, 197–195

Whitehouse, H. 1992, Towards a Kind of Egyptology: The Graphic Representation of Ancient Egypt, 1587–1666, in E. Cropper, G. Perini and F. Solinas (eds), *Documentary Culture. Florence and Rome from Grand-Duke Ferdinand I to Pope Alexander VII*, 63–79. Bologna: Nuova Alfa Editoriale

Wiet, G. (ed.) 1911, *Al-Maqrizi, Al-mawaʻiz wa-l-i tibar fi dhikr al-khitat wa-l-athar*. Cairo: Institut Français d'Archéologie Orientale

Wildung, D. 1977, *Imhotep und Amenhotep*. Munich: Deutscher Kunstverlag

Wilkins, J. 1668, *Essay Towards a Real Character, and a Philosophical Language*. London: S. Gellibrand

Wilkinson, J. 1971, *Egeria's Travels*. London: Society for the Promotion of Christian Knowledge

Wilkinson, J. 1977, *Jerusalem Pilgrims Before the Crusades*. Warminster: Aris & Phillips

Willey, G. and J. Sabloff 1974, *A History of American Archaeology*. London: Thames and Hudson

Wittkower, R. 1977, Hieroglyphics in the Early Renaissance, in R. Wittkower, *Allegory and the Migration of Symbols*, 113–128. London: Thames and Hudson

Woodward, C. 2001, *In Ruins*. London: Chatto and Windus

Woodward, J. 1777, *Of the Wisdom of the Antient Egyptians, & etc. A Discourse Concerning their Arts, their Sciences, and their Learning; their Laws, their Government, and their Religion. With Occasional Reflections upon the State of Learning among the Jews, and some other Nations*. London: W. Bowyer and J. Nichols

Wotton, W. 1694, *Reflections Upon Ancient and Modern Learning*. London: J. Leake, for Peter Buck


Al-Yaʻqubi, Ahmad ibn Abi Yaʻqub 1960, *Tarikh Al-Yaʻqubi*. M. Houtsma (ed.). Beirut: Dar Sader

Yamani, S. 2001, Roman Monumental Tombs in Ezbet Bashendi. *Bulletin de l'Institut Français d'Archéologie Orientale du Caire* 101, 393–414

Yaqut, Ibn ʻAbd Allah Al-Hamawi Al-Rumi 1995, *Muʻjam al-buldan*. F. Wüstenfeld (ed.). Beirut: Dar Sader

Yates, F. 1964, *Giordano Bruno and the Hermetic Tradition*. London: Kegan Paul

Yates, F. 2002, *Giordano Bruno and the Hermetic Tradition*. Revised edition, London: Routledge

Yoffee, N. and G. L. Cowgill (eds) 1988, *The Collapse of Ancient States and Civilizations*. Tuscon: University of Arizona Press

Young, D. 1981, A Monastic Invective Against Egyptian Hieroglyphs, in D. Young (ed.), *Studies Presented to H. J. Polotsky*, 348–360. East Gloucester, Mass: Pirtie and Polson

Young, R. J. C. 1995, *Colonial Desire: Hybridity in Theory, Culture and Race*. London: Routledge


Ibn Zahira 1969, *Al-fadail al-bahirah fi mahasin misr wa al-qahirah*. M. Al-Saqqa and K. Al-Muhandis (eds). Cairo: National Library Press

Zauzich, K-T. 1991, Einleitung, in P. J. Frandsen (ed.), *The Carlsberg Papyri 1: Demotic Texts from the Collection*, 1–11. Copenhagen: Museum Tusculanum Press

Zauzich, K-T. 2000a, Ein Antikes Demotisches Namenbuch, in P. J. Frandsen and K. Ryholt (eds), *A Miscellany of Demotic Texts and Studies*. Copenhagen: Museum Tusculanum Press

Zauzich, K-T. 2000b, Die Namen der Koptischen Zusatzbuchstaben und die Erste Ägyptische Alphabetübung. *Enchoria* 26, 151–157

Zimmerman, A. 2001, *Anthropology and Antihumanism in Imperial Germany*. Chicago: University of Chicago Press

# Index

Note: figure numbers are denoted in bold type.

Abraham: teaching of arts to Egypt 75

Adalberon de Laon 81

Adelard of Bath: on Egyptian geometry 76

Adriani, G. B. 102, 105

Agapius 58

agricultural origins: 74–75, 166, 183

Ahmad, Abu Al-Hassan 'Ali Ibn 47

Akhnukh: equation with Hermes 52

Alberti, L. B. 106; hieroglyphic studies 107–108

alchemy 13, 25, 136; classical knowledge of 94; Islamic study of 47–48; origins of 94; and temples 45, 47–48; *see also* hermetic tradition

Alexander Romance 24, 51, 79–80

Alexander the Great 3, 4; conception myth 24, 80; medieval knowledge of 72; medieval perceptions of 80, 81; Ptolemaic looting of his tomb 42; *see also* Alexander Romance

Alexander VI 111, 119

Alexandria 11; cosmopolitanism 18; foundation of 4; Great Library 27; Mediterranean alignment of 5; Pharos **3:1**, 12, 45, 68, 70, 74; the Serapieion 72; tourism 6; western exodus 18

Alfonsi, Petrus 78

Ali, Mohammed: foreign relations 161; modernization policy 4

Amenophis III: his tomb-chapel, dismantling of 31

American School of Anthropology 168–170, 172–175

Ammianus Marcellinus 11; on Druids 153; rediscovery of 106

Ammon 138

Amun 73

Bi-Amr, Al-Hakim 50; Coptic, use of 60

Bi-Amr, Al-Zahir 61

Amun: Christian interpretations 73; classical perceptions of 74; equation with Jupiter 73; husbandry, introduction of 74–75

Anderson, James: his history of Freemasonry 148

d'Anglure, Seigneur 69–70

Annius of Viterbo 22, 101, 102; *Columna Osiriana* **5:3**, 112, 114; forgeries of 111–112

Antaeus 112

anthropology: Egyptian religion, study of 179; neglect of Ancient Egypt 178; origins of 178

Antiquities Service: establishment of 15

Anubis: classical perceptions of 74; medieval knowledge of 72; Renaissance interpretation of 121

Apis: medieval knowledge of 72; in Renaissance art 111; in Renaissance historiography 112

Apollodorus of Athens 41

Apuleius 73, 77; rediscovery of 106

Arab-Israeli War (1967) 18–19

Arabia: Ancient Egypt, relationship with 40–41; Bes, cult of 51; Isis, cult of 51; Osiris, cult of 51

Arabs: archaeological methods 44–45; astrology 83, 85, 86, 87, 88, 89; astronomy 78, 84, 85, 89; classical translations 58–59, 66; Cleopatra's scientific knowledge, interest in 44; Coptic, knowledge of 59; Egypt, knowledge of 39–40, 45, 47–48, 50, 56, 58–61; Egypt, perceptions of 41–44; geometry texts 76–77; Gnosticism, knowledge of 53; hermetic literature 53, 90, 91–94; hieroglyphs, decipherment of 56, 58–60; holiness of pharaonic monuments, recognition of 54–56, 62; illness, treatment of 51; magic, knowledge of 50–51, 62; monuments, visits to 42, 54; pharaohs, perceptions of 43–44, 62; pharaonic magic, knowledge of 62; religion (pharaonic), knowledge of 51–53, 54–56; protection of pharaonic monuments 42; pyramids, study of 44–45; reuse of monuments 56; temples, knowledge of 45, 47–48, 50–51

archaeology: evolutionary 181–183; historical linguistics 162; Islamic 44–45

Argyll, Duke of 177–178

Aristotle 66, 147; hermetic knowledge, putative transmission of 93

Asclepius 73, 79, 81, 82–83, 91, 109; *see also* hermetic tradition

Ashmonit 58

Ashmoun: temple of 50

Assyria: invasion of Egypt 3

astrology: Arabic 83, 85, 86, 87, 88, 89; classical 87–88; *decans* 87–88; Egyptian **2:1**, 27, 75, 84–85, 87–89; origins of 75

astronomy 84–86, 133, 137; Arabic 78, 84, 85, 89; Chaldean 87; Egyptian 75, 84–86, 133, 137; origins of 75, 84–85

Aswan: tourism 6

Aswan Dam: construction of 18

Athanasius: defence of the doctrine of the Trinity at the Council of Nicaea 138

Aubrey, J. 152

Augustine, St: on astrology 88; on Egypt's antiquity 136; on the hermetic tradition 90, 109, 134–135; on Isis 73

Augustus 6, 105; obelisks of 119

Avebury **6:1**, **7:1**, 145, 163

Ayyubid dynasty 4, 76


Bab al-Bahr palace 60, 61

Babylon: origins of civilization 167

Bacon, Sir Francis: ancient knowledge, rejection of 142–143; on the Sphinx 143

Al-Baghdadi 42, 52

Balfour, Arthur J. 16

Al-Barakat, Abu **3:3**, 56

Barberini, Francesco 127

Barsbay, Al-Ashraf 42

Barthélémy, J-J. 158

Baybars, Al-zahir Rukn Al-Din 60

Bede 72, 73, 78

Bellori, Pietro 127

Belzoni, G. 165; Egyptian Hall exhibition 162

Bembo, Pietro 121

Bernal, Martin 102, 183

Bernard: pilgrimage of 68

Bernini, G. **5:11**, 127, 129, 131

Berosus of Chaldea 111

Bes: Arabian worship of 51

Bible: biblical history and natural philosophy, studies of the relationship between 136–144; chronological studies 136, 145, 176; Egypt, biblical traditions 8, 9, 12–13, 22, 70, 71, 72, 111–112, 123, 134–136, 138–140, 147, 148; Egyptianizing bibles **5:8**, 119; Exodus 70, 71, 72, 140; the Flood 137, 138–139, 141,

175; Genesis 70, 71, 177; *see also Glossa Ordinaria* 70–72

Biondo, F. 106, 107

Birch, Samuel 170

Al-Biyasi, Abu Zakaria 41

*Black Athena* 102

Blumenbach, J. F. 177; antiquity of racial differences 170; mummies, study of 163; racial classification of humanity 162, 165, 169

Boadicea 152

Boas, Franz 178

Boissard, Jean Jacques 121

Bonaparte, Napoleon: Egyptian Campaign 1, 3, 161, 167

Bonomi, Joseph 170

Book of the Fayum 26

Boucher de Perthes, Jacques 175

Braudel, F. 3

British Museum: acquisition of Egyptian antiquities 15, 149; Department of Antiquities, break-up of 181; mummies, acquisition of 149; Parthenon marbles 17

Browne, Peter: classification of a mummy's hair 173

Browne, Sir Thomas 137

Bryant, Jacob 158, 159; Babylonian origins of civilization 167

Bunsen, Baron C. J. K.: on Egyptian chronology 177

Burchard of Strasbourg 68–69

Burnet, Thomas 137

Burnett, James 158


Caesar, Julius: on Druids 153

Cairo: Bab al-Bahr palace 60, 61; tourism 6

Calcagnini, Celio 121

Callisthenes: attributed authorship of Alexander Romance 79

Cambridge Neoplatonists 135

Caracalla 127

Casaubon, Isaac 124, 135

Cassiodorus 70; Jewish teaching of arts to Egypt 75

Catherwood, Frederick 167

Caussin, Nicholas 123

Celtic: its place in Indo-European 162

Celts 148; classical sources of 152–153; Egyptian links (putative) 153; immortality of the soul 153; *see also* Druids

Chaldea: astrology 87; magic 92, 93

Champollion, J-F. 56, 158, 166; Kircher's contribution to 56, 127

Chigi, Agostino 119

Chigi, Flavio: his mummy collection 126, 127

Childe, Gordon 183

China: Egyptians as founders of 156

Christianity: corrupted worship 138, 139, 140, 141; Egypt perceptions of 22, 111–112, 123, 134; Egyptian origins of its beliefs 13, 14; hermetic tradition, perceptions of 134–135; Judaic origins of its beliefs 13, 14; Plato, perceptions of 135; *see also* Bible

Cicero: on Egyptian religion 33–34, 72, 73

Clement of Alexandria 60; on the Jewish origins of Egypt's knowledge 134; on philosophy 34–35, 153; *Stromateis* 24–25, 34

Clement VII 119, 131

Cleopatra 152; Islamic interest in her scientific knowledge 44; medieval knowledge of 72

Cold War 18

Colonna, Pompeo **5:8**, 119

Colossi of Memnon 29, 31

Comestor, Peter 76

Cook, James 156

Copernicus, Nicholas 133

Coptic: Islamic knowledge of 59, 60–61; medieval knowledge of 78; Renaissance study of 127, 129

Coptic bowls: distribution of **1:2**, 12

Copts: Islamic esteem of 42–43; Hermes, association with 52; identification of with pharaonic Egypt 43; as keepers of pharaonic wisdom 56, 58; medieval knowledge of 68

*Corpus Hermeticum*: rediscovery of 13, 14, 65, 81, 109; Christian perceptions of 134–135; *see also* Asclepius, hermetic tradition

craniometry 168–169, 176

Crinito, Pietro 129

Cronaca, Il **5:6**, 115–117

Crossley, James 15

Cudworth, Ralph 135; on the Trinity 138

cult: access to knowledge 29

Curio, Celio Augusto 123

Cuvier, G. 165

Cyriacus of Ancona 106; hieroglyphic decipherment 107

Damietta: Mediterranean alignment of 5

Daniel of Morley 83

Darwin, Charles 175

Davis, Edwin H. 172

Al-Dawadari, Ibn 59

al-Dāya, Ahmad ibn Yūsuf ibn Ibrāhīm: geometry texts 76–77

Delphi, Oracle of 72; rebuilding of 10

Denon, V. 165

Désagulier, John Theophilus 148

*Description de l'Égypte* 165

diffusionism 182, 183

Dime 26

Diodorus Siculus 11, 12, 31–32, 33, 108, 143; on Druids 152, 153; on education 25; rediscovery of 106; Renaissance knowledge of 112

Diogenes Laertius: on Druids 152

Djedi 19, 21

Dodona, Oracle of 33, 72

Domitian: cartouche of 129; Obelisk of 114, 128

Druids 145, 153; classical sources of 152, 153; Egyptian links (putative) 152; as inventors of Pythagoreanism 153; *see also* Celts, Stukeley

Dupérac, Étienne 121

dynastic chronology 8–9, 165

Egeria: pilgrimage of 68

Egypt: alchemy's origins 94; antiquity of 31–32, 136, 165; Arab conquest 3, 4, 8, 12; Arab-Israeli War (1967) 18–19; astrology **2:1**, 27, 84–85, 87–89; astronomy 75, 84–86, 133, 137; biblical traditions 8, 9, 12–13, 22, 70, 71, 72, 111–112, 123, 134–136, 138–140, 147, 148; British colonial administration 16–17; Byzantine period 3; Christian period 12; chronology of 177; classical perceptions 1, 2, 9–11, 22, 23, 31–36, 74; cosmopolitanism 18; Druidic theories 152; dynastic chronology 8–9; education 25–27; ethnographies of 68, 69, 162; geographic definitions 2–5, 65, 70; geometry 137; its

geopolitical context 2, 3, 161; icons of 6, 8;
Hamitic origins 12; Islamic knowledge of
41–45, 47–48, 50–53, 54, 56, 58–61;
knowledge, origins of 9, 10, 11, 13, 32, 36,
52, 84–85, 111, 133, 134, 137, 149; legal texts
27; magic 50–51, 62, 79, 82, 89–90, 92–93, 94;
medieval perceptions 24–25, 26, 72–74, 78–
79; monuments, reuse of 56; nationalism
16–19; origin myths 74–75; Ottoman period
3, 4; philosophy 34–35; Ptolemaic period 11;
racial characteristics 7:3, 163, 165, 166, 168,
169–170, 172–173, 175, 176–177; religion 23–
24, 33–34, 51–53, 54–56, 72–74, 79, 109–111,
138–141, 147, 149, 163, 165, 166;
Renaissance perceptions 109–111; Roman
period 3, 8; Romantic perceptions of 15–16;
science 111, 133, 136–137, 142–144, 149;
social complexity 178–179; stereotypical
representations of 6, 8, 10, 79–80; tourism 6,
19, 136, 149, 159, 161, 167; travellers to 29,
31, 33, 60, 68–70, 76, 102, 103, 105, 107, 126,
136, 149, 159, 167; writing, as the origin of
32–33, 52, 74

Egypt Exploration Fund 180

Egyptian Campaign 3, 161, 167; and the
development of Egyptomania 1

Egyptian Hall: exhibition of Belzoni's
collection 162

Egyptian Society 148, 149, 152, 153, 154

Egyptianizing 18; Bibles 5:8, 119; public
architecture 167; Renaissance 108, 111, 119,
131

Egyptology: academic isolation of 180, 181,
185; development of 6, 8, 15, 65; its
eurocentrism 62; exclusion of Egyptians
from 179; ideological role of 18; origins of
106–109, 111, 179–180; Renaissance 101,
102, 106–109, 111; subject area of 6, 8

Egyptomania: development of 1, 65;
Renaissance 111

Enoch: equation with Hermes 52

Epiphanius 68

Eratosthenes 3, 66

ethnology 163, 165–170, 172–175; end of 176,
178; origins of 162–163

Euclid 76, 77

Eusebius 72; on the hermetic tradition 134–
135

evolution 169, 170, 172, 174; antiquity of 175;
biblical traditions of 163, 165, 166;
chronology of 177–178

Exodus 70, 71, 72, 140

Fabri, Felix: pilgrimage of 103

Fadail Misr 42

Farouk 18

Fatik, Ibn 60

Fatimid Dynasty 76; Bab al-Bahr palace 60,
61; magic, use of 50–51; Night of Fire
celebrations 54

Fayum: identification with the Thebaid 94

Fayum, Book of the 26

Ferrarini, M. F. 115

Ferrata, Ercole 129

Ficino, Marsilio 81, 109, 121, 133, 135; on the
hermetic tradition 109

Fidelis: pilgrimage of 68

Firmicus Maternus: on astrology 87–88

Flood: biblical traditions 137, 138–139, 141,
175

Fludd, Robert 135

Frankfort, H. 183

Frazer, Sir James 179

Freemasonry 22; histories of 148

Gale, Theophilus 134; on the Trinity 138

Galen: De Spermate 81

Genesis 70, 71, 177

Gerard of Cremona 6, 86

Gerbert d'Aurillac 80–81

Al-Gharnati, Abu Hamid: account of Pharos
3:1, 45

Giza: Islamic reports 41, 42; as a granary 103;
medieval visits to 68, 70; Renaissance
knowledge of 5:10, 126

Gliddon, G. R. 170, 172, 180; hieroglyphic
studies 7:2, 170; purchase of mummies 4;
racial characteristics of Ancient Egyptians
7:3, 173–174, 175

Glossa Ordinaria 70–72

Gnosticism 53

Great Library 27

Greaves, John: Giza pyramid, measurement
of 5:10, 124, 136

Greece: admiration of Egypt 23, 32, 32, 35–36;
barbarians, perception of 10, 11, 35;
commerce with Egypt 10; Egypt,
perceptions of 1, 9–11, 22, 23, 31–33, 35–36,
139; Egyptian gods, incorporation of 73;
ethnographic traditions 9, 11; foreigners,

stereotypical representations of 10, 11; invasion of Egypt 3, 4; Persians, perceptions of 10; religion (Egyptian), knowledge of 29, 139; travel to Egypt 29, 31, 33, 60; writing, origin myth of 74

Greenhill, Thomas 136

Gregorius: on pyramids 70

Gregory the Great 139

Gregory, David 142

Grimani, Marco: account of the Great Pyramid of Giza 5:1, 103–104

Hadith 42

Al-Hagag, Abu: Mosque and Tomb of 56

Haiti: Toussaint l'Ouverture's revolt 168

Al-Hakam, Ibn 'Abd 59; on Muqatam Mountain's sacredness 55–56

Al-Hakim, Bi-Amr 50; Coptic, use of 61

Hale, Sir Matthew 144

Ham 12, 68, 138

Al-Hamadani, Abu Al-Hassan 51; archaeological methods of 44

Harmakhes 54

Hartley, David 145

Hauvilla, Johannes de 74

Hearne, Thomas 142

Hecataeus of Miletus 9

Heliopolis: Grand Shrine of 55

Hercules: in Renaissance historiography 112

Hereford mappae mundi: 4:1, 66, 68

Hermann of Carinthia 82; on Amun 73; on Hermes 91, 94; translation of Arabic astrology texts 88, 89; translation of Arabic astronomy texts 85

Hermes 52, 53, 73, 81, 87, 90, 91, 109; Islamic traditions 90, 91; see also Hermes Trismegistus

Hermes Trismegistus 89–96, 134–136; rediscovery of 13, 14, 65, 81, 109; Renaissance perceptions of 128–129, 133, 135; translation of 133, 135; see also hermetic tradition

hermetic tradition 16, 25, 47, 54, 56, 58, 134–136; Asclepius 73, 79, 81, 82–83, 90, 91, 109; Christian perceptions of 109, 134–135; Counter-Reformation use of 124; Islamic knowledge of 53, 90, 91–94; medieval knowledge of 90–96; rediscovery of 13, 14,

65, 81, 109; Renaissance perceptions 101, 109, 124, 128–129; stelae 94, 95

Hermopolis Legal Manual 27

Herodotus 9–10, 11, 12, 14, 23, 31, 36, 143, 163, 165; on the calendar 32; Egypt's place in geography 2, 4, 5; on medicine 25; on mummification 136; Oracle at Dodona 33; racial characteristics of Ancient Egyptians 177; rediscovery of 106; on religion 29, 139; his sources 29, 31; travel to Egypt 29

hieroglyphs: classical perceptions of 11, 56; in decoration 108, 115; end of the use of 12; magic's association with 78; medieval knowledge of 77; negative views of 144, 149; Newton's interpretation of 140; 19th century studies of 7:2, 170; Renaissance studies 5:4, 114–115, 118, 119–121, 123, 124–126, 127–128, 129; as universal language 137

hieroglyphs, decipherment of 14, 56, 62, 137, 154, 158, 166; using Chinese characters 156, 158; classical 106; Islamic 56, 58–60; 19th century 166; Renaissance 107–108, 114, 118, 119, 121, 124, 126, 127–129, 145

Historia de Preliis 79–80, 82, 83

History of Prophethood 43

Hoare, Sir Richard Colt: attitude towards Stukeley's work 163

Hohenburg, Johann Herwarth von: Thesaurus Hieroglyphicorum 121, 123, 124

Horapollo 106, 108; rediscovery of 65; Renaissance knowledge of 121; use of in hieroglyphic decipherment 118

Hordedef 19, 21

Horus: medieval knowledge of 72

Huet, P. D. 156

Hugh of Santalla 95

Hugh of St Victor: Didascalion 75, 86

Hume, David 154–156, 159

Hurun: cult of 54

Hyginus: on Amun 73

hyperdiffusionism 183

Hypnerotomachia Poliphili 5:4, 111, 114, 118, 131

Idris 52, 53

Al-Idrisi, Abu Ja'far: on Acerra's embassy 69; archaeological methods of 44–45; astronomical aspects of monuments, observation of 56; Giza pyramids, his account of 41, 42; on the Grand Shrine of Heliopolis 55; on the Sphinx 54

Imhotep 16, 73, 81; *see also* Hermes Trismegistus

India: Egyptians as founders of 156

Indo-European 159, 162, 182

Innocent X 127

Insinger Papyrus 26

Instructions of Onchsheshonqy 25–26; *see also* Wisdom Texts

Al-Isfahani, Al-Emad: his tour of the pyramids 54

Isidore of Seville 65, 66, 70; *De Natura Rerum* 78; Egyptian history, knowledge of 72; Egyptian invention of astronomy and astrology 75; on geometry 75–76; on Hermes 90; on hieroglyphs 77; Jewish teaching of arts to Egypt 75; on Ptolemy 86, 87

Isis: Arabian worship of 51; Christian interpretations of 73; lamentation over Osiris' death 72; medieval knowledge of 72; origins of farming 75; origins of writing 74; Osiris' body parts, search for 73; in Renaissance art 111; weaving, invention of 75

Islam: Egypt, perceptions of 41–44; and Egyptian identity 17, 18, 19; study of Egypt, its encouragement of 41, 42; Sufism's links with pharaonic religious texts 48; *see also* Arabs

Iyas, Ibn 42, 50


James I 135

Janus: identification with Noah 112

Jerome 66; Egyptian religion, hostility to 74

Jews: Christianity, origins of 13, 14; Egyptian wisdom, as the source of 75, 76, 134; the Exodus 70, 71, 72, 140; religion of, its Egyptian origins 140, 147


Al-Jobry 58

John of Seville: translations of Arabic astrology texts 88

Jones, Inigo 145

Jones, Sir William: classification of Indo-European 159, 162

Josephus: *Antiquitates* 75; Renaissance knowledge of 112

Jubayer, Ibn 48

Julius Caesar: on Druids 153

Julius Honorious 66

Julius II 119

Jupiter: equation with Amun 73

Juvenal 10; on Egyptian religion 23–24, 72, 73–74


Al-Kalbi, Ibn: knowledge of the Heliopolitan sun cult 55

Karnak: Renaissance reports 103

Khaldun, Ibn 50

Khalikan, Ibn 50

Khufu 19, 21

Kinglake, A. 161

king lists 8–9

Kircher, Athanasius 78, 101, 102, 154; Arabic tradition, knowledge of 128; his contribution to Champollion 127; Coptic studies 127, 129; Domitian's cartouche, 'decipherment' of 129; on hermetic tradition 128–129; hieroglyphic decipherment 14, 56, 127–129, 145; obelisk studies 128, 131; obelisks, re-erection of 115; sources of 124–126

Knox, Robert: racial characteristics of Ancient Egyptians 170, 177

Koran *see* Quran


Lactantius: on the hermetic tradition 109, 134–135

Lane, Edward 162

Lawrence, William 165

Le Comte, Louis 156

Leo Africanus 103

Leo X 119, 121, 131

Lepsius, Richard 170

Lethieullier, W. 149

Lhwyd, E. 152

Libya: geographic definitions of 66

Ligorio, Pirro 121

Lubbock, Sir John 181

Lucan: on pyramids 70

Lucian 139

Lucian of Samosata: *Dialogues of the Dead* 24

Luxor massacre 19

Luxor temple: Islamic reuse of 56; Renaissance reports 103

Macpherson, James 152

Macrobius: on the Egyptian discovery of philosophy 75

magic: Chaldean 92, 93; Egyptian 50–51, 62, 79, 82, 89–90, 92–93, 94; hieroglyphs' association with 78; Islamic 50–51, 62

Mameluk dynasty 4

Manetho 112, 165; Arabic translations 58; king lists 8–9; Sabaean veneration of 58

*mappae mundi* **4:1**, 66, 68

Al-Maqrizi 51, 54; on Coptic monasteries 59; on the Fatimid palace in Cairo 60, 61; on Muqatam Mountain's sacredness 55–56; on pharaonic ritual 55

Marcellinus, Ammianus 11; on Druids 153; rediscovery of 106

Mariette, A. 15

Marsham, Sir John: on Egyptian antiquity 136

Martianus Capella: on Egyptian geometry 75

Martin, John 170

Martineau, H. 161

Al-Mas'udi 51, 52, 59, 60; on Alexander the Great's funeral 42; praise of Egypt 43

Ma'shar, Abū 83, 84; astrology texts 83, 85, 86, 87, 88, 89; astronomy texts 84, 85, 89; on Hermes 90, 91

Maurus, Rhabanus 75

Medes 92

Medici: Egyptianizing of 119

Medici, Cosimo de' 109

Mediterranean: in classical thought 2–3

Memnon, Colossi of 29, 31

Memphis: medieval knowledge of 74

Menaus 53

Menes: chronology of 165

Menqaus: treatment of illness through temple construction 51

*Mensa Isiaca* **5:9**, 121–123, 127

Mercati: obelisks, study of 123–124

Mesopotamia: agricultural origins 183

Middle Ages: alchemy, knowledge of 94–95; Alexander the Great, perceptions of 80, 81; Arabic texts, influence of 83–84; astrology 87–88; astronomy 84–86; Copts, knowledge of 68, 78; Egypt, perceptions of 68, 69, 70–72, 74, 78–79, 89–89; fauna (Egyptian), knowledge of 68, 69, 74; geographical knowledge of Egypt **4:1**, 65–66, 68;

geometry 75–76; hermetic tradition 81, 90–96; hieroglyphs, knowledge of 77; history (Egyptian), knowledge of 72–74; magic (Egyptian), knowledge of 79, 89–90; monuments, visits to 68–70; mythology (Egyptian), knowledge of 72–73; Neoplatonism 77–80; pyramids, perception of as granaries 68, 69, 70; religion (Egyptian), perceptions of 72–74, 79; sphinx, knowledge of 68; stereotypical representations of Egypt 79–80; travellers' reports of Egypt 68–70; wisdom of Egypt, perceptions of 74–77, 79

Mill, John Stuart: racial characteristics of Ancient Egyptians 177

Milles, Jeremiah 153

Al-Misri, Dhu Al-Nun 48

Mnemohistory 102

Mohammed: encouragement of the search for wisdom 42; praise of Egypt 42–43

Montelius, Oscar 182

Montagu, John 148

monuments: astronomical links 56; export of 6, 14, 15, 102, 115; Islamic perceptions 54–56, 62, 103; medieval perceptions of 68, 69, 70, 74; negative views 144; protection of 42; Renaissance perceptions **5:1**, 103–104, 107, 109–111, 126, 136; reuse of 56; visitors to 42, 54, 68, 69, 70, 103, 105

More, Henry 135; on the Trinity 138

More, Sir Thomas 135

Morienus 47, 94

Morgan, Henry Lewis 179

Morton, Samuel G.: on the antiquity of racial differences 170; craniometry 168–169, 176; indigenous origins of the Mound-builders, recognition of 169; racial characteristics of Ancient Egyptians 169–170, 172–173; skulls, acquisition of 169

Moses 109, 134, 135; as the inventor of the Trinity 138; medieval perceptions of 71–72; wisdom of 76, 134, 137, 143

Mosque of Abu Al-Hagag 56

Mound-builders: indigenous origins of, anthropological recognition of 169

*mummia* 13, 42

mummies: acquisition of 149, 152; anatomical studies 163, 165; collection of 126, 127; iconic status of 6; sale of 4, 42, 126

mummification: negative views of 144; process of 136

Muqatam Mountain 55–56

Muslim Brotherhood: suppression of 19

Mustafa Kemal Ataturk 17

Myres, Sir John: origins of civilization 182–183

*Mythographus Vaticanus I*: myth of Typhon 73

Al-Nadim, Ibn 45

Nag Hamadi 56, 58

Al-Nahawandi, Abu Al-Qasim 47

Nanni, Giovanni *see* Annius of Viterbo

Napoleon Bonaparte: Egyptian campaign 1, 3, 161, 167

Nasser, Gamel Abdel: non-alignment policy 18, 19

nationalism: Egyptian 16–19

Native Americans: as Egyptian migrants 167–168; Mound-builders 169; origins of, 19th century theories 167–168

Naukratis 10; Mediterranean alignment of 5

Navona obelisk 114

Neckham, Alexander 77

Nectanebo I: granite lions of **5:5**, 115

Nectanebo II: in *Historia de Preliis* 79–80; magic, use of 51, 82, 90; medieval perceptions of 79–81

Needham, John T.: decipherment of hieroglyphs using Chinese characters 156, 158

neoevolutionism 184

Neolithic: definition of 182

Neoplatonism 13, 14, 65, 134, 135; critique of 154; medieval knowledge of 77–78; Renaissance perceptions 109–111; *see also* hermetic tradition

New Archaeology: neglect of Ancient Egypt 184

Newton, Sir Isaac 133, 135, 154; biblical history studies 136–144; hieroglyphic interpretation 137, 140; on natural philosophy and religion 141–142; on Pythagoreanism 142; Stonehenge, dating of 140, 145; on temples 139–141, 147

Nicaea, Council of 138

Niccoli, N. 106; recognition of hieroglyphs on Roman obelisks 107

Nicholas V: relocation of the Vatican obelisk 108

Nile of America 167

Noah 12, 138; identification with Janus 112; Masonic links 148; religion of 138, 139, 140, 141

Norden, F. L. **6:3**, 14, 149, 152; on Copts 163

Nott, Josiah Clark: racial segregation theories 172; racial characteristics of Ancient Egyptians **7:3**, 173–174, 175

Novara, Tomas Obicini da 127

Nu Papyrus 19

Nubia: Egyptian influence in 5

Numenius of Apamea 135

obelisk: of Augustus 119; of Capo di Bove 128; of Domitian 114, 127; Piazza Navona 114; San Macuto 116–118; of the Vatican **5:6**, 108, 115–118

obelisks: hieroglyphs on 107; iconic status of 6; re-erection of 115, 119, 124, 128; relocation of 102, 105, 108–109; Renaissance revival of 108; Renaissance study of **5:6**, **5:7**, 114–118, 124, 128, 131; Roman **5:6**, **5:11**, 105, 108, 114–118

Obicini, Thomas 56

Onchsheshonqy, Instructions of 25–26; *see also* Wisdom Texts

onomasticon 26

Orientalism 15, 162, 178

Origen 77; on the hermetic tradition 134–135

origin myths 74–75

Orpheus 128; trinitarian references 138

Osiris: Arabian worship of 51; body parts, search for 73; Christian interpretations 73; grammar, establishment of 75; Isis' lamentation 72; laceration of 73; medieval knowledge of 72; in Renaissance art 111; in Renaissance historiography 112; Renaissance interpretation of 123

Ovid 73

paratexts 19

Parmenides: dialectic, invention of 75

Peet, T. I. 180

Peiresc, N-C. F. de 127

Perry, C. 149

Perry, W. J. 183

Persia: Greek perceptions of 10; invasion of Egypt 3

Peruzzi, Baldassare **5:6**, **5:7**, 115

Petosiris: on astrology 88–89

Petrie, Sir Flinders 180

Pharos 12; Islamic study of **3:1**, 45; medieval knowledge of 68, 70, 74

Philae 12; Renaissance reports 103

*Picatrix* 92–93

Pico della Mirandola, Giovanni: on Neoplatonism 109–111

Pignoria, Lorenzo 123

Pinturicchio 111

Pitt-Rivers, A. H. L. F. 181

Pius II 114

Plato 128, 133, 134, 147; on alphabetic origins 32–33; Christian perceptions of 135; Egyptian social stability 33; geographical scheme of 2–3; intellectual debt to Egypt 76; *Phaedro* 32–33; praise of Egypt 31; Renaissance knowledge of 109; travel to Egypt 76; trinitarian references 138

Pliny the Elder 66; geographical definition of Egypt 65, 70; on pyramids 36; rediscovery of 106; Renaissance knowledge of 114; on the Sphinx 54

Plotinus 135, 154

Plutarch 143; rediscovery of 106; Renaissance knowledge of 121

Pococke, Richard **6:2**, 14, 149, 152

Poggio Bracciolini 106, 112; recognition of hieroglyphs on Roman obelisks 107

Polo, Marco 156

polygenism 169, 170, 172, 174

Pomponius Mela 66, 70

Posidonius: on Druids 152

Pozzo, Cassiano del 127

predynastic archaeology 184

Prester John 65, 69

Prichard, J. C. 14, 162; biblical account of evolution, his defence of 163, 166; on biblical chronology 176; craniometry, response to 176; on the evolution of Egyptian civilization 166, 167; on human evolution 163, 165; origins of civilization 166; racial characteristics of Ancient Egyptians 163, 165, 176–177; on religious similarities between Ancient Egypt and India 163, 166; his sources 163, 165

Prime, William 167

Psammetichos: experiment with new-born twins 31

Ptah: classical descriptions of 72

Ptahhotep 19

Ptolemy: *Almagest* 133; on astrology 89; geographic definition of Egypt 66; medieval confusion of with a pharaoh 86–87, 90; medieval knowledge of 74; translation of 78

Ptolemy II 40

Ptolemy XIII: medieval knowledge of 74

pyramids: classical perceptions of 36, 70; as granaries 12, 68, 69, 70, 103; iconic status of 6; Islamic study of 44–45; medieval knowledge of 68; negative views 144; Renaissance knowledge of **5:10**, 126, 136; Renaissance revival of 108; visitors to 54

Pythagoras 24, 128, 147; Druidic contacts (putative) 152, 153; gravity, discovery of 142; travel to Egypt 60; trinitarian references 138

Pythagoreanism: Druidic invention of (putative) 153

al-Qabisis 88, 89

Al-Qassim Al'-Iraqi, Abu: his interpretation of twelfth Dynasty stela **3:2**, 48

Quran: Egyptian references 41; perceptions of Ancient Egypt 43; study of Ancient Egypt, its encouragement of 41, 42

Qurra, Thabit ibn 94

racial characteristics of Ancient Egyptians **7:3**, 163, 165, 166, 168, 169–170, 172–174, 175, 176–177

Ramesses II: colossal bust of 15; obelisks of 118

Ranke, Leopold von 178

Raphael 119

Raymond of Marseilles 87

Reggio Emilia 115

Reinach, Salomon 182

Remigius of Auxerre 75

Renaissance: Arabic learning, knowledge of 128; classical learning, knowledge of 105–106, 108, 109, 112, 114, 121, 124; Coptic studies 127, 129; Egypt, perceptions of 13–14, 103–104, 107, 109–111, 126; Egyptianizing 108, 119–121, 131; Egyptology 101, 102, 106–109, 111; Egyptomania 111; hermetic tradition 109, 124, 128–129; hieroglyphic decipherment 118, 119, 121, 124, 128–129, 145;

hieroglyphic studies **5:4**, 114–115, 118, 119–121, 123, 124–126, 127–128, 129; hieroglyphs in decoration 108, 115; historiographical traditions of Egypt 112, 128; monuments, perception of **5:1**, 103–104, 107, 109–111, 126; mythology, study of 123; Neoplatonism 109–111; obelisk studies **5:6**, **5:7**, 114–118, 124, 128, 131; pyramids, perceptions of 103, 126, 136; science (Egyptian), perceptions of 109–111; sources of knowledge of Ancient Egypt 102, 106; Sphinx, perceptions of 103, 109–111, 126; temples, perceptions of 110; travel to Egypt 102, 103, 107

'Alī ibn Riḍwān: 77; on Ptolemy 86–87

Roberts, David 15; 'View on the Nile. Isle of Rhoda and the ferry of Geezeh' **1:1**, 6

Romano, Giulio 115, 119

Rome: Augustus' obelisks 119; Capo di Bove obelisk 128; Domitian's obelisk 114, 127; Egyptian gods, incorporation of 73; Egyptianizing 119–121, 131; import of monuments 115; invasion of Egypt 3; monuments, relocation of 118; Nectanebo I's lions **5:5**, 115; obelisks, relocation of 105, 118; perceptions of Egypt 1, 11, 13–14, 23–24, 33–34; Piazza Navona obelisk 114; pyramids of 105; re-erection of obelisks 115, 119, 124, 128; restoration of Egyptian monuments 119, 127; San Macuto obelisk 116–118; Vatican Obelisk **5:6**, 108, 115–118

Rubens, Peter Paul: mummy collection of 126

Rufinus 72, 78

Sadat, Anwar: association with pharaonic Egypt **1:3**, 19; Islamic fundamentalism, suppression of 19

Said, E.: orientalism 15, 162

Saif Ibn Zi Yazan: epic of 40

Sais: Mediterranean alignment of 5

Saite period: links with Greece 5

Al-Saman: reuse of an Old Kingdom tomb 56

San Macuto obelisk 116–118

Sandwich, Earl of 148, 149

Sangallo, Guiliano da 114–115

Saqqarah: mummies, trade in 126, 127; the Serapieion 55

Al-Sawi: 51, 53; on pharaonic cult 54

*Scala Magna* **3:3**, 56

Schlegel, F. 165

Service, E. 184

Servius: on pyramids 70

Shadat: erection of a statue to Min 51

Al-Shahruzuri, Diau Al-Din: his tour of the pyramids 54

Al-Sharastani 52

Shelley, Mary: *The Last Man* 16

Shelly, Percy: *Ozymandias* 15–16

Shenoute 58

Al-Shu'abi, Sa'adah Ibn Rakan: 47

Shuckford, Samuel 154; natural religion, critique of 147

Siena: the Duomo's mosaic pavement **5:2**, 109

Al-Siqili, Abu Al-Hassan 47

Sir, Abu: Prison of Joseph 55

Sixtus V: re-erection of obelisks 108, 123

slavery, abolition of 168, 175

Smith, Grafton Elliot: hyperdiffusionism of 183

Snake-Charmer's Handbook 27

Sobek: Tebtunis temple 26

Society for Biblical Archaeology 180

Socrates: fable of the origin of writing 32–33

Soemmering, S. T. von 165

Solinus 66, 72; Apis, description of the cult of 72

Solomon's Temple 141, 148

Spencer, John 134

Sphinx: Babylonian urn burials at 54; Bacon's perceptions of 143; medieval knowledge of 68; Renaissance perceptions 103, 109–111, 126; Sabaean cult of 54

Squier, Ephraim George 172

St John, Henry 154

Stephens, John 167

stone circles: Egyptian parallels, theory of 139, 140, 141, 145, 152

Stonehenge: dating of 140, 145; Druidic theory 145; Egyptian origins, theory of 140, 141

Strabo 11, 12, 31, 33; on cultural diversity 35; on Druids 152, 153; medieval knowledge of 66; on Ptolemaic looting of Alexander the Great's tomb 42; rediscovery of 106; sources of 36

Stukeley, William 133, 140, 142, 144, 159; Avebury studies **6:1**, **7:1**, 145, 163; Druidic theories 145, 152, 153; hieroglyphic studies

6:4; membership of the Egyptian Society 148; methods of 163; snake interpretation of Avebury 7:1, 163; Stonehenge, dating of 145; on the Trinity 138, 145

Sutton Hoo: Coptic bowls 1:2

Tacitus 107

Al-Tahtawi, Rifa'a 39

Tanis: Mediterranean alignment of 5

Tebtunis: Sobek, temple of 26

temples: and alchemy 45, 47–48; foreigners' access to 29; Islamic knowledge of 45, 47–48, 50; libraries 2:2, 26, 27, 29; magic, association with 50–51; negative views of 144; Newton's interpretation of 139–141, 147; Renaissance perceptions 103, 110; reuse of 56

*Thesaurus Hieroglyphicorum* 121, 123, 124

Thomas of Acerra 69

Thoth 19, 21, 36, 53; arts, discovery of 75; classical knowledge of 72; identification with hermetic tradition 16, 73; medieval knowledge of 72; *see also* Hermes Trismegistus

Tindal, Matthew 135

Tinnis: Mediterranean alignment of 5

Toland, John 137, 152

Toussaint l'Ouverture, P. D. 168

Trigger, B. 184

Trinity: studies of 138

Tulun, Ibn 60; exploitation of pharaonic gold 42; Sphinx, visit to 54

Tulunid Dynasty 76

Turkey: post-Ottoman national identity 17

Tutankhamun's tomb 1, 17

Tuthmosis I 5

Tylor, E. B. 178, 184; on Egyptian religion 179; evolutionary chronology 177

Typhon: in Greek myth 73; in Renaissance historiography 112

Umail, Ibn: alchemy studies 47–48

Unesco: Abu Simbel temples, its assistance in saving 18

universal history 6:4, 156, 158

universal language 137

Urban VII 127

USA: abolition of slavery 168, 175; Egyptianizing public architecture 167; Nile of America 167; polygenism 169, 170, 172, 174; travel to Egypt 167

Ussher, James 9, 136

Valeriano, Pierio 118, 121; *Hieroglyphica* 121–123

Valerius Maximus: on Druids 152

Valle, Pietro della: acquisition of mummies 126, 127

van Gorp, Jan Becan 121

Varro 73

Vatican obelisk 5:6, 115–118, 108; relocation of 108

Vergil: perceived intellectual debt to Egypt 76

Vico, Enea 121

Vincent of Beauvais 83; Egyptian history, knowledge of 72

Volney, C. 14; on Copts 163

Warburton, William 142, 155–156, 159; on Egyptian history 154; hieroglyphic decipherment 154; Neoplatonism, critique of 154

Warren, Henry 170

Al-Wazan *see* Leo Africanus

Weber, Max 179

Westcar Papyrus 19, 21

William of Boldensele 66, 68, 69, 70

Wisdom Texts 19, 21, 25–26; *see also* Instructions of Onchsheshonqy

Woodward, John 143–144

Wotton, William 143

writing: Ancient Egypt as the origin of 32–33, 52, 74; Arabic alphabet, its basis in Ancient Egypt 62

Al-Ya'qubi 52

Young, Thomas: decipherment of hieroglyphs 166

Zaid, Zaidullah Ibn 40

Zalmoxis 153

Zosimus 94